The Adam Smith Review

Adam Smith's contribution to economics is well recognised, yet scholars have recently been exploring anew the multidisciplinary nature of his works.

The Adam Smith Review is a rigorously refereed annual review that provides a unique forum for interdisciplinary debate on all aspects of Adam Smith's works, his place in history, and the significance of his writings to the modern world.

It is aimed at facilitating debate among scholars working across the humanities and social sciences, thus emulating the reach of the Enlightenment world that Smith helped to shape.

Craig Smith is Professor of the History of Political Thought at the University of Glasgow, UK.

The Adam Smith Review
Published in association with the International Adam Smith Society

The Adam Smith Review is a multidisciplinary annual review sponsored by the International Adam Smith Society. It aims to provide a unique forum for vigorous debate and the highest standards of scholarship on all aspects of Adam Smith's works, his place in history, and the significance of his writings for the modern world. *The Adam Smith Review* aims to facilitate interchange between scholars working within different disciplinary and theoretical perspectives, and to this end it is open to all areas of research relating to Adam Smith. The Review also hopes to broaden the field of English-language debate on Smith by occasionally including translations of scholarly works at present available only in languages other than English.

The Adam Smith Review is intended as a resource for Adam Smith scholarship in the widest sense. The Editor welcomes comments and suggestions, including proposals for symposia or themed sections in the Review. Future issues are open to comments and debate relating to previously published papers.

The website of *the Adam Smith Review* is: http://www.adamsmithreview.org/

For details of membership of the International Adam Smith Society and reduced rates for purchasing the Review, please contact the Membership Secretary, Remy Debes, (rdebes@memphis.edu).

The Philosophy of Adam Smith
The Adam Smith Review, Volume 5: Essays Commemorating the 250th Anniversary of *The Theory of Moral Sentiments*
Edited by Vivienne Brown and Samuel Fleischacker

The Adam Smith Review (Volume 6)
Edited by Fonna Forman

The Adam Smith Review (Volume 7)
Edited by Fonna Forman

The Adam Smith Review (Volume 8)
Edited by Fonna Forman

The Adam Smith Review (Volume 9)
Edited by Fonna Forman

The Adam Smith Review (Volume 10)
Edited by Fonna Forman

The Adam Smith Review (Volume 11)
Edited by Fonna Forman

The Adam Smith Review (Volume 12)
Edited by Fonna Forman

The Adam Smith Review (Volume 13)
Edited by Fonna Forman

The Adam Smith Review (Volume 14)
Edited by Fonna Forman

The Adam Smith Review (Volume 15)
Edited by Craig Smith

For more information about this series, please visit: www.routledge.com/The-Adam-Smith-Review/book-series/ASR

The Adam Smith Review

Volume 15

Edited by Craig Smith

Routledge
Taylor & Francis Group
LONDON AND NEW YORK

First published 2027
by Routledge
4 Park Square, Milton Park, Abingdon, Oxon OX14 4RN

and by Routledge
605 Third Avenue, New York, NY 10158

Routledge is an imprint of the Taylor & Francis Group, an informa business

British Library Cataloguing-in-Publication Data
A catalogue record for this book is available from the British Library

ISBN: 978-1-041-29057-5 (hbk)
ISBN: 978-1-041-29058-2 (pbk)
ISBN: 978-1-003-76782-4 (ebk)

DOI: 10.4324/9781003767824

Typeset in Times New Roman
by Apex CoVantage, LLC

Access the Support Material:

adamsmithreview@glasgow.ac.uk.

https://adamsmithslibrary.gla.ac.uk

http://www.adamsmithreview.org/

Contents

Contributors

Alain Alcouffe is Emeritus Professor of Economics at the University of Toulouse. He served as Director of the Toulouse University Network (2001–2005) and as President of the International Walras Association (2013–2015). His research interests include corporate governance, business intelligence, ecological economics, economic history, and the history of economic thought. He edited the Mathematical Manuscripts of Marx (Economica, 1985) and coedited Business Cycles in Economic Thought: A History (2017, Routledge) and Macroeconomic Theory and the Eurozone Crisis (2018, Routledge). He coauthored Adam Smith in Toulouse and Occitania (Toulouse, 2018) (English edition, 2020, Palgrave). In 2025, he edited a book devoted to Adam Smith's guide in France, Seignelay Colbert de Castlehill (1735–1811): A Bishop Between Scottish Enlightenment and Counter-Revolution, published by Palgrave.

Nir Ben-Moshe is Associate Professor in the Department of Philosophy and Health Innovation Professor in the Carle Illinois College of Medicine at the University of Illinois Urbana-Champaign. His research falls primarily into two areas. The first area lies at the intersection of contemporary moral philosophy and eighteenth-century moral philosophy (esp. Adam Smith). The second area is biomedical ethics (esp. the values at play in the physician-patient relationship). Ben-Moshe is the author of *Idealization and the Moral Point of View: An Adam Smithian Account of Moral Reasons* (forthcoming, Oxford University Press) and co-editor of *The Smithian Mind* (forthcoming, Routledge).

Alfredo Félix Blanco is Consultant Professor at the National University of Córdoba, Argentina, and Online Professor at the Adolfo Ibañez University, Chile. He was Dean of the Faculty of Economic Sciences, National University of Córdoba, Argentina (2009–2012).

Mauricio C. Coutinho is Professor at the University of Campinas, Brazil (Universidade Estadual de Campinas – UNICAMP). His research involves the economics of Adam Smith, pre-Smithian monetary economics, and the diffusion of political economy and of Smith's principles into other countries, especially Brazil. He has recently worked on the first translation of *The Wealth of Nations* into Portuguese (1811–1812) and on some theoretical issues concerning Smith, such as nominal and real prices, revenues, and accumulation of capital (WN, Book II).

Remy Debes is Professor of Philosophy at the University of Memphis. He has published numerous articles and chapters on contemporary ethics and the history of ethics, with an emphasis on the subjects of human dignity, respect, empathy, emotion, and the Scottish Enlightenment, especially David Hume and Adam Smith. He is the editor of *Dignity: A History* (Oxford University Press), co-editor of *Ethical Sentimentalism* (Cambridge University Press), and co-editor of *The Smithian Mind*, forthcoming in the Routledge Philosophical Minds series. He is also Editor-in-Chief of *The Southern Journal of Philosophy*.

Stefano Fiori is Professor of History of Economic Thought at the Department of Economics and Statistics 'Cognetti de Martiis' (University of Torino). His research focuses on the history of economic thought and the connection among philosophy, economics, and other social sciences, viewed from a historical perspective. His scientific interests include pre-classical economics, Adam Smith's theory, Austrian economics, institutional and new institutional economics, methodology, and philosophy of economics.

Franco Godino is Professor of History of Economic Thought at the National University of Córdoba and a master's student at the University of Buenos Aires. His main research interests include the impact of public policy on inequality and development.

F. E. Guerra-Pujol received his Juris Doctorate from Yale Law School and began his academic career at the Pontifical Catholic University of Puerto Rico. He is currently Professor at the University of Central Florida, and his areas of research include markets, property rights, and the philosophy of law. He is also the author of many scholarly papers, journal articles, and book chapters, including 'Gödel's Loophole,' 'Adam Smith's Blind Spot,' and 'Coase's Parable.'

Ryan Patrick Hanley is the J. Joseph Moakley Professor of Political Science at Boston College. Prior to joining the faculty at Boston College, he was the Mellon Distinguished Professor of Political Science at Marquette University and held visiting appointments or fellowships at Yale, Harvard, and the University of Chicago. A specialist in the political philosophy of the Enlightenment period, he is the author of *Adam Smith and the Character of Virtue* (Cambridge, 2009), *Love's Enlightenment: Rethinking Charity in Modernity* (Cambridge, 2017), *Our Great Purpose: Adam Smith on Living a Better Life* (Princeton, 2019), and *The Political Philosophy of Fénelon* (Oxford, 2020). He is most recently the editor of *Love: A History* (Oxford, 2024).

Keith Hankins is the R.C. Hoiles Endowed Chair in Business Ethics & Free Enterprise at Chapman University, where he is also Associate Professor of Philosophy and a founding member of the Smith Institute for Political Economy and Philosophy. He works on issues that lie at the intersection of political philosophy, economics, and social psychology, with an emphasis on developing formal models that shed light on how individuals navigate frictions associated with living in community with others. He also explores how the work of historical figures like Hume and Smith bears on these debates.

Lisa Hill is Professor of Politics at the University of Adelaide. She focuses on the intellectual history of the Western political tradition and has written extensively on two figures of the Scottish Enlightenment: Adam Smith and Adam Ferguson. She is also an authority on classical Stoicism and its impact on the Western political tradition. Her other research interests include democratic theory and electoral studies. She is a Fellow of the Academy of the Social Sciences of Australia, Program Director at the Stretton Institute for Public Policy, and Research Chair of the Centre for Public Integrity, an anti-corruption watchdog.

Jimena Hurtado is Professor of Economics and Vice President for Research and Creation at Universidad de los Andes (Bogotá). As a historian of economic thought, her work examines Adam Smith's moral philosophy and political economy, their dialogues with Rousseau, Mandeville, Tocqueville, and the reception of economic ideas in Latin America. She is President of the International Adam Smith Society, serves on the editorial board of History of Political Economy, and was Co-Editor of the *Journal of the History of Economic Thought* until this year. Recent publications include 'Taste and Commerce in Adam Smith' (Adam Smith Review, 2025) and the co-edited volume *A History of Colombian Economic Thought: The Economic Ideas That Built Modern Colombia* (Routledge, 2024). She holds a PhD in Economics from Université Paris X Nanterre and has held visiting positions at Duke, Stanford, Lille, Lyon 2, and other institutions.

Jorge López Lloret is Professor in the Department of Aesthetics and Theory of the Arts at the University of Seville. He specialises in the history of philosophy and aesthetics of the eighteenth and nineteenth centuries. He has published papers on Descartes, Hutcheson, Diderot, Rousseau, Hume, Alexander von Humboldt, and Darwin. Regarding Adam Smith, in addition to several papers in specialised journals, he has translated and edited the Spanish versions of Considerations Concerning the First Formation of Languages and Lectures on Rhetoric and Belles Lettres. He has also edited and translated into Spanish the writings on aesthetics of Allan Ramsay Jr., including A Dialogue on Taste. He is currently finishing a book, forthcoming, on Adam Smith's *Methodology: Imagination, Rhetoric, and René Descartes*.

Melisa Janet Luc has a master's degree in Economic History from the University of Barcelona, and she is Professor of History of Economic Thought, Economic and Social History, and Gender Perspectives in Economic Sciences at the National University of Córdoba, Argentina.

Adam Marcinkowski received his PhD from York University, Toronto, in 2024. His research examines the interrelated histories of emotions, aesthetics, and theatre. He currently teaches eighteenth-century literature and theatre history at Wilfrid Laurier University and Acadia University.

Hannes Ole Matthiessen has held researcher and assistant professor positions in Frankfurt (Main), Fribourg (Switzerland), and Humboldt-Universität zu Berlin, where he is currently a habilitation candidate. He has published on the philosophy of perception and epistemology (*Epistemic Entitlement: The Right to Believe*, Palgrave Macmillan 2014) as well as on early modern philosophers, especially Thomas Reid. A forthcoming book project is entitled Thomas Reid and the Puzzle of Perspective (with Edinburgh University Press).

Brennan McDavid is Assistant Professor of Philosophy and a member of the Smith Institute for Political Economy and Philosophy at Chapman University. The main focus of her research is ancient philosophy, particularly the theories of human nature, moral psychology, and political organisation in Plato and Aristotle. Her work on Adam Smith primarily explores his reception of arguments in the ancient tradition of virtue ethics.

Ecem Okan is Associate Professor of Economics at the Center for Interdisciplinarity in English Studies, University of Lorraine. Previously, she conducted postdoctoral research at the Center for the Study of Economic Liberty, Arizona State University. She holds a PhD from the University of Paris 1 Panthéon Sorbonne. She is interested in the relationship between economics and the philosophy of history through the works of David Hume and Adam Smith in particular, and the Scottish Enlightenment in general.

Andreas Ortmann is Professor of Experimental and Behavioural Economics at the University of New South Wales in Sydney, Australia. Prior to his move to the land of Oz, he spent a decade at CERGE-EI in Prague, with which he remains affiliated. He holds a PhD in Economics from Texas A&M University. His interests cover Game Theory, Experimental Economics, Industrial Organisation (specifically industries where nonprofits and for-profits compete, certification issues), Corporate Finance, Public Economics, Mechanism Design, Experimental Methods in Economics, Psychology, and other Social Sciences, Behavioral Economics, and the History of Economic Thought (especially Adam Smith).

Maria Pia Paganelli is Professor of Economics at Trinity University. She works on Adam Smith, David Hume, and eighteenth-century monetary theories. She wrote The Routledge Guidebook to Adam Smith's *The Wealth of Nations* (Routledge 2020) and co-edited the Oxford Handbook on Adam Smith (OUP 2013) and Adam Smith and Rousseau (EUP 2018). She has served as the Vice President and President of the History of Economics Society, President of the International Adam Smith Society, and as the book review editor for the *Journal of the History of Economic Thought*.

Zack Rauwald is Research Associate at Fitzwilliam College, Cambridge, and Postdoctoral Researcher at the Hebrew University of Jerusalem. He recently completed his PhD on Adam Smith at the University of Cambridge.

Julio Seoane-Pinilla is Professor of Philosophy at the University of Alcalá (Madrid), dedicated mainly to the study of Enlightenment thought and culture. He has directed several Erasmus+ and national projects as well as three Spanish research centres.

Trevor Shelley is Assistant Professor and Director of Graduate Studies at the School of Civic and Economic Thought and Leadership at Arizona State University. He is the author of *Globalization and Liberalism: Montesquieu, Tocqueville, and Manent* (University of Notre Dame, 2020) and co-editor of *Citizenship and Civic Leadership in America* (Lexington, 2022) and *Renewing America's Civic Compact* (Lexington, 2023). He has also published several book chapters and journal articles on various topics in political theory.

John Skorupski is Emeritus Professor of Moral Philosophy at the University of St Andrews and a fellow of the British Academy and the Royal Society of Edinburgh. He is the author of Being and Freedom and *On Late Modern Ethics in Europe* published in 2021.

Spyridon Tegos is Associate Professor of Early Modern Philosophy at the University of Crete, Greece. He holds a PhD from the University of Paris X-Nanterre with a thesis on the concept of social sentiments in early modern philosophy. In his research, he focuses on the history of moral and political philosophy, particularly the Scottish and French Enlightenment. He is currently preparing a book on the classical French sources (early modern theatre and belles-lettres) that inspired early Scottish liberalism (David Hume, Adam Smith) and, in its aftermath, French liberalism (Germaine de Staël, Alexis de Tocqueville). He also works on a project regarding the legacy of philosophical anthropology in Early Modern moral and political thought.

Benoît Walraevens is Associate Professor of Economics at the University of Caen-Normandy in France. He holds a PhD in Economics from the University of Paris 1 Panthéon-Sorbonne. His work focuses on the history of economic thought, particularly the French and Scottish Enlightenment (especially Adam Smith and Jean-Jacques Rousseau), and on economic philosophy addressing issues of inequality, social justice, and the relationships between the market and democracy. He is currently working on a project on the history of economic thought regarding inheritance.

Eric Entrican Wilson is Associate Professor of Philosophy at Georgia State University (Atlanta, GA). His research focuses on the history of ethics and moral psychology, particularly during the Enlightenment. His work on emotion, self-control, autonomy, and moral judgement has been published in various venues, including *History of Philosophy Quarterly*, *Kantian Review*, *Stanford Encyclopedia of Philosophy*, and *Emotion Theory: The Routledge Comprehensive Guide*.

Editorial introduction and research note

Smith's library and marginalia update

It gives me great pleasure to assume the editorship of *The Adam Smith Review*. My first task is to thank Fonna Forman for her hard work over many years. Fonna will be a hard act to follow. She established the ASR as the home of Smith studies and a vital part of what makes the International Adam Smith Society such a vibrant academic group. In my time as Book Review Editor, I have had the privilege of working with Fonna and her editorial assistants, particularly on the last issue where the reins were being handed over to the new team at Glasgow. I know how much care and work went into each volume. I hope to continue the success that Fonna has created and carry the ASR into the future. With that in mind we have some changes for ASR15. First, our new contact email is adamsmithreview@glasgow.ac.uk.

In taking over as Editor, I'm joined by three Associate Editors, all of whom were based in Glasgow during the Adam Smith tercentenary celebrations. Dr Leo Steeds, Dr Ana Paula Londe Silva, and Dr Hiroyuki Ota will join me in managing the ASR into the future.

Hiroyuki Ota is Assistant Professor in the Department of Philosophy at Toyo University in Tokyo, Japan, and his main research interest is British Intellectual History. Recent publications include a monograph titled *Adam Smith's Moral Theory: The Complexity of the Human Mind and Moral Judgements*, (2024, in Japanese) and a book chapter titled 'Butler and Adam Smith on Conscience, Self-deceit and General Rules' in *Joseph Butler: A Preacher for Eighteenth-Century Commercial Society* (2024, Singapore: Springer).

Ana Paula Londe Silva is a postdoctoral fellow at the Universidade Federal de Minas Gerais, where she coordinates the research project *Political Economy and Abolitionism: Public Debate and Slavery in Brazil During the First Half of the Nineteenth Century*. She served as a research associate at the University of Glasgow from 2023 to 2025, contributing to the project *Adam Smith at 300: Celebrating Adam Smith as Scholar, Educator, and Citizen*. Her research focuses on the history of political economy, antislavery, and abolitionism in the eighteenth and nineteenth centuries, with a recent emphasis on the circulation of economic ideas.

Leo Steeds is currently Research Associate at King's College London. He was previously Research Associate on the Adam Smith 300 project at the University of Glasgow. His research crosses political theory, political economy, and the history of ideas, engaging with contemporary issues in environmental philosophy.

DOI: 10.4324/9781003767824-1

I'm very much looking forward to working with this great team of Smith scholars as they build their careers and contribute to Smith scholarship.

This edition of the ASR includes papers from the IASS conference in Bogota, along with a series of individual submissions that run across Smith's work and that display the cross-disciplinarity and interdisciplinary approaches that characterise both Smith and Smith studies. We have book symposiums on two of the most significant recent monographs on Smith and a research note on an exciting new online resource for Smith scholars. As we celebrate the 250th anniversary of the publication of *The Wealth of Nations* in 2026, I'm happy to report that Smith studies and the ASR are in good health.

Research note

In Volume 11 of *The Adam Smith Review,* we published a research note that detailed the beginning of a project to survey the books that once belonged to Adam Smith. In doing so, Shinji Nohara and I worked with the late Nicholas Phillipson to explore the books in the various libraries and collections around the world. In the intervening years, teams at the University of Tokyo and the University of Glasgow have worked together to examine Smith's library. This project has now been completed, and the results can be found at a new Adam Smith's Library webpage:

https://adamsmithslibrary.gla.ac.uk

Adam Smith's Library provides an open, curated catalogue of the books owned by Smith. You can search the catalogue of Smith's library books by author, title, publication details, and whether the book contains marginalia. Where marginalia is present, you can access images of the markings and either view them online or download them. It is also possible to download the full catalogue data. The project would not have been possible without the assistance of the various libraries around the world that generously allowed us to photograph and upload images from their collections to our website. You can use the website to locate copies of Adam Smith's library books where they are held today in repositories in Japan, Scotland, England, Ireland, Italy, and the United States.

Alongside the searchable database and images, we are also providing introductory materials about Adam Smith's book collecting and identifying Adam Smith's handwriting to assist users in navigating the material. We hope that this will prove to be a valuable resource for those interested in the development of Smith's thinking and his engagement with the authors whose books he owned.

The project was made possible by generous funding from the John Templeton Foundation, the Japan Society for the Promotion of Science, and the Chancellor's Fund of the University of Glasgow.

Craig Smith
The University of Glasgow

Part I

Bogota symposium

1 Introduction

Jimena Hurtado

Emerging from the long season of isolation in 2020, the International Adam Smith Society reconvened with renewed caution and resolve. A first attempt to meet in Madison in 2021 reminded us how fragile in-person scholarly exchange had become. Bogotá (11–13 July 2022) was an experiment in hybridity, not only a technological test but also a deliberate effort to recover the interactions and intersubjective exchange so precious to Smith's moral philosophy. The program at the Department of Economics, Universidad de los Andes, combined plenaries by Vernon Smith and Tyler Cowen with sessions in English and Spanish across moral philosophy, political economy, reception studies, and the arts. All sessions were organised in a hybrid format to widen participation while rekindling face-to-face conversation. More than 50 participants attended; 14 manuscripts were submitted after the meeting, and four were selected for this issue of *The Adam Smith Review*.

Two conversations began in Bogotá structure what follows. The first traces how Smith's political economy travelled into Latin America and what it became in Brazil and in the Río de la Plata. The second re-centres the civic instruments Smith thought made commercial society humane: education broadly conceived and the arts and rhetoric of visibility. Read together, these conversations yield a Smithian politics of recognition – how we learn to see one another, to judge one another, and to educate judgement in modern societies.

The two reception studies by Mauricio C. Coutinho and Alfredo Félix Blanco, Franco Godino, and Melisa Janet Luc show reception not as passive inheritance but as appropriation under constraints. In late-eighteenth and early-nineteenth-century Brazil, diffusion ran through Portugal's institutions, Coimbra's reformed curriculum, and a slave-based colonial economy, with José da Silva Lisboa, Visconde de Cairu, as a pivotal mediator and programmatic Smithian voice. His *Princípios de Economia Política* (Lisbon, 1804), published by the Royal Press and tied to Rodrigo de Souza Coutinho's enlightened statecraft, offered an overt, programmatic Smith in a local quarrel with Lusophone physiocracy, thus providing an early example of Smithian arguments redeployed for metropolitan and imperial policy. As British pressure mounted against the slave trade and Brazil's ports opened, the channels of diffusion shifted from Lisbon's press and patronage to new Brazilian realities. Later nineteenth-century classrooms diversified the canon, including Say and Mill alongside Smith, yielding a hybrid pedagogy of political economy.

DOI: 10.4324/9781003767824-3

Blanco, Godino, and Luc delve into what happens in the Río de la Plata, situating Smith within Bourbon reforms, institutional reconfiguration, and the 'new science' of political economy that animated Buenos Aires on the eve of the May Revolution. Translation politics mattered: the 1794 Spanish *The Wealth of Nations* reached readers like Belgrano and Vieytes in bowdlerised form yet still served as a conduit for liberal doctrines, entering a local discourse also fed by French, Spanish, British, and Italian sources. The result is not a doctrinal transplant, but rather vernacular liberalism with universal principles articulated through local media, institutions, and revolutionary agendas.

The other line of conversation deals with education, visibility, and the art of judgement. It revisits the *Theory of Moral Sentiments*, *The Wealth of Nations*, and the *Lectures in Rhetoric and Belles Lettres* to argue that Smith's remedies for the moral costs of commercial society rely on education and on the rhetorical/aesthetic means by which persons become publicly legible. Zack Rauwald goes beyond a literature that either sidelines inequality or treats taxation as Smith's main instrument, reconstructing Book V to show that education, elementary instruction, civic and moral formation, and the disciplining effects of religious association do the core remedial work. Taxation, though not absent, is limited in redistributive scope; education counters urban anonymity and restores social recognition, addressing what Smith depicts as the poor being 'sunk in obscurity and darkness.'

Complementing this, Jorge López Lloret builds a bridge from Smith's spectator theory to eighteenth-century portraiture. Sympathy is not affective contagion but a compositional labour: the spectator 'pictures out' another's situation, then compares sentiments to judge propriety. This LRBL-inflected pedagogy of seeing clarifies how individuals make themselves visible and how publics learn to read them. In this view, art and rhetoric are not embellishments to moral life; they are techniques of civic legibility in large, anonymous societies.

Three threads tie these contributions together. First, appropriation under constraint. The Latin American essays show ideas moving through censorship, patronage, curricular change, and uneven state formation. This replaces a linear influence story with a historically situated account of how Smithian arguments are selectively redeployed to local ends.

Second, visibility as a moral precondition. Rauwald's emphasis on the poor being overlooked in unequal commercial societies aligns with López Lloret's discussion on the pedagogy of making selves legible and training spectators to see well. Recognition is the hinge: the social damage of inequality is partly a damage to visibility, and the arts of rhetoric and portraiture model how spectatorship can be educated.

Third, civic education serves as Smith's lever. When read together, both articles highlight Book V and LRBL as central to Smith's project. Elementary instruction, associational life, and rhetorical/aesthetic literacies repair the capacities required for mutual judgement; taxation remains ancillary. The result is a revised picture of Smith's political economy where education and the arts are institutional means to sustain recognition, duty, and justice in commercial society.

From Bogotá to the page, the symposium advances two claims: that Latin American receptions are theory-bearing episodes in the global history of Smith's political economy and that Smith's remedies for the moral strains of modern life centre on educating spectatorship through schools, sects, and the arts rather than on ambitious fiscal engineering. May these manuscripts extend conversations initiated across the conference's sessions and panels in Bogotá.

2 Adam Smith's ideas and the May 1810 revolution in Buenos Aires

Alfredo Félix Blanco, Franco Godino, and Melisa Janet Luc

Introduction

The objective of this chapter is to provide a brief review of the influence that Adam Smith's writings and liberal principles had on the ideas of the protagonists of the May Revolution that occurred in Buenos Aires in May of 1810. Its importance lies in understanding the ideas that the May revolutionaries had in mind when building a new economic order, first in the viceroyalty and then in the new independent country, taking into account the influence of Adam Smith's liberal ideas, whether direct or indirect. Moreover, these influences would continue to have weight and shape the minds of those who led Argentina's economic policy until the beginning of the twentieth century.

The new political theories of European thinkers and the birth of a 'new science,' political economy, are very important elements to explain the matrix of revolutionary thought. Scholastics, Late Mercantilists, Physiocrats, and classical economists (mainly Spanish, British, and French) influenced the economic thought of the revolutionaries. But, unlike the existing literature on the May revolutionaries, this chapter will explore in greater depth the influences of Smith and the Smithians, particularly the Spanish, on Manuel Belgrano and Hipolito Vieytes.

The relative economic backwardness of Spain and its political crises were not only catalysts for the revolutionary process but also limits for its aspirations, which were reflected in the disputes and debates that plagued the decades following independence. In this historical context, the growing influence of liberal ideas, both in politics and in economics, played an essential role. Adam Smith's ideas were very relevant during this process, and ultimately economic liberalism would be a driver of development and growth for the Argentine economy in the second half of the nineteenth century and the first decades of the twentieth century.

The 'new science' reached the Viceroyalty of the Río de la Plata at the end of the eighteenth century and the beginning of the nineteenth century, influencing on Manuel Belgrano, generally considered the first Argentine economist, Juan Hipólito Vieytes, Mariano Moreno and Juan José Castelli, among others.

These changes in intellectual paradigms, the crisis of the colonial system, the gradual emergence of institutions that would characterise modern capitalism, and the action of the *Men of May* produced a new reality, one with tensions. It is in this context that the Argentine Republic was born.

DOI: 10.4324/9781003767824-4

In the second section, we offer a brief discussion of the nature of economic thought in the period of independence. Then, the third section describes the political and economic developments that led to the creation of the Viceroyalty of the Río de la Plata, as well as its principal institutional characteristics and intellectual climate. In the fourth section, we discuss the special conditions under which the translation of Smith's *The Wealth of Nations* into Spanish took place, both in Spain and in its colonies, and how it was received by the leading intellectuals of the time. This is to understand the true force with which his ideas reached the principal actors of the May Revolution of 1810.

In the fifth section, we will discuss two intellectuals who played a major role in the May Revolution and were clearly influenced by Smith: Manuel Belgrano and Juan Hipólito Vieytes. Finally, we will offer some concluding considerations on the topic.

The historiography of economic thought during the period

It is generally accepted that Political Economy emerged with the Industrial Revolution and the publication of Adam Smith's *The Wealth of Nations*. Why is that moment considered the beginning of the history of economics? Because it is at that moment in time that economic thought became a science, with a proper method and epistemology (Roncaglia 2006).

A complication in this demarcation arises when we try to incorporate other parts of the world into a history of economic thought. What is considered economic theory was (and still is) mostly developed in Europe and the United States, but economic discussions existed in Latin America (as in other parts of the world, of course) well before the late eighteenth century and continued afterwards, often on its own trajectory. These efforts were pre-scientific and pre-capitalist in nature, given the relative backwardness of Latin American economies compared to Europe's, and therefore should not be considered part of a history of economic thought if we accept the elevation of the discipline to a scientific endeavour as a demarcation (Luc 2021).

Nevertheless, in the history of economics as well as in that of other disciplines, the notion of 'own-knowledge' and the study of the diffusion of economic ideas have given rise to an important debate (Cardoso 2017). Interesting concepts emerged from this debate that reshaped the notion of diffusion (understood as an exercise without influence on theory), the role of the intellectual who adapts a theory, and the understanding of the feedback between existing conditions and theory.

Some authors maintain that the way in which theory is adapted and knowledge is used to develop economic policy is precisely the history of economic thought in a particular country (Cardoso 2003: 625). Thus, following Cardoso (2003) for the case of countries that are not leaders in producing economic theory, five characteristics must be studied to consider the existence of vernacular economic theory: the foreign idea or theory itself; the context in which adoption takes place; the methods, concepts, and techniques of analysis used; the specific conditions of the country or region; and finally, the implications of the theory for economic policy (Cardoso 2003: 623).

Under that focus, the concepts of adaptation, appropriation, and translation of ideas and theories (Cardoso 2017) become central for studying the economic ideas of the colonial period in Latin America. The adaptation of knowledge refers not only to the tweaking of an idea or theory as a finished product but also to a process of reception and creation that moulds it on a larger scale. Appropriation, on the other hand, introduces elements of variation, diversity, and creative thinking into the theory, manifesting the active role of those who participate directly in the process of assimilating ideas. To incorporate this category not only means that we'll no longer talk about one unique universal knowledge but also means that institutional conditions that provide legitimacy to the appropriation of knowledge must be considered: the institutional conditions of the receiving country.[1] Finally, the translation and circulation of texts are acts of communication between the audience, the translators, and the modes and conventions of translation. It demonstrates how knowledge is disseminated through time and space.

The period that is the scope of this work should be considered part of a period of transition (Luc 2021), beginning in the late eighteenth century and culminating with the emergence of structuralism.

The viceroyalty of the Río de la Plata

Among the many crucial elements that led to the revolution of May 1810, the political and institutional organisation of the Spanish Empire and its colonies should be emphasised. The crisis of the colonial economy in the late eighteenth century, along with political developments in the Iberian Peninsula, required responses and solutions from the metropolis. One of the main reasons for crafting the Royal Decree of 1 August 1776, which created the Viceroyalty of the Río de la Plata, was Spain's need to strengthen control over its colonies.[2] However, without intending to, the Decree ultimately contributed to creating the conditions that, together with other factors, led to the end of Spanish control in South America. Eventually, these new institutional arrangements, matched with the political action of the *Men of May*, would give birth to a new nation, one still mired in the same economic issues as its former self.

The measures that accompanied the creation of the new viceroyalty not only freed Buenos Aires from the political tutelage of the Viceroyalty of Alto Peru but also eliminated some obstacles that prevented its commercial expansion. The viceroyalty was followed by a series of measures that contributed to fostering an initially 'shy' spirit of economic liberalism. One year after the inception of the viceroyalty, the port of Buenos Aires was inaugurated, curtailing the interests of traders from Peru and Chile and benefiting the emergent local commercial bourgeoisie. In 1778, King Charles III promulgated the *Rules for the Free Trade of Spain and the Indies,*[3] which allowed reciprocal trade among the ports of Spain and those of its colonies.

The new trade reality was accompanied by the creation of the Customs (Royal Decree, 25 June 1778). The following years witnessed the birth of other modernising institutions: the Consulate of Commerce (1794), the Intendencias (1782), and the Real Audiencia (1783). These reforms not only responded to already existing conditions but also fostered new political and economic structures. This, in turn, led to a recognition and strengthening of commercial interest and ties within the people in the colonies, which also manifested in a considerable increase in the political influence and wealth of the emergent bourgeoisie and local political class. Without intending to, the effort of the Bourbon Reforms laid some groundwork for the growing conflict between the interest of the empire and the local elites, which together with the aid of other elements[4] would eventually lead to revolution.

In the sphere of economic ideas, the emergence of political economy, which attempted to find answers that regarded economic issues in a systematic way, led to the gradual decline of mercantilist doctrines. Cantillon, Quesnay, and the French physiocrats, together with some Spanish authors, pre-announced the emergence of economic liberalism that would find a masterful exposition combined with profound analytical insight and rigor in Adam Smith and the English classical school.[5]

In relation to the influence of the Physiocrats, Lluch and Argemí pointed out that 'the earliest relevant translations [into Spanish] were of an essay by Mirabeau (which later became part of *L'Ami des hommes*), translated by Serafín Trigueros, and of Quesnay's *Maximes générales du gouvernement d'un royaume agricole*, translated by Manuel Belgrano' (Lluch and Argemí 1994: 616).

The ideas of the founders of political economy played a salient role. These ideas, which would influence and then be disseminated by Manuel Belgrano and Juan Hipólito Vieytes, among others, are key to understanding the *Men of May*'s perspective on the economy.[6] The main actors of the May Revolution imagined the future from the perspective of economic liberalism: almost 35 years after the publication of *The Wealth of Nations,* its influence on the intellectual climate of the time is most certainly present. However, they were faced with the conflicts of the historical, political, and social context of a region in which pre-capitalist socio-economic structures were still present and would remain so in the following decades.

Towards 1808, the abdication of Ferdinand VII, together with the appearance of the Junta of Seville and the Supreme Central Junta years later, marked the end of the road for the simmering political developments that began with the Royal Decree of 1776 and eventually ignited by the revolution in 1810 in Buenos Aires.[7]

Smith's work in the viceroyalty of the Río de la Plata

Although Smith's work was far from the only inspiration, and in most cases not even the primary one, the doctrine of economic liberalism that emerged with both practical and theoretical force from *The Wealth of Nations* was a fundamental influence on the intellectual outlook of the men who led the emancipatory struggle. In their hands, many of Smith's most basic principles and conclusions would be so assimilated as to seem absent. Fortunately, a careful examination dispels such misconceptions.

Before examining the influence that English economic liberalism, and in particular the work of Adam Smith, had on the *Men of May*, it is important to highlight the context in which Smith's *The Wealth of Nations* was first translated into Spanish. Manuel Belgrano studied and lived in Spain between 1786 and 1794, so it is unlikely that he would have had access to read the adapted edition of *The Wealth of Nations*. Smith's liberal influence can be seen in his writings, but it is not certain that he read it first-hand.

The first Spanish edition of the book, translated by Jose Alonso Ortiz, a proponent of economic liberalism, was published in 1794 circumventing the ban existing since 1792 on Smith's work due to 'the poverty of his style and the liberality of his morals.' (Leonard and Smith 1944: 89). That year, the Spanish Inquisition had placed the French translation of Smith's work on the index of Prohibited Books (Smith 1957). However, in the 1794 edition, the book was adapted to censorship standards,

> 'purging it of several impious propositions . . . and eliminating entirely an article . . . in which the author favors tolerance in matters of religion, so that it is purged of anything that could lead to error or relaxation in moral or religious matters.'
>
> (Smith 1957: 110)

Nevertheless, Smith's work had a strong influence on Manuel Belgrano through two powerful disseminators of his ideas: the Spaniard Valentín de Foronda and the Irishman Samuel Crumpe (Rojas 2010a). Another author who would greatly influence Belgrano was Jovellanos: 'Though Jovellanos' liberalism was not the product of a single influence, Smith impressed him profoundly. His unpublished papers include a 13-page 'Extract from the Work of Mr. Smith' and a translation of parts of *The Wealth of Nations* (Smith 1957: 106). In Spain, the English version or the French translation of *The Wealth of Nations* was in circulation before the Spanish translation and continued even after its prohibition. Moreover, in the Spanish colonies, *The Wealth of Nations* 'did not take long to reach . . . the enlightened youth that aspired the independence of these territories.' (González Alberdi 1947: 42–43). In fact, in the case of Vieytes, he read it in French before its publication in Spanish, and a French copy was found in his library after his death (Rojas 2010a: 83). Therefore, Smith's influence, at least in Vieyte's case, was also a result of direct contact with his work.

As Rojas (2010a) has proposed, perhaps what also attracted the attention of the *Men of May* was the fact that Buenos Aires was used as an example of an interesting point in *The Wealth of Nations*: the explanation of economic evolution, in particular the characterisation of its first stages. Smith came into contact with data related to the economic structure of South America, especially the Río de la Plata, through the work of Jorge Juan and Antonio de Ulloa, published in Madrid in 1748 and later translated into English (Rojas 2010a: 84).

Ulloa's description of the proliferation of cattle and fishing in the Pampas and its rivers, and especially the consequently low price of meat, illustrated Smith's evolutionary vision of society. In *The Wealth of Nations,* he makes the following reference to Ulloa's work:

> In its rude beginnings, the unimproved wilds, which then occupy the far greater part of the country, are all abandoned to cattle. There is more butcher's meat than bread; and bread, therefore, is the food for which there is

> the greatest competition, and which consequently brings the greatest price. At Buenos Ayres, we are told by Ulloa, four reals, one-and-twenty pence halfpenny sterling, was, forty or fifty years ago, the ordinary price of an ox, chosen from a herd of two or three hundred. He says nothing of the price of bread, probably because he found nothing remarkable about it. An ox there, he says, costs little more than the labor of catching him. But corn can nowhere be raised without a great deal of labor; and in a country which lies upon the river Plate, at that time the direct road from Europe to the silver mines of Potosi, the money-price of labor could be very cheap. It is otherwise when cultivation is extended over the greater part of the country. There is then more bread than butcher's meat. The competition changes its direction, and the price of butcher's meat becomes greater than the price of bread.
>
> (WN I.xi.b.7, 164)

For the Scottish author, societies undergo development through several stages. The first one is that of the 'hunters,' in which the population was sustained by gathering the spontaneous fruits of the earth. This is the stage the viceroyalty was transiting: in the specific case of Buenos Aires, it involved the hunting of wild cattle. Private property was still not present, it being characteristic of the second stage, the 'pastoral' period, in which cattle came to be owned and moved in search of better natural pastures. With the advent of 'agriculture,' the third stage is reached, with land being appropriated by individuals who demand rent for its use. The process ends in the fourth and final stage, the 'commercial' phase, where currency replaces barter and the division of labour prevails, allowing for an increase in population and the consumption of a greater variety of goods (WN V.i).

The limitations of a doctrine created in the centre of the economic world, as England was at the time, to explain the reality of the colonies were and are evident. That is why it is argued in this paper that the adaptation, appropriation, and translation, following Cardoso (2017), of Smith's ideas to an economy in a pastoral state (as he establishes in his writings) were not easy for Belgrano and Vieytes. Even so, they took liberal ideas, among others, to adapt the theory to the reality they observed and to think about what form the economy should take and what role it should have in economic terms in the world.

Economic ideas of the leaders of May

Manuel Belgrano[8]

Belgrano is considered the first Argentine economist, despite having graduated as a lawyer from the University of Valladolid (1793). He was the first secretary of the Buenos Aires Consulate of Commerce (1794). He was well-versed in political economy, philosophy, and law, and also translated physiocratic works into Spanish.

> I confess that I did not apply myself so much to the career I had gone there to pursue, but rather to the study of living languages, political economy and

public law, and that as soon as I had the fortune to find men devoted to the public good who shared their useful ideas with me, the desire to give as much as I could for the benefit of the public and to the acquisition of prestige for my works, aimed at favoring the homeland, took over me.

(Belgrano 1966: 1)

Belgrano had multiple and varied ideological influences. His stay in Spain during the peak of the French Revolution and, as expressed by Ingenieros, the ideological roots of the South American revolutions are

> Rousseau's *Social Contract* as an expression of political liberalism . . .; Quesnay's *General Maxims for the Economic Government* as an expression of economic liberalism, discussed to justify the commercial interests of the colonies against the monopoly of the metropolis. . . . Belgrano imported physiocratic ideas, translating Quesnay's economic maxims and glossing Campomanes.
>
> (Ingenieros 1918: 130)

Belgrano was aware of Smithian doctrine through Carlos Martínez de Irujo's *Compendio,*[9] and later he would produce a summary of Book IV of *The Wealth of Nations* (Smith 1957). The faith in self-correcting markets and economic liberalism, which was on the rise as a consequence of the confluence of real-world economic developments and the intellectual production of Adam Smith and his successors, gradually meant leaving scholastic and medieval worries behind. Such a rise also influenced Belgrano's thought, championing economic liberalism and free trade. However, most of that commitment was not a direct result of Smith's work but of previous authors (Smith 1957: 122).

On the other hand, Belgrano was also influenced by authors such as Galiani,[10] Genovesi,[11] Filangieri[12] (from whom he borrowed the notion of an economic structure integrated by agriculture, manufacturing, and trade), and Feijóo.[13] These influences are highly relevant when judging the more eclectic character of Belgrano's ideas, such as his support for the establishment of an Inca monarchy in the former colonies. Belgrano's ideas on political economy can be found mainly in three different places: (a) his translations of physiocratic works between 1794 and 1796, (b) his memoirs from the Royal Consulate of Buenos Aires, and (c) the articles that he published in the *Correo de Comercio* newspaper.[14]

The translations, being those of the Physiocrats' work, naturally do not shed light on Smith's influence on Belgrano.[15] However, the writings produced for the Consulate of Commerce are an entirely different matter. Belgrano assumed his position as Secretary of the Consulate of Buenos Aires on 2 June 1794, appointed by King Charles IV. He wrote about this event:

> When I finished my degree around 1793, the ideas of political economy were spreading in Spain with frenzy, and I think that this is why I was appointed Secretary of the Consulate of Buenos Aires, created in Minister Gardoqui's time, without me making any arrangements whatsoever for that to happen; and the Secretary's official who was in charge of these issues even asked

> me to name individuals who had this knowledge so as to employ them in other institutions of the sort, which were being created in different business squares around America.
>
> (Belgrano 1966: 2)

For 16 years (1794–1809), he was Secretary of the Consulate,[16] and his ideas on political economy can be appreciated in the memoirs with which the body's sessions were annually opened. For Belgrano, the writing and reading of the memoirs was

> a route for intellectual broadening and a contribution to the common good . . . he expressed all of his enthusiasm and his brilliance, this is the reason why the traditional opinion that the richest and most original of Belgrano's ideas can be found in his memoirs is completely justified.
>
> (Fernández López and Orellana 1984: 353)

In the first memoir, read in June 1796, Belgrano was primarily concerned with 'the general means for the development of Agriculture, as the fertile Mother that supplies all raw materials, . . .' adding almost immediately that 'Agriculture is the true destiny of man' (Belgrano 1996: 12). The strong physiocratic influence can be appreciated in the title of the memoir itself: *General Means to Foment Agriculture, Promote Industry, and Protect Trade in an Agricultural Country.*[17] When Belgrano expressed these ideas, the viceroyalty was far from being the agricultural state that he considered necessary and was closer to being an 'early and rude state of society,' as mentioned by Smith in Chapter VI of *The Wealth of Nations*; Belgrano's concern was how to achieve development for such an economy.

The newspaper *Correo de Comercio* was used by Belgrano to disseminate his ideas. The topics were diverse: the pieces include ones on trade, education, political economy, politics, and geography. He had very clear theoretical economic concepts. He expressed advanced reasoning related to pricing, involving both supply and demand, and combining objective and subjective elements to determine it.

The absence of a debate about value should not be considered a limitation of his theoretical knowledge. Physiocratic views were shaped by the dominant characteristics of the French economy during the mid-eighteenth century, which led them to reason in terms of physical productivity to define 'produit net' without resorting to an exchange value theory. In a similar manner, Belgrano, faced with a pre-capitalist reality, could not (and maybe did not have to) think in terms of the production of exchange values. By that time, English classics had to define an exchange value theory, and they developed a labour theory of value to understand the new economic organisation and the social relationships derived from it.

Belgrano believed that the sources of wealth could be found in agriculture, trade, and industry. At the beginning of his first piece in *Correo de Comercio,* he stated this forcefully:

> Producers, you who provide society with your effort and sweat that allow for society's subsistence, with the gift of products and the raw materials required by the State! Artists, you who know how to settle nature's productions

> by giving them a new shape for a different use from the expected one, and add new value with which to enrich the State and contribute to its prosperity! Traders, you who drive change both internally and externally with your activity and through whose means agriculture and industry are encouraged; the State receives the utilities with which it meets its needs and emergencies!
>
> (in Belgrano 2011: 71)

The concept of interdependence among the different sectors of the economy was also present: 'the mutual dependency of agriculture and trade is such that one cannot flourish without the other' (in Varo and Coria 1998: 7) and talking about the foundation of trade, he states that

> [A]griculture and industry are its essence; they are joined in such a way that if one weighs more than the other it destroys itself. The products of the land with no industry will have no value, if agriculture is neglected the channels for trade are obstructed.
>
> (in Varo and Coria 1998: 7)

Notwithstanding his not having developed a theory of value, he defined productivity in a broader way than the Physiocrats because he did not link it to an exclusively physical event but rather associated it with economic values. He did not limit the production of economic surplus (the physiocratic 'produit net') to agriculture.

On monetary matters, he expressly recognises the functions of money as a unit of measure and as a medium of exchange, approaching the idea of the money veil, typical of classical thought. He offered a basic perception of the quantity theory of money by saying that the extraordinary rise in all prices is related to 'that infallible principle that states that the value of things arises from the total amount of cash in circulation' (in Varo and Coria 1998: 9).

Juan Hipólito Vieytes[18]

Vieytes is mainly remembered for his participation and political commitment to the revolutionary movement of May 1810.[19] His role as the head of the newspaper *Semanario de Agricultura, Industria y Comercio*[20] made him the first 'criollo journalist.' However, it is relevant to highlight his significance as an economist, which is often not properly recognised. He has been treated with a certain intellectual contempt by Robert S. Smith (1957) and Luis Roque Gondra (1927), but as Carlos Rodríguez Braun pointed out, 'although Vieytes was no innovative theoretician nor a scholarly prepared thinker, he was an early and able disseminator of smithian economics and deserves to be counted among the foremost Spanish and Spanish-American economists of his day' (Rodríguez Braun 1997: 444).

Vieytes was a great admirer of, and an expert on, Adam Smith and his acolytes. He refers to the Scottish philosopher as 'the sublime economist'[21] (Vieytes 2003: 111–114) and draws his main concepts from *The Wealth of Nations*.[22] Just like in Belgrano's case, another important influence was the works of the physiocrats, which suggested the need to obtain maximum profit from the land and advocated for the development of farming activities. He considered agriculture the only noble and honest activity that would allow for the production of true wealth, and he even believed it to be a patriotic activity.

As it has already been stated, stockbreeding was more developed than agriculture in the viceroyalty, but Vieytes believed there was a need to expand the latter, maintaining that the long-term growth of a capitalist economy required the growth of agriculture's productivity. Moreover, during this stage of development, stockbreeding seemed less compatible with liberal ideas because it promoted the monopoly of land use by those who possessed it.

Vieytes believed that the development of farming would soon take place in the Río de la Plata because it would be unavoidable after a correct delimitation of property rights, education, and trade. In his own words: 'For our fields to succeed, property must be ensured so that no one feels restless about it; the ease with which it is upset is the cause of the slow growth which can be seen in our beautiful fields' (Vieytes 2003: 19), and again:

> The desire to possess is born together with man; those who do not own a property are those who do not have enough means to get one; let us ease the way towards satisfying this wish and we will have settlers to spare.
>
> (Vieytes 2003: 273)

He was equally clear with his opinions about free trade and vehemently rejected monopoly and the existence of barriers to international trade, showing an evident influence of Smith's writings.

His view of the economic system was presented in the articles published in the *Semanario de Agricultura, Industria y Comercio* and in the *Correo de Comercio (1810–1811)*. In fact, the title of the newspaper itself gives us a perspective on his concerns: the development and interrelation of agriculture, industry, and trade. Vieytes expects the economy to be a system of interrelated parts:

> Producers: No Nation can prosper without the development of industry; its extension is enormous, its products countless and its usefulness is beyond words. Everything that is produced by the three kingdoms of nature can be subjected to industry, and all of what industry embraces is useful for men.
>
> (Vieytes 2003: 10)

Vieytes highlighted the importance of personal interest as an engine of human conduct, as well as productive work, the division of labour, and trade, which allows for the creation and distribution of wealth. With a statement that could have been included in Adam Smith's *Theory of Moral Sentiments*, he expressed his belief that personal interest is the main motivation of human conduct: 'For man to get rid of inaction and laziness, no other path is known but that of using interest as bait' (Vieytes 2003: 16).

He suggested that one of the prerequisites for economic growth is the availability of a labour force and, therefore, he advocated for measures to populate the territory. He was also concerned about the importance of productivity and, referring to the incorporation of innovative technologies, he wrote for *Semanario* about the new tanning methods in England: '[W]e can make in one day what used to take months before, saving time, efforts and handling costs' (Vieytes 2003: 345).

Just like in Belgrano's case, Foronda was an important source of inspiration for Vieytes, and his influence can be clearly perceived in a couple of letters published in *Correo de Comercio*, both attributed to Vieytes. One of them deals with trade unions, while the other addresses 'the unfair tax on food products.' Additionally, in *Correo de Comercio*, Vieytes recommended reading texts about education, philosophy, and logic, which had been translated into Spanish by Foronda (Rojas 2010a).

Crumpe was also a great influence on Vieytes' economic ideas.[23] Between February and June 1805, Vieytes published translations of several parts of Crumpe's work.[24] Physiocracy also had a decisive influence on Vieytes' ideas, even though, as has already been stated, Belgrano was the main scholar and purveyor of Quesnay and his disciples' doctrine in the Río de la Plata.[25] Jovellanos, who also advocated for the encouragement of agriculture, the mercantilist Uztáriz,[26] and the Italian Galiani also contributed to the formation of Vieytes' economic ideas.

To summarise these influences, it is worth noting that Vieytes was inspired by the ideas of the thinkers who have been mentioned and the liberal spirit of the time, despite the relative backwardness of the Spanish territories in the Río de la Plata. He stated, '[A]ll wise Nations have agreed on granting indefinite freedom to their own businessmen' (in Rojas 2010b: 230).

His belief that the interdependency of countries is only natural, and one of the bases of free trade, was summarised in *Semanario* when he wrote:

> The world is no other thing but a large population shared out in many headquarters even if there are seas, vast deserts and terrible, almost inaccessible mountain ranges between them; industry has eased the difficulties which impeded social contact, and there is no longer any region which is unaware of the existence of the others, with which it holds an uninterrupted wisdom involving active and passive trade.
>
> (Vieytes 2003: 171–172)

In the society contemplated by the *Men of May*, respect for property was essential:

> For our lands to succeed property must be ensured so that no one feels restless about it. . . . He who lives in a country ruled by peace and respect for property shall be happy: without these, it cannot be enjoyed, farming involves fear, the products are collected with anxiety, and work is done with no hope of improving.
>
> (Vieytes 2003: 19)

That respect for property rights, a basic prerequisite for the construction of a modern capitalist society, would be encouragement enough for people to produce more.

Final considerations

The revolutionary process of May 1810 had a multiplicity of causes. The French Revolution, the independence of the United States, the economic transformations in Europe since the mid-eighteenth century, and the changes it brought to social and economic relations and their subsequent evolution all contribute to the context in which the independence of this Spanish colonial territory took place. In that historical era, the growing influence of liberal ideas, in both the political and economic spheres, had a decisive role in the revolutionary events of 1810. The new political ideas of European intellectuals, together with the publication of works on the 'new science' of economics, constituted the matrix of revolutionary thought.

The opinions of Belgrano and Vieytes, among others, are key to understanding the perspective that the *Men of May* had on the economy. Late mercantilists, Physiocrats, and classical economists all left a mark on these men's ideas. Smith's influence was naturally present, albeit in different degrees, with Belgrano's being mediated through Smith's Spanish acolytes and Vieytes' more directly through his reading of *The Wealth of Nations*. The comments and citations from these two leaders of the May Revolution of 1810 are evidence of the dominant presence of the ideas of economic and political liberalism. Vieytes and Belgrano adopted and translated ideas and theories from many European authors. They adapted them to the context of the viceroyalty and appropriated them to design economic policy, both during the last days of the viceroyalty and in the early years of independence. Thus, their work can be included in the discussions that are now taking place around the processes of adaptation, appropriation, and translation of ideas and theories.

However, the relative economic backwardness of the Spanish mainland, its successive political crises, and the consequences they had for the viceroyalty were both catalysts for the revolutionary process and limits that can be seen in the arguments and debates among the leaders of that historical period. The change of intellectual paradigms, the crisis of the colonial economy, the gradual emergence of modern capitalist institutions, and the political events that took place in the Iberian Peninsula, together with the actions of the *Men of May*, would give birth to a new reality, along with its tensions. The convictions (some of them radical, others eclectic) of those who decisively contributed to the end of the Spanish colonial system in South America took time to consolidate. The ideas of freedom, property, and free trade, which vigorously took over after the arrival of European capitalism, were not consolidated with the May Revolution. The issue of Argentina's national unity would remain unresolved for 50 years after that.[27]

Finally, the leaders of the national emancipation of Argentina reached the end of their lives with discouraging feelings. They could have easily ended their lives with the comment attributed to Juan José Castelli on his deathbed: 'If you see the future, tell him not to come.'

Notes

1 'The idea of universal science to which national or regional characteristics are totally irrelevant has been gradually replaced by a new approach in the cultural and intellectual history of science that vigorously includes the "local manifestations of universal science"' (Cardoso 2017: 34).
2 Other reasons for implementing these reforms were to modernise the Spanish economy, carry out territorial reorganisation, and centralise and strengthen control over the colonies.
3 It is important to note that this 'free trade' did not allow freedom to trade as Adam Smith understood it. These rules were made to trade only between the Spanish colonies and with the Kingdom of Spain, tied to an exhaustive control by the latter. They were not tied to the logic of economic liberalism or Smith's absolute advantages.
4 The independence of the United States and the French Revolution had influenced the men of May, particularly Manuel Belgrano. These events were key to the May leaders' thinking about independence from the Kingdom of Spain.
5 It is essential to highlight the great influence that the ideas of Valentín Tadeo de Foronda (1755–1821) and other Spanish intellectuals had over the *Men of May*. For an exposition on the topic, consult Fernández López (2005).
6 Among others that deserve to be mentioned are:

   a) Juan José Castelli (1764–1812), He is remembered as the 'speaker of the revolution,' was Secretary of the Consulate, and actively helped spread the ideas and events of the May Revolution.
   b) Mariano Moreno (1778–1811) was one of the most distinguished men of the May Revolution of 1810. Owner of a powerful intelligence, endless energy, and complete commitment to the cause.

7 A detailed analysis of the fall of the Spanish Empire in the Río de la Plata, and its transition to a new institutional context has been done by Adelman (1999), 'Section I: The Age of Revolution, 1780s–1820s.'
8 Manuel Belgrano (1770–1820), son of Domingo Belgrano y Peri and María J. González Casero, attended the Real Colegio de San Carlos and continued his education in Salamanca and Valladolid.
9 *Compendio de la obra inglesa intitulada Riqueza de las naciones, hecho por el marqués de Condorcet* (1792).
10 Ferdinando Galiani (1728–1787) wrote *Dialogues on the Commerce in Wheat* (1770).
11 Antonio Genovesi (1712–1769) wrote *Lezioni di commercio o sia d'economia civile*, one of the first Italian texts to address the topics of political economy in a systematic way.
12 Gaetano Filangieri (1752–1788) is the author of *Scienza della legislazione*, written between 1780 and 1785. The work is considered an essential contribution regarding legal philosophy and highlighted the tight interrelationship between the laws of politics and the laws of economics.
13 Fray Benito Jerónimo Feijóo y Montenegro (1676–1764). His work is made up of nine volumes of *Universal Critical Theater* and five volumes made up of his 163 *Erudite and Peculiar Letters*.
14 On 3 March 1810, the first issue of *Correo de Comercio* was published.
15 For an exposition of these works, see Blanco (2015).
16 His role during this period had some brief interruptions; in 1796 and 1800, he took a health-related leave of absence and was replaced by Juan José Castelli. In 1806, he interrupted his work as a consequence of the English invasion of Buenos Aires.

17 The similarities with *Quesnay's General Maxims of the Economical Government in an Agricultural Kingdom*, which Belgrano had translated, are evident.
18 Juan Hipólito Vieytes (1762–1815) was the son of Juan Vieytes and Petrona Mora Fernández de Agüero. After the death of Mariano Moreno, to whom he was politically close, Vieytes replaced him as Secretary of the Primera Junta (or 'First Assembly').
19 Vieytes set up a business (a soap factory) together with his friend Nicolás Rodríguez Peña, the premises of which were frequently used as clandestine meeting place for the revolutionary men.
20 Vieytes edited the *Semanario* between 1802 and 1807. He also wrote for *Correo de Comercio de Buenos Aires*, published between 1810 and 1811.
21 The quotation is from the *Carta 12* of the *Semanario* from the 24 December 1806.
22 The first Spanish edition of Adam Smith's work was published in Madrid in 1794, and Vieytes owned several editions of the *Wealth of Nations* (Smith 1957).
23 Samuel Crumpe (1766–1796) was the author of *An Essay on the Best Means of Providing Employment for the People*. It has been suggested that Vieytes was more interested in Crumpe's works than in Adam Smith's himself because the style of the former was closer to journalism (Rodríguez Braun 1997).
24 For example, a translation of Crumpe's memoir entitled *Economic Freedom, Low and Fair Taxes and Property Security are Necessary for the Development of Economy. Taxes should not Impede or Stop Trade* [La libertad económica, la imposición justa y la garantía de la propiedad son necesarias para el desarrollo de la economía. Los impuestos no deberían impedir ni detener el comercio], published in the issue of 27 March 1805 (Vieytes 2010: 235–240).
25 Physiocratic influences made Vieytes reflect upon farming topics. In these matters, he was influenced by Jean-Baptiste François Rozier (1734–1793), author of the *Cours complet d'agriculture théorique*.
26 Gerónimo de Ustáriz (1670–1732) is best known for his main work *The Theory and Practice of Commerce and Maritime Affairs* (1724).
27 In the four decades that followed the May Revolution, a civil war between 'federalists' and 'unitarians' broke out and impeded almost completely the existence of a central government. This period ended with the battle of Caseros (3 February 1852), in which Urquiza defeated Rosas. The following year, a constitution was enacted, but the country remained divided: Buenos Aires on the one hand and the Confederation (the other provinces) on the other. This division lasted until 1861, when Bartolomé Mitre defeated Urquiza (battle of Pavón) and unified the country under his authority.

Bibliography

Adelman, J. (1999) *Republic of Capital: Buenos Aires and the Legal Transformation of the Atlantic World*. Stanford: Stanford University Press.

Argemí d'Abadal, L. (2012) 'Physiocrats', in J. G. Backhaus (ed.) *Handbook of the History of Economic thought*. New York: Springer.

Belgrano, M. (1954) *Escritos económicos*. Buenos Aires: Raigal.

Belgrano, M. (1966) *Autobiografía y otras páginas*. Buenos Aires: Eudeba.

Belgrano, M. (1996) *Memorias,* (ed.) M. Fernández López. Buenos Aires: Biblioteca Página 12.

Belgrano, M. (2011) *Escritos sobre educación,* (ed.) R. Gagliano. La Plata: UNIPE, Editorial Universitaria. Online. http://biblioteca.clacso.edu.ar/Argentina/unipe/20171121062036/pdf_347.pdf (accessed 26 September 2022)

Blanco, A. F. (2015) 'Some Considerations on the Influence of Economic Liberalism in the May Revolution of 1810 in Buenos Aires, Argentina', *Iberian Journal of the History of Economic Thought*, 2(1): 36–47. Online. https://revistas.ucm.es/index.php/IJHE/article/download/49772/46267/ (accessed 26 September 2022)

Cardoso, J. L. (2003) 'The International Diffusion of Economic thought', in W. Samuels, J. Biddle and J. Davis (eds.) *A Companion to the History of Economic thought*. Oxford: Blackwell.

Cardoso, J. L. (2017) 'Circulating Economic Ideas: Adaptation, Appropriation, Translation', in A. M. Cunha and C. E. Suprinyak (eds.) *The Political Economy of Latin American Independence*. London: Routledge.

Correo de Comercio de Buenos Aires. (1810–1811) *Buenos Aires: Imprenta de Niños Expósitos*. https://catalogo.bn.gov.ar/F/?func=direct&doc_number=001181512

Fernández López, M. (2005) 'Cartas de Foronda: su influencia en el pensamiento económico argentino', in La Asociación (eds.) *Anales de la Asociación Argentina de Economía Política*. Buenos Aires: La Asociación. Online. https://docplayer.es/22493158-Cartas-de-foronda-su-influencia-en-el-pensamiento-economico-argentino-1.html (accessed 26 September 2022)

Fernández López, M. and Orellana, D. (1984) 'Manuel Belgrano y las Máximas de Quesnay', *Revista De Economía Y Estadística*, 25(1): 83–124. Online. https://revistas.unc.edu.ar/index.php/REyE/article/view/4423 (accessed 26 September 2022)

Foronda, V. (1994) *Cartas sobre los asuntos más exquisitos de la Economía Política y sobre las Leyes criminales*. Vitoria: Gobierno Vasco, Departamento de Economía y Hacienda.

Gondra, L. R. (1927) *Las Ideas Económicas de Belgrano*. Buenos Aires: Universidad de Buenos Aires.

González Alberdi, P. (1947) *Los economistas Adam Smith y David Ricardo*. Buenos Aires: Futuro.

Ingenieros, J. (1918) *La evolución de las ideas argentinas*. Buenos Aires: Talleres Gráficos Argentinos. Online. https://www.marxists.org/espanol/ingenieros/1918-la-revolucion.pdf (accessed 26 September 2022)

Leonard, I. A. and Smith, R. S. (1944) 'A Proposed Library for the Merchant Guild of Veracruz, 1801', *The Hispanic American Historical Review*, 24(1): 84–102.

Lluch, E. and Argemí, L. (1994) 'Physiocracy in Spain', *History of Political Economy*, 26(4): 613–627. Online. http://diposit.ub.edu/dspace/bitstream/2445/9172/1/137068.pdf (accessed 26 September 2022)

Luc, M. J. (2021) 'Periodization in Prehistory, Transition and the History of Economic thought in Latin America: An Expanded View', in L. Fiorito, S. Scheall and C. E. Suprinyak (eds.) *Research in the History of Economic Thought and Methodology: Including a Selection of Papers Presented at the 2019 ALAHPE Conference*. Bingley: Emerald Publishing Limited.

Rodríguez Braun, C. (1997) 'Early Smithian Economics in the Spanish Empire: J. H. Vieytes and Colonial Policy', *The European Journal of the History of Economic Thought*, 4(3): 444–454.

Rojas, R. (2010a) *El pensamiento económico de Juan Hipólito Vieytes*. Buenos Aires: Fundación San Antonio. Online. http://www.hacer.org/pdf/Rojas05.pdf (accessed 26 September 2022)

Rojas, R. (2010b) 'Propiedad, productividad y comercio: el Pensamiento económico de Juan Hipólito Vieytes', *Revista de Instituciones, Ideas y Mercados*, 53: 203–238. Online. http://www.eseade.edu.ar/files/riim/RIIM_53/53_7_rojas.pdf (accessed 26 September 2022)

Roncaglia, A. (2006) *The Wealth of Ideas: A History of Economic thought*. Cambridge: Cambridge University Press.

Smith, A. (1976) *An Inquiry into the Nature and Causes of the Wealth of Nations*, (eds.) R. H. Campbell and A. S. Skinner, Glasgow edition. Oxford: Oxford University Press.

Smith, R. S. (1957) 'The Wealth of Nations in Spain and Hispanic America, 1780–1830', *Journal of Political Economy*, 65(2): 104–125.

Varo, R. and Coria, L. (1998) 'Conceptos económicos de los escritos de Manuel Belgrano', in Universidad Nacional de Córdoba (eds.) *Anales de la Asociación Argentina de Economía Política*, Córdoba: Universidad Nacional de Córdoba. Online. http://portal.eco.unc.edu.ar/files/Biblioteca/conceconmb.pdf (accessed 26 September 2022)

Vieytes, J. H. (2003 [1802–1807]) *Semanario de Agricultura, Industria y Comercio*, versión facsimilar de Editorial Docencia, Buenos Aires. Publicado originalmente por la Imprenta de los Niños Expósitos, Buenos Aires.

Vieytes, J. H. (2010) *Semanario de Agricultura Industria y Comercio*, (ed.) Fundación Hernandarias. Buenos Aires: Fundación Hernandarias.

3 The first translation of *The Wealth of Nations* into Portuguese

Accumulation of capital

Mauricio C. Coutinho

Introduction

The first translation of *The Wealth of Nations* (*WN*) into Portuguese was released in 1811 in Rio de Janeiro, Brazil, by the Royal Press. In 1807, the invasion of Portugal by Napoleon's troops led the Royal Court to flee from Lisbon, and from 1808 until 1821, Rio de Janeiro remained the seat of the Portuguese empire. In its flight to Rio de Janeiro, the Portuguese court had transferred the Royal Press, an institution that, in addition to issuing decrees and official texts, published selected books to the transitory capital. The 1811 translation of *The Wealth of Nations* was, thus, an official initiative, surely promoted by two special personages, José da Silva Lisboa and Rodrigo de Souza Coutinho.[1]

José da Silva Lisboa, an intellectual from Coimbra origin and a high official of the colonial administration, was appointed as the head of the Royal Press in 1808. Silva Lisboa had already published a pioneering political economy book in Lisbon (1804) titled *Princípios de Economia Política* (*Principles of Political Economy*), which demonstrates the author's enthusiasm for Adam Smith. Backing Silva Lisboa in the Royal Press was Rodrigo de Souza Coutinho, a high-grade official of the Portuguese government, then chief minister of the Portuguese government in Rio de Janeiro. Souza Coutinho himself was an admirer of Adam Smith's ideas.[2] Indeed, Silva Lisboa and Souza Coutinho were high expressions of Portuguese political economy in their time.[3]

It is arguable that the translation of WN was conceived as part of the effort to support a set of governmental policies implemented between 1808 and 1810, which were under attack at the time. Effectively, D. João, the prince regent, upon arriving in Brazil immediately opened trade to all 'friendly nations' – in that context, England. In 1810, the *Trade and Navigation Treaty* established British commodities as preferential imports. Several Brazilian and Portuguese traders reacted against the opening of trade and the low import rates, as they represented a loss of the metropolitan privileges assured by the prevailing colonial rules up to that point. Rio de Janeiro was invaded by British merchants and manufacturers, causing Portuguese-Brazilian manufacturers and merchants to lose a previously secured market. José da Silva Lisboa, who had already published pamphlets and books in defence of the new policies,[4] possibly conceived the dissemination of Smith's magnum opus as intellectual support for the new Portuguese 'liberal' policies.[5]

DOI: 10.4324/9781003767824-5

It is worth noting that the Portuguese version of WN was edited as a 'compendium,' meaning an abridged version of the original work. In the foreword ('Prologue'), the editor explains that, although France and Spain had opted for integral translations, an abridged version seemed adequate to 'generalize the knowledge of doctr*ines*' that would be useful to the 'prosperity of each country.' Additionally, an abridged version would make the reading 'softer,' avoiding some 'prolix discussions that especially interest England.'[6] It is worth noting that the prologue mentions other political economy authors, such as Say, Sismondi, Canard, and references Playfair's and Garnier's editions of the original work. The foreword aims to show a broad knowledge of political economy, involving Smith's successors and varied national efforts in disseminating Smith's works.

The editors – or the translator – included a few notes along with the translation and emphasised several passages with italics. The notes, the stressed passages, and most of all, the choice of passages to be kept or suppressed from the original text provide a good indication of the preferences of the editor or translator. These preferences also lead us to a tormenting question: what is the real authorship of the translation? Officially, the translation is attributed to Bento da Silva Lisboa, the son of José da Silva Lisboa, an official of the Foreign Affairs and War Ministry then serving at the Royal Press. The fact is that Bento da Silva Lisboa – who, after Brazilian independence (1822), would achieve high positions in government – was an 18-year-old young man in 1811, whose familiarity with the English language and political economy is difficult to assess, to say the least. Given the high standards of the translation and the expertise required to engage in the efforts of translating, selecting passages, stressing passages, it is not difficult to conclude that the real authorship, or even the existence of a team behind the editorial effort, is a permanent puzzle. I assume that José da Silva Lisboa's behind-the-scenes tutorship during the translation process should be taken into consideration. The shadow of his ideas, expressed in his several books and pamphlets, is easily found both in the general style of the translation and in several specific solutions.[7]

I have been engaged in the study of the 1811 WN's Portuguese edition for some years.[8] The current chapter will focus on Book II, on 'the nature, accumulation, and employment of stock,' specifically in its chapters I, II, III, and V. I believe these chapters will be helpful in understanding some concerning issues related to the translation of WN into Portuguese. These issues include (i) terminological dilemmas, such as the distinction between 'stock' and 'capital,' or how to translate 'revenue'; (ii) the special challenges posed by specific institutional contexts, such as those present in Book II's chapter on money; (iii) the *ad usum* or instrumental aspects of the 1811 translation, such as the editors' use of Smith's stratification of sectors of economic activity in chapter V to reinforce José da Silva Lisboa's main point, that is, the scarcity of capital in Brazil suggested the concentration of endeavours in the most productive sector – agriculture. In short, Book II provides a good insight into terminological challenges, institutional specificities, and politically fruitful uses of translations – issues that seem to be important in any translation effort applied to a science devised as instrumental to support proposals for economic policies.

Apart from this introduction, the second section will focus on the general extension of the compressions and on some terminological specificities of the 1811 translation. The third section will focus on institutional or environmental differences that may impact translation. The fourth section will be attentive to the instrumental usage of Smith's work. The fifth section presents a very brief conclusion.

Compressions and some terminological challenges

As mentioned, WN's 1811 Portuguese edition is an abridged version of the original work. In the whole Book II, the overall remaining text – a measure of the remaining (or translated) parts, once considered the exclusions from the original text – is 49%. In each chapter, the remaining or translated parts are in chapter I, 75%; II, 21%; III, 54%; IV, 92%; V, 79%. As seen, chapter II, the longest chapter in Book II, abounding in examples from Scotland and England, suffered severe compression.

Chapter I is of special interest because it entails a contrast between two terms or two economic categories that are difficult to translate: stock and capital. In current Portuguese, we translate both words as 'capital,' and modern translated editions of WN are not always attentive to the distinction between stock and capital. The 1811 edition applied to 'stock,' in most situations, the alternative 'fundos.' According to a very authoritative dictionary of the end of the eighteenth century,[9] apart from its general uses meaning 'bottom' or 'rearguard,' 'fundo' '*in modern times means capital, or substance.*' That is, one of the possible and alternative meanings for 'fundo' is capital or substance, which somehow indicates amassed resources.

I guess, however, that Silva Lisboa's 'fundo' has another, more evident origin. It is simply an adaptation of the French word 'fonds,' largely used by French economists, including the physiocrats, to designate amassed resources, either material or financial. Garnier's edition of WN, praised in the 1811 Portuguese/Brazilian edition's foreword, resorts to 'fonds.'

Apart from 'stock,' there are other terminological challenges in the Portuguese translation. One of the most important challenges is 'revenue.' Revenue, which was a term usually associated with public funds – the revenue of the state – became widely used by Smith in WN to designate the resources or remunerations attributed to labour (wages), stock (profit), or land property (rent). Situating wages, profit, and rent as the 'original revenues' is a characteristic of Smith's work. Indeed, Samuel Johnson's dictionary defines revenue, an originally French word, as: 'Income; annual profits received from land or other funds.' And, in Book I, chapter V, Smith concludes:

> Whoever derives his revenue from a fund which is his own, must draw it either from his labour, from his stock, or from his land. The revenue derived from labour is called wages. That derived from stock . . . is called profit. . . . The revenue which proceeds altogether from land, is called rent, and belongs to the landlord.
>
> (WN I.vi.18, 69–70)

In this and other passages, Silva Lisboa translates 'revenue' as 'redito.' 'Redito' can be assumed as a synonym of 'rendimento'[10] – the latter, to date used as the Portuguese equivalent of 'revenue.' In the just-transcribed passage of WN, 'revenue' is translated as 'redito'; 'labour' as 'trabalho,' which is usual; 'wage' as 'salario,' which is also usual; 'stock' and 'profit' as 'fundo' and 'proveito'; and 'rent' as 'renda.' I will comment on 'renda' later, but it is interesting to note two words: 'redito,' Silva Lisboa's solution for 'revenue,' and 'proveito,' for profit. 'Proveito' was accepted by the dictionaries of the time (Bluteau and Moraes Silva 1789) as a synonym of 'lucro,' the word still commonly used in Portuguese to specify the revenue associated with stock or capital. We will see that, although 'proveito' was the most common choice, the 1811 edition sometimes uses 'lucro.' However, 'proveito' is by far the most frequent. For instance, we can find, in Book II, chapter I (p. 7), this solution: 'capital' (capital) can be used to '. . . *extract resources from the land, or manufacture them, or in buying them for later selling with profit ('proveito').*' Or, as in chapter III:

> a part of the produce of land rebuilds the capital of the farmer ('lavrador'), the other part pays its profit ('proveito'), and the land rent; . . . thus constituting a revenue ('redito'), of the owner of this capital as a profit ('proveito') for his stock ('fundo')
>
> (p. 37)[11]

In Book II, Silva Lisboa establishes 'redito' as the translation of 'revenue.' The Smithian distinction between 'stock' and 'capital,' which is crucial in these passages, is not always preserved in the text. In paragraph II, Smith states that 'the whole stock . . . is distinguished in two parts' (WN II.i.2, 279), designating 'capital' as the part which provides the revenue to be expected from the stock not immediately consumed. 'Stock' remains associated with immediate consumption. In this specific passage, Silva Lisboa translates 'capital' as 'capital,' but avoids associating immediate consumption with any specific word. Effectively, the latter sentence of paragraph II – 'In one, or other, or all of these three articles, consists the stock which men commonly reserve for their own immediate consumption' (WN II.i.2, 279) – was suppressed in the 1811 edition.

The division of capital into fixed and circulating capital, an important specificity of Book II, brings us to another difficult term. Smith mentions the fixed and circulating capital of the farmer, and the farmer represents in Smith's text the typical agricultural capitalist, whose circulating capital is employed in the wages and maintenance of his workers. Silva Lisboa translates 'farmer,' in this and in all situations, as 'lavrador,' a word that can designate Smith's 'farmer,' but effectively designates anyone who cultivates the land. According to Bluteau and Moraes Silva (BMS), the word 'fazendeiro,' which nowadays designates Smith's 'farmer,' was already current in Portuguese. 'Lavrador' seems to be an understatement since it means anyone who ploughs or cultivates the land.

Let me point out some words that suggest difficulties, indecisions, or even inaccuracies in Silva Lisboa's translations. I will just list these words, followed by the page on which they appeared in Book II of our '*Compendio*' (CRN). Silva Lisboa usually translates 'workman' (or 'workmen') as 'obreiro(s)' – for instance, in chapter I, p. 5. According to our dictionary (BMS), 'obreiro' means someone who works in 'obras.' 'Obra,' in turn, means 'product,' not to mention general outcomes from nature, art, or unearthly grace. The word 'trabalhador,' which currently designates anyone who works in any trade and was already in use in the 1800s, was not mentioned by Silva Lisboa. With 'workman,' Smith clearly refers to workers in general, in any trade. It is not clear why Silva Lisboa attaches 'obreiro' to workman.

'Labour' is another troublesome word. Silva Lisboa more frequently translates it as 'industria,' which is the Portuguese equivalent of 'industry.' The current Portuguese word for labour (or 'labour') is 'trabalho,' which, however, in the 1800s (according to the BMS dictionary) meant rustic labour. 'Industria' meant, in the 1800s – and still means – ingenious or cunning labour. Diligence, or diligent labour, is the meaning attributed by Samuel Johnson to 'industry,' and I think this was also Smith's perception and use of the term. Silva Lisboa, however, avoids 'trabalho' and insists on 'industria,' even in situations where Smith clearly did not mean 'diligence.' My strong guess, in this case, is that Silva Lisboa's 'industria' is a pure reflex of the French word 'industrie,' which was not only current in France but very much used by Say exactly to designate – as in English and in Portuguese – ingenious or inventive labour. José da Silva Lisboa (Silva Lisboa's father) was a great admirer of Say, even though his more intense connections with Say's works were built after 1811.[12]

'Trade' is another difficult word. Silva Lisboa translates it as 'emprego' (see p. 7), which literally means 'employment.' Additionally, 'instruments of trade,' which are simply instruments to be used in any way of making a living, are translated by Silva Lisboa as 'instrumentos de comércio' (see pp. 8, 9, 12, 18); 'comércio,' here, in the literal meaning of buying and selling. 'Gross' and 'net' revenue are crucial concepts in chapter II. Silva Lisboa sometimes translates them as 'renda grossa' and 'renda liquida' (p. 17), using the term 'renda' to refer to 'revenue.' In some instances, he uses 'rendito' – for example, 'rendito grosso' and 'rendito liquido' (p. 18). However, on page 20, 'rendito' is the solution adopted for 'rent' – a term that clearly defines the revenue attributed to the landowner or the owner of a rented house.

Although we will not examine chapter IV (*Of Stock Lent at Interest*), it is interesting to note that Silva Lisboa translates the English term 'interest' as 'interesse' in all situations. 'Interesse' could in deed designate in the 1800s the revenue (or returns) associated with money lending. However, it had a more imprecise or fluid meaning: general profit, gain, utility. 'Interesse' is not improper, but it was not a specific term – as 'interest' was in Smith's or in any economist's text at that time. 'Stock lent at interest' becomes 'fundo emprestado a interesse.' On the other hand, Smith's 'moneyed interest' is translated by Silva Lisboa (see p. 58) as 'interesse dos capitalistas,' which may be literally considered as 'interest of capitalists,' 'capitalistas' here designating anyone who has – and so can lend – money.

In chapter V, three words or expressions caught my attention. Silva Lisboa translates 'prejudices' as 'preocupações,' and 'preocupações' simply means 'preoccupation.' Smith's important classification of the branches of foreign trade includes 'foreign trade of consumption,' translated by Silva Lisboa as 'comercio de consumo' (p. 78), or simply as 'consumption trade,' or 'trade of consumption goods,' with no reference to external trade. Finally, Smith's important export of the 'surplus produce' is translated as 'exportar o produto,' the literal equivalent of 'export the product,' with no reference to 'surplus produce.'

Institutional or environmental differences (and difficulties)

For several reasons, chapter II (*Of Money Considered as a Particular Branch of the General Stock of the Society*) provides a good illustration of the difficulties in translating WN when there are several specificities, or institutional differences, on the horizon. Effectively, the British monetary system was quite different from the Portuguese one, not to mention that the Brazilian currency and credit system had its particularities within Portugal's community. And, as mentioned, the original WN text underwent significant suppressions in chapter II: the 1811 translation cut 79% of the original text. The abundance of examples and institutional specificities might be a reason for the suppression of so many passages, as argued in the 1811 edition's foreword. I add to the avoidance of specificities that would interest English readers only, as argued in the foreword, the fact that the Silva Lisboas, father and son, did not exhibit great fluency in monetary matters. At least José da Silva Lisboa's several texts and books concerning economic matters,[13] on both applied and theoretical matters, do not insist on or even pay particular attention to monetary issues.

Apropos, Silva Lisboa's translation of chapter II is difficult to comprehend, because the compressions were quite significant. The Portuguese text also contains a great number of emphases (in italics), and some footnotes are not always clear. For instance, the fifth paragraph concludes with: 'Their real wealth too is in proportion, not to their gross, but to their net revenue' (WN II.ii.5, 286–87). The 1811 edition added a footnote to this sentence that translates into English as follows: 'This must be understood of that part of the revenue that can be spared from the yearly consumption, to accumulate in the capital stock' (footnote, p. 17). The text itself is hardly understandable, simply because the Portuguese version of the footnote is unacceptable.

Up to paragraph seven, the translator followed the original edition's content.[14] In paragraph seven, the suppressions begin. I will present a few examples, trying to evince their context or position in the original edition, as well as their relevance or irrelevance. In paragraph seven, which is initiated with 'The intention of the fixed capital is to increase the productive powers of labour,' Silva Lisboa goes until 'The expence which is properly laid out upon a fixed capital of any kind, is always repaid with great profit, and increases the annual produce by a much greater value than that of the support which such improvements require' (WN II.ii.5, 287). The continuation is simply cut off until the sentence 'It is upon this account that all such improvements in mechanicks,' where CRN retakes the original text.

Other examples. WN paragraph 10 goes as 'The circulating capital of a society is in this respect different from that of an individual.' Silva Lisboa had cut the last sentence of paragraph nine, which goes in WN as 'The maintenance of those three parts of the circulating capital, therefore, withdraws no portion of the annual produce from the net revenue of the society, besides what is necessary for maintaining the fixed capital.' The first part of paragraph ten is kept, but Silva Lisboa cut the last sentence, which goes as 'Though the whole goods in a merchant's shop must by no means be placed in his own stock reserved for immediate consumption, . . . without occasioning any diminution either of his capital, or of theirs' (WN II.ii.10, 288). In this case, the compression clearly results in a loss in the meaning of Smith's arguments.

The next, and decisive, WN paragraphs (11 and 12) are kept. Paragraph 11 is, 'Money, therefore, is the only part of the circulating capital of a society, of which the maintenance can occasion any diminution in their revenue.' And paragraph 12: 'The fixed capital, and that part of the circulating capital which consists in money, so far as they affect the revenue of the society, bear a very great resemblance to one another.' Paragraph 13, which compares the expenditures necessary for the upkeep of the fixed capital and those necessary to make and keep gold and silver coins, is reasonably well translated. However, paragraph 14, in which Smith presents money as 'the great wheel of circulation,' is translated until this precise point. The last sentence was suppressed: 'In computing either the gross or the neat revenue of any society, we must always, from their whole annual circulation of money and goods, deduct the whole value of the money, of which not a single farthing can ever make any part of either' (WNII.ii.14, 289). Paragraph 15 was also suppressed, and from that point on, a great number of paragraphs were not incorporated into CRN.

The Portuguese edition returns to the original text only in paragraph 23, in which Smith engages in his superb synthesis:

> Money, therefore, the great wheel of circulation, the great instrument of commerce, like all other instruments of trade, though it makes a part and a very valuable part of the capital, makes no part of the revenue of the society to which it belongs.
>
> (WNII.ii.23, 291)

Indeed, Silva Lisboa makes a not-so-inspiring adaptation of paragraph 23. It is important to note that, from paragraph 24, Smith enters the discussion on paper money, a crucial issue in monetary economics in general and in Smith's argument in particular. Exactly here, there is an immense increase in the suppressions. Effectively, Silva Lisboa presents the general idea, well expressed in WN's paragraph 26: 'The substitution of paper in the room of gold and silver money, replaces a very expressive instrument of commerce with one much less costly, and sometimes equally convenient' (WN II.ii.26, 292). In Portuguese, it goes as follows: 'A substituição de papel de credito em lugar da moeda de oiro e prata, faz succeder a hum mui dispendioso instrumento de commercio, (qual he o dinheiro metallico) outro que he muito menos custoso, e, algumas vezes, igualmente conveniente' (CRN, p. 24). In brackets, Silva Lisboa added an explanation to Smith's 'a very expressive instrument or commerce': (qual he o dinheiro metallico), in English, 'which is metallic Money.' The addition seems depreciatively trivial.

However, the fact is that, from paragraphs 28 and 29, Smith settles on more detailed explanations about the working of a credit system, choosing bank notes as an example of paper money. We have from this point an increase in examples referred to Scotland but, most of all, a display of Smith's perception of the credit system and of the possibility that notes reduce the use of metallic money. In short, banknotes and paper money in general replace an element of circulating capital – coins – that, apart from its acknowledged benefits, adds expenses to commercial societies. In addition, and possibly most important, WN's text approaches in a very peculiar manner several issues that had been raised by the 17th and 18th monetary debates. The fact is that the immense suppressions made by the 1811 edition in the last two-thirds of chapter II, approximately, from paragraph 30 until the end of the chapter, in paragraph 106 – smash Smith's versions of these debates.

Among the smashed issues, I would mention the several approaches to the quantity of money necessary for circulation, an issue elaborated by Petty, crucial for Locke's and Cantillon's understanding of money and circulation, and that had been revisited by Smith. Although Smith proposes that 'What is the proportion which the circulating money of any country bears to the whole value of the annual produce circulated by means of it, it is, perhaps, impossible to determine' (WNII.ii.40, 296), he advances some guesses. Smith's decisive proposition that 'The whole paper money of every kind which can easily circulate in any country never can exceed the value of the gold and silver, of which it supplies the place' (WN II.ii. 48, 300) came as a sequence to these debates on the quantity of money in circulation. All this material was either lost or very badly disposed of in Silva Lisboa's translation.

To be fair, the passage just mentioned was fairly translated by Silva Lisboa – see CRN, p. 29. However, we are here in WN's paragraph 48, partially translated by Silva Lisboa. Suddenly, the Portuguese version jumps from WN's paragraph 49 into paragraph 67: 'The customs of merchants, which were established when the barbarous laws of Europe did not enforce the performance of their contracts' (WN II.ii.67, 309). The suppressed part holds a very important exposition of the relations between bankers and merchants that was entirely lost. This suppression engulfs Smith's exposition of the Scottish banking system, and we can argue that these examples hardly apply to the Portuguese-Brazilian context. I would rather stress that, in Smith's system, general principles, or even theories, are frequently elucidated by examples that make these principles understandable. In these passages on money, the examples certainly make Smith's general view of money understandable. For instance, when Smith chose as a forceful example 'The paper currency of North America' (WN II.ii. 100, 326), his purpose was not only to present the American system to readers but also to ponder on the relations between paper money and coins. The 1811 edition simply suppresses this possibility, losing part of the spirit and method of Smith's work.

I think chapter II does not represent a full and comprehensive example of Silva Lisboa's undertaking and achievements, because, as mentioned, the compressions from the original text were extensive. In other chapters, the adherence to the original text and to the spirit of Smith's work is greater. Anyhow, chapter II is not only essential to establish Smith's view on money and credit. It is also crucial to pave the way for the decisive criticism of the 'mercantile system' in Book IV. Thus, under the guise of suppressing examples that supposedly interested English readers only, Silva Lisboa may have sacrificed Smith's overall intent.

The instrumental usage of a translation

This section will focus on chapter V of Book II (Of the Different Employment of Capital), a chapter largely used by José da Silva Lisboa to combat the critics of the measures enacted by the Portuguese government immediately following its arrival in Brazil, more precisely, from 1808 to 1810. These measures included opening trade to all 'friendly nations' and reducing import taxes, thus favouring British traders and the import of British manufactures. According to the critics, the new policy would hinder the development of manufactures in colonial Brazil and would block the traditional commercial nexuses that favoured Portugal's exports to Brazil. The Brazilian economy would thus remain restricted to agriculture. Silva Lisboa defended the new policies and argued in his writings[15] that, 'as Smith taught,' capital should be first employed in agriculture. Smith's ideas on the existence of a preferential ordering of employment of capital were most of all developed in chapter V.

Chapter V is also representative of the editorial criteria of the 1811 edition, because what was stated in the Foreword as the main criterion for selecting passages to be excluded was followed in its pages. Indeed, examples and illustrations from other countries constituted the bulk of suppressed passages. As seen earlier, 79% of the original text was translated, and examples and illustrations effectively constitute the bulk of the suppressed 21%. Up to paragraph seven (WN II.v.7, 361), the translation is quite comprehensible. In the middle of this long paragraph, there is some confusion. Smith's sentence is: 'He is thus enabled to furnish work to a greater value, and the profit, which he makes by it in this way, much more than compensates the additional price which the profit of the retailer imposes upon the goods' (WN II.v.7, 361). Silva Lisboa's translation is as follows:

> Assim he habilitado a fornecer obra de muito maior valor, e o ganho que por esse modo obtem, lhe compensa, muito mais do que o lesa, a maioria do preço que o vendedor por miudo requer pelas cousas que distribue ao povo.
> (CRN, p. 69)

It is difficult to translate this sentence into English, because its meaning is not clear even in Portuguese. Then, Smith says that the prejudices of political economy writers against 'shopkeepers and tradesmen' have no foundation at all. Silva Lisboa translates 'tradesmen,' a general word applied to anyone who trades, as 'vendedores de retalho,' or retail traders, which has a much more restricted meaning. After that, there is some confusion concerning the 'grocery trade.'

Subsequently – we are still in paragraph seven – Smith says that competition, in the case of too many (20) sellers, 'might perhaps ruin some of themselves; but to take care of this is the business of the parties concerned, and it may safely be trusted to their discretion' (WN II.v.7, 362). Silva Lisboa adopts for this concise conclusion a long solution: 'mas o cuidar nisso, he o negocio das partes, que interessão em prevenir o seu prejuízo; e deve-se com segurança confiar na prudencia das mesmas, que assim o hão de fazer' (CRN, p. 69). Here, Lisboa uses a long and unnecessary formula to express what could be perfectly understood by means of a short sentence. In addition, the last sentence of paragraph seven was suppressed, which precluded Portuguese-speaking readers from accessing one of the many spirited sentences of the original WN: 'It is not the multitude of ale-houses . . . that occasions a general disposition to drunkenness.'

In paragraph 12, Smith starts the development of one of his strong axioms: 'No equal capital puts into motion a greater quantity of productive labour than that of the farmer' (WN II.v.12, 363). Smith's defence of this proposition is effectively complicated, but – and as mentioned – the idea was cherished by Silva Lisboa, who emphasises (italics) the passage 'In agriculture too nature labours along with man.' Further in this paragraph, again in italics: *'This rent may be considered as the produce of those powers of nature, the use of which the landlord lends to the farmer.'* Still further: 'In them, nature does nothing; man does all; and the reproduction must always be in proportion to the strength of the agents that occasion it.' Here, the last part of the sentence (after the last semicolon) was stressed in italics.

In paragraph 13, Smith introduces another issue, the residence (local) of the employer of capital. Paragraph 13 focuses on agriculture and retail trade, paragraph 14 on wholesale merchants, and paragraph 15 on manufacturers. Silva Lisboa simply omitted paragraph 14, preserving the others. Silva Lisboa skipped the examples used by Smith to reinforce his arguments on the capitals of manufacturers (Lyon, Sicily, Spain). In WN's paragraph 17, an option that was frequent in CRN: Smith's '*exports of the surplus produce*' is presented as 'exports of the produce.'

In paragraph 18, another illustration is suppressed. Smith mentions the possibility of a country – like a particular person – lacking sufficient capital to conduct all activities: agriculture, manufacture, and long-distance transport. He adds: 'The inhabitants of many different parts of Great Britain have not capital sufficient to improve and cultivate all their lands' (WN II.v.18, 365). This is part of a long illustration that was suppressed by Silva Lisboa, who directly (and in the same paragraph) connected it to WN's following paragraph, 'When the capital of any country.'

WN's paragraphs 19 and 20 were very important to Silva Lisboa, because in them Smith affirms that, 'When the capital of any country is not sufficient for all those three purposes' (WN II.v.19, 366), it would not be wise to spread the available capital in many sectors. Silva Lisboa translates these paragraphs, but in the end, some adaptations are difficult to grasp. The adopted solutions disrupt the fluency of the text, to say the least. Moreover, the last sentence, which was not translated, reaffirms an important Smithian formula: 'But the revenue of all the inhabitants of the country is necessarily in proportion to the value of the annual produce of their land and labour' (WN II.v.20, 366).

In addition to this important suppression, the Portuguese edition omitted the whole paragraph 21, in which Smith displays the virtues of the North American case, based on an emphasis in agriculture. Paragraph 22, which added the cases of China, Indostan, and India, was also suppressed. Paragraphs 23 and 24 were translated, and in paragraph 24, Silva Lisboa introduces a very strange and lengthy footnote, aiming to explain the meaning of carrying trade.

In paragraph 25, the suppression of the example at the end of the paragraph is unfavourable to the understanding of Smith's idea. The paragraph deals with capitals internal to the country, and the example mentions an exchange of Scottish and English commodities. In this case, Smith concludes, 'The capital which sends Scotch manufactures to London and brings back English corn and manufactures to Edinburgh, necessarily replaces, by every such operation, two British capitals, which had both been employed in the agriculture or manufactures of Great Britain' (WN II.v.25, 368). The example and the entire paragraph clarify that we are dealing with internal exchanges – even though we have, in this case, two different (internal) spaces, namely Scotland and England. The problem is that Silva Lisboa uses the term 'export'; literally 'Quando ambas as mercadorias exportadas são o produto da industria nacional' (CRN, p. 79), and the word 'exportadas,' as the verb 'exportar' – literally, to export – suggests or even implies transferring commodities to a different nation. In the end, if readers consider Silva Lisboa's translation literally, they will be induced to believe that the two capitals involved were internal, even though 'exports' (and imports) are the focus.

The following paragraph (26) immediately delves into the use of capitals employed in 'purchasing foreign goods for home-consumption, when this purchase is made with the produce of domestick industry.' There is a clear contrast between this and the previous paragraph. Silva Lisboa's translation is fine, and, curiously, it preserves WN's example that deals with exports and imports involving Great Britain and Portugal. However, the suppression of examples continues. In paragraph 28, which deals with 'foreign goods for home consumption' imported with commodities produced in any other country,' a very long example was entirely suppressed. In order to establish continuity in the text, Silva Lisboa was led to introduce a small – and not entirely comprehensible – passage.

The adaptations also made it difficult to understand the translation of paragraph 29, which mentions Brazil. Specifically, 'If they – foreign commodities for home consumption – are purchased with the gold of Brazil . . . or with the silver of Peru, this gold and silver, like the tobacco of Virginia, must have been purchased with something that either was the produce of the industry of the country, or that had been purchased with something else that was so' (WN II.v.29, 370). Silva Lisboa revises this passage and makes significant adaptations to ensure that Smith's idea is comprehensible. Ultimately, Smith is explaining the advantages of trading in gold or silver coins, regardless of their origin. It must be admitted that Silva Lisboa succeeded in conveying this idea, which would have been much more easily conveyed without the omission of the example.

In WN's paragraph 30, the same difficulty arises. This is a long paragraph dedicated to the carrying trade, enriched by examples involving Holland, Portugal, and Poland. In the end, Smith mentions coal trade from Newcastle to London to account for the ships involved, thus estimating the total advantages and employment in each case. Silva Lisboa leverages only this last illustration, which is sufficient to transmit Smith's perception of the uselessness of giving 'extraordinary encouragements' to the carrying trade. Smith's general idea, complemented by WN's paragraphs 31 and 32, is well represented by the 1811 translation, which is effectively engaged in conveying the notion of the importance of the diverse branches of trade.

Most importantly, Smith's insistence on the convenience of letting the surplus – demand vs. produce of 'any particular branch of industry' – be sent abroad is enthusiastically received by Silva Lisboa. The CRN edition suppresses the reference to Great Britain and reinforces the word 'demand' in the passage '*The surplus part of them, therefore, must be sent abroad, and exchanged for something for which there is a demand at home*' (WN ii.v.372) with an emphatic formula: '*demanda e precisão (real ou de phantasya)*' (CRN, p. 85), which can be approximately translated into English as 'demand and need (whether real or out of phantasy).'

Smith's text proceeds by recalling 'Great Britain' – which is surely directed at combating the many national strategies of the 'mercantile system.' In suppressing the mentions of Great Britain, the 1811 abridged version spares space, but loses part of its clarity. It seems Silva Lisboa is interested in going directly into the last paragraph (37), to settle the conclusion. This paragraph suffered some compression, and it is worth noting that Smith opens the paragraph with a typical phrasing: 'The consideration of his own private profit, is the sole motive who determines the owner of any capital to employ it either in agriculture, in' (WN II.v.37, 374). Well, Silva Lisboa, in this case, translates 'profit' as 'interesse,' which means 'interest.' We have seen that 'profit' has been translated as 'proveito' or 'lucro,' without a clear distinction between these two admissible words. 'Interesse' or 'interest' adds imprecision to a solution that was not very precise.

Conclusion

This chapter focuses on chapters I, II, and V of Book II, which does not imply that Silva Lisboa conceived no interesting solutions for translating the remaining chapters of Book II – which are not examined here. Chapters I, II, and V were chosen because I believe they provide a good understanding of the characteristics and problems of the first Portuguese translation of WN. These chapters consider three elements: idiomatic difficulties, differences in institutional environments and trade mechanisms of distinct economies, and the political and theoretical choices of the translators.

By 'idiomatic difficulties,' I mean not only the usual pitfalls of any translating effort but also the crucial fact that the political economy discourse was still under development, in a sense being shaped by Smith's work. Several terms were acquiring a more precise or unique dimension in political economy: profit, revenue, interest, produce, value. . . . Obviously, the dissemination of these and other terms and concepts in the different economies and throughout different expert communities was unequal. The 1811 edition somehow reflects these imprecisions or indecisions, and it is surely much less clear and precise than the original text. However, despite all the imprecisions, I would say that Silva Lisboa's efforts were laudable in this respect.

On the other hand, excessive compression can result in unacceptable problems. This was typically the case in Book II, chapter II, as well as in the many other highly compressed passages. Silva Lisboa's choices – and most of all the radical compression – stemmed from various perceptions, formative vices, and choices. The differences in institutional settings – monetary systems and trade practices differ across countries – explain part of the difficulties. However, we should also keep in mind the hurdles raised by this specific branch of the economy and economic thought, as well as the lack of interest or knowledge of the Silva Lisboas – and here I include father and son – in monetary topics. This lack of interest and precision comes as a surprise, because precisely at the time Portugal and Brazil were facing problems and innovations in their money and banking systems.

Finally, regarding inclinations, or what I termed *ad usum* or instrumental orientation of translations, it seems that the 1811 biases are quite evident. Anyone who has read José da Silva Lisboa's texts, especially those addressing the stormy debates of the 1808–1810 policies, will feel that the comments, emphases, and even the choices of passages to be suppressed are entirely consistent with José da Silva Lisboa's inclinations. The 1811 Portuguese edition of WN was an instrumental initiative – an observation that can surely be applied to many translations, without diminishing their merits.

Notes

1 On the transfer of the Royal Press to Brazil, see Schwarcz (2022). On the dilemmas of the Portuguese empire in the period, see Alexandre (1993).
2 On José da Silva Lisboa's life, see Kirschner (2009). On Rodrigo de Souza Coutinho, see Silva (1993, 2006).
3 More details on the diffusion of political economy in Portugal can be seen in Cardoso and Cunha (2012), Cardoso (2001), Cardoso and Almodovar (1998), Cardoso (2009a), and Cardoso (2009b).
4 Indeed, the first book published by the Royal Press in Brazil, in 1808 and 1809, was José da Silva Lisboa's *Observações sobre o Comércio Franco do Brasil* (*Observations on Brazilian Free Trade*) (Silva Lisboa, 1808–09).
5 The Portuguese policies and the 1810 treaties are examined by Cantarino and Oliveira (2017) and Arruda (2022).
6 The 1811 edition of the *Wealth of Nations* and any other Portuguese texts were translated into English by the article's author.
7 More details on Bento da Silva Lisboa's political career are presented in Blake's Biographical Dictionary. See Blake, (1883–1902).
8 See Coutinho (2017) and Coutinho (2022).
9 *Diccionario da Lingua Portugueza*, Bluteau and Moraes Silva (1789). The word 'fundo' is found in page 644. Bluteau e Moraes Silva will be our reference for the Portuguese language standards of the 1811 edition.
10 According to Bluteau and Moraes Silva (1789).
11 When the original WN's passages are presented, they are identified with (WN, book, chapter, page). Passages from the 1811 edition are identified by page number.
12 For instance, *Estudos do bem-commum e Economia Politica* (Studies on common good and Political Economy), Silva Lisboa (1819–20).
13 José da Silva Lisboa also wrote extensively on political problems and translated passages from Edmund Burke in *Extractos das obras politicas e economicas de Edmund*

Burke (Extracts from the political and economic works by Edmund Burke) (Silva Lisboa 1812).

14 Paragraph numbers refer to the original WN edition. I have not indicated paragraph numbers of the 1811 edition because WN's original paragraphs were very often divided into more than one paragraph; or, conversely, two paragraphs from WN were compacted into one.

15 Silva Lisboa (1810).

References

Alexandre, V. (1993) *Os Sentidos do Império: Questão Nacional e Questão Colonial na crise do Antigo Regime Português*. Porto: Edições Afrontamento.

Arruda, J. J. (2022) *Planos para o Brasil, projetos para o mundo: o novo imperialismo britânico e o processo de independência*. São Paulo: Alameda.

Bluteau, R. and Moraes Silva, A. (1789) *Dicionário da língua portuguesa composto pelo padre D. Rafael Bluteau, reformado, e acrescentado por Antonio de Moraes Silva natural do Rio de Janeiro*. Lisboa: Officina de Simão Taddeo Ferreira.

Cantarino, N. M. and Oliveira, M. F. (2017) 'The Treaties of 1810 and the Crisis of the Luso-Brazilian Empire', in A. M. Cunha and C. E. Suprinyak (orgs). *The Political Economy of Latin American Independence*. London: Routledge.

Cardoso, J. L. (2001) *A Economia Politica e os Dilemas do Império Luso-Brasileiro (1790–1822)*. Lisboa, Comissão Nacional para as Comemorações dos Descobrimentos Portugueses.

Cardoso, J. L. (2009a) 'Free Trade, Political Economy and the Birth of a New Economic Nation: Brazil 1808–1810', *Revista de Historia Econômica – Journal of Iberian and Latin American Economic History*, 27(2): 183–204.

Cardoso, J. L. (2009b) 'The Transfer of the Court to Brazil, 200 Years Afterwards', *E-journal of Portuguese History*, 7(1): 1–19.

Cardoso, J. L. and Almodovar, A. (1998) *A History of Portuguese Economic thought*. London and New York: Routledge.

Cardoso, J. L. and Cunha, A. M. (2012) 'Enlightened Reforms and Economic Discourse in the Portugues-Brazilian Empire (1750–1808)', in *History of Political Economy* (Vol. 44), pp. 619–641.

Coutinho, M. C. (2017) 'Silva Lisboa on Free Trade and Slave Labor', in A. M. Cunha and C. E. Suprinyak (orgs) *The Political Economy of Latin American Independence*. London: Routledge.

Coutinho, M. C. (2022) 'José da Silva Lisboa: liberalismo e economia política', in I. C. Salomão (ed.) *Ideias econômicas no Brasil oitocentista*. Porto Alegre: Editora UFRGS.

Kirschner, T. C. (2009) *José da Silva Lisboa, Visconde de Cairu. Itinerários de um ilustrado luso-brasileiro*. São Paulo: Alameda.

Schwarcz, L. (2022) *A Longa Viagem da Biblioteca dos Reis: Do Terremoto de Lisboa à Independência do Brasil*. São Paulo: Companhia das Letras.

Silva, A. M.-D. (1993) 'Introdução', in R. S. Coutinho (ed.) *Textos Políticos Económicos e Financeiros (1783–1811)*. Lisboa: Banco de Portugal.

Silva, A. M.-D. (2006) *Portrait d'un Homme d'état: D. Rodrigo de Souza Coutinho, Comte de Linhares* (Vol. I: 'Les années de formation 1755–1796'; Vol. II: 'L'homme d'Etat, 1796–1812'). Paris: Centre Culturel Calouste Gulbenkian, pp. 1755–1812.

Silva Lisboa, J. (1804) *Princípios de Economia Política*. Lisboa: Impressão Régia.

Silva Lisboa, J. (1808–09) *Observações sobre o Comércio Franco do Brasil*. Rio de Janeiro: Impressão Régia.

Silva Lisboa, J. (1810) *Refutação das declamações contra o commercio inglez, extraídas de escritores eminentes*. Rio de Janeiro: Impressão Régia.

Silva Lisboa, J. (1812) *Extractos das obras politicas e economicas de Edmund Burke*. Rio de Janeiro: Impressão Régia.
Silva Lisboa, J. (1819–20) *Estudos do bem-commum e Economia Politica*. Rio de Janeiro: Impressão Régia.
Smith, A. (1811) *Compendio da Obra da Riqueza das Nações de Adam Smith*. Rio de Janeiro: Impressão Régia.

4 Adam Smith and the sympathetic portrait

Jorge López Lloret

Introduction

This chapter is concerned with the nature and construction of sympathy by Adam Smith in *The Theory of Moral Sentiments* (1759) and in *Lectures on Rhetoric and Belles Lettres* (1762–1763). In general terms, my hypothesis will be that in TMS, Smith dealt with the hermeneutics of the spectator, but in LRBL, he placed more importance on the semiotics of the actor, the way in which the orator and the writer defined their public presentation, which can be applied to the social actors who construct their public presence to be morally judged by others. From a conceptual point of view, LRBL is thus complementary to TMS and should be included more often in analyses of Smithian sympathy.

In my view, the inclusion is the main contribution of this chapter, and I believe that Smith's approach can best be understood by looking at it alongside the portraiture of the period, particularly the work of his acquaintance Allan Ramsay. Smith argued in TMS that when we evaluate another person's moral behaviour, we must create a mental *portrait* of it before responding sympathetically. He also stated that we all wish to be praiseworthy. In this case, we must present a *portrait* of ourselves that is easily interpretable, and this is where the rhetorical construction of our public presence becomes pertinent if we want to evoke a sympathetic response in others. This construction should be based on two basic principles of Smith's rhetoric in LRBL, namely naturalness and perspicuity. Since these are also two characteristic principles of Ramsay's strictly contemporary portraiture, I believe that Smith's connection with the world of Ramsay's public presences is a good case study to reinforce the complementary relationship between TMS and LRBL.

Generally speaking, the question to which Smith gave a sympathetic solution was articulated in Xenophon's *Memorabilia* III, 10, a text well known to Smith, though not explicitly referred to by him in this regard. It was a dialogue between the painter Parrhasius and Socrates. The two were discussing the extent to which painting could represent the inner self, or more generally, the possibility of reading a person's character traits and moral condition from their outward appearance.

DOI: 10.4324/9781003767824-6

Painters of the Georgian period often reflected on this because, as Joshua Reynolds noted:

> [T]he habits of my profession unluckily extend to the consideration of so much only of character as lies on the surface, as is expressed in the lineaments of the countenance.
>
> (Reynolds 1952: 66)

Reynolds knew, as Socrates did, that his skill as a portraitist went beyond the contours of the face and encompassed colour, pose, gesture, clothing, setting, and so on. However, this did not settle the question: the painter recreated the outer appearance, but it was up to the spectator to imagine a possible interior. Adam Smith read Xenophon and was in personal contact with Reynolds in later life, so he would be familiar enough with the topic to open TMS with it:

> As we have no immediate experience of what other men feel, we can form no idea of the manner in which they are affected, but by conceiving what we ourselves should feel in the like situation . . . our senses . . . never did, and never can, carry us beyond our own person, and it is by the imagination only that we can form any conception of what are his sensations. Neither can that faculty help us to this any other way, than by representing to us what would be our own, if we were in his case. It is the impressions of our own senses only, not those of his, which our imaginations copy. By the imagination we place ourselves in his situation . . . we enter as it were into his body, and become in some measure the same person with him, and thence form some idea of his sensations, and even feel something which, though weaker in degree, is not altogether unlike them.
>
> (TMS I.i.1.2; Smith 1976a)

Such an assurance was important for Smith because it was the condition of possibility for moral judgements. If we are to understand the conditions and emotions of a person whose behaviour we are trying to judge morally, we have to recreate their situation in order to *enter into* it. In everyday life, this would invariably be an indirect description, as is usual in the theatre (the most famous example being Act II, Scene I of Shakespeare's *Hamlet*), because we cannot know the character of another person directly from within, but from the outside, through their words, gestures, clothes, and such. This is indirect, but, as Smith said when he discussed historical description in LRBL, it is the most effective and engaging for human beings. To use an example of my own, I might report that an earthquake in Lisbon has destroyed the city and caused the death of 60,000 people. However, if I describe people running, injured, naked, crying, and calling for their loved ones amidst the ruins, then I invite the reader to enter sympathetically into the scene because 'we feel for them as it were for ourselves' (LRBL ii.28; Smith 1983). The indirect description transforms the collective scene into a series of individual experiences into which we can enter because 'the incidents of private life tho' not so important would affect us more deeply and interest us more than those of a Publick nature' (LRBL ii.66). Smith's mechanism of sympathy is always (and I will develop this as a semiotic model in Parts V, VI, and VII) an indirect description of personal relationships, whether face-to-face or otherwise.

Smith adopted this theatre-like strategy, making spectators of those passing moral judgements, but it should also be seen in the context of painting, which was then enjoying a 'golden age' in Britain (Macmillan 1986). Smith put it like this: we have to 'take time to *picture out* in our imagination the different circumstances of distress which must occur to him' (TMS I.i.3.4; italics mine). It is literally a matter of *portrayal*, in line with the mimetic principles of Aristotle's poetics: seeing the other person, imaginatively imitating their situation, *entering into* it, passing judgement on it, and feeling sympathy or antipathy. Although Smith's later theory of imitation in painting was less concerned with the formal and thematic similarity of the painting to reality and more with the material disparity between reality and the pictorial medium,[1] it was still imitative. It evidenced the triumph over material disparity that generated similarity of form, crucial in the case of portraiture.

In any case, we could *enter* a picture as we would enter a real social and personal situation. In Lecture 21 on rhetoric, Smith put into practice, without explicitly mentioning it, what George Turnbull called his 'Hampton Court experiment' in 1740 (Turnbull 1971: 14). This experiment involved looking at Raphael's cartoons for the Sistine Chapel tapestries and noting down how he felt in front of them, leading to the following conclusion:

> When one takes a view of the Chartoons of Raphael, it is not Paul Preaching at Athens or Elias Struck with Blindness that first attract our attention but Peter receiving the Keys, Peter feed my Sheep. This piece represents a state of mind in all the figures not much different from that we are in. . . . Whereas the emotions in the others are so violent that it takes a considerable time before we can work ourselves up so far as to enter into the Spirit of the pieces.
> (LRBL ii.95; Smith 1983)

This *entering into* another, out of which sympathy arises, concerns the spectator, but what about the person being portrayed and judged? After all, as Smith said in TMS, we want to be laudable and not blameable. This desire to elicit the sympathy of others is also a feature of portrait painting, where sympathy is not only *interpreted* but also *produced.* These two facets of sympathy are complementary and share two basic characteristics: their visual nature and the operative presence of the imagination.

We will focus on the connection to painting in TMS and LRBL (leaving aside the more technical treatment received in 'Imitative Arts') for two reasons. First, the two works take a contemporary and complementary approach, and second, because in this case artistic imitation was a kind of 'interpretive lens' for Smith, as Jonathan B. Wight pointed out (Wight 2006: 169). Smith's interest in the instrumental use, rather than the intrinsic pleasure (Wight 2006: 163), of painting brings us to portraiture, bypassing historical painting, where sympathy was of lesser importance.

I have chosen the connection with Ramsay's painting for a number of reasons, not least of which are his links with the philosophical context that grew up around David Hume (Macmillan 1986: 27–30), which also happened to be Smith's own. Additionally, Ramsay, more than any other artist, can be called a 'sympathetic portraitist,' as Alasdair Smart has sometimes pointed out (Smart 1992: 70, 84, 104, 104, 157, 167, 179). Nevertheless, my conclusion will show that the visual means of painting are only part of a broader set of semiotic resources with which the self can construct a character that arouses sympathy in the spectator.

Smith and Ramsay's interests converge

Ramsay and Smith were prominent figures in the Scottish Renaissance that followed the union with England in 1707, a glittering period of cultural and intellectual development known as the Scottish Enlightenment. Both grew up under the tutelage of John Clerk of Penicuik, a friend of both Allan Ramsay senior (Smart 1992: 14–15), who was a regular visitor to their home, and Adam Smith senior (Ross 1995: 12–13), who named him as his son's guardian in his will. John Clerk epitomised the cultural and learned spirit of the Scottish elite of the time. After studying in Leiden with Hermann Boerhaave, he travelled around Italy in pursuit of his archaeological and antiquarian interests, taking an interest in music, painting, literature, and architecture. This lent a sophisticated, cosmopolitan air to his social circle at his Palladian villa at Mavisbank (built by William Adam), from which Ramsay and Smith reaped the benefits (Brown 1987: 13–15).

Two cultural priorities of the day were the development of an indigenous school of painting and the oratorical improvement of the Scottish elite. Ramsay, Scotland's foremost mid-eighteenth-century painter, took a keen interest in his country's rhetorical development, while Smith, whose public life began when he lectured on rhetoric in Edinburgh in 1748, turned his attention to the theory and practice of painting. Both epitomised a similar convergence of rhetoric with painting that culminated in 1759, when Ramsay painted a portrait of his wife, Margaret Lindsay, and Smith published TMS.

Here, I will set aside the evidence of Ramsay's interest in rhetoric and instead focus on Smith's interest in painting. His library was well stocked with titles on the subject, including classical references from the Renaissance up to his own time.[2] In addition, general works on aesthetics[3] and numerous works on rhetoric discussing the parallel between the orator and the painter were also present.[4] This is not exhaustive, but it points to a keen interest that must have influenced Smith's thought. There are two biographical facts that are worthy of note in connection with this interest.

The first concerns is study of rhetoric, as the use of painting to illustrate rhetorical concepts had been customary in the history of the discipline since the time when Cicero compared his idea of rhetoric with the painting of Zeuxis (*De Inventione* II.i.1). Moreover, if rhetoric sometimes conceived of itself based on painting, from the Renaissance onwards, painting conceived of itself based on rhetoric, as shown, for example, in Castiglione's *Il Cortegiano* and Alberti's *On Painting*. From the time of John Dryden's translation and notes on Du Fresnoy's *De Arte Graphica* and, most notably, Shaftesbury's *Second Characters*, the idea of the connection between rhetoric and painting, as a variation on the theme of the 'sister arts,' was widely held in Great Britain (Hagstrum 1958: 129–150).

The second is related to the school of art and design founded by Robert Foulis in 1753 on the grounds of the University of Glasgow (Fairfull-Smith 2001: 17–26), one year before the establishment of the Edinburgh Select Society, the brainchild of Allan Ramsay (Flessenkämper 2010: 115–116). Smith's connection with the Foulis Academy and Ramsay during these two years brought him into contact with the technical literature of the time and the evolution of pictorial trends from the seventeenth century to his own time. This contact could have been through engravings at the Foulis Academy or through direct personal contact with Ramsay. By this time, after abandoning his early Italianate style, Ramsay had embraced the French pictorial model of Jean-Marc Nattier, a delicate style of portraiture that had evolved from florid Rococo to the more sober Neoclassicism. He was also preparing *A Dialogue on Taste*, which was known to Smith, in which he argued that empirical and imitative painting was the only acceptable form of the art (Smart 1992: 110, 139).

In 1752 Smith became a founding member of the Glasgow Literary Society, which Foulis joined in 1753. Lord Cardross stated that 'the Literary Society gave origin to Dr. Adam Smith's *Essay on Language*, to his *Theory of Moral Sentiments*' (Murray 1913: 38). Smith's many references to painting in LRBL and TMS are therefore understandable, and it is not implausible to hypothesise that between 1753 and 1759 he was laying the groundwork for his pictorial vision of the spectator's moral judgement (in TMS) and the actor's aesthetic production (in LRBL) and, with them, a complex hermeneutic and semiotic model of productive and interpretative sympathy that would be embodied in Ramsay's mature painting.

The distinctive nature of Adam Smith's sympathy

For Smith, sympathy was something *constructed* by the subject as a spectator and as an actor, unlike Hume, for whom it was a state immediately *produced* in the spectator by seeing the actor (Fleischacker 2012: 276–282). This can be clarified by a musical comparison to which both resorted. Discussing sympathy in *A Treatise on Human Nature* (1739–1740), Hume wrote that 'as in strings equally wound up, the motion of one communicates itself to the rest; so all the affections readily pass from one person to another, and beget correspondent movements in every human creature' (Hume 2002, III.iii.1: 368). For his part, in a long note in TMS Smith drew on the concept of 'harmony':

> Before we approve the sentiments of any person as proper and suitable to their objects, we must not only be affected in the same manner as he is, but we must perceive this harmony and correspondence of sentiments between him and ourselves. . . . The approbation of propriety therefore requires, not

> only that we should entirely sympathize with the person who acts, but that we should perceive this perfect concord between his sentiments and our own.
> (TMS II.i.5.11)

Smith was responding to Hume, as is clear from the second edition of TMS, where he differentiated between 'the sympathetic passion of the spectator' and 'the emotion which arises from his observing the perfect coincidence between this sympathetic passion in himself, and the original passion in the person principally concerned' (TMS I.iii.1.9). Sympathetic approval of the behaviour of another person lies in the former, which is an intellectual act of comparison, not in the latter, which is an impassioned response that Hume never went beyond. Both draw on Jean Philippe Rameau's harmonic theory, grounded in the physical fact that when a note sounds, the harmonics that have some mathematical relationship with it also resonate[5]; if a string was plucked and another string of the same proportion was nearby, the latter would vibrate. From this point on, a musician could use strings whose sounds would be enhanced, turning a mechanical fact into a deliberate composition. Hume likened the sympathiser to the resonating string and Smith to the musician constructing a chord. For him, sympathy was constructed as an artistic composition, which was equally applicable to rhetoric, narrative, and painting.

We can *enter into* a painting as we would a real person, and a real person as we would a painting. In Smith's cultural context, the quintessential pictorial genre was the portrait, constructed by a painter in a tense compromise between the person being depicted and the codes of pictorial representation, oscillating between idealisation and naturalisation (West 2004: 21–29). Indeed, in TMS, Smith compared moral judgement with two trends in pictorial criticism, one idealistic and the other not:

> When a critic examines the work of any of the great masters in poetry or painting, he may sometimes examine it by an idea of perfection, in his own mind, which neither that nor any other human work will ever come up to; and as long as he compares it with his standard, he can see nothing in it but faults and imperfections. But when he comes to consider the rank which it ought to hold among other works of the same kind, he necessarily compares it with a very different standard, the common degree of excellence which is usually attained in this particular art.
> (TMS I.i.5.10)

Critical judgement reflects the fact that the painter can either idealise the sitters or depict them as realistically as possible, subject to the prevailing socially acceptable norms. Both pictorial models coexisted in Smith's time, with Reynolds depicting the *idealist* and Ramsay the *empiricist*. While Reynolds explained the neoclassical idealist model in his famous *Discourses on Art*, Ramsay wrote on empiricism in *A Dialogue on Taste*, both of which were well known to Smith (Mizuta 2000: no. 2011). In portrait painting, there was an uneasy relationship between the urge to idealise the sitters, presenting them in a better light, and the impulse to portray them as they are. In other words, approbation could be derived either from admiration and detachment or from sympathy and proximity to someone. Susan C. Jarratt, who focused on ekphrasis, the verbal description of real or imaginary pictures, a topic of undoubted interest to Smith,[6] related his use of painting to detachment and impartial spectatorship (Jarratt 2008: 43–44). However, I believe it has more to do with sympathy and proximity, and that Smith saw pictorial reconstruction as a means of achieving the proximity necessary to *enter into* the observed, generating sympathy in the case of the portrait.

Ramsay constructed his pictorial work to evoke sympathy for someone personally close to him. A desirable prerequisite for this was familiarity between the portraitist and the sitter. The better acquainted the painter is with their subject, the better their portrayal will be. Ramsay knew almost all his subjects well, in many cases intimately, as in the portrait of his wife Margaret (Dulau 2013: 67–88). The sympathy we feel in front of his portraits is the same as he felt for those he portrayed, constructing their presence using relevant details that let us *enter into* and sympathise with them. This is how we must construct the context of others in everyday life to pass judgement on their behaviour sympathetically. Although we may never see the world through their eyes, only through our own, the devices by which we can *enter into* their situation bring us as near as possible to seeing it through theirs. James Engell's remarks about Smith's sympathy are apposite:

> The more accurately and completely our imagination reproduces the circumstances of another in our mind, the more readily the feeling of sympathy is excited. Imagination, therefore, encourages us to know a situation, to ascertain events surrounding a person, and even to learn the character and passions of the person who is the object of sympathy.
>
> (Engell 1981: 150)

Arousing sympathy requires knowledge of the people to be sympathised with by reconstructing their life story and their environment through what Michael L. Frazer called a 'multistage process' (Frazer 2012: 100). In painting, this can only happen in portraiture and, more specifically, in the version that Macmillan called 'empirical portraiture' (Macmillan 1986: 18), which was the second form of critical judgement identified by Smith in TMS.

Not just any personal construction will trigger a sympathetic response. As Smith's metaphor of musical harmony shows, sympathy stems from a constructive process that requires as much knowledge as possible of the people we sympathise with and their specific situation. Yet, he would suggest that some situations are easy to *enter into*, and others are not. I observed this in the Hampton Court *experiment*: we are more likely to engage with things that are closer to our everyday lives and less emotionally intense. In portraiture terms, we would be more sympathetic to Margaret Lindsay arranging her vase of flowers in Ramsay's painting than, for example, to Queen Marie Leszczynska doing the same in her portrait by Carle van Loo (made in 1747), as the theatrical and ornate array of objects around her mark her out as a superior *figure*. Unlike Margaret's, it is more difficult to see through the eyes of the queen. The presentation of the painter's wife evokes proximity and sympathy, while that of the queen creates a sense of detachment and admiration.

This contrast is important because Smith sometimes wrote, especially in TMS, on the 'disposition to admire, and almost to worship the rich and powerful,' but for him, this was 'the great and most universal cause of the corruption of our moral sentiments' (TMS I.iii.3.I). From an economic standpoint, in his famous statement about the invisible hand (TMS IV.I.10), he regarded this as positive because it led to the redistribution of wealth, but from a moral judgement perspective, it was always negative (Dwyer 1998: 23). That is why his descriptions of the rich, with their obscene ostentation, have an air of the ridiculous, perhaps even of a moral lesson (Dwyer 1998: 48, 74). For example, the wonderful invisible hand argument from TMS begins like this: 'The poor man's son, whom heaven in its anger has visited with ambition, when he begins to look around him, admires the condition of the rich' (TMS IV.I.7). Admiration is negatively associated with the wrath of the gods; it is seen as a punishment. Moreover, for Smith, the greatest triumph of the well-heeled, with their parade of wealth, is 'to figure at a ball' (TMS I.iii.2.5; Dwyer 1998: 40). For Smith, admiration was a corrupted form of sympathy, and it was best to admire the rich without sympathising with them because this was necessary to maintain the social order. The object of our sympathy should be people who are more modest and virtuous: 'The most perfect modesty and plainness, joined to as much negligence as is consistent with the respect due to the company, ought to be the chief characteristics of the behaviour of a private man' (TMS I.iii.2.5). Smith described the economic benefit of excessive spending, but I think his sympathy lay with the *plain* style of the artisans who produced the work, not with the *high* style of the rich consumer and their parade of obsolescent and superfluous wealth (Keppler 2013: 52). As Forman-Barzilai stated, TMS was a 'manifesto of middle-class mores' joined to the 'morality of ordinary people' (Forman-Barzilai 2011: 111).

The rhetorical and pictorial arousal of sympathy

In TMS, Smith stated that we all want to elicit a sympathetic response from others. That would certainly be the wish of Ramsay and his models, for it is difficult not to respond sympathetically to his mature portraits, designed as they are to elicit such a response. Smith also attached great importance to sympathy being both interpreted and produced, especially in LRBL, where he advocated the most direct communication of thought possible between writer and reader, but also in TMS, where he asserted that we all want to be praised and to be praiseworthy, not blamed or blameworthy. Not only do we construct the outward appearance of others to interpret and evaluate their behaviour sympathetically, but we also construct our own appearance to arouse sympathy. This we do every day in the domestic realm, the place where empirical portraiture achieves its most human and artistic achievements. Smith covered this in greater depth in LRBL, and his students, colleagues, and friends who read about sympathy in 1759 in TMS may also have heard something similar along the lines of Lecture 6 on rhetoric in 1762, when he said:

> When the sentiment of the speaker is expressed in a neat, clear, plain and clever manner, and the passion or affection he is possessed of and intends, *by sympathy*, to communicate to his hearer, is plainly and cleverly hit off, then and then only the expression has all the force and beauty that language can give it.
>
> (LRBL i.v56)

After analysing certain elocutionary devices, particularly metaphor, and before studying the character of certain writers,[7] Smith reiterated this idea at the beginning of Lecture 8, a sign of the importance he attached to it:

> [T]hat really gave beauty to stile: That when the words neatly and properly expressed the thing to be described, and conveyed the sentiment the author entertained of it and desired to communicate by sympathy to his hearers; then the expression had all the beauty language was capable of bestowing on it.
>
> (LRBL i.96)

If Smith were talking about painting rather than literary expression, this could well explain the visual rhetoric of Ramsay's mature style. It is true that painting is a static and visual medium, and language, written or spoken, is a dynamic and imaginative one. However, just as Smith found it preferable to arouse sympathy with as few literary figures as possible, using clear and direct language, Ramsay also eschewed trappings and ostentation, reducing the pictorial space to the *simplest* possible depiction of the sitter, except in his court portraits. This is not a fanciful comparison between the rhetoric and painting of the time on my part, given that two leading figures in British painting theory, Jonathan Richardson and Turnbull, believed that painting was as effective a language as the written and spoken word (Richardson 1971: 3; Turnbull 1971: ix). Smith and Ramsay were peculiar in that here the former focused on everyday speech and the latter on everyday personal appearance. As Smith contended, it was wrong to believe that beauty of form was something other than what we see ordinarily (LRBL i.103).

As we have seen, arousing sympathy was best achieved with a situation that we could easily *enter into*. Ideally, this should be an everyday situation that did not take a long time to understand, as Smith said when describing Raphael's cartoons. Ramsay agreed with Smith on this point, setting aside the narrative nature of historical painting that aimed to represent historical and mythological events rather than real people. In 1755, André Rouquet, who considered Ramsay to be one of the best portraitists of the day, and the portrait to be the pictorial genre most in demand by the English, wrote these significant words on how a sitter should behave:

> It is impossible to chuse from amongst animated objects, an attitude so permanent as to be absolutely analogous to the immobility of painting; but

> reason requires that we chuse such one as comes nearest to it. In portraiture every thing should contribute to resemblance: now the more we chuse such circumstances in nature as come nearest to those to which painting is subject, the more we shall be convinced of our having collected such illusive circumstances, as must contribute to render the portrait like the original, or, if we may be permitted the expression, the original like the portrait.
>
> (Rouquet 1970: 68)[8]

Here Rouquet touched on something that had been of interest to Western aesthetic theory since the second half of the seventeenth century and throughout the eighteenth century, namely how well the spatial arts could represent temporal phenomena (the so-called Laocoön problem). Smith was no stranger to this problem, as he owned copies of relevant texts on the subject and devoted part of Lecture 21 on rhetoric to it, casting doubt on whether painting could represent phenomena over time: '[T]he Painting can only represent one moment or Point of time and the situation things were in at that time' (LRBL ii.87).[9] In Smith's view, painting, in order to be easily understood, should not depict actions stretching over a long, complex time period but can depict a single action spanning a short period of time, particularly if it is an everyday action. In a sense, Smith rejected the viability of historical painting shortly before Lessing did, thereby affirming the pictorial suitability and human interest of portraiture.

Once again, this can be illustrated by Ramsay's portrait of his wife Margaret (Smart 1992: 155–156). The action was domestic, simple, and every day. We find Margaret arranging a vase of roses that occupies the right half of the painting. She has been doing this for some time because the vase is filled with roses. Margaret is shown in profile, facing the vase, and bathed in the light from the open shutter in the left background. It is her home environment, which also happens to be Ramsay's. Margaret's face is turned slightly towards the viewer, originally her husband, but now each of us. She has heard us while arranging the vase and looks at us with warm curiosity. That alone is what Ramsay faithfully captured. Thanks to the subtle and endearing way the painter has arranged her features, Margaret's face shows sobriety, serenity, curiosity and, above all, affection, without any hint of unbridled passion. The *quiet* and geometrically minimalist composition is masterfully constructed so that our eyes meet Margaret's *quiet* gaze: her face against a dark background between the shutter and the vase, the most brightly lit surface in the painting. This culminates in a slightly off-centre compositional pyramid that guides our exploration of the image until we reach her eyes. We feel Margaret's sympathy for us, and in a play of glances that could linger as long as we like, we respond with sympathy. Sympathy has been aroused (by the painter, sitter, or actor) and interpreted (by the spectator).

The fundamental element of this whole ethical, aesthetic, and pictorial framework was character. Let us return to van Loo's portrait of Marie Leszczinska, also depicted arranging a vase of roses. Here, the pose and props take precedence over character since what is important is her social standing, not who she is as a person. In Margaret's case, on the other hand, the mask of pomp and circumstance seems to have fallen away, and we behold her as a person, or, at any rate, the painter manages to convince us of this through his insightful presentation of her character against the backdrop of a credible and inconsequential act. Ramsay did much the same in almost all the portraits of his second period, giving effect to the words of Richardson, one of the main driving forces behind a British school of portrait painting, who in 1715 declared that a portrait painter must understand and '*enter into* their Characters' (Richardson 1971: 22; italics mine). It must be said, however, that he was thinking of more formal and idealised portraits than Ramsay's later works. We cannot be sure if Smith read these words (although the similarity of the language is striking), but they would have been known to the Foulis Academy. At the heart of the matter was the possibility of getting to know a person's inner self through a composition of their presence, depicting their character (Wendorf 1983: 110–112). The convincing presentation of the character allows the imagination, an essentially visual faculty since Addison's time, to sense the inner self of another person.

Character presentation was a central theme in LRBL. Immediately after his discussion of how to arouse sympathy in Lecture 6, Smith analysed the work of various writers from Lectures 6 to 11, focusing on style as an indicator of each writer's character. He then spent Lectures 13 and 15 describing the nature of demonstrative rhetoric that tries to praise the praiseworthy *ethos* of the honourable. Although he did draw on examples from painting, especially in Lecture 13, the main theme was literature. Despite the argument deriving from painting carrying more weight than might first appear, as we shall see.

The arousal of sympathy through plain style: the Lysias model

Smith used many literary references in LRBL to help explain why he gave so much attention to character. I will focus on the influence of the reflection of the ancients on style on Smith, notably the literary criticism of Dionysius of Halicarnassus, whose contribution to Smith's rhetoric has not yet been studied. I find Dionysius particularly interesting because his reflections on style as an indication of character were accompanied by numerous examples from painting.

Dionysius introduced Smith to two themes that were to attune him to Ramsay's empirical portraiture as a way of *entering into* and sympathising with other people. These were the '*ethos-charakter-stylus*' sequence and the axiological predominance of plain style, or what I will call the 'Lysias model.' These references may also have partially influenced the painting of an artist as thoroughly versed in literary and visual antiquity as Ramsay.

In *On Literary Composition* 10.2, Dionysius said:

> It seems to me that the two most important effects which those who write both poetry and prose should aim at are attractiveness and beauty. The ear craves for both of these, being affected in much the same way as the eye: for the latter, when it views moulded figures, pictures, carvings, or any other human artefacts, and finds both attractiveness and beauty in them, is satisfied and desires nothing more.
>
> (Dionysius of Halicarnassus 1985: 69–71)

On the basis of such a comparison, Dionysius reflected on the relationship between style and character and on the different types of style, establishing a hierarchy among them, which, as we shall see, Smith took advantage of.

In the same place, Dionysius established this foundational schema:

> I also think that, as in personal appearance, so in literary composition, an individual character (χαρακτῆρα) is associated with each of us; and I find not a bad illustration in painting. As in that art all painters mix their pigments together in a variety of shades, in the same way in poetry and all other literature, though we all use the same words, we do not put them together in the same manner.
>
> (Dionysius of Halicarnassus 1985: 167)

As he summarised in *On Demosthenes* 13, the style of an expression (λέξει) shows a particular character, and this can tell us about the individual's nature (ἤθει) (Dionysius of Halicarnassus 1974: 287). We then find three basic elements that define a visual or textual composition. First, there is what we might call 'style,' or what Dionysius called 'lexis' and the Latin '*stylus*' (from the stylus used to write on wax tablets). These are directly perceptible elements that define the emergent peculiarities of a composition, such as a long, flowing brushstroke in painting or the use of alliteration in writing. The description of these elements, whether real or fictional, is direct. Second, we have what could be called 'character,' or what Dionysius called '*charakter.*' This was a more holistic notion, defining the distinctive traits of the author as expressed in his work on the basis of the set of stylistic features: simple or contrived, modest or pompous, and such like. This description of the character is partly direct and partly interpretive and reconstructive. Third and finally, we come to the condition of the person, or as Aristotle put it, '*ethos*' (*Rhetoric* 1356a1–4), which, along with '*pathos*' and '*logos*,' was one of the fundamental pillars of rhetoric, as embraced by Smith through Cicero (Kapust and Schwarze 2016: 106–108; McKenna 2006: 40). Style leads to character, which in turn leads to the condition of the person (a semiotic model I will develop in the next section). The 'ethos' of the person can only be described indirectly through style and character.

Based on this framework, applicable to both painting and writing, Dionysius identified three styles: plain, mixed, and grand. The mixed style, epitomised by Demosthenes, was not pure but instead exhibited characteristics of both the plain and grand styles. The pure styles were the plain and the grand, the latter being typical of Thucydides. Smith knew and appreciated Dionysius' stylistic analysis of Thucydides' words, as well as his analysis of Thucydides' narrative construction that gave priority to spatial rather than temporal connections (Dionysius of Halicarnassus 1974: 481–483; Smith LRBL ii.33–34). Smith's assessment of Thucydides' literary style – sudden, concise, forceful, and loosely connected – mirrored that of Dionysius. However, while Dionysius was somewhat negative about Thucydides' historical construction, Smith was positive (Dionysius of Halicarnassus 1974: 527, 543; Smith LRBL ii.33, 53, 57). Unlike Smith, Dionysius was more concerned with Thucydides' style as a sign of his character than in his historical narrative.

He interpreted Thucydides as a literary writer rather than as a historian. Our interest lies in assessing style as a sign of character, so we leave aside the question of historical construction.

The distinction between the two pure styles was that the grand style used literary figures and made obvious artistic efforts, which was not the case with the plain style, as we shall soon see. (I will call it the 'Lysias model' because Dionysius used Lysias' speeches as the best example). Dionysius thought that the best way to understand both styles was by comparing them, which he prefaced with another reference to painting:

> There are some old paintings which are worked in simple colours without any subtle blending of tints but clear in their outline, and thereby possessing great charm; whereas the later paintings are less well-drawn but contain greater detail and a subtle interplay of light and shade, and are effective because of the many nuances of colour which they contain.
>
> (Dionysius of Halicarnassus 1974: 179–181)

In translating this into Smith's rhetoric and Ramsay's painting, we might substitute Jonathan Swift and Margaret Lindsay for Dionysius' Lysias, and replace Isaeus – Lysias' disciple who embellished his master's plain style – with Shaftesbury and Marie Leszczinska. Dionysius preferred a plain style, as no doubt did Smith and Ramsay.

Dionysius' characterisation of the Lysias model is of great interest, as Smith was familiar with it and, I believe, used it to some extent in his literary analysis of Swift. It was, moreover, a rather pictorial characterisation that was suitable to describe the portraits of Ramsay's second period, as we shall see.

In his Lectures 23 and 29, Smith presented a synthesis of the Lysias style that originated with Dionysius. In Lecture 29, Smith said:

> Lysias is the most ancient of all the Orators whose works have come to our hands. He wrote private Orations to be delivered by the persons concerned; and in these he studied to adapt them to the Character of a simple good natured man not at all versed in the Subtility and Chicane of the Law.
>
> (LRBL ii.218)

In Lecture 23 he further stated that Lysias 'lost himself much when he attempted anything florid and extraordinary such as this subject required' (LRBL ii.123). This laid the ground for his characterisation of Swift, and just as Dionysius compared Lysias favourably with Isaeus, so Smith compared Swift favourably with Shaftesbury. According to Dionysius, central to the Lysias model is his ability to express 'ideas in standard, ordinary, everyday language' (Dionysius of Halicarnassus 1974: 25). In other words, without too much effort, Lysias used perspicuous 'everyday language' to reveal the truth, especially to present individuals appropriately, 'so that their words seem to reflect their good moral character' (Dionysius of Halicarnassus 1974: 33). Working from the premise of the appropriateness of style to the character of a real person speaking on a subject in a seemingly impromptu oratorical address, Dionysius set out a catalogue of Lysias' virtues. I highlight two because of their relevance to the question at hand. The first can be called the 'art of disguising art' or the gift of making work appear spontaneous rather than deliberate. For Dionysius, this is the most elusive level of excellence, more so than highly decorated stylistic evidence:

> The distinctive nature of its melodious composition seems, as it were, not to be contrived or formed by any conscious art, and it would not surprise me if every layman, and even many of those scholars who have not specialized in oratory, should receive the impression that this arrangement has not been deliberately and artistically devised, but is somehow spontaneous and fortuitous. Yet it is more carefully composed than any work of art. For this artlessness is itself the product of art: the relaxed structure is really under control, and it is in the very illusion of not having been composed with masterly skill that the mastery lies.
>
> (Dionysius of Halicarnassus 1974: 35)

The second virtue, a natural consequence of the first, is that this style 'is suited not so much to the display of rhetorical power as to the *portrayal* of the realities of human nature' (Dionysius of Halicarnassus 1974: 47; italics mine). Rouquet said something similar of Ramsay, that of 'acknowledging no other guide than nature' and being moved by a 'rational taste of resemblance' (Rouquet 1970: 36). With both virtues, the most convincing possible connection between style, character, and the moral condition of the person is established, which was not possible in the case of the grand style.

Smith adopted both Dionysian principles, including their pictorial value. He developed the Lysias model in Lecture 7, splitting it into two sub-styles, plain and simple. In my view, the closest to the Lysias model was the plain one, of which Smith said:

> He is not at all sedulous to please, on the conterary he affects a sort of austerity and hardness of behaviour, so that when the common civilities of behaviour would be the most natural and easy manner, he industriously avoids them. He is so far from affecting any graces or civilities that he affects the conterary, and renders himself more severe than his nature would naturally lead him to be. [He despises the fashion in every point and neither conforms himself to it in dress, in language nor manners, but sticks by his own downright ways].
>
> (LRBL i.86)

According to Smith, this requires superior skills, such as Swift had, as well as careful planning to avoid the semblance of planning:

> He is so far from studying the ornaments of language that he affects to leave them out even when naturall; and in this way he often throws out pronouns

> etc. that are necessary to make the sentence full but would at the same time lead him into the uniformity of cadence which he industriously avoids. This however makes his stile very close, no word can be passed over without notice, every other one must be strongly accented to draw the attention of the hearer, for a word lost would spoil the whole.
>
> (LRBL i.92)

The link with Dionysius becomes clearer when Smith concludes his interpretation of Swift through painting, as in his plain style, 'he *paints* but each thought in the best and most proper manner and with the greatest strength of colouring must be visible to anyone at first sight' (LRBL i.106; italics mine).

Smith chose Shaftesbury to illustrate the grand style and, given his obvious distaste for him, to underline his preference for plain style. Swift was at pains never to use literary devices, while Shaftesbury took advantage of the practice of his time, which was to think that the 'perfection of language is very different from that we commonly speak in,' or that 'a good stile is almost conterary to that which we generally hear' (LRBL i.103). Thus, the main conclusion of Smith's critique was that Shaftesbury 'formed to himself an idea of beauty of Stile abstracted from his own character, by which he proposed to regulate his Stile' (LRBL i.138). While Swift (or Lysias as orator or Ramsay in his portrait of Margaret) succeeded in making the connection between style, character, and the condition of the person with perspicuity, Shaftesbury (or Dionysius' Thucydides or van Loo in his portrait of Marie Leszczinska) did not. Although in both cases the process was fictitious because it called for the use of imagination in the public construction of the self, only plain style conformed to Smith's ideal of communicative sympathy. Grand style, at best, could connect style with an admired character, but plain style helped us to *enter* more easily *into* the condition of the person we were relating to through sympathy in moral judgement.

In short, the productive model of communicative sympathy in LRBL helps us better understand the 'portraiture' strategies that we need to put into practice so that the person who will judge our situation using the interpretative sympathetic model of TMS can *enter into* it.

A semiotic and demonstrative model of sympathy

For Smith, the productive and interpretative power that allowed us to interpret others and construct ourselves for others during personal interactions was the imagination, the quintessential visual-pictorial power since the days of Addison. Imagination was the agent of a multifaceted, multistage process that created 'mental portraits.'

In both Smith's mental portrait and Ramsay's physical portrait, a semiotic approach to arousing and interpreting the sympathetic process was at work. This approach was appropriate to the interpretation of portraitures, texts, and the presentation of self in 'everyday life'. It was made up of three levels: the *signifier*, in which a series of discrete perceptual elements (Dionysius' 'stylus') is used to construct an overall form that has a two-level *meaning*; the *denotative*, that is, what the *signifier* explicitly means in the representation without transcending the canvas or the page (Dionysius' '*charakter*'); and the *referential*, the intended meaning beyond the representation (the Aristotelian '*ethos*').

Both Smith, with his sympathetic model of construction and interpretation, and Ramsay, with his empirical painting based on first-hand knowledge of the sitter, believed that '*ethos*' could be guessed from '*charakter*' and '*stylus*,' although not in the case of grand style. According to Smith, Shaftesbury did not go beyond the signifier-denotative meaning relationship, providing no referential meaning whatsoever, unlike Swift. It is the equivalent of Ramsay's and van Loo's portraits. Ramsay did not present Margaret in an ostensibly studied pose but as if he had met her by chance and depicted her spontaneously as she was. This concealment of the art was supposed to lead more easily to sympathetic identification, which was not possible in van Loo's portrait of Queen Marie. Here, it was clear that the model's pose and the meticulous artistic care given to the overelaborate staging of the composition made it difficult to access her '*ethos*' sympathetically because it only presented her role as a queen. An intimate relationship with her was inconceivable, as the goal was admiration, not sympathy.

This brings us to demonstrative rhetoric as found in LRBL and TMS. Smith was well acquainted with this type of rhetoric, having made it the subject of Lectures on Rhetoric 23 and 24. He was known to cultivate the genre at times, as in his dedication to William Crawford in the second edition (dated in 1758) of William Hamilton's *Poems on Several Occasions* or, more notably, in his letter published by William Strahan upon Hume's death. Demonstrative rhetoric set out to extol cities, virtues, and so on, but above all people who were deserving of such flattery, or *praiseworthy* people. The whole idea of portrait painting was also to make the sitter appear praiseworthy. As Henry Newcome argued in the second half of the seventeenth century when he was persuaded to have his portrait taken, 'a man should study both to be blameless and eminently active, that presumes to leave a picture behind him,' for 'if it put in mind of evil or of no good done by him, it is to little or bad purpose' (Piper 1978: 126). A portrait invariably has a measure of demonstrative rhetoric, letting others *enter into* us with sympathetic approval.

This longing to be praiseworthy or, for that matter, to be the rightful subject of a piece of demonstrative oratory moves us all in our daily lives. Smith thought so too and, in addition to the aforementioned lectures on rhetoric, wrote TMS III.2 on the subject, which opened with the following beautiful and obsessively symmetrical passage:

> Man naturally desires, not only to be loved, but to be lovely; or to be that thing which is the natural and proper object of love. He naturally dreads, not only to be hated, but to be hateful; or to be that thing which is the natural and proper object of hatred. He desires, not only praise, but praiseworthiness; or to be that thing which, thought it should be praised by nobody, is, however, the natural and proper object of praise. He dreads, not only blame, but

> blame-worthiness; or to be that thing which, though it should be blamed by nobody, is, however, the natural and proper object of blame.
>
> (TMS III.2.1)

All of us, at all times, act and present ourselves mindful of our potential for *encomium,* whether it is a speech extolling our ethical worth or a portrait showing how righteous we are as individuals. This is integral to the genesis of the impartial spectator, as Smith showed in TMS III.1–2. The first step in creating the impartial spectator, by which we measure ourselves, is to see ourselves (and be seen) as objects of praise or portraiture. In other words, upon seeing our true selves in a mirror, we may feel as if we are essentially righteous (Raphael 2007: 39–40), but the impartial spectator could always dash our hopes by showing that perhaps we could be reprehensible.

Our everyday need to appear kind and praiseworthy as articulated in TMS flows into the productive concept of sympathy in LRBL: we have to arouse it in others and in ourselves. This does not necessarily mean that we have to put on an act, pretending to be something we are not. Pretending to be what we are not, an ever-present possibility, means that we could be held accountable if the fiction were to be discovered. As Smith said, this would be deceitful, and 'the man who had the misfortune to imagine that nobody believed a single word he said, would feel himself the outcast of human society' (TMS VII.iv.26). This calls for the ideal of communicative transparency, relevant not only in a literary work or the construction of a portrait but also in our everyday life, something that is not strictly aesthetic. Here again we have to turn to perceptible elements ('*stylus*' or signifier) with which to construct a performance and an appearance (denotative '*charakter*'), allowing others to correctly judge our personal condition (referential '*ethos*') placing themselves in our place 'with their eyes.' A certain kind of literature (Swift, but not Shaftesbury) or painting (Ramsay, but not van Loo) would be a good preparation for this.

Conclusion: the complexities of Smith's sympathy

Adam Smith observed that for us, nature is an 'opera house,' behind the scenes of which we are not admitted (Astronomy II.9; Smith 1980). Our relationship with other human beings was similar, but in this case the mechanism of sympathy did allow us to go 'behind the scenes' because of two dimensions identified and studied conclusively by Forman-Barzilai, who called them 'the stage of surveillance' and 'the stage of discipline' (Forman-Barzilai 2011: 63). The first stage, which goes from the outside in, is the one in which 'a "spectator", any ordinary person, observes and judges the behaviour of an "agent" and through some means communicates this judgment' (Forman-Barzilai 2011: 63). The second stage, which goes from the inside out, 'refers to the impact that the spectator's surveillance and judgment have upon the agent, the extent to which they motivate him to modify his conduct' (Forman-Barzilai 2011: 63). That is, the mechanism of sympathy has a hermeneutic dimension of interpretation and another semiotic dimension of construction. As I anticipated in the introduction, in TMS Smith gave more weight to the hermeneutics of the spectator, but in LRBL he placed more importance on the semiotics of the actor, the way in which the orator (at the podium, the lectern, the pulpit, or on the bench) and the writer defined their public presentation, which can be applied to the social actors who construct their public presence to be morally judged by others. From a conceptual point of view, LRBL is complementary to TMS.

At the end of TMS, Smith referred to the need for a synthesis of the spectator's interpretation and the actor's construction. In a section on trust, he stated the following:

> We all desire, upon this account, to feel how each other is affected, to penetrate into each other's bosoms, and to observe the sentiments and affections which really subsist there. The man who indulges us in this natural passion, who invites us into his heart, who, as it were, sets open the gates of his breast to us, seems to exercise a species of hospitality more delightful than any other.
>
> (TMS VII.iv.28)

Here, Smith used a visual metaphor to identify the two dimensions of sympathy as defined by Forman-Barzilai. The semiotics of the constructive process that, in my analysis of the influence of Dionysus on LRBL, I have defined as the 'Lysias model,' is based on the perspicuous connection between style, character, and the ethical condition of the person. This development gives concrete form to the second part of Smith's text just cited. It is telling that the first word we retain from LRBL is 'perspicuity' (LRBL i.1), one of the meanings of which in Samuel Johnson's dictionary is 'easy to be understood.' In LRBL, Smith said that perspicuity would be achieved by reducing as much as possible the literary figures common in the 'grand style' in order to more easily arouse the sympathy of the listener or reader (LRBL i.56v). I believe that this also applies to the moral behaviour of the actor who wants to make it easier for others to put themselves in his or her place in sympathetic judgement. This dual and perspicuous mechanism of sympathy requires a certain degree of proximity, in any of the three types defined by Forman-Barzilai: physical, affective, and historical (Forman-Barzilai 2011: 135–195). Putting this together, once again thanks to Forman-Barzilai, with Smith's resulting 'anti-cosmopolitanism,' I conclude that the sympathy mechanism arising from the combination of TMS and LRBL is important in the world of personal relationships that underlies WN, quite different from the caricature of a stark and anonymous market that continues to prevail in the popular interpretation of Smith's thought.

Keppler stated that WN's world of personal relationships 'constitutes a direct, but partial, extension of' TMS (Keppler 2013: 6), because the exchange of goods was a consequence of the exchange of looks, sentiments, and values and, like them, 'always supposes the coincidence of two mental universes' (Keppler 2013: 20). Starting from the premise that 'the *homo oeconomicus* in an intensely social being' (Keppler 2013: 8, 32), he went on to say that 'the sympathy mechanism is, in fact, at the origin of the formation of an economic rationality' (Keppler 2013: 20) and therefore that the economic behaviour described by Smith served to control egoistical and antisocial passions (Keppler 2013: 8). According to him, the sympathy mechanism was the essential basis of the market, so 'economic deliberations . . . are the logical and necessary consequences of the sympathy mechanism' (Keppler 2013: 34). This could be so because 'Adam Smith's view of the economy is indeed that of a world of small-scale shopkeepers' (Keppler 2013: 61).

Meanwhile, Dwyer went into a little more detail about WN's world of personal relationships, which for him were not limited to the 'crude cash nexus of profit motive' because, 'for Smith and his contemporaries, ethics and economics were inseparable' (Dwyer 1998: 46). Dwyer thought that it was a world of small-scale capitalism, where close personal relationships and the sympathetic mechanism were important (Dwyer 1998: 24). It was a world of 'country gentlemen,' 'farmers,' 'pre-industrial capitalists,' 'gentry and yeomanry,' and so on, a socioeconomic group that Ramsay, our secondary protagonist, knew intimately and portrayed on numerous occasions, beginning with his wife, Margaret (Dulau 2013: 67–88). These economic actors possessed a 'certain mediocrity' that generated sympathy that the great landowners and the aristocracy, with their selfishness and conspicuous consumption of luxury goods, did not (Dwyer 1998: 25, 26, 41). In short, this economic world of Smith helped build a 'good neighbourhood,' endowed with ethical values (Dwyer 1998: 45).

In my view, all of this shows the importance of the sympathy mechanism in WN, understood in the hermeneutic, semiotic, and perspicuous sense that I have called 'the Lysias model.' While it is not possible to go into this in greater detail, I do wish to present an example from the textual environment of the famous 'invisible hand.' The argument of this part of WN is generally interpreted as follows: when traders only look out for their own interests, the entire market benefits. For many, this is at odds with the sympathetic structure of TMS, giving rise to the also well-known 'Adam Smith problem.' However, I believe that the sympathy mechanism and personal proximity are very much present in the argument. Shortly before coining his now-famous expression, Smith explained the reasons why a trader would prefer to invest in local markets:

> In the home-trade his capital is never so long out of his sight as it frequently in the foreign trade of consumption. He can know better the character and situation of the persons whom he trusts.
>
> (WN IV.ii.6; Smith 1976b)

According to these words, merchants are not short-sighted egoists, but rather people moved by knowledge and sympathy, who decide to limit themselves to the local market because their knowledge of others is more direct and reliable there. Smith used terminology that refers to the sympathy mechanism: merchants preferred to exchange goods and capital with those whose character and situation they *knew*, that is, those with whom they could have more certainty. In this market situation, there is no doubt that it was also important for others to make the effort to *perspicuously* demonstrate their trustworthy character (this had been the purpose of individual and corporate group portraits of Dutch merchants since the seventeenth century). I am not claiming that for Smith economic exchanges were based on relationships of genuine friendship, uncontrollable passionate responses, or normative judgements, but rather on the confidence derived from the sympathetic mechanism, which in the market was also a mental and conscious process on the part of the spectator, of observation, interpretation, and identification with the actors, who built their presence to facilitate that process. This was possible within the spatial and social scale of the groups identified by Keppler and Dwyer, and it was also the economic version of one of the conclusions of Smith's critique of Stoic cosmopolitanism in TMS (Forman-Barzilai 2011: 19):

> To man is allotted a much humbler department, but one much more suitable to the weakness of his powers, and to the narrowness of his comprehension; the care of his own happiness, of that of his family, his friends, his country.
>
> (TMS VI.ii.3.6)

We may wonder if this makes sense today, when face-to-face proximity and direct visual presence are the exception rather than the rule in our social relationships. Bearing in mind Forman-Barzilai's statement that physical proximity matters but is neither necessary nor sufficient (Forman-Barzilai 2011: 143), I think the treatment of sympathy that emerges from LRBL's semiotic model allows us to answer in the affirmative. I have defined the constructive part of the sympathy mechanism as semiotic due to the abundance of resources available for constructing the sympathetic character. First, there are the resources of close and face-to-face interaction, such as personal image and behaviour, use of language, gestures, clothing, and the like. However, in LRBL, there are other resources for building personal character that work without personal presence or visual representation. In my chapter, I have focused particularly on the resources of painting and the literary text. Painting and painters appear several times in LRBL as something that we might be able to enter into. Painted portraits, in Smith's time, were flat and static mimetic representations of an actor who may be very far away (in space and time) from the spectator. However, each portrait, just like any literary text, provided signs with which to build the sympathetic character of that actor. Something similar, but not visual, happens with writing. Smith was explicit about this when, following Dionysius, he analysed the character of certain writers (Lucian, Swift, Shaftesbury, and others) from their texts. Written texts are abstract and distant signs that allow us to reconstruct the character of writers and *enter into* their ethical condition, a process that, according to Smith, is favoured whenever the writer is perspicuous. Hence, if we study it in conjunction with the semiotic complement of LRBL, the sympathy mechanism will turn out to be a resource of such richness and value in so many diverse social situations that it will be as relevant today as when Smith analysed it in the second half of the eighteenth century.

Notes

1 Imitative Arts I.1–7, Smith 1980; De Marchi 2006: 150–151; Jones 1992: 69; Malek 1972: 50.

2 Such as *On Painting* by Leonardo da Vinci (Mizuta 2000: no. 973), *Le Vite* by Vasari (Mizuta 2000: no. 1713), *Le Vite de' Pittori* by Bellori (Mizuta 2000: no. 142), *Conférences de l'Académie Royale* by Felibien (Mizuta 2000: no. 599), *Abrege de la Vie des Peintres*

and *Cours de Peinture* by Piles (Mizuta 2000: nos. 1304 y 1305), *Réflexions Critiques*, by Du Bos (Mizuta 2000: no. 540), *Three Treatises* by James Harris (Mizuta 2000: no. 749), *The Present State of the Arts in England* by Rouquet (Mizuta 2000: no. 1445), *Seven Discourses* by Joshua Reynolds (Mizuta 2000: no. 1427) or *An Essay on Painting* by William Hagley (Mizuta 2000: no. 761).

3 Such as those by Aristotle, Shaftesbury, Addison, Hutcheson, Hume, Akenside, Gerard, Rousseau, and Diderot.

4 From Cicero and Quintilian to Fénelon, taking in Philostratus, Lucian, Dionysius of Halicarnassus, Pseudo-Dionysius, Castiglione, and Arnauld and Nicole, among others.

5 Smith owned a 1737 copy of Rameau's *Génération Harmonique*; Mizuta (2000: no. 1400).

6 Smith owned Philostratus' work on the subject (Mizuta 2000: no. 1298).

7 Swift, Lucian, Shaftesbury, and Addison, for example.

8 Smith owned a copy of this work by Rouquet (Mizuta 2000: no. 1445).

9 Text as Shaftesbury's *Second Characters* (Mizuta 2000: no. 1512) or Harris' *Three Treatises* (Mizuta 2000: no. 749).

Bibliography

Brown, I. G. (1987) *The Clerks of Penicuik: Portraits of Taste and Talent*. Edinburgh: Penicuik House Preservation Trust.

De Marchi, N. (2006) 'Smith on Ingenuity, Pleasure, and the Imitative Arts', in K. Haakonssen (ed.) *The Cambridge Companion to Adam Smith*. Cambridge: Cambridge University Press, 2006.

Dionysius of Halicarnassus. (1974) *Critical Essays I*, (ed.) J. Henderson. Cambridge, MA: Harvard University Press.

Dionysius of Halicarnassus. (1985) *Critical Essays II*, (ed.) J. Henderson. Cambridge, MA: Harvard University Press.

Dulau, A. (2013) 'Women of Sense and Education', in M. Campbell (ed.) *Adam Ramsay: Portraits of the Enlightenment*. Munich: Prestel.

Dwyer, J. (1998) *The Age of Passions: An Interpretation of Adam Smith and Scottish Enlightenment Culture*. East Linton: Tuckwell Press.

Engell, J. (1981) *The Creative Imagination. Enlightenment to Romanticism*. Cambridge, MA: Harvard University Press.

Fairfull-Smith, G. (2001) *The Foulis Press and the Foulis Academy*. Glasgow: The Glasgow Art Index.

Fleischacker, S. (2012) 'Sympathy in Hume and Smith: A Contrast, Critique, and Reconstruction', in C. Fricke and D. Føllesdsal (eds.) *Intersubjectivity and Objectivity in Adam Smith and Edmund Husserl*. Berlin: De Gruyter.

Flessenkämper, I. (2010) *Considerations, Encouragements, Improvements. Die Select Society in Edinburgh 1754–1764*. Berlin: Akademie Verlag.

Forman-Barzilai, F. (2011) *Adam Smith and the Circles of Sympathy: Cosmopolitanism and Moral Theory*. Cambridge: Cambridge University Press.

Frazer, M. L. (2012) *The Enlightenment of Sympathy: Justice and the Moral Sentiments in the Eighteenth Century and Today*. Oxford: Oxford University Press.

Hagstrum, J. H. (1958) *The Sister Arts: The tradition of Literary Pictorialism and English Poetry from Dryden to Gray*. Chicago, IL: The University of Chicago Press.

Hume, D. (2002) *A Treatise of Human Nature*, (eds.) D. F. Norton and M. J. Norton. Oxford: Oxford University Press.

Jarratt, S. C. (2008) 'Ekphrastic Rhetoric and National Identity in Adam Smith's Rhetoric Lectures', in L. L. Gaillet (ed.) *Scottish Rhetoric and Its Influences*. New York: Routledge.

Jones, P. (1992) 'The Aesthetics of Adam Smith', in P. Jones and A. S. Skinner (eds.) *Adam Smith Reviewed*. Edinburgh: Edinburgh University Press.

Kapust, D. J. and Schwarze, M. A. (2016) 'The Rhetoric of Sincerity: Cicero and Smith on Propriety and Political Context', *American Political Science Review*, 110: 100–111.
Keppler, J. H. (2013) *Adam Smith and the Economy of the Passions*. London: Routledge.
Labio, C. (2013) 'Adam Smith's Aesthetics', in C. J. Berry, M. P. Paganelli and C. Smith (eds.) *The Oxford Handbook of Adam Smith*. Oxford: Oxford University Press.
Macmillan, D. (1986) *Painting in Scotland: The Golden Age*. Oxford: Phaidon.
Malek, J. S. (1972) 'Adam Smith's Contribution to Eighteenth-Century British Aesthetics', *The Journal of Aesthetics and Art Criticism*, 31: 49–54.
McKenna, S. J. (2006) *Adam Smith: The Rhetoric of Propriety*. Albany: State University of New York Press.
Mizuta, H. (2000) *Adam Smith's Library: A Catalogue*. Oxford: Clarendon Press.
Murray, D. (1913) *Robert and Andrew Foulis and the Glasgow Press*. Glasgow: James Maclehose and Sons.
Piper, D. (1978) *The English Face*. London: The National Gallery Portrait.
Raphael, D. D. (2007) *The Impartial Spectator: Adam Smith Moral Philosophy*. Oxford: Oxford University Press.
Reynolds, J. (1952) *Portraits: Character sketches of Oliver Goldsmith, Samuel Johnson, and David Garrick, Together with Other MSS of Reynolds Recently Discovered among the Private Papers of James Boswell*, (ed.) F. W. Hilles. New York: McGraw-Hill.
Richardson, J. (1971) *An Essay on the Theory of Painting*. Menston: Scholar Press.
Ross, I. S. (1995) *The Life of Adam Smith*. Oxford: Clarendon Press.
Rouquet, A. (1970) *The Present State of the Arts in England*. London: Cornmarket Press.
Shawe-Taylor, D. (1990) *The Georgians: Eighteenth-Century Portraiture and Society*. London: Barrie and Jenkins.
Smart, A. (1992) *Allan Ramsay: Painter, Essayist and Man of the Enlightenment*. New Haven: Yale University Press.
Smith, A. (1759) *The Theory of Moral Sentiments*. London: A. Millar.
Smith, A. (1976a) *The Theory of Moral Sentiments*, (eds.) D. D. Raphael and A. L. Macfie, Glasgow edition. Oxford: Oxford University Press. Reprinted, Liberty Press (1982).
Smith, A. (1976b) *An Inquiry into the Nature and Causes of the Wealth of Nations*, (eds.) R. H. Campbell and A. S. Skinner, Glasgow edition. Oxford: Oxford University Press. Reprinted, Liberty Press (1981).
Smith, A. (1980) *Essays on Philosophical Subjects*, (ed.) W. P. D. Wightman, Glasgow edition. Oxford: Oxford University Press. Reprinted, Liberty Press (1982).
Smith, A. (1983) *Lectures on Rhetoric and Belles Lettres*, (ed.) J. C. Bryce, Glasgow edition. Oxford: Oxford University Press. Reprinted, Liberty Press (1985).
Turnbull, G. (1971) *A Treatise of Ancient Painting*. München: Wilhelm Fink Verlag.
Wendorf, R. (1983) 'Ut Pictura Biographia: Biography and Portrait Painting as Sister Arts', in R. Wendorf (ed.) *Articulated Images: The Sister Arts from Hogarth to Tennyson*. Minneapolis: University of Minnesota Press.
West, S. (2004) *Portraiture*. Oxford: Oxford University Press.
Wight, J. B. (2006) 'Adam Smith's Ethics and the "Noble Arts"', *Review of Social Economy*, 64: 155–180.

5 Adam Smith on the remedies to economic inequality

Zack Rauwald

In the eighteenth century, England's '[p]rosperity extended a long way down the social scale.' An average labourer in England annually consumed more than three baskets of subsistence goods, whereas most workers elsewhere barely consumed more than one basket (Allen 2019: 111–112). Only the poorest vagrants and paupers in England consumed so little during this time. And yet, the number of poor people in England tripled in the eighteenth century, as the 'greatest income gains were made by the landed classes and the bourgeoisie, the two richest groups in society' (Allen 2019: 112). Real income inequality grew between 1500 and 1815, as food prices increased 'much more than prices of what the rich consumed' (Hoffmann et al. 2002: 323). Although eighteenth-century England was flourishing and most people benefitted from this economic prosperity, inequality also grew significantly. Most scholars contend that the rise of economic inequality, particularly *relative* poverty, was unproblematic for most contemporary British thinkers and emphasise commerce's role in reducing absolute poverty (e.g. Boyd 2008).

This interpretation has also dominated scholarship on Adam Smith (1723–1790). Smith's philosophy of history, which charted human development from hunter-gatherers to commercial society, showed that the division of labour increased most people's wealth and thereby improved the general standard of living in a given society. Emphasising this general improvement through the development of society, Istvan Hont and Donald Winch, the pioneers of modern Smith scholarship, contended that Smith was primarily concerned with poverty rather than inequality (Hont and Ignatieff 1983; Winch 1996). Winch, for instance, claimed that the central point of *The Wealth of Nations* (*WN*) was to show that 'in the midst of so much oppressive inequality' the division of labour was capable of explaining how the 'lowest and most despised member of civilised society' enjoyed 'superior affluence and abundance' compared to what 'the most respected and active savage can attain to' in a more equal society (Winch 1996: 61). As a result of this dominant interpretation of Smith's philosophy of history, his thoughts on economic inequality have been sidelined.

Recently, this interpretation has been challenged. Ryan Patrick Hanley first discussed Smith's ideas on the adverse moral effects of inequality, asserting that for Smith 'inequality is inimical to sympathy, and that commercial societies,

DOI: 10.4324/9781003767824-7

insofar as they require some degree of inequality, also inhibit a certain degree of sympathy' (Hanley 2009: 46, fn. 44). Hanley emphasised the significance of *semblable* in Smith's moral thought: for a spectator to fully sympathise with an agent, they must be well-acquainted and belong to the same social station and affluence. Economic inequality weakens people's likeness, meaning they cannot fully sympathise with one another (Hanley 2009: 47). Building on Hanley's analysis, Dennis Rasmussen showed that Smith was concerned with the damaging consequences of extreme inequality, independently from poverty. He demonstrated that, for Smith, inequality was a 'double-edged sword' that was beneficial for society but had adverse moral consequences for individuals. He especially emphasised that relative poverty was problematic for Smith, as the poor are overlooked because people are more likely to sympathise with the rich, according to Smith (Rasmussen 2016). Most recently, Benoît Walraevens has claimed that Smith was more concerned with the causes of inequality – natural or unnatural, fair or unfair – rather than its level *per se* (Walraevens 2021). Walraevens connected Smith's analysis of inequality's effects with his assessment of mercantilism: 'Smith combines economic and moral arguments . . . to criticise the mercantile system and defend . . . the system of natural liberty, which affords economic efficiency, a fairness of distribution and more independence and social mobility' (Walraevens 2021: 211).[1]

Although these scholars have examined the causes and effects of economic inequality for Smith, they overlooked his ideas on the remedies to economic inequality.[2] This paper seeks to analyse these remedies, namely taxation and education, to ascertain their effectiveness in alleviating the most severe drawbacks of economic inequality in commercial society. Satoshi Niimura, the only scholar who has considered Smith's thought on this matter, argued that commercial society would naturally become more equal for Smith (Niimura 2016).[3] According to Niimura, rising wages, occasioned by increasing labour scarcity, and the reform of succession laws, which would decrease the amount of land held by each landowner, would naturally diminish economic inequality for Smith. Niimura added that Smith recommended policies like redistributive taxation and state-sponsored education to accelerate this process (Niimura 2016). However, Niimura focused exclusively on Smith's political economy. He thus neglected the predominantly moral consequences of economic inequality and the centrality of Smith's educational proposals as a remedy to these effects. This paper therefore has three main arguments: first, that Smith thought sovereigns should and could remedy the effects of economic inequality; second, that the adverse effects of economic inequality were principally *moral*; and third, that Smith's educational proposals most effectively remedied these moral effects.[4]

To make this case, this paper first briefly outlines Smith's thoughts on the adverse effects of economic inequality. The second section explores Smith's ideas on taxation and argues that his suggestions do not permit a significant redistribution of wealth, which would neutralise the adverse effects of economic inequality on individuals. The third section emphasises the salience and effectiveness of Smith's ideas on education as a remedy to the ills of economic inequality.

Smith on the effects of economic inequality

This paper begins with a short overview of Smith's moral psychology in *The Theory of Moral Sentiments* (*TMS*), as that is fundamental to any understanding of the effects of inequality on people's moral judgements. Smith's moral thought is founded on sympathy, a fellow-feeling, 'which interest[s]' a man 'in the fortune of others, and render[s] their happiness necessary to him, though he derives nothing from it except the pleasure of seeing it' (TMS I.i.1). According to Smith, there are two kinds of sympathy: natural sympathy and a fuller, interactive sympathetic process. The former is a very limited, natural, and immediate sentiment: when we see somebody happy, we momentarily feel a part of their joy. The latter includes a complex adjustment of the passions of both the agent and the spectator to reach a concord of emotions. For this to be possible, spectators must first gain insight into the context within which someone acted before a judgement can be made; rather than generating sympathy, it awakens curiosity to determine the reasons that prompted the agent to behave in that way (TMS I.i.6–10). The spectator envisions himself in the position of the agent to measure his imagined response to the actual reaction of the agent. This adjustment is based on the spectator's humanity to amplify his sentiments and the agent's self-command to control his emotions. We approve of actions that we can fully sympathise with and disapprove of ones we cannot fully sympathise with (TMS I.i.3.1–2; TMS I.i.3.9–10; I.i.5.1). This principle also operates when men assess their own behaviour: they envision themselves as a well-informed 'impartial spectator,' who judges their conduct neutrally (TMS III.1.1–7). Crucially, men desire others' approval and attention and enter 'into the great school of self-command' to regulate their emotions to gain the approval of spectators (TMS III.3.22). However, according to Smith, people do not only want to be praised; they want to be praise-worthy. The approbation of spectators, when confirmed by the imagined impartial spectator, 'necessarily strengthens our own sense of our own praise-worthiness' (TMS III.2.3). Through recurrent moral judgements, we can infer 'general rules' of behaviour. While reason deduces these maxims, they originate in the sentiments of individual judgements that constitute them: 'It is by finding in a vast variety of instances that one tenor of conduct constantly pleases in a certain manner, and that another as constantly displeases the mind, that we form the general rules of morality' (TMS VII.iii.2.7). Morality and the general rules of conduct are learned through social interactions for Smith, making continued social contact crucial for individuals to remain virtuous.

Rasmussen explained that '[i]n Smith's view, extreme economic inequality leads people to sympathise more fully and readily with the rich than the poor, and this distortion in our sympathies in turn undermines both morality and happiness' (Rasmussen 2016: 342). In addition to living in poverty, the poor suffer as they are disregarded:

> Nothing is so mortifying as to be obliged to expose our distress to the view of the public, and to feel, that though our situation is open to the eyes of all mankind, no mortal conceives for us the half of what we suffer.
>
> (TMS I.iii.2.1)

Poor people are always overlooked as though they were 'in the midst of a crowd,' while '[t]he man of rank and distinction . . . is observed by all the world' (TMS I.iii.2.2). A poor man 'is ashamed of his poverty,' as he senses that people do not perceive him or do not engage in his misery (TMS I.iii.2.2). This exacerbates the poor man's situation because he suffers from his poverty and from his companions' 'real and gross inhumanity' (TMS I.i.2.4). Smith claimed that '[t]he bitter and painful emotions of grief and resentment more strongly require the healing consolation of sympathy' than pleasant sentiments, highlighting that the poor more urgently required the solace of sympathy (TMS I.i.2.4). Unlike the poor man, the rich man

> glories in his riches, because he feels that they naturally draw upon him the attention of the world, and that mankind are disposed to go along with him in all those agreeable emotions with which the advantages of his situation so readily inspire him.
>
> (TMS I.iii.2.1)

Consequently, 'his heart seems to swell and dilate itself within him, and he is fonder of his wealth, upon this account, than for all the other advantages it procures him' (TMS I.iii.2.1).

Since Smith's moral philosophy is founded on sociability and his theory of conscience, the imagined impartial spectator, depends on real spectators to ensure its judgements remain accurate, the inconspicuousness of poor people could have significant consequences. According to Smith, '[n]o action can properly be called virtuous, which is not accompanied with the sentiment of self-approbation' (TMS III.6.13). To conduct oneself virtuously, one must intend to be virtuous and hence one must be praiseworthy. However, if one's impartial spectator is not calibrated through comparing one's own judgements with those of real spectators, because one is overlooked due to one's poverty, people's ability to be virtuous is undermined. For Smith, virtue played a salient role in people's pursuit of happiness, which 'consists in tranquillity and enjoyment' (TMS III.3.30). Hence, the relative poverty of the poor may contribute to their unhappiness.

Although Rasmussen did not call attention to the drawbacks of the division of labour in his analysis of Smith's thoughts on economic inequality, these are also important to note, especially in conjunction with his ideas on education. The drawbacks of the division of labour exacerbate the miserable situation of the poor as they are socially isolated further, undermining their ability to be virtuous. As a labourer does monotonous work, he loses the 'habit' to exert his mind,

> and generally becomes as stupid and ignorant as it is possible for a human creature to become. The torpor of his mind renders him, not only incapable of relishing or bearing a part in any rational conversation, but of conceiving any generous, noble, or tender sentiment, and consequently of forming any just judgment concerning many even of the ordinary duties of private life. . . . The uniformity of his stationary life naturally corrupts the courage of his mind. . . . His dexterity at his own particular trade seems . . . to be acquired

> at the expence of his intellectual, social, and martial virtues. But in every improved and civilized society this is the state into which the labouring poor, that is, the great body of the people, must necessarily fall, unless government takes some pains to prevent it (WN V.i.f.50).
>
> (Passage 1)

The many benefits of the division of labour are contrasted with its lamentable effects on labourers. Workers cannot discuss subjects beyond their job or current needs and are deprived of the fortitude to endure irregular lives, like that of soldiers (WN V.i.f.50). In the *Lectures on Jurisprudence* (*LJ*), Smith maintained that '[n]othing tends so much to corrupt and enervate and debase the mind as dependency' (LJA vi.8). Hence, labourers' characters may corrupt, as they are likely weak and reliant on their employer. They are also deprived of the capacity to make accurate moral judgements, which, as aforementioned, is a prerequisite to living virtuously and happily. Workers are so entrenched in their stage of the manufacturing processes that they cannot discuss their work with their neighbour because it is too specialised, promoting social isolation (Lamb 1973: 283–284). The negative impact of corruption is not restricted to labourers: society more broadly may also be affected, as Smith identified workers as an important source of improvement and innovation (WN I.i.8).

While scholars have associated these drawbacks with corruption in commercial society, few have connected them with Smith's thought on economic inequality (Hill 2006; Tegos 2013). The association is clear: these workers' monetary situation necessitated their employment in manufacturing to support themselves; they did not own land, or at least were highly unlikely to have done so, whereas lords or rich merchants did not have to work in manufacturing for their subsistence. This is not absolute poverty but rather *relative* poverty, as these people were employed and, for this to be sustainable, they must have earned enough to afford essentials like food (WN I.viii.15).[5]

Smith explained that these drawbacks, in conjunction with man's disregard for the poor, enhanced social isolation:

> A man of rank and fortune is by his station the distinguished member of a great society, who attend to every part of his conduct . . . he is obliged to a very strict observation of that species of morals, whether liberal or austere. . . . A man of low condition, on the contrary, is far from being a distinguished member of any great society. While he remains in a country village his conduct may be attended to, and he may be obliged to attend to it himself . . . he may have what is called a character to lose. But as soon as he comes into a great city, he is sunk in obscurity and darkness. His conduct is observed and attended to by nobody, and he is therefore very likely to neglect it himself, and to abandon himself to every sort of low profligacy and vice (WN V.i.g.12).
>
> (Passage 2)

This passage demonstrates the severity of the effects on the poor. The rich remain on a path to happiness and virtue and preserve their characters because they are seen, maintaining a stringent regard for morality. Conversely, the situation of the poor is dire. In pre-commercial states of society, they lived within village communities and were unseen. However, in commercial society, when they move to urban areas for work, they are 'sunk in obscurity and darkness' because they lose this community, becoming socially isolated (WN V.i.g.12). Due to their relative poverty, strangers overlook them, making it challenging to make new social connections. In short, for Smith, economic inequality could socially isolate individuals and thereby significantly impact their capacity for virtue and happiness. For Smith, there were two remedies to this great cost – taxation and education – to which we now turn.

Taxation as a remedy to the effects of economic inequality

Niimura accentuated taxation as Smith's remedy to economic inequality, arguing that Smith's policy 'is intended to impose a tax that is progressively greater than proportional to income on the rich, particularly on the landowner class' (Niimura 2016: 899). He claimed that most scholars considering Smith's ideas on wealth redistribution neglected taxes on luxuries and rent and instead overemphasised 'expressly progressive burdens, such as house-rent tax or road tolls' (Niimura 2016: 899).[6] However, according to Niimura, taxes on luxuries and on land eventually amount to progressive taxes on income, since the rich are more likely to purchase luxuries and own land (Niimura 2016: 899). While Niimura rightly claims that Smith's tax proposals fall disproportionately on the rich, I will argue that this progression was fairly limited by examining Smith's ideas on taxes on land and consumables as these were, according to Niimura, the most progressive.

Smith's four maxims of taxation form the foundation of his thoughts on taxes.[7] The first maxim outlined by Smith was equity: 'The subjects of every state ought to contribute towards the support of the government, as nearly as possible, in proportion to their respective abilities; that is, in proportion to the revenue which they respectively enjoy under the protection of the state' (WN V.ii.b.3). Smith compared the costs of government to maintenance costs of a vast estate, asserting that it is fair that people 'contribute in proportion to their respective interests in the estate' (WN V.ii.b.3).[8] This first maxim demonstrates that Smith advocated for some progressive taxation. Second, certainty: 'The tax which each individual is bound to pay ought to be certain, and not arbitrary.' Uncertainty threatened people's liberty as tax collectors could demand payment at any time (WN V.ii.b.4). Third, convenience: 'Every tax ought to be levied at the time, or in the manner in which it is most likely to be convenient for the contributor to pay it' (WN V.ii.b.5). Fourth, efficiency in collection: 'Every tax ought to be so contrived as both to take out and to keep out of the pockets of the people as little as possible, over and above what it brings into the publick treasury of the state' (WN V.ii.b.6). Importantly, Smith thought that only taxes that aligned with these maxims would raise revenue justly (Berry 2018: 93).

Smith divided land taxes into two categories: first, taxes on agricultural land; and, second, taxes on inhabited land which he called ground rent. Smith supported agricultural land taxes if their rate was fixed based on acreage rather than rent, as a variable tax would impede improvement (WN V.ii.c.1–2; V.ii.c.18; LJB 317). Since different parts of the country were more improved than others, and land taxes should remain constant, this tax was unequal, offending the maxim of equity. However, this tax 'is perfectly agreeable to the other three' maxims: first, it was certain, as the amount was fixed; second, it was convenient as tenants advanced the tax; and, third, its collection was efficient, as it could be levied by fewer tax officers than would be required to raise a similar amount of revenue through a tax on consumables (WN V.ii.c.2). Nevertheless, Smith thought land taxes should be moderate, making it unlikely that this tax would fundamentally alter wealth distribution. Smith considered the taxation of ground-rent as the most appropriate tax, as it existed because of the sovereign's good governance and not landlords' good management (WN V.ii.e.11). Ground-rent was constituted by any excess building rent, which recompensed the construction of the building and its maintenance. The amount of rent charged by landowners depended on the desirability of the location (WN V.ii.e.9). Hence, a ground-rent tax would have fallen more heavily on areas where people could afford to pay a higher rate of ground-rent. That people could do this was, according to Smith, 'altogether owing to the good government of the sovereign,' as he protected 'the industry either of the whole people, or of the inhabitants of some particular place' (WN V.ii.e.11). Thus, while this tax fell disproportionately on the rich, it would have affected wealthy townspeople, who owned property in urban areas where rents were higher, more than large landowners.

Smith's tax proposals were not only about what should be taxed but also about what should not. He opposed taxes on necessities because they increase the price of subsistence. This, in turn, occasions an increase in the price of labour, which increases the price of all other commodities (WN IV.ii.35). The problems caused by taxing necessities were grave and could only be sustained by the richest countries. They were most common in Holland, but Smith claimed the country 'continues to prosper, not by means of them, as has been most absurdly supposed, but in spite of them' (WN IV.ii.36). Thus, the country would have flourished much more if it had freed itself from the shackles of improper taxation, highlighting the importance of a proper tax policy. If a country thrived less than it could, this affected the poor most.

This is especially important because for Smith necessities were not limited to subsistence needs. Instead, he considered necessities to be relative: they were dependent on what was deemed respectable in a society. As he writes, '[b]y necessaries I understand, not only the commodities which are indispensably necessary for the support of life, but whatever the custom of the country renders it indecent for creditable people, even of the lowest order, to be without' (WN V.ii.k.3). A linen shirt is not essential to survival, and the Greeks and Romans lived comfortably without linen,

> [b]ut in the present times . . . a creditable day-labourer would be ashamed to appear in publick without a linen shirt, the want of which would be supposed

> to denote that disgraceful degree of poverty, which, it is presumed, no body can well fall into without extreme bad conduct.
>
> (WN V.ii.k.3)

Therefore, Smith explained that '[u]nder necessaries . . . I comprehend, not only those things which nature, but those things which the established rules of decency have rendered necessary to the lowest rank of people. All other things I call luxuries' (WN V.ii.k.3). Necessities are *relative*; they include essentials like food and items needed to appear honourable, requiring everyone to have a certain amount of wealth. Any price increase of necessities made it more likely that more poor people would fall below this relative poverty threshold, suggesting that taxes on necessities would amplify inequality rather than remedying it.

Smith was more open to taxing luxuries. Taxes on luxuries did not affect the price of labour in the way taxes on necessities did, as they only increased the price of the luxury that was taxed, with its cost falling entirely on the consumer (WN V.ii.k.9). Smith explained that taxes on luxuries observed three of the four maxims. First, they were equitable. Although they did not fall equally on people by wealth, as rich people could abstain from consuming luxuries to avoid paying tax, they were voluntary and therefore fair. Nevertheless, since Smith considered 'luxuries and vanities' as 'the principal expence of the rich,' while the poor spent most on necessities, these taxes can still be considered progressive (WN V.ii.e.6). Second, these taxes were 'perfectly certain,' as an item's price already included the tax (WN V.ii.k.59). Third, they were convenient to the taxpayer, as they could be 'paid piece-meal, or in proportion as the contributors have occasion to purchase the goods upon which they are imposed' (WN V.ii.k.60). However, Smith lamented that taxes on luxuries 'offend in every respect against the fourth' maxim because they are expensive to collect (WN V.ii.k.60). Nonetheless, he posited that Britain was less affected than other countries by this inefficiency in collection, as '[o]ur state is not perfect, and might be mended; but it is as good or better than that of most of our neighbours' (WN V.ii.k.66).

For Smith, luxuries of the poor should be taxed similarly to luxuries of the rich. In an undated letter to Sir John Sinclair of Ulbster, Smith wrote:

> I dislike all taxes that may affect the necessary expenses of the poor. They, according to circumstances, either oppress the people immediately subject to them, or are repaid with great interest by the rich, *i.e.* by their employers in the advanced wages of their labour. Taxes on the *luxuries* of the poor, upon their beer and other spirituous liquors, for example, as long as they are so moderate as not to give much temptation to smuggling, I am so far from disapproving (Corr. Letter 299 to Sir John Sinclair of Ulbster, undated: 327).
>
> (Passage 3)

This passage raises two important points: first, Smith was not wholly against taxes affecting the poor but strongly disapproved of taxes on essentials. While Smith thought most luxury taxes would fall on the rich, he did not think they would solely fall on them, undermining the view that they would support any wholesale redistribution. Unusually for eighteenth-century Britain, Smith did not consider beer a necessity, as he thought people could abstain from alcohol 'without any reproach' (WN V.ii.k.3). In the eighteenth century, beer was 'the universal drink of all members of society,' as people thought it was safer to drink than water while also being a source of calories (Muldrew 2011: 65–66). Smith's views on beer as a luxury thus illustrate the limits of relative necessities. Second, this passage demonstrates that, for Smith, taxes must be moderate to not encourage smuggling.[9] That taxes on luxuries could only be marginal further weakens the view that they could occasion significant wealth redistribution. Moreover, taxes are not necessarily used to directly redistribute wealth; instead, they may be used to pay for government expenditures, such as the military. Therefore, while the wealth of the poor would be taxed disproportionately less, they may not benefit from any direct monetary support to limit economic inequality in society. According to Smith, who was a commissioner of Scottish customs between 1778 and 1790, high duties on foreign luxuries failed to discourage consumption and instead encouraged smuggling, which 'reduced the revenue of the customs below what more moderate duties would have afforded' (WN V.ii.k.27; Stewart 1980: 325). Therefore, for Smith, a lower tax rate, which may restrict wealth redistribution, more effectively raises tax revenue than a high tax rate, which only encourages smuggling. In *LJ*, Smith added that while high land taxes may ruin a great landowner, as 'few people have so much self-command as to lay up money to be ready' to pay the tax, this does not apply to luxury taxes as '[w]hen a person finds that he is spending too much on the elegancies of life, he can immediately diminish his consumption' (LJB 316). In short, Smith's proposals for taxes on luxuries were only limitedly progressive, as he suggested taxing the luxuries of both the rich and the poor and because taxes had to be reasonable to be effective.

Importantly, there is only a clear link between taxation and wealth redistribution when the taxes collected are spent on specific measures that reallocate wealth, such as on poor relief. Smith explained that political economy, 'considered as a branch of the science of a statesman or legislator,' had two objects:

> first, to provide a plentiful revenue or subsistence for the people, or more properly to enable them to provide such a revenue or subsistence for themselves; and secondly, to supply the state or commonwealth with a revenue sufficient for the publick services.
>
> (WN IV.1)

The central question then is how this revenue is spent.

This exposes a tension in Niimura's argument that Smith's tax proposals permit a redistribution of wealth that would significantly restrict the effects of economic inequality in society. Smith's comments on direct wealth redistribution through the poor laws were very limited. He advocated an amendment of these laws to ensure labour could move freely. The freedom of movement of labour permits an abundance of labour in one area to counterbalance scarcities in another; thus, wage differences across the country would even out and extreme wages, both very low through an overabundance of labour and very high through a scarcity of labour, would be less likely (WN I.x.c.41–58). He made no further comments concerning the poor laws. As Gertrude Himmelfarb argued, this does not necessarily imply that Smith was unsympathetic to an amended version of the poor laws (Himmelfarb 1984; Dean 1991). Smith may have criticised the Act of Settlement, but stopped short of criticising the principle of poor relief. Moreover, Himmelfarb explained that Smith did not condemn the increasing costs of poor relief in the years after *WN* was published (Himmelfarb 1984: 61). As this was his only discussion of direct tax redistribution, it leaves the extent to which taxation could be a remedy to economic inequality for Smith moot. Hence, one must focus on his other remedy for economic inequality, education, to which we turn now.

Education as a remedy to the ills of economic inequality

Education was Smith's principal remedy for economic inequality, as it countered the most harmful effect of inequality in commercial society: social isolation. As outlined earlier, social isolation could impede people's capacity for moral judgement and virtue. Therefore, even though Smith did not propose to eliminate economic inequality directly through taxation and redistribution, he offered an alternative that alleviated the effects of this inequality. This route addressed the moral problems associated with economic inequality without removing the foundation for opulence.

Smith's ideas on education not only covered literacy and numeracy but also included social learning. As Berry explained, 'A pervasive theme in *The Theory of Moral Sentiments* is that morality is a learnt phenomenon' (Berry 2006: 133).[10] The educational element of Smith's moral psychology is evident when Smith discusses the process by which children learn self-command. A young child does not have control over its passions, and their parents happily enter into their violent passions. The only emotion they learn to control is anger, but this control is occasioned by fear and concern for their safety, and not by any real moderation through their impartial spectator, as parents frighten their children into not displaying anger. However,

> [w]hen it is old enough to go to school, or to mix with its equals, it soon finds that they have no such indulgent partiality. It naturally wishes to gain their favour, and to avoid their hatred or contempt. Regard even to its own safety teaches it to do so; and it soon finds that it can do so in no other way than by moderating, not only its anger, but all its other passions, to the degree which its play-fellows and companions are likely to be pleased with. It thus enters into the *great school of self-command*, it studies to be more and more master of itself, and begins to exercise over its own feelings a discipline which the practice of the longest life is very seldom sufficient to bring to complete perfection (TMS III.3.22).[11]
>
> (Passage 4)

Mastering self-command through the impartial spectator is a lifelong process, a 'school,' which necessitates constant social interactions to sustain.[12] Since self-command is the foundation for all virtues, including justice, education was central to Smith's 'Science of Man' and his vision of sociability and happiness. Smith distinguished between the educational institutions for children and those for everyone in society: the former emphasised learning to read, write, and account, whereas the latter focused on social learning through creating communities (WN V.i.f-g). Together, they alleviated more effectively the adverse effects of economic inequality than Smith's limited progressive tax proposals.

Smith was concerned that economic inequality created educational inequalities. He explained that '[t]he education of the common people requires, perhaps, in a civilised and commercial society, the attention of the publick more than that of people of some rank and fortune' (WN V.i.f.52). The wealthy gladly support the education of their children, who are often educated until their late teens. If these children are not properly educated, 'it is seldom from the want of expence laid out upon their education; but from the improper application of that expence' (WN V.i.f.52). Money was available to support their education, but it may have been spent on incompetent teachers, hampering the educational progress of their children. Smith acknowledged that the occupations of 'people of some rank or fortune . . . are not, like those of the common people, simple and uniform' (WN V.i.f.52). The considerable drawbacks of the division of labour might not affect them as severely. This also further strengthens the aforementioned point that these drawbacks are occasioned by economic inequality. Whereas a poor man's skill at his occupation was 'acquired at the expence of his intellectual, social, and martial virtues,' wealthy men were mostly engaged in complex jobs, which required them to 'exercise the head more than the hands' (WN V.i.f.50; WN V.i.f.52). Rich people also had more leisure time, allowing them to pursue further knowledge for which their extensive education had given them the foundation (WN V.i.f.52). By contrast, the poor

> have little time to spare for education. Their parents can scarce afford to maintain them even in infancy. As soon as they are able to work, they must apply to some trade by which they can earn their subsistence. That trade too is generally so simple and uniform as to give little exercise to the understanding; while, at the same time, their labour is both so constant and so severe, that it leaves them little leisure and less inclination to apply to, or even to think of any thing else (WN V.i.f.53).
>
> (Passage 5)

The sovereign should thus focus on the education of the poor, as I have shown elsewhere (Rauwald 2024). Unlike the rich, the poor could not pursue learning in adulthood, as they had to work for their subsistence. Yet, they may have required education more, as they experienced the adverse effects of economic inequality more intensely. Smith explained that in rude states of society, the sovereign did not need to support this education, as everyone was a warrior and a statesman, who 'naturally' learned to make accurate private and public judgements. While everyone was decently skilled, most did not reach a great degree of 'knowledge, ingenuity, and invention' (WN V.i.f.49; WN V.i.f.51). The situation was different in commercial societies: through corruption, many 'fall into that drowsy stupidity, which . . . seems to benumb the understanding of almost all the inferior ranks of people' (WN V.i.f.51). While some attained hitherto unknown levels of understanding, the majority suffered. In commercial societies, Smith claimed, 'some attention of government is necessary . . . to prevent the almost entire corruption and degeneracy of the great body of the people' (WN V.i.f.49). Economic inequality, which occasioned corruption and educational inequalities, was thus a central reason for the need for state support.

Smith's educational proposals followed the Scottish model, which was founded on state legislation rather than philanthropy as in England (Houston 1985: 112). From the late sixteenth century, Protestant reformers in Scotland strongly advocated the provision of schools to promote the public good by fostering talented children and preserving religiousness. This would be achieved by improving literacy, making the Bible accessible to everyone (Houston 1985: 5, 112). Landowners or burgh councils had to fund schools and teachers, making education more affordable to the poor (Houston 1985: 112).[13] However, as Houston noted, 'education was not free, it was not compulsory and it was not universal until the very end of the nineteenth century' (Houston 1985: 113). Nonetheless, Scotland's system was widely considered superior to the English system during the eighteenth century (Houston 1985: 6–7). Daniel Defoe (c. 1660–1731), for example, praised Scotland's educational system which ensured that the poor would learn how to read and write. Conversely, Defoe asked, '[H]ow full of Ignorance are the dark Villages in our Land of Light, and how many thousand Parishes are there in England, where a third Part of the People can neither write nor read?' (Defoe 1708: 318).

Smith's advocacy for the Scottish system may thus be unsurprising. Following the Scottish system, Smith contended that parish schools should be established in every district or parish. Although he conceded that poor children could not be as thoroughly educated as the rich, Smith claimed they could be taught 'the most essential parts of education . . . to read, write, and account' before they became workers (WN V.i.f.54). The public could facilitate this elementary education for 'a very small expence' and acquiring it may even be 'impose[d] upon almost the whole body of the people' (WN V.i.f.54; WN V.i.f.57). Children could thereby become more productive labourers, which may support Alex Thomas' suggestion that education could boost workers' wages, making it less likely they would fall below the relative poverty threshold (Thomas 2017: 112–113). Smith questioned the value of learning 'a little smattering of Latin' and instead advocated classes 'in the elementary parts of geometry and mechanicks' (WN V.i.f.55). If this were implemented, 'the literary education of this rank of people would perhaps be as complete as it can be' (WN V.i.f.55). Smith maintained that teachers should not be completely paid for by the state, as this would promote indolence and lower teaching standards, which could lead pupils to lose interest in education (WN V.i.f.2–7; WN V.i.f.17; WN V.i.f.55). If parents contributed a small fee, they might also be interested in ensuring that their children received a proper education, as they would essentially be customers.

Smith argued that the education of poor children had several benefits: first, it counteracted 'gross ignorance and stupidity,' and superstition and enthusiasm, which Smith considered dangerous (WN V.i.f.61). Smith demonstrated the folly of superstition by examining how 'great phenomena of nature,' like lightning, initially sparked wonder and curiosity about their causes: 'Superstition first attempted to satisfy this curiosity by referring all those wonderful appearances to the immediate agency of the gods' (WN V.i.f.24). People originally thought that 'the invisible hand of Jupiter' was intervening in earthly affairs to cause these natural events (Astronomy III.2). Through science, which Smith labelled 'the great antidote to the poison of enthusiasm and superstition,' people could overcome these false explanations and seek natural causes (WN V.i.f.61; WN V.i.g.14). Echoing David Hume (1711–76), Smith claimed that enthusiasm and superstition were dangerous because 'an ignorant and stupid' population was more prone to 'occasion the most dreadful disorders' (Hume 1994: 46–50; WN V.i.f.61). By contrast, an educated population was more respectable and decorous. They considered themselves more decent and more likely to gain their superiors' respect, which enhanced their own regard for their superiors. Importantly,

> [t]hey are more disposed to examine, and more capable of seeing through, the interested complaints of faction and sedition, and they are, upon that account, less apt to be misled into any wanton or unnecessary opposition to the measures of government.
>
> (WN V.i.f.61)

Educated individuals could make more accurate public judgements, a trait lost through corruption in commercial society. This was especially important in free societies, where people's 'favourable judgement' determined 'the safety of government,' meaning it was 'of the highest importance' that government ensured they did not make public judgements too 'rashly or capriciously' (WN V.i.f.61). As we will see, this element of the education of the young – shielding people from enthusiasm and superstition – supports the proper functioning of the institutions for the instruction of people of all ages (WN V.i.g.14).

Second, the education of children, if it included gymnastic exercises, would strengthen individuals' martial spirit, which supports the preservation of freedom and safeguards a society's security. Smith noted that people's martial spirit, upon which a society's security depends, decays with improvement (WN V.i.f.59). This created the need for standing armies, which could threaten liberty if the army was not controlled by the sovereign and nobility, who were most interested in maintaining the status quo (WN V.i.a.41; WN V.i.f.59–60). If the martial spirit were preserved through proper education, this 'would necessarily diminish very much the dangers to liberty, whether real or imaginary, which are commonly apprehended from a standing army' (WN V.i.f.59).

While Smith explicitly discussed these two advantages, educating poor children may have further benefits. Smith's remarks in passage four illustrate the importance of attending school to a child's development of self-command, upon which accurate moral judgements and virtuous conduct depend (TMS III.3.22). This could further support people's sense of their respectability and thus deter disorder. Moreover, considering that part of Smith's discussion of corruption exacerbating social isolation was occasioned by people becoming overly specialised, which impeded their capacity to speak about anything other than their work, a basic education may give people something to discuss, alleviating social isolation. In sum, Smith's educational proposals for the disadvantaged young counteracted the adverse effects of corruption on poor people's intellectual and martial virtues and thus alleviated the drawbacks of economic inequality and provided a foundation for the proper functioning of moral and political judgement in commercial society.

Smith also commented extensively on the education 'of people of all ages,' which was 'chiefly those for religious instruction' (WN V.i.g.1). As we will see, his proposals were analogous to eighteenth-century dissenting academies, which were established after the exclusion of nonconformists from the Universities of Oxford and Cambridge (Kramnick 1990: 51; Claeys 1999: 141). Dissenting academies were funded by voluntary contributions and teachers were usually also ministers. They primarily aimed to offer university-level teaching to educate future ministers, but many also taught subjects like commerce, medicine, and law (Reid 2010: 98). The independence of these academies freed them from traditional restrictions on curricula, allowing them, through their zeal, 'to make considerable contributions to virtually every area of eighteenth- and nineteenth-century life' (Claeys 1999: 141). Isaac Kramnick concluded that it was in these academies 'where learning flourished in the eighteenth century' (Kramnick 1990: 51). This highlights the inherent link between religion and education in the eighteenth century and demonstrates how independent religious groups could likewise become centres of learning.

For Smith, religion's role in supporting social learning was most important. To counteract the negative effects of social isolation, Smith argued that religion could create new communities that replaced the agricultural age's village communities in urban areas (WN V.i.g.12).[14] However, according to Smith, religion had to be properly organised to perform this educational role effectively. Before outlining his ideal type of religious organisation, Smith considered the history of religion to expose the shortcomings of established religions, which he defined as a dominant religious group supported by political power (WN V.i.g.1–7). This distinguishes Smith's ideas on religion from Hume's, who thought established religions averted religious zeal and enthusiasm most effectively (Hume 1983: 135–136). In contrast, as we will see, Smith considered the zeal and industriousness of clergy as fundamental for religion to properly provide a sphere for social learning.

Much as with teachers, Smith claimed that preachers' 'exertion, . . . zeal and industry, are . . . much greater' when they are paid by voluntary contribution instead of a guaranteed salary (WN V.i.f.4–7; WN V.i.g.1). They are incentivised to provide their students – their congregation – a good experience so students would properly recompense them. Conversely, when teachers are guaranteed their remuneration, they become idle. This laziness undermines the austere system of morals, by which common people must live.[15] Preachers begin as common people who stringently follow the austere standard. Once a religious group becomes an established religion, as they are supported politically, preachers become financially independent, which occasions them to slowly become gentlemen that follow liberality. Originally, people respected preachers for their austere conduct, which commoners could relate to since they had to be as stringent (WN V.i.g.10–11). Once preachers transform into gentlemen, they lose their spiritual authority over commoners, as they adhere to a different standard of moral conduct (WN V.i.g.10–11; WN V.i.g.38). According to Smith, this had occurred in England, as the Church of England was more scholarly but thereby lost the 'arts of popularity' to the Methodists (WN V.i.g.1). For Smith, the change from religious sects to an established religion is destructive for common people, who lose moral role models, and for preachers, whose moral and spiritual authority is weakened. This diminishing respect for spiritual teachings challenges religion's capacity to counteract social isolation, the most destructive effect of economic inequality.

To preserve and moderate this zeal, Smith outlined an ideal type of religious organisation: a thought experiment that considered the situation where politics and religion had never combined to create a religious monopoly. According to Smith's ideal, there would be thousands of small sects, with every preacher leading their own group. Preachers would work hard to increase their following, as sectarians would pay them voluntarily (WN V.i.g.8). This industriousness may permit Smith's thought experiment to become reality, as the idleness of established religion's clergy allows new religious groups to gain followers. Smith described preachers of new sects as 'hungry Tartars' charging at the 'effeminate nations of southern Asia,' representing preachers of established religions (WN V.i.g.1). Therefore, Smith's ideal was not a wholly abstract vision of religious organisation: much like mercantile policies led governments to sanction monopolies, an established religion's monopoly could only be sustained through unfair political interventions (WN I.x.c).[16]

Like monopolies in other sectors, Smith thought established religions did not serve the needs of adherents as well as independent sects, undermining religion's capacity to alleviate the adverse effects of economic inequality. Unlike established religions, where preachers become lazy and lose their austerity in favour of liberality, the competition between sects would ensure preachers continue practising the austere system of morality. Practising the austere system is fundamental to their moral authority; deviating from it would disinterest followers, who would leave the sect to join one whose leader subscribed to the austere system (WN V.i.g.1; WN.V.i.g.10–11). Moreover, they would attempt to set themselves apart by acquiring knowledge, which would diffuse to their congregation through sermons, highlighting the similarity between Smith's proposals and eighteenth-century dissenting academies (WN V.i.g.8; WN V.i.g.39). Since sectarians become cognisant of proper virtue through preachers' teachings, they would try to be virtuous and therefore pursue further education, which would counteract superstition and enthusiasm and develop their intellectual virtues that were lost through corruption.

With an established religion, such zeal is perilous, but if there are thousands of sects, the danger is minimal. Even if some preachers taught enthusiastic or superstitious maxims, no group 'could be considerable enough to disturb the publick tranquillity' (WN V.i.g.8). The sovereign must ensure peace between groups by hindering 'them from persecuting, abusing, or oppressing one another' (WN V.i.g.16). The strong competition between sects promotes peace, as 'the consumers of religion will tend to patronize sects that are vigorous but non-violent in pursuing converts' (Griswold 2003: 76). Smith claimed that competition 'might in time probably reduce the doctrine of the greater part of them to that pure and rational religion, free from every mixture of absurdity, imposture, or fanaticism, such as wise men have in all ages of the world wished to see established' (WN V.i.g.8). Positive law could not establish this 'pure and rational religion' because it 'always has been, and probably always will be, more or less influenced by popular superstition and enthusiasm' (WN V.i.g.8). The competition of sects, therefore, not only promotes moderation but also creates the conditions for belief free of superstition and enthusiasm to emerge. Smith thus thought that competition not only prevented factions from interfering with morality by warping perceptions of impartial judgement but also turned religious factions into positive institutions that promoted impartial judgement. Instead of promoting plurality, intense competition between sects will make them much more similar than if there were only a handful of sects. As will be discussed shortly, this was crucial in distinguishing Smith's proposals from the violent religious sects of the English Civil War (1642–1651).

For Smith, the most important educational purpose of these sects was to provide a space for social learning, which is required throughout one's life to calibrate one's impartial spectator, improve one's self-command, and preserve one's regard for morality. This space was needed as Smith thought that, unlike the rich, who were constantly seen, the poor were isolated after leaving their intimate village communities. To counteract this social isolation occasioned by economic inequality, Smith argued that small religious sects could replace the village communities of the agricultural age in urban areas (WN V.i.g.12). This community ensures that their conduct is closely observed, allowing sectarians, irrespective of wealth, to retain the capacity to make moral judgements, behave virtuously, and thus pursue happiness. As they are seen, their impartial spectators would likely be well (or at least better)-calibrated, reinforcing their regard for the general rules of morality. Should a sectarian conduct themselves viciously, this would reflect badly on them and their group and could have significant consequences:

> All his brother sectaries are, for the credit of the sect, interested to observe his conduct, and if he gives occasion to any scandal, if he deviates very much from those austere morals which they almost always require of one another, to punish him by what is always a very severe punishment, even where no civil effects attend it, expulsion or excommunication from the sect (WN V.i.g.12).
>
> (Passage 6)

This negatively affects the agent in several ways: first, they are penalised by other sectarians and their conscience. If they know they behaved viciously, they will consider themselves the proper object of this blame, which alone is already the 'most mortifying and most offensive' but coupled with their impartial spectator's blame, other sectarians' 'disapprobation mortifies us beyond all measure' (TMS III.1.4; TMS III.2.6). Second, the threat of excommunication is severe, as sectarians believe it is the right way of serving God – otherwise, they would have joined another sect – and thus exclusion means they cannot serve God in their preferred manner. Moreover, an excommunicated individual no longer benefits from the community, suggesting they would again experience the adverse effects of social isolation and corruption. It might also be difficult to join another sect, as the agent's previous conduct may have tarnished their reputation. Third, the agent is not only blamed by their conscience and other sectarians, but also considers themselves the proper object of God's blame, as they have broken the deity's maxims (TMS III.5.12–13). Thus, Smith's ideal effectively alleviates the negative effects of economic inequality – most notably social isolation – by creating a space that supports people's social learning, which preserves their regard for morality and their capacity to make moral judgements.

Smith conceded that '[t]he morals of those little sects . . . have frequently been rather disagreeably rigorous and unsocial' (WN V.i.g.12). He was likely referring to the English Civil War's sects, which had stirred political and social instability (Ahnert 2014: 11). However, Smith suggested two remedies to counter this drawback. First, Smith advocated the 'study of science and philosophy' and a minimum requirement of education for all 'liberal' occupations. The 'middling rank' would thus reject enthusiastic and superstitious preachers, as '[s]cience is the great antidote to the poison of enthusiasm and superstition' (WN V.i.g.14). For Smith, 'science demystifies superstition,' which offsets assertions by superstitious spiritual teachers that they are superior (Griswold 2003: 78). Educated individuals would reject these teachings and consult more moderate teachers. According to Smith, the poor cannot be significantly affected by this superstition and enthusiasm if the superior ranks are guarded against them. Although he does not explicitly explain why, this is likely a consequence of the poor's disposition to admire and emulate their superiors (WN V.i.g.14; TMS I.iii.3.7). Frequent public celebrations form the second remedy, as they are contrary to 'that melancholy and gloomy humour which is almost always the nurse of popular superstition and enthusiasm' (WN V.i.g.15).

Smith's educational proposals form a salient part of his remedies to economic inequality's destructive effects. His ideas on educational institutions for the young ensure they are taught basic skills that would deflect superstition and enthusiasm and further boost their productivity. Since Smith thought adults were usually freely interested in education, teaching children essential literacy and numeracy skills may make it possible for them to pursue further learning in adulthood (WN V.i.f.15). His ideas on religious sects may be even more important as a remedy for the consequences of economic inequality. Social isolation, which affects the poor most, is restricted, as anyone could join a religious sect that replaced the agricultural age's village communities. Instead of socially isolated and corrupted individuals who are taught by lazy teachers, Smith's ideal type of religious organisation permits interactions with passionate preachers, which strengthen people's religious sentiments and further protect the deity's general rules of morality. At the same time, the potentially adverse effects of factions are contained by competition.

Smith's ideal creates another level of spectatorship: in addition to the imagined disapprobation of one's conscience or God when one behaves viciously, one is blamed by fellow sectarians. The negative outcomes of social isolation could thereby be averted, limiting moral corruption and protecting individuals' sense of duty and justice. For Smith, education strengthened people's 'intellectual, social, and martial virtues,' effectively alleviating the most destructive consequences of economic inequality (WN V.i.f.50). Education was a more targeted remedy to the drawbacks of economic inequality than Smith's limited progressive taxation proposals, although they work together: if the sovereign generates less tax revenue, less can be spent on education.

Conclusion

Recent scholarship has shown that Smith was concerned with the causes and effects of economic inequality (Rasmussen 2016; Walraevens 2021). However, Smith went further: he offered suggestions on how these effects could be remedied. For Smith, the effects of economic inequality were primarily *moral* – and, as I have argued, so were his suggested remedies. Smith's tax proposals did not allow for significant redistribution of wealth, and he did not outline a redistributive mechanism in any of his works. Instead, one must look to Smith's thoughts on education and religion; they were Smith's principal remedies for the adverse effects of economic inequality, rather than taxation as Niimura (2016) argued. This paper therefore provides a revised picture of his vision of commercial society and the role of education and religion within it.

Acknowledgements

I am very grateful to Sylvana Tomaselli for her support and guidance. I also thank Craig Muldrew for his helpful advice. I am grateful to the anonymous reviewers for their useful suggestions. Research for this project was supported by the Israel Science Foundation (grant no. 2809/24; PI: Yiftah Elazar).

Notes

1 This new reading of Smith has been disputed: for example, Harris (2020).
2 Rasmussen claimed Smith's tax and educational proposals were 'motivated chiefly by his palpable concerns about poverty' and did not effectively remedy the effects of economic inequality (Rasmussen 2016: 345).
3 Boucoyannis (2013) makes a similar case.
4 I thereby also challenge Harris (2020), who claimed that a sovereign both cannot and should not interfere claim that for Smith '[t]here is nothing that the sovereign can or should do about inequality and its social consequences' (Harris 2020: 142).
5 Sen (2009) made a similar point. Although there is ample scholarship on the role of education as a response to the adverse effects of the division of labour, this literature does not address economic inequality.
6 For example, Fleischacker (2004); Pack (1991).
7 For a more detailed discussion of taxation in WN, see Hollander (1973).

8 See also WN V.ii.e.6.
9 Smith made the same point in WN V.ii.b.6.
10 For similar readings, see Thomas (2017) and Weinstein (2007).
11 The italicisation is my own.
12 Peart (2015) provides an insightful discussion of 'the great school of self-command.'
13 Contemporaries frequently observed the cheapness of elementary education in Scotland, for example, Smollett (2012: 4).
14 Griswold (2003) provides a study of Smith's thought on the community-building function of religion.
15 Smith claimed that there were two standards of conduct, liberal and austere. The former accepts 'luxury . . . the pursuit of pleasure to some degree of intemperance, [and] the breach of chastity, at least in one of the two sexes,' whereas the latter stresses self-command and prudence (WN V.i.g.10).
16 Anderson (1988) provides a discussion of Smith's economic analysis of religion.

References

Ahnert, T. (2014) *The Moral Culture of the Scottish Enlightenment, 1690–1805*. New Haven: Yale University Press.

Allen, R. C. (2019) 'Class Structure and Inequality during the Industrial Revolution: Lessons from England's Social Tables, 1688–1867', *The Economic History Review*, 72(1): 88–125.

Anderson, G. M. (1988) 'Mr. Smith and the Preachers: The Economics of Religion in the Wealth of Nations', *Journal of Political Economy*, 96(5): 1066–1088.

Berry, C. J. (2006) 'Smith and Science', in K. Haakonssen (ed.) *The Cambridge Companion to Adam Smith*. Cambridge: Cambridge University Press, pp. 112–135.

Berry, C. J. (2018) *Adam Smith: A Very Short Introduction*. Oxford: Oxford University Press.

Boucoyannis, D. (2013) 'The Equalizing Hand: Why Adam Smith Thought the Market Should Produce Wealth Without Steep Inequality', *Perspectives on Politics*, 11(4): 1051–1070.

Boyd, R. (2008) 'Manners and Morals: David Hume on Civility, Commerce, and the Social Construction of Difference', in C. Wennerlind and M. Schabas (eds.) *David Hume's Political Economy*. Routledge: Abingdon, pp. 65–85.

Claeys, G. (1999) 'Virtuous Commerce and Free Theology: Political Economy and the Dissenting Academies 1750–1800', *History of Political Thought*, 20(1): 141–172.

Dean, M. (1991) *The Constitution of Poverty: Toward a Genealogy of Liberal Governance*. London: Routledge.

Defoe, D. (1708) '30 September 1708', *A Review of the State of the British Nation*, 5(80): 317–320.

Fleischacker, S. (2004) *On Adam Smith's Wealth of Nations: A Philosophical Companion*. Princeton: Princeton University Press.

Griswold, C. (2003) 'Religion and Community: Adam Smith on the Virtues of Liberty', *Theoria: A Journal of Social and Political Theory*, 102: 65–93.

Hanley, R. P. (2009) *Adam Smith and the Character of Virtue*. Cambridge: Cambridge University Press.

Harris, J. (2020) 'The Protection of the Rich against the Poor: The Politics of Adam Smith's Political Economy', *Social Philosophy and Policy*, 37(1): 138–158.

Hill, L. (2006) 'Adam Smith and the Theme of Corruption', *The Review of Politics*, 68(4): 636–662.

Himmelfarb, G. (1984) *The Idea of Poverty: England in the Industrial Age*. New York: Alfred A. Knopf.

Hoffmann, P. T., Jacks, D. S., Levin, P. A. and Lindert, P. H. (2002) 'Real Inequality in Europe since 1500', *The Journal of Economic History*, 62(2): 322–355.

Hollander, S. (1973) *The Economics of Adam Smith*. Toronto: University of Toronto Press.

Hont, I. and Ignatieff, M. (1983) 'Needs and Justice in the Wealth of Nations: An Introductory Essay', in I. Hont and M. Ignatieff (eds.) *Wealth and Virtue: The Shaping of Political Economy in the Scottish Enlightenment*. Cambridge: Cambridge University Press, pp. 1–44.

Houston, R. A. (1985) *Scottish Literacy and the Scottish Identity: Illiteracy and Society in Scotland and Northern England 1600–1800*. Cambridge: Cambridge University Press.

Hume, D. (1983) *The History of England: From the Invasion of Julius Caesar to the Revolution in 1688, Volume III*, (ed.) W. B. Todd. Indianapolis: Liberty Fund.

Hume, D. (1994) 'Of Superstition and Enthusiasm', in K. Haakonssen (ed.) *Political Essays*. Cambridge: Cambridge University Press, pp. 46–50.

Kramnick, I. (1990) *Republicanism and Bourgeois Radicalism: Political Ideology in Late Eighteenth-Century England and America*. Ithaca: Cornell University Press.

Lamb, R. (1973) 'Adam Smith's Concept of Alienation', *Oxford Economic Papers*, 25(2): 275–285.

Muldrew, C. (2011) *Food, Energy, and the Creation of Industriousness: Work and Material Culture in Agrarian England, 1550–1780*. Cambridge: Cambridge University Press.

Niimura, S. (2016) 'Adam Smith: Egalitarian or Anti-Egalitarian? His Responses to Hume and Rousseau's Critique of Inequality', *International Journal of Social Economics*, 43(9): 888–903.

Pack, S. J. (1991) *Capitalism as a Moral System: Adam Smith's Critique of the Free Market Economy*. Aldershot: Edward Elgar.

Peart, S. J. (2015) 'Comment: Entering the "Great School of Self-Command": The Moralizing Influence of Markets, Language, and Imagination', in R. Garnett, P. Lewis and L. Ealy (eds.) *Commerce and Community: Ecologies of Social Cooperation*. London: Routledge, pp. 77–81.

Rasmussen, D. (2016) 'Adam Smith on What Is Wrong with Economic Inequality', *American Political Science Review*, 110(2): 342–352.

Rauwald, J. L. Z. (2024) 'Adam Smith on the Public Provision of Education', *History of European Ideas*, 50(5): 733–749.

Reid, D. A. (2010) 'Rational Dissent and the Rhetoric in Educational Philanthropy in the Dissenting Academies of Lancashire, Hackney and Exeter', *Northern History*, 47(1): 97–116.

Sen, A. (2009) 'Introduction', in R. P. Hanley (ed.) *The Theory of Moral Sentiments*. London: Penguin Books, pp. vii–xxvi.

Smith, A. (1976a) *The Theory of Moral Sentiments*, (eds.) D. D. Raphael and A. L. Macfie, Glasgow edition. Oxford: Oxford University Press.

Smith, A. (1976b) *An Inquiry into the Nature and Causes of the Wealth of Nations*, (eds.) R. H. Campbell and A. S. Skinner, Glasgow edition. Oxford: Oxford University Press.

Smith, A. (1978) *Lectures on Jurisprudence*, (eds.) R. L. Meek, D. D. Raphael and P. G. Stein, Glasgow edition. Oxford: Oxford University Press.

Smith, A. (1980) *Essays on Philosophical Subjects*, (ed.) W. P. D. Wightman, Glasgow edition. Oxford: Oxford University Press.

Smith, A. (1987) *Correspondence of Adam Smith*, (eds.) E. C. Mossner and I. S. Ross, 2nd edition, Glasgow edition. Oxford: Oxford University Press.

Smollett, T. (2012) *The Adventures of Roderick Random*, (eds.) J. G. Basker, N. Seary, P. Boucé and O. M. Brack. Athens: The University of Georgia Press.

Stewart, D. (1980) 'Account of the Life and Writings of Adam Smith, L.L.D.', in W. P. D. Wightman (ed.) *Essays on Philosophical Subjects*, Glasgow edition. Oxford: Oxford University Press, pp. 269–332.

Tegos, S. (2013) 'Adam Smith: Theorist of Corruption', in C. J. Berry, M. P. Paganelli and C. Smith (eds.) *The Oxford Handbook of Adam Smith*. Oxford: Oxford University Press, pp. 353–371.

Thomas, A. M. (2017) 'Adam Smith on the Philosophy and Provision of Education', *Journal of Interdisciplinary Economics*, 30(1): 105–116.
Walraevens, B. (2021) 'Adam Smith's View of Economic Inequality', *Cambridge Journal of Economics*, 45: 209–224.
Weinstein, J. (2007) 'Introduction: Adam Smith's Philosophy of Education', *The Adam Smith Review*, 3: 51–74.
Winch, D. (1996) *Riches and Poverty: An Intellectual History of Political Economy in Britain, 1750–1834*. Cambridge: Cambridge University Press.

Part II

Papers

6 Adam Smith in the city of light

F. E. Guerra-Pujol and Alain Alcouffe

Qu'elle me semblait la plus belle et la plus charmante de toutes les villes barbares.[1]

Adam Smith's travels in Europe have been retold many times, but little is known about his comings and goings in Paris. He began his sojourns in the French capital by permanently resigning his professorship; he concluded them by mourning the death of one of the teenage boys who had been entrusted to his care. In total, Adam Smith made three separate visits to Paris. His first visit occurred in February 1764 and lasted less than a fortnight (Rae 1895: 174; Ross 2010: 210), but his second and third stays lasted much longer – from February to July 1766 and then from September to October 1766 – interrupted only by a short interlude in Compiègne in August. Part 1 of our work revisits Smith's first visit to Paris in February 1764. Part 2 explores Smith's second sojourn in Paris, from February to July 1766. Part 3 then concludes by revisiting Smith's final days in Paris.

Part 1: Adam Smith's first visit to Paris (February 1764)

This part retraces the pivotal role Charles Townshend played in Adam Smith's travels, revisits the Scottish philosopher's fateful decision to resign his Glasgow professorship for good soon after his arrival in Paris, and highlights a great controversy over France's royal finances that Smith may have taken notice of during his travels.

A powerful patron

When Smith first arrived in Paris on 13 February 1764, he had a powerful patron to thank for this chapter in his life: Charles Townshend, a prominent British politician who had married into the British aristocracy. In 1755, Townshend had wed a wealthy heiress, Caroline Campbell, the eldest daughter of the second Duke of Argyll and widow of Francis, Lord Dalkeith, the eldest son of the second Duke of Buccleuch. Townshend thus became the stepfather to Lady Dalkeith's three surviving children: Henry Scott (1746–1812), Hew Campbell Scott (1747–1766), and Frances Scott (1750–1817). The eldest child, Henry, was the heir to the title of

DOI: 10.4324/9781003767824-9

Duke of Buccleuch. Henry was not only a direct descendant of King Charles II of England and King Henry IV of France (see Duke Henry's family tree in Alcouffe and Massot-Bordenave 2020: 30); he was born into one of the wealthiest and most prestigious families in Scotland. Upon reaching the age of majority in September 1767, Duke Henry would become one of Scotland's largest landowners.[2]

Townshend was contemplating sending Henry to continental Europe upon the completion of his stepson's studies at Eton (cf. Hume's 12 April 1759 letter to Smith; Corr. 31). At the time, the 'grand tour' was a rite of passage for the sons of elite British families, 'the 'crown' of [their] education' (Cohen 2001: 129). Smith himself describes this aristocratic custom in Book V of *The Wealth of Nations* as follows:

> In England it becomes every day more and more the custom to send young people to travel in foreign countries immediately upon their leaving school, and without sending them to any university. Our young people, it is said, generally return home much improved by their travels. A young man who goes abroad at seventeen or eighteen, and returns home at one and twenty, returns three or four years older than he was when he went abroad.
>
> (WN V.i.f.36, 773 Smith 1981)

At some point in the summer of 1759, Townshend travelled to Scotland and met with Smith personally in Glasgow to discuss Townshend's plans for Duke Henry's grand tour, including Smith's appointment as Henry's private tutor.[3] Smith agreed in principle to accept this opportunity and drew up a list of 53 classical works for the young duke to study in preparation for his grand tour; among Smith's syllabus were all the classics of ancient Greek and Roman literature, including Homer, Sophocles, and Virgil (see Corr. #41, note 2, in Mossner and Ross 1987). But by the time Duke Henry completed his studies at Eton and was ready to embark on his grand tour, the 1763/64 academic year at Glasgow University had already begun. Townshend wrote to Smith on 25 October 1763 (Corr. #76) to confirm his willingness to travel with Duke Henry, but Smith tried to postpone the date of departure until after the end of the academic year. In a letter dated 12 December 1763 to his friend David Hume (Corr. #78), Smith reports:

> The day before I received your last letter I had the honour of a letter from Charles Townshend, renewing in the most obliging manner his former proposal that I should travel with the Duke of Buccleugh, and informing me that his Grace was to leave Eton at Christmas, and would go abroad very soon after that. I accepted the proposal, but at the same time expressed to Mr Townshend the difficulties I should have in leaving the University before the beginning of April, and begged to know if my attendance upon his Grace would be necessary before that time. I have yet received no answer to that letter, which, I suppose, is owing to this, that his Grace is not yet come from Eton, and that nothing is yet settled with regard to the time of his going abroad. I delayed answering your letter till I should be able to inform you at what time I should have the pleasure of seeing you.

Although the remaining correspondence between Smith and Townshend is lost, Townshend must have rejected any postponement of Duke Henry's grand tour, for Smith was in London by mid-January 1764 (Phillipson 2010: 183; Ross 2010: 210; Rae 1895: 174), and he and the young duke departed for the coast of France soon thereafter.

Smith's letter of resignation

We know two things for sure about Smith's first visit to Paris in February 1764. One is that it was a short visit, about ten or 12 days (see Rae 1895: 174; Ross 2010: 210). Less than two weeks after arriving in the French capital, Smith and Duke Henry proceeded to Toulouse in the south of France, where they lived and travelled for most of the next 18 months (see generally Alcouffe and Massot-Bordenave 2020). The other thing we know is that Smith resigned his professorship on his first full day in the City of Light: Valentine's Day, 14 February 1764. On that day, Smith wrote a letter addressed to one of his former students, Thomas Miller (Ross 1995: 148), who was the Lord Rector of Glasgow University from 1762 to 1764 (Corr. #81, note 1, in Mossner and Ross 1987). In this letter, Smith does two things. First, he officially resigns his professorship for good (previously, he had taken a temporary leave of absence), and next, he asks that the remainder of his salary go to Thomas Young, another former student of Smith's, who had taken over the Scottish philosopher's lectures at Glasgow University when he (Smith) had first taken his leave of absence in the fall of 1763 (see Corr. #81).

Why did Adam Smith decide to resign his prestigious professorship instead of just extending his temporary leave of absence? (See Guerra-Pujol and Rashid forthcoming) Whatever the reason, when the Scottish philosopher arrived in Paris in February 1764, his friend and intellectual mentor David Hume was already there. Hume had been in the City of Light since October 1763, serving as the unconfirmed Secretary to Francis Seymour Conway (Lord Hertford), the first peacetime British Ambassador to France since the outbreak of the Seven Years' War (see Mossner 1970: 441. See also Corr. #73, note 1, in Mossner and Ross 1987). As a result, Smith and Hume would have had the opportunity to meet and resume their friendship during Smith's first visit to the French capital (Rasmussen 2017: 125–126). Perhaps they even shared the same living quarters at the Hôtel de Grimberg on the rue Saint-Dominique on the Left Bank of Paris, where Lord Hertford (and presumably David Hume as well) had been residing before relocating the British Embassy to the luxurious Hôtel de Brancas at the junction of rue de l'Université and rue de Bourbon. (According to Mossner 1970: 490, Lord Hertford did not take possession of the Hôtel de Brancas until March of 1764 – in other words, *after* Smith had left Paris for Toulouse.) In any event, this was to be the only time Smith and Hume would meet on French soil, for by the time Smith returned to Paris in February 1766, Hume had already departed (with Jean-Jacques Rousseau) to London. In the meantime, did Smith – or Hume, for that matter – take notice of one of the most pressing topics of public controversy at the time?

A provocative Parisian pamphlet

When Adam Smith arrived in Paris in February 1764, an enormous public controversy was swirling around the French capital. The ostensible culprit was a recently published pamphlet titled *Richesses de l'etat, ou Lettre écrite à l'auteur de ce systeme, par un de ses confrères*. (See Anon. [Roussel de la Tour] 1763.) Although this pamphlet was published anonymously, it was subsequently attributed to Roussel de la Tour (see Darnton 2024: 75; Higgs 1897: 61). Within two years of its original publication in May 1763, more than 40 pamphlets were circulated in response to Roussel's proposal (Shovlin 2006: 96).

Roussel's pamphlet had kindled the embers of public debate in Paris for several reasons. First and foremost, it was provocative. Roussel proposed nothing less than an end to France's 'unjust system of taxation' (Darnton 2024: 72). At the time, commoners contributed a disproportionate share of the kingdom's taxes, while nobles and clergy were excluded from most taxes (Hauser 1933). Under Roussel's proposed reform, by contrast, France's complicated plethora of direct and indirect taxes, including the *taille* (a land tax) and the *vingtième* (a 5% property tax), would be scrapped and replaced by a single graduated tax on the incomes of the wealthiest two million families in the kingdom. For Roussel, France's complicated tax system not only had to be simplified; nothing less than a 'radical reorganization' of the tax system would be required (Shovlin 2006: 95).

Another reason why Roussel's work received so much attention was the kingdom's dire financial straits: France was bankrupt. Roussel, however, had projected that his proposed 'single tax' reform would generate 700 million livres per annum, more than double France's tax revenues (Darnton 2024: 72–73; Shovlin 2006: 96). In short, Roussel's provocative proposal not only purported to replenish the royal coffers; it also took direct aim at the inequity of France's complex tax system in which the poorest people generally paid the most in taxes, while the wealthiest paid little or no tax, a mind-boggling lack of proportionality that may have informed Smith's four maxims of taxation in Book V of *The Wealth of Nations* (Guerra-Pujol 2025).

Was Smith aware of *Richesses de l'Etat* or of the intense public debate it had provoked, and if so, was he thinking of Roussel's proposal when he (Smith) formulated his maxims of taxation in *The Wealth of Nations*? Although Smith does not refer to Roussel or to *Richesses de l'etat* by name in any edition of his *The Wealth of Nations*, the title of his second magnum opus most certainly does, since a literal translation of the words 'richesses de l'etat' means 'wealth of the state.' In addition, Smith was in Paris at the height of the controversy generated by this pamphlet, and as it happens, a copy of Roussel's work made its way into Smith's library (Bonar 1932: 157; see also Klein and Humphries 2019: 455), so perhaps the question we should be asking instead is, *How could Smith have not been aware of the controversy surrounding Roussel's pamphlet?*

In the alternative, even if Smith had not read Roussel's work himself or debated its merits with the *économistes* and *philosophes* of pre-revolutionary France, it is also possible that Smith learned about the kingdom's archaic system of taxation during his subsequent travels in the South of France (Alcouffe and Massot-Bordenave 2020: 198–207). For some ten or 12 days after their arrival in Paris in mid-February 1764 (Rae 1895: 174; Ross 2010: 210), Adam Smith and his pupil Duke Henry travelled south and took up residence in the tranquil town of Toulouse. They would not return to Paris until two years later.

Part 2: Adam Smith's second stay in Paris (February to July 1766)

We fast-forward to Smith's second visit to the French capital in 1766. Among other things, this part of our paper narrows down the date of Smith's return to Paris, describes his lodgings in the fashionable neighbourhood where he lived during his second stay in the City of Light, surveys Smith's reputation among the famed *philosophes*, chronicles some of Smith's possible interactions with several contemporary Parisian luminaries – including *salonnière* Madame du Deffand as well as two of the leading *économistes* of Europe, the royal physician François Quesnay, and the royal *intendant* Anne Robert Jacques Turgot – and concludes by describing one or more possible romantic attachments Smith may have developed during his second sojourn in Paris.

Request to relocate

> With respect to Tholouse, I consent to your leaving it when you please for the very reasons which you alleged, but when you settle at Paris, I must entreat you will still think the place of residence only changed and not your age, nor your plan of improvement, nor the propriety of continuing the same study and the same exercises.
>
> (Lord Townshend to Duke Henry, 22 April 1765, reprinted in Alcouffe and Massot-Bordenave 2020: 284–285)

After taking up residence in the tranquil French town of Toulouse, Smith and Duke Henry were subsequently joined by Henry's younger brother, Hew Campbell Scott. As a result, the Scottish philosopher now had two teenage boys under his care: Duke Henry, who was 17 when he began his grand tour in Paris in 1764, and Hew, who was just a year younger than Henry. At some point, however, perhaps after the arrival of his brother Hew, Duke Henry wrote a letter to his stepfather, Charles Townshend, requesting permission to relocate to Paris. [As an aside, according to Alain Alcouffe and Philippe Massot-Bordenave, it was Smith – not his teenage pupils Henry and Hew – who wanted to relocate from Toulouse to Paris. Alcouffe and Massot-Bordenave also speculate that Smith was becoming 'impatient' to relocate to the French capital. (Alcouffe and Massot-Bordenave 2020: 283)]

For his part, Townshend granted the request to relocate in a letter addressed to Duke Henry dated 22 April 1765 (Ross 1974: 182–184). For some unknown reason, though, Smith was in no hurry to leave Toulouse. Smith and his teenage pupils remained in the South of France until the fall of 1765 before travelling to Geneva and then to Paris (see timeline in Alcouffe and Massot-Bordenave 2020: xiii–xiv).

In addition, when Townshend finally granted Duke Henry's request to relocate to Paris, he also warned his stepson 'against any female attachment' (Alcouffe and Massot-Bordenave 2020: 284; Ross 1974: 184). The relevant (and juiciest) part of Townshend's letter contains the following injunction:

> If you go much into mixed company, as I suppose you will, let me warn you against any female attachment. Your rank & fortune will put women of subtle characters upon projects which you should not be the dupe of, for such connexions make a young man both ridiculous & unhappy. Gallantry is one thing; attachment is another; a young man should manifest spirit & decorum even in this part of his character, & preserve his mind entire & free in lesser as well as greater things.

Could Townsend's dire admonition 'against any female attachment' have also been meant for Adam Smith? (See Guerra-Pujol 2021). Either way, Townsend's warning may not have been an academic or abstract one, for an aristocratic female contemporary with direct knowledge of Lord Townsend's habits and dispositions, Lady Louisa Stuart (1985/1827: 38), once described Duke Henry's stepfather as 'a man of pleasure, a libertine.' In any case, Smith eventually returned to the City of Light sometime in February 1766, almost two years to the day of his first visit to Paris in 1764.

Date of Adam Smith's return to Paris

When did Smith's second sojourn in the City of Light begin? One source has Smith's pupil Henry, the 3rd Duke of Buccleuch, arriving in Paris as early as 26 October 1765 (Cole 1931: 80), so presumably Smith would not have been far behind, while another contemporary source has them arriving as late as 3 March 1766 (Toynbee 1904: 430). By contrast, most biographers of Adam Smith have him arriving in Paris in December 1765. John Rae (1895: 194), for example, citing Dugald Stewart, conjectures that 'Smith left Geneva in December for Paris, where he arrived, according to Dugald Stewart, about Christmas 1765.' Rae thus concludes: 'It may be taken . . . that [Smith and Duke Henry] arrived in Paris about the middle of December, just in time to have a week or two with Hume before he finally left Paris for London with Rousseau on the 3rd of January 1766' (John Rae 1895: 194). Similarly, E. G. West (1976: 160) states that 'Smith and his party came to Paris from Geneva at the end of 1765,' while Ian Simpson Ross (2010: 209) confirms that

> [i]t has been assumed that 'Smith and his pupils [Duke Henry and Henry's younger brother Hew] travelled to Paris from Geneva in December 1765, in time to see Hume and possibly Rousseau before they left the French capital for England on 4 January 1766.'

But this conjecture is most likely wrong. If Smith had arrived in the Parisian capital prior to 4 January, the date of David Hume's hasty departure from the City of Light, it is likely that the professor of moral philosophy and the historian would have met at some point before Hume's departure. However, as Ross himself correctly indicates, there is no evidence to suggest that such a meeting ever took place.[4] Instead, Ross reports: 'The first news from Paris of Smith being there comes from Horace Walpole, who recorded on 2 March 1766 that [they] had gone to an "Italian play" . . . at the Comedie-Italienne.'[5] In fact, Walpole's first reference to Smith appears in his travel journal two weeks earlier: 15 February 1766. His journal entry for that date begins thus: 'Dr. Smith came'[6] (see also Appendix #1). By contrast, another contemporary source, the Reverend William Cole (1931: 80), has Smith's pupil, Duke Henry, arriving in Paris as early as 26 October 1765. Although Reverend Cole's account does not mention Adam Smith or Duke Henry's younger brother Hew Scott Campbell by name, it is unlikely that Duke Henry would have travelled to Paris from Geneva alone. Of these two primary sources, however, we find Horace Walpole to be far more credible than the Reverend Cole for several reasons.

First, Horace Walpole, who was in Paris from September 1765 to April 1766, annotated his activities in the French capital on a daily basis during his seven-month stay, while the Reverend Cole began writing his Paris travel *memoire* almost six months after he left Paris. Second, Walpole was not only keeping a contemporaneous journal; he was also residing in the Hôtel du Parc Royal, where Smith and Duke Henry would stay during their second Paris sojourn. Walpole had moved to the Hôtel du Parc Royal on 3 October 1765. His journal entry for that date (Lewis 1939: 266) reads, 'Took a new apartment at the Hôtel du Parc Royal, Rue du Colombier.' So, if Smith or Duke Henry had arrived there prior to 1766, Walpole would no doubt have taken notice of this fact. In addition, yet another contemporary source – a personal letter authored by George-Louis Le Sage (1723–1803), a prominent Genevan scientist who had contributed articles to the *Encyclopédie* (Kafker 1989: 148–149) and addressed to Louise Elisabeth Nicole de La Rochefoucauld, the Duchesse d'Enville (1716–1797) – suggests that Smith was still in Geneva as late as 5 February 1766.[7]

Another piece of evidence regarding Smith's arrival date is his decision to hire David Hume's manservant during his (Smith's) second Paris stay. As it happens, Hume had recommended a servant to Smith in a letter written sometime in January of 1766 (Corr. #90). This letter is addressed to 'A Monsieur Adam Smith Chez Monsieur Foley, Banquier a Paris.'[8] Among other matters, Hume writes:

> I recommended my Servant St Jean to you: If he be with you or the Duke, I am sure you will like him and keep him on; and you need say nothing of this to him. But if you did not engage him, please send to him and tell him, that as I cannot promise on my Return to Paris soon, I do not wish he wou[l]d deprive himself of any other good Service that offers. He lives at Collet's, a Hirer of Coaches in the Rue des vieux Augustins, a few Doors from the Hotel du Parc ro[y]ale where you intended to lodge. He is known either by the Name of St Jean or Jean Garneau.[9]

In other words, the fact that Hume's letter is addressed to the home of Smith's banker in Paris (Chez Monsieur Foley) and not to Smith himself at the Hotel Parc

Royal, combined with the fact that Hume's manservant recommendation appears in a letter, is further evidence that Smith must have arrived in Paris after Hume and Rousseau's departure on 4 January 1766. Otherwise, if Smith had arrived prior to Hume's departure, Hume would no doubt have addressed his letter directly to Smith at the Parc Royal or made his recommendation directly to Smith in person, without the formality of a letter, since Hume too was residing at the Parc Royal.

Regardless of the precise date of Smith's return to Paris, he would take up residence in some of the finest lodgings that Paris had to offer: the Hôtel Parc Royal on the rue du Colombier.

Hôtel Parc Royal

Eighteenth-century Paris was the capital of luxury, and the epicentre of this bygone world was the *hôtels particuliers* of the *Faubourg Saint-Germain*, where Smith resided during his 1766 sojourn in Paris. Originally, this district was an agricultural suburb located beyond the old city walls of early medieval Paris, but by the time of Adam Smith's second stay in Paris, this quiet quarter was becoming one of the most exclusive and fashionable parts of the City of Light. Smith's primary residence in this upscale neighbourhood was the Hôtel Parc Royal on the rue du Colombier.

Three of Smith's contemporaries had lodged at the Parc-Royal during their stays in Paris. Thomas Pennant, who stayed at the Hôtel du Parc Royal from 25 February to 11 April 1765, informs us that his lodgings at 'l'hotel du Parc royale, Rue Colombier, Fauxberg St Germains, were handsome apartments, consisting of four rooms and one for my Servant, for which I paid twelve guineas a month' (Pennant 1948/1765: 9, punctuation and spelling in the original). For his part, Horace Walpole stayed at the Hôtel du Parc Royal from 3 October 1765 until his departure from Paris on 17 April 1766,[10] while David Hume had relocated from his apartment in the British Embassy to the Parc-Royal in November of 1765 and stayed there until his departure from Paris on 4 January 1766 (Mossner 1970: 504). That such luminaries as David Hume, Thomas Pennant, and Horace Walpole would stay at the Parc-Royal is some indication of this hotel's quality.[11] It is even possible that David Hume recommended the Parc-Royal to Adam Smith and that Smith occupied Hume's rooms after the latter's hasty departure on 4 January 1766.

The 1768 edition of *The Gentleman's Guide in his Tour through France* includes the 'Hotel du Parc Royal, from 24 to 450 livres per month'[12] among 'the best hotels or lodging houses' in the 'Quartier S. Germain des Pres' (Playstowe 1768: 234).[13] At the time, the best *hôtels* or townhouses in Paris had their own private water wells, and the best apartments in the city had their own bathtubs.[14] Alas, the precise location of the Hôtel du Parc Royal remains a mystery. A street-numbering ordinance was not enacted in Paris until 1768, two years after Smith's stay in the French capital,[15] and the 'rue du Colombier' was subsequently renamed 'rue Jacob' (Hillairet 1964, Vol. 1: 665). Prior to this name change, the Rue du Colombier and the rue Jacob formed 'one long street' (Cole 1931: 52–53) that ran next to the original abbey complex of Saint-Germain-des-Prés.[16] (For a close-up of the Rue du

Colombier *circa* 1739, see Appendix #2.) Today, the Rue Jacob is a quiet street in the 6th arrondissement of modern-day Paris.[17]

In addition to the Hôtel Parc Royal, a publisher named 'Chez J. W. imprimeur' may have also been located on the rue du Colombier in the Hôtel de Saxe. For example, a 1766 pamphlet titled 'Protest against the bill to repeal the American stamp act, of last session. Great Britain' states that it was published 'À Paris: Chez J. W. imprimeur, rue du Colombier, Fauxbourg St. Germain, à l'hôtel de Saxe.'[18] Did this publisher, however, really exist, or was it a ruse to hide the identity of the true publisher in London?[19] Either way, the Hôtel de Saxe was a real place, for it is listed in the 1770 edition of *The Gentleman's Guide in His Tour Through France* (Playstowe 2018: 233–234) as one of eight of the 'best hotels or lodging houses' on the rue du Colombier in Paris.[20]

The Hôtel du Parc Royal was also located close to the prestigious *Comédie-Française*, one of the three theatres in the City of Light receiving royal patronage, and to the famed Café Procope, said to be the oldest café in Paris in continuous operation.[21] Although there is no evidence that Adam Smith frequented the Café Procope, given its fame and proximity to the Parc-Royal (this celebrated café was located on the Rue des Fosses Saint-Germain, not far from the Parc-Royal and the Rue du Colombier), we imagine he paid a visit. Perhaps he even met the leading *économistes* of his day there. At the time of Adam Smith's visit to Paris, the Café Procope was a hub of the artistic and literary community, the place where actors, writers, musicians, poets, statesmen, scientists, dramatists, stage artists, playwrights, and literary critics went to see and be seen. Given Smith's erudition, he must have been very eager and excited to meet many of these *lumières*. In fact, the famed *philosophes* of France may have also been equally honoured to meet the Scottish philosopher.

Smith's reputation among the **philosophes** *of Paris*

When Adam Smith installed himself in the *Faubourg Saint-Germain* in Paris in 1766, he was already one of the foremost philosophers of his age. In summary, his reputation in Parisian intellectual circles and in the wider *République des lettres* of the European Enlightenment was a function of two variables. One is the reception in France of Smith's first magnum opus, *The Theory of Moral Sentiments* (Smith 1976 [1790]); the other is his close connection with David Hume, who had already befriended many of the leading *philosophes* and *salonnières* of the French capital and spoken highly of Smith during his (Hume's) celebrated residency in Paris from October 1763 to January 1766. Much has already been written about Hume's Parisian sojourn and his friendship with Smith (Mossner 1970; Rasmussen 2017), so we will focus instead on the early reception of *The Theory of Moral Sentiments* in France.

First off, soon after the publication of Smith's *Theory of Moral Sentiments* in 1759, the first French-language publication to take notice of Smith's new treatise was a subscription periodical, the *Journal encyclopédique*, which published a prominent and favourable review of the first edition of *The Theory of Moral Sentiments* as early as October 1759.[22] This review appears on pages 3–18 of the

15 October 1759 edition of the *Journal encyclopédique*. This issue of the journal consists of 168 pages in all, and '*The Theory of Moral Sentiments*, by Adam Smith, Professor of Moral Philosophy in the University of Glasgow' is the first work to be reviewed there.

The next chapter in the French reception of Smith's first book was the publication in 1763 or 1764 of an anonymous French translation of the first edition of *The Theory of Moral Sentiments*.[23] We know it was the first edition from 1759 that was translated because Smith added an entirely new chapter to the second edition of his great work (Of the Influence and Authority of Conscience), but this chapter does not appear in the first French translation of Smith's *Theory of Moral Sentiments*. This translation of Smith's work was titled *Métaphysique de l'âme*.[24] One contemporary source (none other than David Hume) identifies Mr Fitzmaurice as the translator,[25] while another contemporary source identifies the translator as Eidous.[26] Others have suggested that the French translator was Abbé Blavet (see Sudo and Shinohara 1985, cited in note 4 to 'Appendix E New Letters' in Mossner and Ross 1987). The historical consensus, however, is that Smith's translator was indeed Marc-Antoine Eidous (see Eche 2015; see also Biziou 2013: 19 n.14; cf. Alcouffe and Massot-Bordenave 2020: 26–27). Eidous was not only a tireless translator[27]; he was also a prolific *Encyclopédiste* who contributed over 400 articles to the first five volumes of Diderot and d'Alembert's *Encyclopédie*. In any case, according to James Bonar's 1894 catalogue of Smith's library, two copies of the French-language translation of *The Theory of Moral Sentiments* appear on Smith's bookshelf (Bonar 1932: 168; Mizuta 1967: 55). Did he obtain either of these copies during one of his sojourns in Paris?

The Theory of Moral Sentiments had not only been translated into French, the lingua franca of Europe at the time[28]; this new translation had also been reviewed in two of Paris' great literary journals: the prestigious periodical *Correspondence littéraire, philosophique et critique* had published a short one-paragraph review of this new French translation in December 1764,[29] while the *Année littéraire*, a French literary periodical led by Élie-Catherine Fréron (1718–1776), a leading light of the 'Counter-Enlightenment' (see generally Balcou 1975), published a much longer, 24-page review of the French translation of Smith's work, also in 1764.[30] (A fourth Parisian literary newsletter – *Mémoires secrets pour servir à l'histoire de la république des lettres en France, depuis 1762 Jusqu'à nos jours* – did not take any notice of Smith's *Theory of Moral Sentiments*.[31]) In short, by the time of Smith's return to Paris in 1766, his first great work had been translated into French, the *lingua franca* of the Enlightenment, and had also been reviewed in three important Parisian periodicals. Smith's growing fame and intellectual reputation among the *philosophes* may have thus opened the doors for him to the famed *salons* of pre-revolutionary Paris.

The salon *of Madame du Deffand*

On Easter Sunday, 30 March 1766, we find this intriguing entry in Walpole's journal: 'To Mme du Deffand. Mr Smith came' (Lewis 1939: 310; see also Appendix #1).[32] The reference to 'Mme du Deffand' in the passage above is to none other than

Marie Anne de Vichy-Chamrond, la marquise du Deffand (1696–1780), a *salonnière*, wealthy patroness of the arts, and spirited woman of letters with a sharp tongue who presided over her *salon* from her *tonneau*, her great straw-canopied chair (Bradford 1915: 570). In private correspondence, Walpole provides one of the most memorable descriptions of Madame du Deffand:

> [she] is now very old and stone blind, but retains all her vivacity, wit, memory, judgment, passions and agreeableness. She goes to operas, plays, suppers, and Versailles; gives suppers twice a week; has everything new read to her; makes new songs and epigrams, ay, admirably, and remembers every one that has been made these fourscore years. She corresponds with Voltaire, dictates charming letters to him, contradicts him, is no bigot to him or anybody, and laughs both at the clergy and the philosophers. In a dispute, into which she easily falls, she is very warm, and yet scarce ever in the wrong: her judgment on every subject is as just as possible; on every point of conduct as wrong as possible: for she is all love and hatred, passionate for her friends to enthusiasm, still anxious to be loved, I don't mean by lovers, and a vehement enemy, but openly.
>
> (Horace Walpole's letter to Thomas Gray dated 25 January 1766, reprinted in Cunningham (1857: 467)

As it happens, Adam Smith himself may have become acquainted with the sumptuous and celebrated *salon* society of Paris through none other than Madame du Deffand. Her *salon* was located on the third floor of her crowded apartment on the rue Saint-Dominique (now the Boulevard Saint-Germain; see Collins 2006: 109), just a few blocks from the Hôtel du Parc Royal on the rue du Colombier, where Smith, along with Horace Walpole, was lodging.

Broadly speaking, the *salons* of the City of Light were the social spaces of Parisian high society, or *le monde*, and in its pre-revolutionary heyday, the famed *salon* of Madame du Deffand had gained international renown and attracted famous diplomats, great ladies, *philosophes*, and prominent politicians. By all accounts, foreign visitors to Paris flocked to participate in her celebrated evening repasts. Her *salon* not only attracted diplomats from all over Europe – including such leading lights as Johan Bernstorff, the Danish extraordinary envoy to Paris from 1744 to 1751; Marquis Caraccioli, the Neapolitan ambassador from 1771 to 1781; and Count Ulrik Scheffer, the Swedish minister to Paris from 1744 to 1751 – but it also became a popular destination for British writers and eccentrics, men of state, and enthusiast of art, literature, philosophy, and politics. Among the many distinguished English-speaking guests to grace her *salon* were Lord Bath, Gilbert Elliot, Lord Robert Darcy, Charles FitzRoy, Edward Gibbon, David Hume, James Macdonald, and Lord Shelburne, just to name a few.

Was Smith among the distinguished guests of Madame du Deffand? Smith scholar Edith Kuiper has emphasised the role that cultivated women like Madame du Deffand played in Parisian high society and in expanding Smith's intellectual horizons (Kuiper 2006: 41, 49). Although there are no references to Madame du

Deffand in *The Wealth of Nations* or in Smith's surviving correspondence, Smith may have coveted an invitation to her famed *salon* during his residency in the French capital (Rae 1895, ch. 14; see also Blom 2010: 4). After all, Smith himself admired artistic and literary pursuits – no less than 1/5th of the books in his personal library were on 'Literature and Art,' including many literary works in French (Bonar 1932: xxviii). Also, what better place than the *salons* of Paris to discuss his first great work, *The Theory of Moral Sentiments*, which had been translated into French in 1764 and had been well-received in France. Smith was something of a minor intellectual celebrity – minor, that is, in comparison to Hume – and the leading *salonnières* of Paris would no doubt have been eager to host such a distinguished and erudite visitor.

By the time of Smith's second visit to Paris, however, du Deffand's *salon* was in decline. Her protégé, Jeanne Julie Éléonore de Lespinasse (1732–1776), had opened a competing *salon* of her own just down the street in 1764 (Zaretsky and Scott 2009: 81; Mossner 1970: 453). In any case, although Smith does not mention Madame du Deffand in his correspondence, according to Walpole, he paid her a visit on Easter Sunday (30 March 1766) during his second sojourn in Paris. More generally, it was at these *salons* where Smith would have met, and perhaps befriended, some of the leading lights of the Enlightenment. These *lumières* not only provided grist for Smith's intellectual mill; they were also invaluable sources of information for Smith's fertile mind. Perhaps, even, it was through Madame du Deffand that Smith obtained introductions to Marie-Jeanne Riccoboni, an illustrious *femme de lettres* and one of the most well-known and best-selling European novelists of her day, or to Anne Robert Jacques Turgot, one of the most original and preeminent political economists of the Age of Enlightenment.

*Smith and the economists (*les économistes*)*

According to Ian Simpson Ross (1984: 185; Ross 2010: 231), Smith's various 'encounters with the economic theorists of France can be considered one of the most exciting passages in Smith's intellectual development, second in importance only to his early contacts with Hume.' But is this assessment an accurate one, or is it pure hyperbole? What, in short, did Adam Smith learn from the French economists? (Carey 2020) At a minimum, we know Smith met with both Anne Robert Jacques Turgot and François Quesnay during Smith's second and third visits to Paris in 1766, and we know this because Smith himself refers to his personal discussions with Turgot and Quesnay in his correspondence during this time (Corr. #93, #94, and #97), but when and where did they meet?

The most celebrated French economist at the time, François Quesnay, is said to have received many visitors at his apartment or *entresol* in the Palace of Versailles (for a description of Quesnay's 'cramped' lodgings in Versailles, see Vardi 2012: 40–42). However, it is highly unlikely that he and Smith ever met there for two reasons: one is that we have no direct evidence that Smith ever visited Versailles; the other is that Quesnay most likely relinquished his *entresol* after the death of his primary patroness and protector, Madame de Pompadour, in 1764. In the alternative, the famed *salons* of Paris may have been a possible point of contact between Smith and the French economists. Turgot, for example, was close to Madame du Deffand's protégé, Julie de Lespinasse, who held a prominent *salon* of her own on the rue Saint-Dominique, just a few blocks from where Smith was staying during his second visit to Paris. Moreover, Mademoiselle Lespinasse not only attracted the leading lights of the Enlightenment to her *salon*, including d'Alembert, Diderot, and Hume; she also (along with Smith and Turgot) closely followed the latest developments in 'the philosophers' quarrel' between Hume and Rousseau (Zaretsky and Scott 2009: 174).[33]

Regardless of where Smith and *les économistes* met, what did they talk about? Did Smith, for example, ask Quesnay or Turgot about their respective entries in the famed *Encyclopedia*? Did Smith discuss any of the ideas in Turgot's *Reflections on the Formation and Distribution of Wealth*, which the Frenchman was writing at the time? Did Smith confer with either *économiste* about the problems of taxation or take notice of the commotion caused by the recent publication of *Richesses de l'Etat* in May of 1763, a provocative political pamphlet whose title is similar to Turgot's *Reflections* and Smith's *The Wealth of Nations*? By the same token, was Smith aware of the *Tableau économique* or any of the five political economy papers that Quesnay himself may have published in 1766 (see Fonseca n.d.), including Quesnay's '*Analyse de la formule arithmétique du Tableau Économique de la distribution des dépenses annuelles d'une Nation agricole*,' which was published in the June 1766 issue of Pierre Samuel du Pont de Nemours' *Journal de l'agriculture, du commerce et des finances*? Above all, was Smith aware of the 1763 and 1764 royal decrees liberalising the grain trade in most of France?

As it happens, one of the most remarkable natural experiments in the annals of political economy was occurring on French soil at this very moment in history. At the instigation of the so-called Physiocrats (Bloomfield 1938: 733–734), Louis XV had recently promulgated two edicts deregulating the sale of grain, the kingdom's most essential agricultural staple. These decrees, however, were doomed to fail because in Paris the old police regulations and price controls still applied. (Kaplan 2016; Baker 1978: 701; Charbit 2002: 875; Touzery 1994: 516). As an aside, we are placing the label 'physiocrat' inside scare quotes because the eminent luminaries of the famed *laissez-faire* school referred to themselves as *les économistes*, and the term 'physiocracy' was not coined until 1767, the year after Smith had concluded his travels, when Pierre Samuel du Pont de Nemours published his treatise *Physiocratie, ou Constitution Naturelle du Gouvernement le Plus Avantageux au Genre Humain* (G. Smith 2008: 378).

Alas, there is no direct evidence that Smith discussed any of these topics or problems of political economy with either Quesnay or Turgot, and any statement to the contrary is pure speculation. The first point to consider is the opportunity of a meeting while Smith was in Paris. As we have seen, Adam Smith visited the French capital on three occasions: ten or 12 days in February 1764, followed by two extended stays in 1766. Specifically, Smith remained in Paris from February 1766 to July 1766, was in Compiègne for an extended visit in August 1766, and then returned to Paris in September or October 1766. What about Quesnay or Turgot?

François Quesnay was a royal physician and was therefore based for most of the year in the Palace of Versailles or the Château de Compiègne, Louis XV's place of residence during the summer months (Plax 2017). Thus, it is most likely that Smith and Quesnay first met during Smith's extended stay in Compiègne in August 1766. The first time the name of Quesnay is mentioned in Smith's correspondence is in a letter by Smith to Lord Townshend dated 26 August 1766 (Corr. #94), with Smith's return address being Compiègne. Moreover, the only other reference to Quesnay in Smith's surviving correspondence appears in his 15 October 1766 letter to Lady Frances (Corr. #97), the sister of Smith's teenage pupils, Henry and Hew Campbell Scott. Neither of these letters, however, makes any mention of political economy. Instead, both letters are devoted to the physical ailments of the pupils under Smith's care and to the efforts of Quesnay and other eminent physicians to treat their respective illnesses.

For his part, Turgot was based in Limoges in central France from 1761 to 1774. Turgot was a royal *Intendant* (tax collector) for the French provinces of Angoumois, Basse-Marche, and Limousin, a region later known as Limoges. Furthermore, we know that Turgot could not have been in Paris during the first half of 1766, as his own correspondence shows that he spent the first part of 1766 in Limoges (Groenewegen 1993: 107, 116 n.6). Turgot was, however, 'definitely in Paris from July to September 1766.'[34] Smith and Turgot's main opportunity to meet would have occurred either in July 1766 or in September 1766, depending on how long Smith's August 1766 stay in Compiègne lasted.

According to one contemporary source (André Morellet), Smith and Turgot may have met on several occasions:

> M. Turgot, who like me loved things metaphysical, estimated [Adam Smith's] talents greatly. We saw [Smith] several times; [Smith] was presented at the house of M. Helvetius; we talked of commercial theory, banking, public credit and several points in the great work he was meditating.
>
> (Morellet, *Mémoires*, Vol. 1: 237)

Although this excerpt makes reference to Turgot's *Reflections*, there is no additional evidence to show whether Smith discussed any problems of political economy with Turgot. What we do have direct evidence of, however, is that Smith and Turgot took close notice of *l'affaire Rousseau-Hume* (Zaretsky and Scott 2009: 176–177). In a letter to his friend David Hume dated 6 July 1766 (Corr. #93), Smith writes:

> I am thoroughly convinced that Rousseau is as great a Rascal as you, and as every man here believes him to be; yet let me beg of you not to think of publishing anything to the world upon the very great impertinence which he has been guilty of to you. . . . Your whole friends here [Paris] wish you not to write, the Baron [d'Holbach], D'Alembert, Madame Riccaboni, Mademoiselle Riancourt, Mr Turgot etc. etc.

Although he refers to Rousseau as a 'rascal,' Smith also strongly disapproves of Hume's rash decision to assail the Swiss philosopher in print. Doing so would not only add fuel to the flames of this quarrel and convert Rousseau into a secular martyr of sorts; it would also tarnish Hume's reputation as *le bon David.* Smith saw that if Hume wanted to be remembered as 'a man of mild disposition, of command of temper, of an open, social, and cheerful humour . . . little susceptible of enmity, and of great moderation in all my passions' (Hume 1987 [1777]: xl), then attacking Rousseau would be counterproductive. On this note, Smith singles out the opinion of his fellow political economist Turgot at the very end of his 6 July letter to Hume (Corr. #93):

> Mr Turgot, a friend every way worthy of you, desired me to recommend this advice to you in a Particular manner, as his most earnest entreaty and opinion. He and I are both afraid that you are surrounded with evil counsellours, and that the Advice of your English literati, who are themselves accustomed to publish all their little gossiping stories in Newspapers, may have too much influence upon you.

This second passage suggests that Smith and Turgot discussed the Hume-Rousseau affair at length among themselves, but there is no direct evidence, either in Smith's own meagre correspondence or in that of Turgot, that they discussed any of the great issues of political economy of the day, such as the ongoing debate over taxation or the effects of the liberalisation of the grain trade or the economic table of Quesnay. Also, although Smith and Turgot had many friends in common (Hoyng 2011), the total absence of subsequent correspondence between them – or between Smith and Quesnay, for that matter – speaks volumes. (But see Hoyng 2011, who explains why a correspondence between Smith and Turgot may have nevertheless existed.) In any case, the direction of influence between Smith and the French economists is a matter of great controversy (Guerra-Pujol and Rashid, forthcoming). On the one hand, no less a contemporary authority than Pierre Samuel du Pont de Nemours (the French economist who coined the term 'physiocracy') is reported to have said that 'all that is worthwhile in Adam Smith can be found in Turgot's *Reflections*' [Du Pont de Nemours 1782, quoted in Vardi (2012: 10 n.25)]. On the other hand, it is also possible that the direction of influence went in the opposite direction (from Smith to Turgot) since Turgot did not complete his *Reflections* until November of 1766, that is, after his meetings with Smith. By the same token, Dugald Stewart (1982/1793: 304) reports that Smith was going to dedicate *The Wealth of Nations* to Quesnay ('If he had not been prevented by Quesnai's death [in 1774], Mr Smith had once an intention (as he told me himself) to have inscribed to him his *The Wealth of Nations*'), but unlike his putative mentor (Quesnay), Smith does not present any economic table or other visual arguments in *The Wealth of Nations* and ultimately rejects Quesnay's system as a viable theory of political economy.

To recap, we know for certain that Smith and Quesnay discussed the health of Smith's pupils, and we also know for certain that Smith and Turgot discussed the Hume-Rousseau affair. Of course, it is plausible to assume that Smith, Quesnay, and Turgot also discussed problems of political economy, but to quote one scholar

(Groenewegen 1993: 107), 'it appears just as likely that they discussed philosophy, history, law, philology and literature.'[35] Moreover, the *économistes* were not the only leading lights that Smith met during his second Paris sojourn, for he also befriended a best-selling literary lady and possible love interest, Madame Marie-Jeanne Riccoboni.

A love interest in Paris?

> The poets and romance writers, who best paint the refinements and delicacies of love and friendship, and of all other private and domestic affections, Racine and Voltaire, Richardson, Marivaux, and Riccoboni, are, in such cases, much better instructors than Zeno, Chrysippus, or Epictetus.
>
> (TMS III.3.14, 143)

> *Je suis bien vaine,* my dear Mr Garrick, *de pouvoir vous donner, ce que je perds avec un regret très vif, le plaisir de voir monsieur Smith. . . . Je suis comme des folles jeunes filles qui écoutent un amant sans penser au regret, toujours voisin du plaisir. Grondez-moi, battez-moi, tuez-moi! Mais j'aime monsieur Smith, je l'aime beaucoup. Je voudrois que le diable emporta tous nos gens de lettres, tous nos philosophes, et qu'il me rapporta Mr Smith.*[36]
>
> [Letter from Madame Riccoboni to David Garrick, reprinted in Nicholls (1976: 88–89), and in Leddy (2013: 11)]

Are these the words of a woman with a mere 'schoolgirl crush on the Scot' (Leddy 2013: 11), or are they a passionate romantic confession of a woman madly in love with Adam Smith? The author of this love letter was none other than Marie-Jeanne Riccoboni, an accomplished actress in the famed Théâtre-Italien as well as an illustrious *femme de lettres* (Dawson 2018), one of the most well-known and best-selling European novelists of her day (Darnton 1998: 255). But she was not only 10 years older than Smith; perhaps she was also prone to literary exaggeration.

At the same time, her love letter is addressed to a close friend and confidant, fellow actor and author, David Garrick, whom she had befriended during his visit to Paris in 1763 and with whom she maintained a years-long correspondence (Nicholls 1976: 18–19; Dawson 2018). But could Madame Riccoboni's letter have been meant for Adam Smith himself? That is, was it a confession of sorts? According to one Smithian scholar (Fay 1956: 6), Madame Riccoboni may have given this letter to the object of her affections for him to deliver in person to Garrick upon his return to London, but Smith never delivered Riccoboni's letter.

Moreover, the first reference to or mention of Smith in Madame Riccoboni's correspondence occurs as early as May 1766, during Smith's second visit to Paris. Specifically, in a letter dated 21 May 1766, Riccoboni writes:

> *Il vient ici deux Anglois, l'un est ami de Garrick, l'autre est* éscossois; mon Dieu quel *Escossois! Il parle durement avec grandes dents – il est laid*

> *comme un diable. C'est Mr Smith, autheur d'un livre que je n'ai point lu. Je lui parle de l'Escosse et sur tout des montagnes.*[37]
>
> (Letter reprinted from Madame Riccoboni to Robert Liston, reprinted in Nicholls 1976: 70–72)

Why does Madame Riccoboni report this initial encounter with Smith, and why is it significant? As it happens, her 21 May letter is addressed to Sir Robert Liston, a Scotsman who at the time had much in common with Smith. Like the Scottish philosopher, Liston was also residing in Paris in his capacity as a tutor to two sons of a British political figure, Sir Gilbert Elliot, the 3rd Baronet of Minto (see Charrier-Vozel n.d.; Nicholls 1976: 20). It is thus most likely that Riccoboni is simply informing Liston about the arrival of a fellow Scotsman and fellow tutor in Paris. But at the same time, despite Smith's difficulty in speaking, his big teeth, and his ugly face ('*Il parle durement avec grandes dents – il est laid comme un diable*'), it sounds like she might be flirting with Smith, talking about Scotland and mountains. Could they have fallen in love that summer?

Alas, all we know for certain is that they must have met on more than one occasion after their initial meeting in May of 1766. According to Smith himself, in a letter to his friend David Hume dated 6 July 1766 (Corr. #93), Smith had discussed the news of the so-called Hume-Rousseau affair with Riccoboni, along with several other persons as well. Specifically, they discussed whether Hume should respond to Rousseau's incendiary accusations. The timing of this letter is itself a significant revelation because Rousseau's first open declaration against Hume, accusing his Scottish host of abject treachery, does not occur until 23 June 1766 (Zaretsky and Scott 2009: 151–154). Most likely, Smith and Riccoboni, along with the rest of their intellectual and artistic circle, discussed *l'affaire Rousseau-Hume* at length at one or more of the famed *salons* of Paris sometime between receiving news of Rousseau's 23 June indictment and the 6 July, that is, the date of Smith's letter to Hume. Beyond this, however – beyond their initial meeting and subsequent discussions about Hume and Rousseau – it is impossible to say with any degree of certainty whether Smith and Riccoboni were involved in a romantic relationship.

Aside from Madame Riccoboni, did Adam Smith develop any other romantic attachments during any of his three visits to Paris? Did he fall in love? The Abbé Colbert, Smith's closest confidant during his time in Toulouse (March 1764 to October 1765; see Alcouffe 2025), alludes to this possibility in a letter to Smith dated 18 September 1766[38]:

> *Et toi, Adam Smith, Philosophe de Glasgow, héros et idole des highbroad Ladys, que fais-tu mon cher ami? Comment gouvernes-tu La Duchesse d'Anville et Mad. de Bouflers, ou ton coeur est-il toujours épris des charmes de Mad. Nicol et des appas tant apparens que cachés de cette autre dame de fife que vous aimiéz tant?*[39]
>
> (Corr. #91, reprinted in Buchan 2006: 77; Fay 1956: 157; Mossner and Ross 1987: 111; Ross 2010: 227)

Is this passage a 'smoking arrow,' so to speak (Guerra-Pujol 2021: 135–136), or was Colbert writing in jest – the equivalent of literary banter among close friends? Either way, putting aside the 'lady of Fife,'[40] Colbert's letter refers to three possible love interests who are Frenchwomen – the Duchess of Anville, Madame de Boufflers, and Madame Nicol – two of whom had town homes in Paris (Madame de Boufflers and Duchess of Anville).

To begin with, the 'Duchess of Anville' most likely refers to Marie-Louise-Nicole Elizabeth, duchesse d'Enville (1716–1794), a *salonnière* and Enlightenment matron. Smith first made her acquaintance in Geneva in late 1765 or early 1766 (Alcouffe and Guerra-Pujol, forthcoming), and they may have crossed paths again during Smith's second sojourn in Paris. At that time, she was residing at her townhouse, the Hôtel de La Rochefoucauld on the Rue de Seine, which was within walking distance of Smith's Paris lodging, the Hôtel du Parc Royal. What about 'Madame Nicol'? Alas, her precise identity is unclear. She may have been the wife of Jacques Nicol de Montblanc, a wealthy landowner who presided over the Mont Blanc Estate in the present Croix Daurade district of Toulouse (Alcouffe and Massot-Bordenave 2020: 262), but aside from this conjecture, we have no idea who 'Madame Nicol' was or where she was from.[41] That leaves 'Madame de Boufflers.'

Adam Smith and la Comtesse de Boufflers

Marie Charlotte Hippolyte de Saujon (Madame la Comtesse de Boufflers), the 'principal mistress' of Louis François de Bourbon, the 6th Prince of Conti (Mossner 1970: 434), was not only one of the leading *salonnières* of pre-revolutionary France (Mossner 1970: 459–460); she was also 'one of the most prominent Anglophiles in Paris' (Stewart 1970: 184), having befriended both David Hume and Adam Smith during their respective stays in Paris, but that said, we have no other evidence, beyond the reference in Colbert's letter (see earlier), to suggest a romantic attachment between Smith and Madame de Boufflers.

Nevertheless, Smith and Madame de Boufflers met on more than one occasion. She hosted a sumptuous *salon* on Friday evenings in the Prince of Conti's urbane residential headquarters, *Le Temple*, a medieval compound that was originally built in the thirteenth century by the Knights Templar and subsequently destroyed during the tumult of the French Revolution (Mossner 1970: 459). Although neither Boufflers nor the Prince of Conti is mentioned in Smith's surviving Paris correspondence, other evidence indicates that Smith was personally acquainted with the Comtesse and was a guest at her *salon*, which attracted some of the foremost men of letters of the Enlightenment era, including leading lights such as David Hume, who lived in Paris from 1763 to 1766 and became close friends with the Comtesse; Horace Walpole, who attended many a soiree in the *Temple* during his five visits to Paris; and Jean-Jacques Rousseau, who resided there before departing with Hume to London in January 1766 (Mossner 1970: 511). Was Adam Smith among her famed guests?

In a letter addressed to her close friend and confidant David Hume, dated 6 May 1766, the Comtesse de Boufflers writes: '*Je vous ai dit, ce me semble, que j'ai fait connoissance avec M. Smith, et que, pour l'amour de vous, je l'avois fort accueilli.*'[42] In other words, the Comtesse de Boufflers tells Hume that she 'warmly welcomed' Smith ('*je l'avois fort accueilli*'). This declaration implies that Smith must have attended her famed *salon* at least once in the spring of 1766, that is, during his second visit to Paris. In fact, Smith may have visited the *Temple* and Madame de Boufflers more than once, for in another letter addressed to David Hume, dated 25 July 1766, the Comtesse reports: '*Je fait priet votre ami Mr Smith de venir chez moi. Il me quitte a l'instant.*'[43]

What did Smith and Boufflers and her dinner-party guests discuss during their *soirées*? In her 6 May letter to Hume, the Comtesse de Boufflers reports that she is reading Smith's *Theory of Moral Sentiments*: '*Je lis actuellement sa théorie des sentiments moraux: je n'en suis pas fort avancée, mais je crois de cela me plaira.*'[44] Did she begin reading Smith's *Theory of Moral Sentiments* in anticipation of meeting Smith, or did meeting Smith leave such a great impression on the Comtesse as to motivate her to read his first magnum opus? Either way, it is also possible that these *soirées* were mere 'frivolous and light-hearted' affairs (Ketton-Cremer 1966: 211). Although some scholars have described the central role the Paris salons played in Europe's literary and intellectual circles (Goodman 1989; 1996), others have painted a less rarified and more snobbish picture of these sumptuous *salons* (Collins 2006; Lilti 2005).[45] Whichever of these pictures of the pre-revolutionary *salon* is the more accurate one, the highlight of Smith's grand tour travels occurred in August 1766 when Smith and his pupils visited Compiègne, about 80 kilometres northeast of Paris.

Part 3: Adam Smith's last days in Paris (September to October 1766)

The third and final part of our paper revisits Adam Smith's last days in Paris. But first, we describe an oft-overlooked aspect of Smith's travels: his short stay in Compiègne in August 1766.

Château de Compiègne

Adam Smith's second sojourn in Paris (February to July 1766) concluded when Smith and his pupils travelled to Compiègne sometime in August 1766 (Rae 1895: 197). As an aside, both John Rae and Ian Simpson Ross incorrectly describe the Scottish philosopher's stay in Compiègne as a mere excursion. Rae (1895: 22), for example, reports that Smith

> had been in the habit while in Paris of taking his pupils for excursions to interesting places in the vicinity, . . . and in August 1766 they went to Compiègne to see the camp and the military evolutions which were to take place during the residence of the Court there,

while Ross (2010: 227) writes, '[Smith] took his protégés, Buccleuch and his brother, on excursions to places of interest such as Compiègne when the Court went there for the diversion of hunting.'

But the visit to the royal hunting park at Compiègne was not just a 'day trip' or weekend excursion. Instead, it was most likely one of the highlights of Adam Smith's three-year grand tour travels and probably deserves a chapter or paper of its own, for it was in Compiègne that Smith and his pupils got to reside at a royal château and attend one or more hunts with the King of France. The pristine 20,000-acre forest at Compiègne was not only one of the oldest royal hunting grounds in France, dating back to the time of the Merovingian King Clovis; the whole area was saturated with the history of past French kings and the origins of the monarchy: 'French kings, beginning with Francis I, began the habit of short, but frequent, stays to enjoy the hunt' (Plax 2017: 109).

As it happens, Compiègne was also the site of Louis XV's favourite chateau and hunting grounds, and the Château de Compiègne was the centre of court life and the exercise of royal power when Louis XV and his Court were in town during the summer months. In the words of art historian Julie Anne Plax, 'Versailles was and always would be associated with Louis XIV, but Compiègne, with its well-ordered hunting park, would bear the mark of Louis XV' (Plax 2017: 116). Among other things, Louis XV commissioned the construction of a new royal château, the plans for which were drawn by Ange-Jacques Gabriel. Every summer, the king moved his royal court to Compiègne, where he hunted an average of four to five days a week (Plax 2017: 103). In 1764, for example, David Hume, in his capacity as Secretary of the British Embassy, followed the French Court to Compiègne and spent the months of July and August there (Mossner 1970: 461). Perhaps Duke Henry, who was Louis XV's cousin, received an invitation directly from the king himself, or perhaps it was Smith who had secured the invitation through his contacts at Britain's embassy in Paris.

Either way, it is unclear how long Smith's sojourn in Compiègne lasted. In a letter addressed to Adam Smith from David Hume dated August 1766, Smith's Paris mailing address 'Anglois Hotel du Parc roiale, Fauxbourg St Germain a Paris' is crossed out and a new forwarding address, consisting of the words 'a Compiègne,' is added twice, in another hand (see Corr. #96, note 1, in Mossner and Ross 1987). Additionally, in a letter dated 26 August 1766 (Corr. #94), Smith reports to Lord Townshend that Duke Henry became ill 'on Thursday last' (Mossner and Ross 1987). Following the Gregorian calendar, which was adopted in France in 1582 (Cohen 2000), 26 August 1766 would have been a Tuesday. We can therefore surmise that Smith and his pupils had arrived in Compiègne towards the middle part of August, perhaps even earlier. But how long did they stay there? Smith's only other letter from Compiègne is dated 27 August 1766 (Corr. #95), so he must have remained there until the end of August or the beginning of September, at least until Duke Henry recovered from his illness.

In any case, upon their return to the French capital at the end of the summer/beginning of fall 1766, Smith's last days in Paris would be sombre ones, marred by the death of Duke Henry's younger brother, Hew Campbell Scott.

The death of Hew Campbell Scott

Two pieces of personal correspondence, both written in Smith's hand only four days apart (15 and 19 October 1766; Corr. #97 & #98), report that Hew had contracted a fatal fever. Both missives are addressed to Lady Frances, Henry, and Hew's sister.[46] Of all Smith's extant letters postmarked in France, his 15 October letter to Lady Frances is the longest, totalling 894 words. (The second-longest piece of correspondence Smith wrote during his travels in France, a letter addressed to Charles Townshend, contains 626 words. See Corr. #95.) By his own account, Smith wrote this letter late at night – 11 P.M. – and it contains many gruesome details of Hew's illness. Among other things, Smith reports on Hew's many 'vomitings,' 'purgings [that] continued with great violence,' and 'delirium,' and he also describes how Hew had 'bled very copiously at the nose' (Corr. #97). By comparison, Smith's next letter to Lady Frances, dated 19 October 1766 (Corr. #98), is laconic and to the point:

> It is my misfortune to be under the necessity of acquainting you of the most terrible calamity that has befallen us. Mr Scott dyed this Evening at seven o'clock. I had gone to the Duke of Richmonds in order to acquaint the Duke of Buccleugh that all hope was over and that his Brother could not outlive tomorrow morning: I returned in less than half an hour to do the last duty to my best friend. He had expired about five minutes before I could get back and I had not the satisfaction of closing his eyes with my own hands. I have no force to continue this letter; The Duke, tho' in very great affliction, is otherwise in perfect health. I ever am etc. etc.

Alas, although Smith had consulted with two eminent doctors – Quesnay and Richard Gem, the doctor assigned to the British embassy in Paris (Armbruster 2019: 131) – and Hew had received the best medical care he could have possibly received in the Paris of his day and age, Hew's illness was fatal. Upon Hew's untimely demise, moreover, Smith's grand tour and his third and last sojourn in Paris would also come to an abrupt close.[47]

Conclusion: the end of Smith's grand tour travels

An entry in the journal of Lady Mary Coke, Hew's aunt and Lady Dalkeith's youngest sister, informs us that 'The Duke of Buccleuch . . . is arrived. He and Lady Frances are all she [Lady Dalkeith] has left of six' (quoted in Fay 1956: 158). Lady Coke's journal entry is dated 27 October 1766, so if her account is accurate, it would mean that Duke Henry and his tutor had cut short their grand tour and returned to London as early as the end of October. However, aside from his date of departure, this final chapter of Smith's Paris sojourn poses additional unanswered questions. Why, for example, did Smith address his letters announcing Hew's illness and death to Hew's young sister, Lady Frances, and not to his mother, Lady Dalkeith, or stepfather, Lord Townshend? Also, in his correspondence with Lady Frances, Smith had initially described Hew's condition as a 'fever,' but what was the true cause of his death?

However these mysteries are solved, we conclude with one final observation. It is reported that Smith and Duke Henry brought back from France no less than three trunks (Alcouffe and Massot-Bordenave 2020: 204), presumably full of books, souvenirs, and other keepsakes. Among their Paris mementos was a sensitively-rendered miniature of Hew Campbell Scott painted by the famed French artist Jean-Baptiste Greuze (Ross 2010: 234).[48] This one tangible artefact of Smith's time in Paris is an oil on canvas, relatively small, measuring 64.1 × 52.7 centimetres or about 25.2 × 20.7 inches (Buccleuch Collections/Bridgeman Images n.d.). It shows Hew Campbell Scott in the uniform of the 3rd Foot Guards in half-length, presenting Hew's visage and his body from the waist up.[49] It was Smith's sombre task to place this little portrait in the hands of Hew's mother, Lady Dalkeith (Ross 2010: 234). Hew's remains were subsequently interred at Dalkeith, the ancestral home of the Buccleuchs (Ross 2010: 232).

Notes

1 Sorbière (1660: 574). Our translation: 'She [Paris] appears to me the most beautiful and charming of barbarian cities.' The author of this quotation, Samuel (de) Sorbière (1615–1670), was a French physician and man of letters.

2 See generally Bonnyman (2014). See also Alcouffe and Massot-Bordenave (2020: 28–34; Valentine (1970, Vol. 2: 773).

3 See Smith's 17 September 1759 letter to Townshend (Corr. #39), where Smith writes, 'I had the pleasure of seeing you at Glasgow.'

4 More revealing, there is no mention of any such meeting between Hume and Smith in December 1765 or January 1766 – or between Smith and Rousseau, for that matter – in their surviving correspondence.

5 Ross (2010: 209). See also Appendix #1.

6 Lewis (1939: 302). See also Appendix #1. At the same time, a letter from Walpole to Lord Mary Coke, which is dated 3 March 1766, states: 'Your nephews [Duke Henry and his younger brother Hew Campbell Scott], Madam, and Dr. Smith are coming to the Hôtel I inhabit.' See Toynbee (1904: 430). This letter presents a puzzle, since Horace Walpole refers to Smith as early as 15 February 1766 – in his journal entry for that day. Either Walpole started writing the 3 March letter on an earlier date or the 15 February journal entry is based on mistaken hearsay.

7 Specifically, Le Sage writes in his 5 February 1766 letter: 'Of all the people I meet at your house, . . . I continue to see only the excellent Mylord Stanhope and somewhat Mr. Smith.' Prevost (1805: 226), footnote omitted, our translation, cited in Ross (2010: 209). See also Rasmussen (2017: 286 n.61).

8 As an aside, 'Foley' is identified by name in several editions of *The Gentleman's Guide in his Tour through Paris* (1768, 1770, and 1783, p. 10) as one of the bankers in Paris who could provide letters of credit to foreign visitors: 'It will naturally occur to you to get letters of credit on Mssrs. Foley, Wolfe, or some other banker at Paris.'

9 See Corr. #90 in Mossner and Ross (1987). As a further aside, the 1768 and 1770 editions of *The Gentleman's Guide in his Tour through France* (1768 & 1770, p. 235) mention a 'Register Office for Servants,' which at that time was located at the Cour de Lamoignon. (The Cour Lamoignon was a former court in Paris that no longer exists today. It was located in the crowded Île de la Cité district. See Lazare and Lazare 1844: 364.) According to both the 1768 and 1770 editions of *The Gentleman's Guide*, 'This office furnishes servants of every kind, and of both sexes: the master, on applying for a servant, pays 30 sols; and if, after a short trial, the servant does not answer his purpose, the office procures another without farther expence' (Mossner and Ross 1987). Smith and Duke Henry, however, would have no need to visit the Register Office for Servants. Duke Henry already had his own servant, one 'Mr. Cook' (Rae 1895: 182), and David Hume had recommended a servant to Smith in his January 1766 letter to Smith.

10 See Lewis (1939: 266 n.72). Indeed, Horace Walpole returned to the Parc-Royal during each of his four subsequent visits to the City of Light. The editor of Walpole's

correspondence and his 1765/66 Paris journal, Wilmarth Sheldon Lewis, states that the Hôtel du Parc Royal 'remained [Walpole's] hotel during all his visits to Paris.'

11 Cf. Lefeuve (1875, Vol. 3: 23): '*N'est-ce pas à l'hôtellerie du Roi-Georges, dite alors du Parc-Royal, que ne craignit pas de descendre le protecteur des lettres Horace Walpole, qui devait être difficile sur le choix de son pied-à-terre? Il avait à Strawberry-Hill une résidence princière, dans laquelle s'imprimaient ses propres ouvrages.*' ('Wasn't it at the hôtellerie du Roi-Georges, then called the Parc-Royal, that Horace Walpole, protector of letters, was not afraid to stay, who must have been difficult about the choice of his pied-à-terre? He had a princely residence at Strawberry-Hill, in which his own works were printed.')

12 Likewise, according to the 1766 earlier edition of *The Gentleman's Guide in his Tour through France* (1766: 10), a livre was worth 'about ten-pence half-penny Sterling.' How much was a *livre* at the time? (See generally D'Avenel 1925; Fourastié 1958). According to the 1768 edition of *The Gentleman's Guide* (p. 7), 'A livre is no coin, but computation, and is twenty-pence French, or ten-pence English.' This 10 to 1 exchange rate remained stable until the eve of the Revolution; according to the 1770, 1772, and 1783 editions of *The Gentleman's Guide*, one French *livre* was still worth 'about ten-pence Sterling.'

13 In all, a total of eight hotels are listed under 'Rue du Colombier' in the *Gentleman's Guide* (233–234), including the Parc-Royal. Additionally, two of 'the best ordinaries and eating houses' were also located on this same street, one being 'De la Salle, Traiteur, from 20 sols to 3 livres'; the other, the 'Hotel d'Espagne, at all prices' (28).

14 Recently, a typical day in the life of an eighteenth-century St Germain town-house was recreated at the Getty Museum in Los Angeles in 2011 as part of an art exhibition *Paris: Life and Luxury in the 18th Century*. The exhibition opened at the Getty on 26 April 2011 and ended on 7 August 2011. See Bremer-David (2011). For additional examples of luxury goods in eighteenth-century Paris, see Vanpée (2013).

15 See Conlin (2013: 80–81). Even then, the implementation of the ordinance was uneven, since the aristocracy would refuse to bemean their town houses with numbers. Conlin (2013: 80–81).

16 It is possible that the old Parc Royal was located on today's 37 rue Jacob or the present 41 rue Jacob – the entries for those particular street numbers in the *Dictionnaire Historique des Rues de Paris* read 'Ex-hôtel' (Hillairet 1964, Vol. 1: 666). According to another source (Lefeuve 1875, Vol. 3: 23), the Parc-Royal subsequently became the 'hôtellerie du Roi-Georges,' but as of this writing (winter of 2024), we have not been able to discover any information about the Roi-Georges.

17 Rue du Colombier was renamed 'Rue Jacob' on 14 July 1836. See Hillairet (1964 Vol. 1: 665. See also Lefeuve (1875, Vol. 5: 389): '*Dès 1838 une rue du Colombier s'est engloutie dans la bouche de la rue Jacob* . . . .' ('As early as 1838 a rue du Colombier was swallowed up in the mouth of rue Jacob . . . .'). The original 'Rue du Colombier' is thus not to be confused with the existing 'Rue du Vieux Colombier.' (Julian Baggini makes this mistake in his intellectual biography of David Hume. See Baggini (2021: 192).

18 This 1766 pamphlet is available online at https://hdl.handle.net/2027/yale.39002071112057. See also A complete collection of the genuine papers, letters, &c. in the case of John Wilkes, Esq: late member for Aylesbury, in the county of Bucks, Paris: chez J. W. imprimeur, rue du Colombier Fauxburgh, St. Germain, à l'hôtel de Saxe' (1767).

19 See, for example, the note to 'Report on William Pitt's Speech in the House of Commons [14 January 1766] from Benjamin Franklin to William Strahan,' National Archives (n.d.), available online at https://founders.archives.gov/documents/Franklin/01-13-02-0013.

20 In addition, the 'Hotel de Saxe, rue du Colombier' is listed in the 1783 edition of *The Gentleman's Guide in His Tour Through France* as one of the best eating houses in Paris. See Gentleman's Guide (1783: 228–229). There is, however, no reference to the Hotel de Saxe in the 1766 edition of the *Gentleman's Guide*.

21 It was to the Café Procope, for example, that Jean-Jacques Rousseau retired on 18 December 1752, before the performance of his last play *Narcisse* had even finished, saying

publicly how boring it all was on the stage, now that he had seen it mounted (Shaw 1955: 116). As an aside, the claim of 'oldest café in continuous operation' is not entirely true since the original café closed in 1872. It reopened, however, in the 1920s. See Friedrich (1990). Today, Café Procope is located on rue de l'Ancienne Comédie in the 6th arrondissement of Paris. See https://www.procope.com/en/.)

22 The *Journal encyclopédique* was founded in 1756 by Pierre Rousseau, who was also its editor. This journal became the *Journal Encyclopédique ou Universel* in 1775 and was later merged into the *Esprit des journals* in 1793. See generally Wagner (1991), Article #730, available online at https://dictionnaire-journaux.gazettes18e.fr/journal/0730-le-journal-encyclopedique.

23 The second edition of *The Theory of Moral Sentiments* was published in 1761. For a survey of the main revisions Smith made in the second edition of his work, see Ross (2010: 178–185).

24 This translation was reviewed in *L'Année littéraire* (1764, Vol. 6, pp. 145–168); see also Chisick (2004: 242–243; Faccarello and Steiner 2002).

25 In a letter dated 28 October 1763 and addressed to Adam Smith, Hume informs Smith that 'The Baron d'Holbac . . . told me that there was one under his Eye that was translating your Theory of moral Sentiments' and that a second savant, one 'Mr Fitzmaurice,' was involved in some way in this translation project (see Corr. #77). (As an aside, this 'Mr. Fitzmaurice' may refer to Sir William Petty, Viscount Fitzmaurice, who later became the 2nd Earl of Shelburne. See note 1 to Corr. #28 in Mossner and Ross (1987).) The relevant part of Hume's 28 October letter to Smith reads (Corr. #77):

The Baron d'Holbac, whom I saw at Paris, told me, that there was one under his Eye that was translating your Theory of moral Sentiments; and desir[e]d me to inform you of it: Mr Fitzmaurice, your old Friend, interests himself strongly in this Undertaking: Both of them wish to know, if you propose to make any Alterations on the Work, and desire you to inform me of your Intentions in that particular.

26 See the footnote corresponding to the review of Smith's *Theory of Moral Sentiments* in the 1 December 1764 issue of the *Correspondence littéraire, philosophique et critique*, which is reprinted in Tourneux (1878: 143–144, 144 n.1).

27 According to French historian Jacques Kafker (1989: 139), Eidous had translated more than 40 works during his lifetime, including Robert James's Dictionary of Medicine. See Kafker (1989: 139). See also entry for 'Eidous' in the *Biographie universelle ancien et moderne*, Vol. 12 (1855: 324).

28 For a history of the French language as the *lingua franca* of Europe, see Wright (2016).

29 This review is reprinted in Tourneux (1878 [1764]: 143–144). The author of the short and anonymous review observes that Smith's work has not enjoyed as much success in France as it has in England, mainly because of the poor quality of the translation. As mentioned in the text, a footnote identifies one 'Eidous' as the translator of Smith's first magnum opus. See Tourneux (1878 [1764]: 143–144), p. 144 n.1.

30 See *L'Année littéraire* 1764, Vol. 6, pp. 145–168, available online at https://gallica.bnf.fr/ark:/12148/bd6t53745812/f154.item.

31 Fréron had published eight issues of his literary journal in 1764, and the review of the *Métaphysique de L'âme* appears on pages 145–168 of the sixth issue. See Chisick (2004: 260 n.23). The *Mémoires secrets* was first published in London as a multi-volume set from 1781 to 1789, but this literary journal originally circulated in pre-revolutionary Paris as a manuscript newsletter. See, for example, Goodman (1996: 43).

32 As an aside, before Walpole's departure from Paris on 17 April, Smith appears in his journal four more times – once on 1 April, twice on 7 April, and one last time on 9 April. During this same span of time (i.e., 30 March to 9 April), Madame du Deffand is mentioned no less than ten times – every single day except for 8 April. (The relevant journal entries are reprinted in Lewis (1939: 310–312).) Walpole and du Deffand became especially close friends. Upon her death in 1780, for example, du Deffand left her papers and her dog Tonton to Walpole. Her correspondence to Walpole, which took up four volumes, was first published at Walpole's Strawberry Hill printing press in 1810.

33 According to one source (Dalkin 1972: 16), however, Turgot may have dissociated himself from certain Paris *salons* – specifically, those of Madame de Geoffrin, Mademoiselle de Lespinasse, and the Baron d'Holbach: 'For Mme de Geoffrin's salon – and the same is true of those founded by Mlle de Lespinasse and by d'Holbach, . . . – attracted especially the *philosophes* and the *encyclopédistes*, from whom Turgot ultimately dissociated himself because of their cynical, shallow, and atheistical doctrines.'

34 For evidence in support of this conjecture, Groenewegen (1993: 116 n.7) cites three letters from Turgot addressed to David Hume, which are reprinted in Hill Burton (1849: 130–148).

35 Cf. Groenewegen (1993: 116 n.14): 'Both Turgot and Smith had written on these subjects and they therefore shared many more interests than just economics,' citing Feilbogen (1892: 17).

36 Our translation: 'I am very vain, my dear Mr. Garrick, to be able to give you, what I lose with a very keen regret, the pleasure of seeing Mr. Smith. . . . I am like a foolish young girl who listens to her lover without ever thinking of loss, which always accompanies pleasure. Scold me, beat me, kill me! But I love Mr. Smith, I love him greatly. I wish the devil would take all our men of letters, so long as brings Mr. Smith back to me.'

37 Our translation: 'Two Englishmen have arrived here. One is a friend of Garrick's; the other is Scottish; my God what a Scot! He speaks with difficulty through big teeth – and he's ugly as the devil. He's Mr. Smith, author of a book I haven't read. I talk to him about Scotland, and especially about mountains.'

38 Ernest Campbell Mossner and Ian Simpson Ross incorrectly date the letter as 'February 18, 1766' (Corr. #91 in Mossner and Ross 1987); as a result, at least two scholarly sources (Buchan 2006: 77; Kuiper 2013: 76 n.11) incorrectly identify the date of this letter as 18 February 1766 instead of 18 September 1766. Also, Kuiper (2013: 76 n.11) incorrectly attributes the authorship of this letter to David Hume.

39 Our translation: 'And you, Adam Smith, Glasgow philosopher, high-broad Ladies' hero and idol, what are you doing my dear friend? How do you govern the Duchess of Anville and Madame de Boufflers, where your heart is always in love with Madame Nicol and with the attractions as apparent as hidden of this lady of Fife that you loved.'

40 As an aside, Alain Alcouffe and Andrew Moore (2018: 15 n.18) identify Smith's 'lady of Fife' as Lady Janet Anstruther, who 'was renowned for her beauty and for her reputation as a flirt.'

41 Cf. Fay (1956: 157): Is there a lead to the Nicol in Lord Holland's postscript to Townshend of 27 May 1765, 'I could say a great deal of Nicoll now at Thoulouse, but I think you know him?'

42 Stewart (1970: 185). Our translation: 'I told you, it seems to me, that I became acquainted with Mr. Smith, and that, for your sake, I warmly welcomed him.'

43 Stewart (1970: 185). Our translation: 'I prayed for your friend Mr Smith to pay me a visit. He's leaving me right now.'

44 Stewart (1970: 185). Our translation: 'I am currently reading his theory of moral sentiments: I am not very advanced, but I think I will like it.'

45 Cf. Lilti (2005: 10): 'Salons were mostly organized as little courts, revolving around the hostess, and ruled by the ideals of *politesse*, witty conversation, social distinction, and *galanterie*.'

46 In fact, Smith may have addressed three letters in all to Lady Frances, the first of which, however, is lost, for Smith himself refers to 'my last letter' in his letter to Lady Frances dated 15 October 1766. See Corr. #97.

47 According to Ian Simpson Ross (2010: 231), 'In all likelihood Smith would have stayed in France until 1767, the year of the majority of the Duke of Buccleuch' had it not been for 'a dramatic change of plans occasioned by the fatal illness of the Hon. Campbell Scott in October 1766.' See also Phillipson (2010: 199).

48 Although we do not know exactly when or where Hew Campbell Scott sat for his portrait, the artist, Jean-Baptiste Greuze, was settled in the French capital at this time (Dilke 1911). Moreover, Greuze was a highly regarded painter, especially for his

portraits and scenes of family (Barker 2005). In fact, by the time Hew Campbell Scott sat for his portrait in 1766, Greuze had reached the zenith of his powers and reputation (Barker 2005). The previous year, for example, Greuze was represented in the Salon with no less than thirteen works, including *La Jeune Fille qui pleure son oiseau mort*, *La Bonne Mère*, *Le Mauvais fils puni*, and *La Malediction paternelle*, two of which are currently on display at the Louvre. The works on display at the Louvre are *Le Mauvais fils puni* and *La Malediction paternelle*. See Dilke (1911). Among his Greuze's works is a 1777 portrait of Benjamin Franklin, which today is housed in the American Philosophical Society (APS) Library & Museum, located at 104 South Fifth Street in Philadelphia, Pennsylvania.

49 As an aside, Ian Simpson Ross (2010: 234) mentions in a parenthetical that this painting is 'now at the Hirsel, residence of the Earl of Home.' According to another source, however, Hew's portrait is now located in Bowhill House on the Scottish Borders. See Buccleuch Collections/Bridgeman Images (n.d.).

Works Cited

Alcouffe, A. (2025) *Seignelay Colbert de Castlehill (1735–1811): A Bishop between Scottish Enlightenment and Counter-Revolution*. London: Palgrave Macmillan.

Alcouffe, A. and Guerra-Pujol, F. E. (forthcoming) 'Adam Smith in Geneva', *To Be Presented at the 2025 Conference of the International Adam Smith Society*, March 28–30, 2025.

Alcouffe, A. and Massot-Bordenave, P. (2020) *Adam Smith in Toulouse and Occitania: The Unknown Years*, London: Palgrave Macmillan.

Alcouffe, A. and Moore, A. (2018) 'Smith's Networks in Occitania – March 1764–October 1765', *Presented at the 31st Annual Conference of Eighteenth-Century Scottish Studies Society (Glasgow), Eighteenth-Century Scottish Studies Society*, pp. 1–18. https://hal.science/hal-02614246/.

Anon. [Roussel de la Tour] (1763) *Richesses de l'etat, ou Lettre écrite à l'auteur de ce systeme, par un de ses confrères*. Paris: Chez Bonaventure Ruinart.

Armbruster, I. (2019) 'The Doctor of the Rights of Man', *Midwest Journal of Undergraduate Research*, 10: 130–147.

Baggini, J. (2021) *The Great Guide: What David Hume Can Teach us about Being Human and Living Well*. Princeton, NJ: Princeton University Press.

Baker, K. M. (1978) 'State, Society, and Subsistence in Eighteenth-Century France', *Journal of Modern History*, 50: 701–711.

Balcou, J. (1975) *Fréron contre les philosophes*. Geneva: Droz.

Barker, E. (2005) *Greuze and the Painting of Sentiment*. Cambridge: Cambridge University Press.

Biziou, M. (2013) 'Traductions et retraductions françaises de la *Théorie des sentiments moraux* d'Adam Smith. L'insoutenable légèreté de (re)traduire', *Noesis*, 21: 229–263. https://journals.openedition.org/noesis/pdf/1864.

Blom, P. (2010) *A Wicked Company: The Forgotten Radicalism of the European Enlightenment*. New York: Basic.

Bloomfield, A. (1938) 'The Foreign-Trade Doctrines of the Physiocrats', *American Economic Review*, 28(4): 716–745.

Bonar, J. (1932) *A Catalogue of the Library of Adam Smith*, 2nd edition. London: Royal Economic Society.

Bonnyman, B. (2014) *The Third Duke of Buccleuch and Adam Smith: Estate Management and Improvement in Enlightenment Scotland*. Edinburgh: Edinburgh University Press.

Bradford, G. (1915) 'Portrait of a Lady: Madame Du Deffand', *North American Review*, 201(713): 567–579.

Bremer-David, C. (2011) *Paris: Life and Luxury in the 18th Century*. Los Angeles: J. Paul Getty Museum.

Buccleuch Collections/Bridgeman Images. (Not dated) *Portrait of the Hon. Campbell Scott (Oil on Canvas)*. https://www.bridgemanimages.com/en-US/greuze/portrait-of-the-hon-campbell-scott-oil-on-canvas/oil-on-canvas/asset/7287559

Buchan, J. (2006) *The Authentic Adam Smith: His Life and Ideas*. New York: Norton.

Carey, T. V. (2020) 'What Did Adam Smith Learn from François Quesnay?', *Journal of Scottish Philosophy*, 18(2): 175–191.

Charbit, Y. (2002) 'The Political Failure of an Economic Theory: Physiocracy (translated by A. Virmani)', *Population*, 57(6): 855–884.

Charrier-Vozel, M. (Not dated) 'Marie-Jeanne Riccoboni', in *The Digital Encyclopedia of British Sociability in the Long Eighteenth Century* ("DIGIT.EN.S"). Online. https://www.digitens.org/en/notices/marie-jeanne-riccoboni.html.

Chisick, H. (2004) 'The Representation of Adam Smith and David Hume in the *Année littéraire* and *Journal Encyclopédique*', in D. Dawson and P. Morère (eds.) *Scotland and France in the Enlightenment*. Lewisburg: Bucknell University Press, London: Associated University Presses, pp. 240–263.

Cohen, E. (2000) 'Adoption and Reform of the Gregorian Calendar', *Math Horizons*, 7(3): 5–11.

Cohen, M. (2001) 'The Grand Tour: Language, National Identity, and Masculinity', *Changing English: Studies in Culture and Education*, 8(2): 129–141.

Cole, W. (1931) *A Journal of My Journey to Paris in the Year 1765 by the Rev. William Cole*, 1st Am edition. New York: Richard R. Smith.

Collins, N. (2006) *The Problem of the Enlightenment Salon: European History or Post-European Politics, 1755–1850*. PhD dissertation, University College London. https://discovery.ucl.ac.uk/id/eprint/1348921/1/432003.pdf.

Conlin, J. (2013) *Tales of Two Cities: Paris, London and the Birth of the Modern City*. New York: Counterpoint.

Cunningham, P. (ed.). (1857) *The Letters of Horace Walpole*, Vol. 4. London: Bentley.

Dalkin, D. (1972) *Turgot and the* Ancien Régime *in France*. New York: Octagon.

Darnton, R. (1998) 'Two Paths through the Social History of Ideas', *Studies on Voltaire and the Eighteenth Century*, 359: 251–294.

Darnton, R. (2024) *The Revolutionary Temper: Paris, 1748–1789*. New York: Norton.

D'Avenel, G. (1925) *Les Enseignements de l'Histoire des Prix*. Paris: Payot.

Dawson, D. (2018) 'La Plus Distraite Creature: Adam Smith in the Correspondence of Marie-Jeanne Riccoboni', *Paper presented at a conference on the Networks of Enlightenment at the University of Glasgow*, July 17–21, 2018, panel on Continental Networks 1: Smith, Sympathy and France, on file with the authors.

Dilke, E. F. S. (1911) 'Greuze, Jean Baptiste', in H. Chisholm (ed.) *Encyclopaedia Britannica*, 11th edition, Vol. 12. Cambridge, UK: Cambridge University Press, pp. 584–585.

Du Pont de Nemours, P. S. (1782) *Memoires sur la vie et les ouvrages de m. Turgot, ministre d'état*. Hathi Trust. https://catalog.hathitrust.org/Record/000602373.

Eche, A. (2015) 'L'abbé Prévost (1697–1763) et Marc-Antoine Eidous (1724–1790): esquisse comparée de traducteurs de récits de voyages au XVIIIe siècle', *Convergences francophones*, 2(2): 12–24. http://mrujs.mtroyal.ca/index.php/cf/index.

Faccarello, G. and Steiner, P. (2002) 'The Diffusion of the Work of Adam Smith in the French Language: An Outline History', in K. Tribe (ed.) *A Critical Bibliography of Adam Smith*, London: Pickering & Chatto, pp. 119–134.

Fay, C. R. (1956) *Adam Smith and the Scotland of His Day*. Cambridge, UK: Cambridge University Press.

Feilbogen, S. (1892) *Smith und Turgot: Ein beitrag zur geschichte und theorie der nationalökonomie*. Vienna: Alfred Holder.

Fonseca, G. L. (Not dated) 'The Physiocratic Journals', *History of Economic Thought*. https://www.hetwebsite.net/het/schools/physioc_journal.htm#journalphys.

Fourastié, J. (1958) *Documents pour l'histoire et la théorie des prix*. Paris: A. Colin.

Friedrich, O. (1990) 'The Greatest Cafes of Paris', *Time*, May 21, 1990, available at https://perma.cc/N9WB-TV78

Goodman, D. (1989) 'Enlightenment Salons: The Convergence of Female and Philosophic Ambitions', *Eighteenth Century Studies*, 22(3): 329–350.

Goodman, D. (1996) *The Republic of Letters: A Cultural History of the French Enlightenment*, Rev. edition. Cornell University Press.

Groenewegen, P. D. (1993) 'Turgot and Adam Smith', in J. C. Wood (ed.) *Adam Smith: Critical Assessments*. London and New York: Routledge, pp. 106–119.

Guerra-Pujol, F. E. (2021) 'Adam Smith in Love', *Econ Journal Watch*, 18(1): 127–155.

Guerra-Pujol, F. E. (2025) 'Adam Smith's Blind Spot', *Journal of Public Finance and Public Choice*, 40: 1 (in press).

Guerra-Pujol, F. E. and Rashid, S. (forthcoming) 'Die Adam Smith Probleme', *Social Science Research Network*. https://papers.ssrn.com/sol3/papers.cfm?abstract_id=4430263.

Hauser, H. (1933) 'The Characteristic Features of French Economic History from the Middle of the Sixteenth to the Middle of the Eighteenth Century', *Economic History Review*, 4(3): 257–272.

Higgs, H. (1897) *The Physiocrats: Six Lectures on the French Économistes of the 18th Century*. London: Macmillan.

Hill Burton, J. (1849) *Letters of Eminent Persons Addressed to David Hume*. Edinburgh: William Blackwood and Sons, p. 130.

Hillairet, J. (1964) *Dictionnaire historique des rues de Paris*, 2nd edition. Paris: Les Éditions de Minuit.

Hoyng, A. C. (2011) *Turgot en Smith; een paar apart*. PhD dissertation, University of Amsterdam (on file with the authors).

Hume, D. (1987) [1777] 'My Own Life', in Miller, E. (ed.) *Essays, Moral, Political, and Literary*, Rev. edition. Indianapolis: Liberty Fund, pp. xxxii–xli.

Kafker, J. (1989) 'Notices sur les auteurs des dix-sept volumes de "discours" de l'Encyclopédie', *Recherches sur Diderot et sur l'Encyclopédie*, 7: 125–150.

Kaplan, S. (2016) *Bread, Politics, and Political Economy in the Reign of Louis XV*, 2nd edition. London: Anthem.

Ketton-Cremer, R. W. (1966) *Horace Walpole, a Biography*, 3rd edition. Ithaca, NY: Cornell University Press.

Klein, D. and Humphries, A. (2019) 'Foreword and Supplement to Adam Smith's Library: General Check-List and Index', *Econ Journal Watch*, 16(2): 374–474.

Kuiper, E. (2006) 'Adam Smith and His Feminist Contemporaries', in L. Montes and E. Schliesser (eds.) *New Voices on Adam Smith*. Routledge, pp. 40–60.

Kuiper, E. (2013) 'The Invisible Hands: Adam Smith and the Women in His Life', *Adam Smith Review*, 7: 62–78.

Lazare, F. and Lazare, L. (1844) *Dictionnaire administratif et historique des rues de Paris et de ses monuments*. Paris: Chez Félix Lazare.

Leddy, N. B. (2013) 'Grave, Philosophical, and Cool Reasoner: Mary Wollstonecraft on the Use of Gender in Adam Smith', *Adam Smith Review*, 7: 8–17.

Lefeuve, C. (1875) *Histoire de Paris, rue par rue, maison par maison*, 5th edition. Paris: C. Reinwald et Cie.

Lewis, W. S. (1939) *The Yale Edition of Horace Walpole's Correspondence*, Vol. 7. New Haven: Yale University Press.

Lilti, A. (2005) *Le monde des salons: Sociabilité et mondanité à Paris au XVIIIe siècle*. Paris: Fayard.

Mizuta, H. (1967) *Adam Smith's Library: A Supplement to Bonar's Catalogue with a Checklist of the Whole Library*. Cambridge, UK: Cambridge University Press.

Mossner, E. C. (1970) *The Life of David Hume*, 2nd edition. Oxford: Oxford University Press.

Mossner, E. C. and Ross, I. S. (1987) *Correspondence of Adam Smith*. Indianapolis: Liberty Fund.

Nicholls, J. C. (ed.). (1976) *Mme Riccoboni's Letters to David Hume, David Garrick, and Sir Robert Liston, 1764–1783*. Oxford: Voltaire Foundation.

Pennant, T. (1948) [1765] *Tour on the Continent, 1765*. London: Adlard.

Phillipson, N. (2010) *Adam Smith: An Enlightened Life*. New Haven: Yale University Press.

Plax, J. A. (2017) 'J.-B. Oudry's *Royal Hunts* and Louis XV's Hunting Park at Compiègne: Landscapes of Power, Prosperity and Peace', *Studies in the History of Gardens & Designed Landscapes*, 37(2): 102–119.

Playstowe, P. (1768) *The Gentleman's Guide in His Tour Through France*, 3rd edition. London: G. Kearsly.

Playstowe, P. [Millard, J.] (2018) [1770] *The Gentleman's Guide in His Tour Through France*, 4th edition. London: G. Kearsly, Hathi Trust. https://catalog.hathitrust.org/Record/008612368.

Prevost, P. (1805) *Notice de la vie et des écrits de George-Louis Le Sage de Genève*. Geneva: Chez J. J. Paschoud.

Rae, J. (1895) *Life of Adam Smith*. London: Macmillan.

Rasmussen, D. (2017) *The Infidel and the Professor: David Hume, Adam Smith, and the Friendship that Shaped Modern Thought*. Princeton, NJ: Princeton University Press.

Ross, I. S. (1974) 'Educating an Eighteenth-Century Duke', in G. W. S. Barrow (ed.) *The Scottish Tradition: Essays in Honour of Ronald Gordon Cant*. Edinburgh: Scottish Academic Press, pp. 178–197.

Ross, I. S. (1984) 'The Physiocrats and Adam Smith', *Journal for Eighteenth-Century Studies*, 7(2): 177–189.

Ross, I. S. (1995) *The Life of Adam Smith*, 1st edition. Oxford: Oxford University Press.

Ross, I. S. (2010) *The Life of Adam Smith*, 2nd edition. Oxford: Oxford University Press.

Shaw, E. (1955) 'The Chevalier de Mouhy's Newsletter of 20 December 1752', *Modern Language Notes*, 70(2): 114–116.

Shovlin, J. (2006) *The Political Economy of Virtue: Luxury, Patriotism, and the Origins of the French Revolution*. Ithaca, NY: Cornell University Press.

Smith, A. (1976) [1790] *The Theory of Moral Sentiments*, Glasgow edition. Oxford: Oxford University Press.

Smith, A. (1981) *An Inquiry into the Nature and Causes of the Wealth of Nations*, Glasgow edition. Indianapolis: Liberty Fund.

Smith, G. (2008) 'Physiocracy', in Ronald Hamowy (ed.) *Encyclopedia of Libertarianism*. Los Angeles: SAGE, pp. 378–379. https://www.libertarianism.org/topics/physiocracy.

Sorbière, S. (1660) *Lettres et discours de M. de Sorbière, sur diverses matières curieuses*. Paris. https://gallica.bnf.fr/ark:/12148/bpt6k316511r.

Stewart, D. (1982) [1793] '*Account of the Life and Writings of Adam Smith, LL.D.*', in W. P. D. Wightman (ed.) *Essays on Philosophical Subjects*, Glasgow edition. Indianapolis: Liberty Fund, pp. 269–351.

Stewart, M. M. (1970) 'Adam Smith and the Comtesse de Boufflers', *Studies in Scottish Literature*, 7(3): 184–187.

Stuart, L. (1985) [1827] *Memoire of Frances, Lady Douglas*. Edinburgh: Scottish Academic Press.

Sudo, Y. and Shinohara, H. (1985) 'A Forgotten Letter of Adam Smith to David Hume, 12th December, 1763', *Journal of Economics of Kwansei Gakuin University*, 39: 124–127.

Tourneux, M. (1878) [1764] *Correspondence littéraire, philosophique et critique par Grimm, Diderot, Raynal, Meister, etc.* Paris: Garnier Frères, https://gallica.bnf.fr/ark:/12148/bpt6k5784261h

Touzery, M. (1994) *L'Invention de l'impôt sur le revenu: la taille tarifiée, 1715–1789*. Vincennes: Comité pour l'histoire économique et financière de la France.

Toynbee, P. (1904) *The Letters of Horace Walpole*, Vol. 6. Oxford: Clarendon Press.

Valentine, A. (1970) *The British Establishment, 1760–1784: An Eighteenth-Century Biographical Dictionary*. Norman: University of Oklahoma Press.

Vanpée, J. (2013) 'Creating an Online Exhibit in a First-Year Seminar: Luxury Objects in the Age of Marie Antoinette', *ABO: Interactive Journal for Women in the Arts, 1640–1830*, 3(1). https://digitalcommons.usf.edu/abo/vol3/iss1/4/

Vardi, L. (2012) *The Physiocrats in the World of Enlightenment*. Cambridge: Cambridge University Press.

Wagner, J. (1991) 'Le Journal encyclopédique', in J. Sgard (ed.) *Dictionnaire des journaux, 1600–1789*. https://dictionnaire-journaux.gazettes18e.fr/journal/0730-le-journal-encyclopedique

West, E. G. (1976) *Adam Smith: The Man and His Works*, 2nd edition. Indianapolis: Liberty Press.

Wright, S. (2016) 'French: The Rise and Fall of a prestige lingua franca', in S. Wright (ed.) *Language Policy and Language Planning: From Nationalism to Globalisation*, 2nd edition. London: Palgrave Macmillan, pp. 134–153.

Zaretsky, R. and Scott, J. (2009) *The Philosophers' Quarrel: Rousseau, Hume, and the Limits of Human Understanding*. New Haven & London: Yale University Press.

Appendix 1

Date of Horace Walpole's Paris Journal Entry	*Reference to Smith or Duke Henry (followed by page number)*
Saturday, 15 February	'Dr Smith came. Went to an auction of prints. To Mme d'Uson. To Mme de Bentheim, Mme Lillebonne there. To Duchesse de la Vallière, Mme de Ferté-Imbault and Count Golowski there. To Mme Geoffrin's.' (302, footnote omitted)
Sunday, 2 March	'To Italian play with Lord and Lady G. Lennox, Duke of Buccleuch, Dr Smith, Sir H. Echlin and Captain Jones, *Tom Jones*.' (305, footnotes omitted)
Monday, 3 March	'King went suddenly to the Parliament – packing up and writing letters till late in the evening. Dr Smith and Baron d'Holbach came. To the Temple.' (306)
Saturday, 8 March	'Ditto. Mme Geoffrin, Mr Smith, Mme du Deffand, Lord and Lady George came.' (306, footnote omitted) [Note: The word 'Ditto' refers to Walpole's journal entry for the previous day (March 7): 'Cold in my eyes.']
Sunday, 9 March	'Ditto. Ditto, and Duke of Buccleuch and M. Schuwalof.' (306) [Note: The second 'Ditto' refers to the individuals who visited with Walpole on the previous day (March 8).]
Tuesday, 11 March	'Mr Smith and M.de Sarsfleld. To take the air. To Mme du Deffand.' (307)
Thursday, 13 March	'Dr Smith and Gordon, Principal of the Scotch College came.' (307)
Saturday, 15 March	'With Dr Smith to the Scots College.' (307, footnote omitted) [See also pp. 358–360 of Walpole's 'Anecdotes Written in 1766.']
Sunday, 16 March	'To Hôtel de Brancas, Duke of Buccleuch etc. There.' (308)
Thursday, 20 March	'Mr Young, Mr Lyttelton, Duke of Buccleuch and Mr Smith came. To shops.' (309)
Saturday, 22 March	'To shops. With Lady and Lord George, Mr and Mrs Carr, Duke of Buccleuch, Mr Scot, and Mr Nicholson to the Foire St-Germain, and supped afterwards at Lord George's.' (309)
Monday, 24 March	'Dined at Duke of Buccleuch's with several English.'
Tuesday, 25 March	'To manufacture at Sevè with Lady George, Mrs Ker, Duke of Buccleuch and Mr Scot.' (309, footnote omitted)

(*Continued*)

(Continued)

Date of Horace Walpole's Paris Journal Entry	*Reference to Smith or Duke Henry (followed by page number)*
Wednesday, 26 March	'To Mme d'Usson, Duke of Buccleuch etc. Abbé Colbert, and M. de Barbantane, and Mme de Gacé there.' (309)
Friday, 28 March	'Supped at Hôtel de Brancas with Duke of Buccleuch, Lord Fitzwilliam and others.' (310)
Sunday, 30 March 30	'To Mme du Deffand. Mr Smith came.' (310)
Tuesday, 1 April	'M. de Schuwalof and Mr Smith came.' (311)
Monday, 7 April	'The Rena, Lord Tavistock and Mr Smith came.' (312, footnote omitted)
Monday, 7 April	'Supped at Lady Mary Chabot's with Lady Browne, Mme de Bouzols, Mr Smith and Chevalier de Barfort.' (312)
Wednesday, 9 April	'Lord Edward Bentick and Mr Smith came.' (312)

Appendix 2

Image 6.1 Detail from 1739 map of Paris (plan de turgot), showing the Rue Du Colombier

Source: Wikimedia Commons, https://en.wikipedia.org/wiki/File:Foire_Saint-Germain_-_detail_Turgot_map_of_Paris_Plate_11.jpg

7 Adam Smith's curious theatre

The paradox of tragedy and the problem of Smith's praise of Racine's *Phèdre*

Adam Marcinkowski

In *The Theory of Moral Sentiments* (TMS), Adam Smith cites the initially poor reception of Jean Racine's *Phèdre et Hippolyte* (1677) to illustrate a writer's sensitivity to public opinion.[1] He deduces from Racine's ensuing 12-year hiatus from the theatre that the playwright 'was so disgusted by the indifferent success of his Phaedra, the finest tragedy, perhaps, that is extant in any language, that, though in the vigour of his life, and at the height of his abilities, he resolved to write no more for the stage' (TMS III.2.19).[2] To support his argument that this example represents the quintessential case of even a genius author's vulnerability to wayward public opinion, Smith cites what had become the verdict of eighteenth-century French critics: that *Phèdre* is unparalleled as a tragedy. Yet, this claim has troubled those seeking to reconcile Smith's taste with his moral philosophy.[3] It is not obvious how the same writer who insists that 'We are disgusted, with that clamorous grief, which without any delicacy, calls upon our compassion with sighs and tears and importunate lamentations' could so laud a tragedy fixated on the emotional outpourings of an overwrought woman like Phaedra (TMS I.i.5.3).

Some have chosen to discount this problem. Gloria Vivenza, for instance, infers from this ostensible discrepancy that 'we should be a little wary of Smith's definition of Racine's *Phèdre*' given that he seems 'far more at ease experiencing the quiet sentiments of the elegiac poets than the moving sentiments of the lyric poets' that inform Racine's drama (Vivenza 2001: 168–169).[4] But trivialising Smith's affinity for *Phèdre* risks distorting our understanding of what motivates the sympathetic imagination in Smith's TMS. Ever since David Hume first aligned this question with the paradox of tragic pleasure, or the 'difficult Problem to account for the Pleasure received from the Tears and Grief and Sympathy of Tragedy,' to warn Smith that the 'Hinge of your system' – that sympathy was necessarily agreeable – was insufficiently proven, researchers have referred to a note added to TMS' second edition to outline Smith's response to Hume's challenge (Corr. Letter 36).[5] There, Smith addresses what makes painful spectacles pleasing by distinguishing between the potential for sympathy to induce pain and the 'always agreeable' sentiment of approbation, which occurs when the spectator observes 'the perfect coincidence between this sympathetic passion in himself, and the original passion in the person principally concerned' (TMS I.iii.1.9 note b*). When assaulted by spectacles of pain and torture, spectators wince or flee, which is why Smith regards

DOI: 10.4324/9781003767824-10

Sophocles' attempt to elicit compassion for Philoctetes' putrid foot 'as among the greatest breaches of decorum of which the Greek theatre has set the example' (TMS I.ii.1.11). However, if tragedy invites spectators to determine whether the painful expression is right and why, then a favourable moral and aesthetic judgement will manifest as a pleasurable sympathetic response.

While approbative pleasure can strengthen our resolve when confronted by painful spectacles, it does not explain why we seek them out in the first place. Nor can it alone account for Smith's praise for *Phèdre* since Smith claims that this pleasure is most intensely brought forth by admirable spectacles of stoic or sublime masculine self-command rather than feminine surrender. Approbation, he says, 'heightened by wonder and surprise, constitutes the sentiment which is properly called admiration, and of which applause is the natural expression'; and it is 'The man, who under the severest tortures allows no weakness to escape him, vents no groan, gives way to no passions which we do not entirely enter into, commands our highest admiration' (TMS I.i.4.3; I.ii.1.12). Smith, moreover, claims that Cato – a character popularised in the eighteenth century by Joseph Addison's *Cato* (1713) – evokes this pleasure best because his 'tranquility' and 'fatal resolution' in the face of tragedy stages 'a spectacle which even the gods themselves might behold with pleasure and admiration' (TMS I.iii.1.13).[6] But if approbation felt most strongly as admiration resolves the paradox of tragedy, and if Cato is who we admire most, then why is *Phèdre* rather than *Cato* Smith's favoured tragedy? While Smith approves of Cato's character, he never applauds Addison's play except offhandedly, when he affirms that Cato showcases 'The sentiment of complete sympathy and approbation, mixed and animated with wonder and surprise, [which] constitutes what is properly called admiration, as has already been more than once taken notice of' (TMS I.iii.1.13).[7]

In what follows, I consider how the problem of Smith's unexpected appreciation of *Phèdre* invites reassessing the psychological dynamics motivating the sympathetic imagination by requiring alternative solutions to the paradox of tragedy. There are currently two competing explanations for Smith's praise. The first is that Smith approves of this play because it teaches readers and audiences how the impartial spectator encourages moral feelings like shame and guilt.[8] This hypothesis has three related advantages. It can be grounded in a tradition that begins with Aristotle's claim in the *Poetics* that instructive representations can please even when the 'things are painful to look upon – corpses, for instances, or the shapes of the most revolting animals' (Aristotle 2013: 20). This pleasure accounts for the seeming contradiction that Smith's theory tends to glorify masculine stoicism while his 'most potent examples are drawn from tragedy, most often the she-tragedy of a previous generation, plays known for their focus on distress' endured and expressed by women such as Monimia, Isabella, and Phaedra (Marsden 2019: 25).[9] Although these distraught women might be difficult to watch, if they and their performance provide moral edification, then we will 'take pleasure in viewing highly realistic images of them' (Aristotle 2013: 20). Finally, this proposed link between education and pleasure can help explain Smith's concession that literature often educates better than philosophy – or that 'The poets and Romance writers, who best paint the refinements and delicacies of love and friendship, and of all other private and domestic affections, Racine and Voltaire; Richardson, Marivaux, and Riccoboni; are, in such cases, much better instructors than Zeno, Chrysippus, or Epictetus' (TMS III.3.14). However, while moral education might be necessary for excellence, it does not sufficiently justify Smith's conviction about *Phèdre*'s greatness. Smith later rates Voltaire's *Mahomet* (1741) as 'one of the most interesting, and perhaps the most instructive spectacles that was ever introduced upon any theatre,' yet he ranks *Phèdre* rather than *Mahomet* as the finer tragedy (TMS III.6.12).

The second possibility looks to *Lectures on Rhetoric and Belle Lettres* (LRBL) to understand Smith's preference for the kind of formalism that, according to Dugald Stewart, influenced Smith's taste for French Neoclasscism rather than bourgious British drama:

> The principles of dramatic composition had more particularly attracted his attention; and the history of the theatre, both in ancient and modern times, had furnished him with some of the most remarkable facts on which his theory of the imitative arts was founded. From this theory it seemed to follow as a consequence, that the same circumstances which, in tragedy, give to blank verse an advantage over prose, should give to rhyme an advantage over blank verse; and Mr. Smith had always inclined to that opinion. Nay, he had gone so far as to extend the same doctrine to comedy; and to regret that those excellent pictures of life and manners which the English stage affords, had not been executed after the model of the French school.
>
> (Stewart 1858: 49)

This approach has uncovered Smith attacking curiosity for hindering sympathy with fictional characters. Some readers of LRBL, moreover, posit that Smith venerates *Phèdre*'s capacity to transcend curiosity to elicit a more robust sympathetic effect. David Reisman, for instance, reasons that Smith favours French neoclassical playwrights like Racine over their British counterparts because their adherence to the unities reduces the audience's curiosity and keeps them more attentive to the performance by compressing the timeframe of events. Reisman notes that 'An audience in the theatre may be willing to suspend its disbelief' but will 'never be willing to suspend its curiosity, and will never forgive a playwright for not providing it with adequate information' (Reisman 1976: 46). Similarly, Nicolas Phillipson contends that Smith praises *Phèdre* because

> Racine had followed Euripides' excellent practice of using prologues to explain the plot so that "we may be free to attend to the Sentiments and Actions of each scene," clearing the ground for the central dramatic purpose of showing the characters struggling to control the passions,

giving us an opportunity to better understand and sympathise with them (Phillipson 2010: 62).[10] My aim in this essay is to develop this second line of reasoning, expanding upon the insight that *Phèdre* invites and then overcomes curiosity to model an overlooked tension in Smith's TMS between the pleasures of approbative sympathy and curiosity's delights, one that both catalyses and yet sometimes impedes the sympathetic imagination.

A torturous curiosity

If scholars recognise the function of curiosity in TMS at all, they typically confine its significance to just the '*first step*' towards the superior moral pleasure of sympathy (Kopajtic 2020: 13, original emphasis).[11] However, a comparison of Racine's play and Smith's TMS exposes why this view needs further examination. Consider, for instance, an oft-quoted passage from Smith's TMS:

> Even our sympathy with the grief or joy of another, before we are informed of the cause of either, is always extremely imperfect. General lamentations, which express nothing but the anguish of the sufferer, create rather a curiosity to inquire into his situation, along with some disposition to sympathize with him, than any actual sympathy that is very sensible. The first question which we ask is, What has befallen you? Till this be answered, though we are uneasy both from the vague idea of his misfortune, and still more from torturing ourselves with conjectures about what it may be, yet our fellow-feeling is not very considerable.
>
> (TMS I.i.1.9)

Smith analyses here a formal scene – what I call a scene of inquiry – whereby a character encounters someone suffering and asks them, 'What's wrong?' Scenes of inquiry facilitate the creation of what Aristotle describes in the *Poetics* as, after plot, the second most important element of tragedy: *ēthos*. For Aristotle, *ēthos* or '"Moral character" is what makes us evaluate agents in particular ways,' and the presence of *ēthos* differentiates what Aristotle classifies as the historical from the poetical or 'what actually happened, and . . . the kinds of events that *would* happen' (Aristotle 2013: 28, original empahsis). Moral character typically emerges from the further combination of Aristotle's third and fourth most important elements of tragedy: speech (*lexis*) and thought (*dianoia*). When historical agents rationalise the why of what they did, the process transforms them into more than the sum of their actions. They become universalisable character types who, under similar circumstances, would do the same thing again and again.

Racine features a version of this formal scene in *Phèdre*, when the titular character steps onstage grieving before collapsing into a chair:

> *Phèdre*
>
> N'allons point plus avant. Demeurons, chère Œnone.
> Je ne me soutiens plus. Ma force m'abandonne.
> Mes yeux sont éblouis du jour que je revois,
> Et mes genoux tremblants se dérobent sous moi.

> Hélas! (*Elle s'assied*)
> [No further, stay, dear Oenone!
> I can no longer support myself. My strength abandons me.
> My eyes are dazzled by the daylight I again see.
> And my trembling knees give out from under me.
> Ah! (*she sits*)].[12]
>
> (Racine *Phèdre* 1999: 1.3:153–157)

Racine's contemporaries identified this scene as repeating much from Euripides' *Hippolytus*, even proposing that this part of the play was merely a translation.[13] In both versions, Phaedra enters in anguish, and her nurse inquires into what has befallen her. Phaedra's resistance to answering soon wavers, and she acquiesces to her nurse by admitting her incestuous desire for Hippolytus and what 'she intends to do right and how and why' (Kovacs 1980: 291). She admits her love is perverse, and because she cannot control it, she determines suicide to be the correct path forward.

In his sole reference in TMS to the content of this play, Smith analyses this moment to define a comparable Aristotelian distinction between primary and secondary passions:

> The reserve which the laws of society impose upon the fair sex with regard to this weakness, renders it more peculiarly distressful in them, and upon that very account, more deeply interesting. We are charmed with the love of Phaedra, as it is expressed in the French tragedy of that name, notwithstanding all the extravagance and guilt which attend it. That very extravagance and guilt may be said, in some measure, to recommend it to us. Her fear, her shame, her remorse, her horror, her despair, become thereby more natural and interesting. All the secondary passions, if I may be allowed to call them so, which arise from the situation of love, become necessarily more furious and violent; and it is with these secondary passions only that we can properly be said to sympathize.
>
> (TMS I.ii.2.4)

For Smith, primary passions are limited to what he terms the individual's 'situation or disposition of the body,' and they take as their object something peculiar to that person alone (TMS I.ii.1.1). Secondary passions take these primary passions as their object, and this derivation can be followed by the spectator. We cannot, as Smith argues, love as the lover does because we lack the specific attraction that defines their object of love. We can, however, imagine what Smith describes as a situation of passion, a more universal or poetical 'situation of love' rather than the historical situation of the lover (TMS I.ii.2.4).[14] Although we never 'enter into the attachment of the lover,' by generalising their situation to ourselves, we can 'enter into all the anxiety, and concern, and distress of the lover,' whose courtship faces the hazards that make up the plots that fascinated Smith (TMS I.ii.2.2). *Phèdre*'s scene of inquiry eases this transformation from the historical Phaedra into a poetical one. It provides room for her to demonstrate that she recognises the immorality of her incestuous yearning, thereby developing her moral character. While we do not sympathise with her desire, we can sympathise with her painful yet far more moral secondary passions – her fear, her shame, her remorse, and her despair.

If Phaedra's dialogue copies much from Euripides' version, the magnitude of the nurse's heartache in Racine's play is original. Pained by Phaedra's affliction, Oenone mimics that sorrow, dropping to her knees to beg her ward to speak:

Œnone

Madame, au nom des pleurs que pour vous j'ai versés,
Par vos faibles genoux que je tiens embrassés,
Délivrez mon esprit de ce funeste doute.
[Madam, in the name of these tears that I shed for you,
By these feeble knees that I clasp
Deliver me from this fatal uncertainty.]
(*Phèdre* 1.3:243–5)

Racine's Oenone underscores what Smith figures as curiosity's painful torturousness. If curiosity hurts, then its resolution must alleviate it in a manner reminiscent of Edmund Burke's portrayal of delight as a reduction in pain that is 'far from distressing, or disagreeable in its nature' (Burke 2015: 31). Smith draws further attention to the delightfulness of curiosity when he argues that Phaedra's peculiarity generates that initial recommendation to overcome our distaste for her outpourings to instead become drawn to sympathise with her secondary passions. We are, Smith suggests, more tolerant of and curious about a woman's misery because the laws of society leave them more vulnerable than men to the consequences of courtship gone wrong. Learning about such curious cases becomes correspondingly much more satisfying.

Phèdre's indifferent success

As an enthusiast of French neoclassical theatre and its history, Smith must have known about the circumstances that contributed to *Phèdre*'s failure – namely, that a rival cabal had sabotaged its 1 January 1677 premiere.[15] According to legend, they spoiled Racine's opening night by purchasing the most expensive seats at the Hôtel de Bourgogne, leaving them empty. Two days later, the conspirators debuted a competing *Phèdre et Hippolyte* written by Jacques Pradon at the Hôtel Guénégaud. They also initiated the Affaire des Sonnets by circulating a poem (now attributed to Antoinette Deshoulières) that contemptuously reviewed Racine's play:

Dans un fauteuil doré, Phèdre tremblante et blême,
Dit des vers où d'abord personne n'entend rien;
Sa nourrice lui fait un sermon fort chrétien,
Contre l'affreux dessein d'attenter à soi-même.

Hyppolite la hait presque autant qu'elle l'aime;
Rien ne change son cœur ni son chaste maintien:
La nourrice l'accuse, elle s'en punit bien;
Thésée a pour son fils une rigueur extrême.

Une grosse Aricie, au cuir rouge, aux crins blonds,
N'est là que pour montrer deux énormes tetons,
Que, malgré sa froideur, Hyppolite idolâtre.

Il meurt enfin traîné par ses courciers ingrats;
Et Phèdre, après avoir pris de la mort-aux-rats,
Vient, en se confessant, mourir sur le théâtre.

In a gilded chair, Phaedra, trembling and pale,
Recites verses which at first no one understands;
Her nurse gives her a great Christian sermon,
Against the awful plan to harm herself.

Hippolytus hates almost as much as she loves;
Nothing changes his heart nor his chaste bearing:
The nurse accuses him, she pays dearly for it;
Theseus is extremely harsh to his son.

A big Aricia, with red hide and blond mane,
Only there to flaunt her two enormous breasts,
Which Hippolytus worships despite her coldness.

He finally dies dragged by his ungrateful stallions;
And Phaedra, after taking rat poison,
Comes confessing to perish in the theatre.
(Deshoulières and Deshoulières 1764: 30)[16]

While the sonnet mostly lampoons the play's events by interpreting them as silly and exaggerated, exhibiting a grand bosom rather than sublime style or substance, the first couplet specifically accuses Phaedra's scene of inquiry of misfiring. It portrays the scene as having a jarring presence that shatters the viewer's absorption in the dramatic events. Phaedra stumbles on stage with tears streaming and then sits. Her nurse cries too. And no one knows why.

What is strange – and perhaps what the sonnet writers notice – is that Racine bolsters the unintelligibility of this theatrical intensity by altering Euripides' version. He discards the prologue spoken by Aphrodite (which establishes for the audience her role in causing Phaedra's incestuous longing), and he shortens the scene where the nurse and the chorus speculate about Phaedra's illness to just a few lines. In his adaptation, Oenone only announces to Hippolytus that Phaedra is unwell before shooing him away. By comparison, Jacques Pradon also removes the prologue. Yet, his version remains closer to Euripides in terms of structure. Although he substitutes Aricia for the nurse in the scene of inquiry, he, like Euripides, dedicates several lines before Phaedra's entrance to speculating about different reasons for her illness. And, unlike in Racine's version, the mystery is soon solved. Phaedra confesses the real reason for her suffering in less than half as many lines and after only her third turn to speak.

If, as the sonnet writers seem to believe, the scene requires knowing the cause of Phaedra's illness to succeed, then it is possible Racine had in mind an audience already familiar with the myth. However, this knowledge could not be taken for granted. There was no guarantee that the playwright would follow versions that audiences were acquainted with, a fact attested to by Racine's previous play *Iphigénie* (1674). This play's final act may have surprised some when it revealed that Agamemnon's daughter had survived, that Eriphile was secretly born with the name Iphigenia, and that she was the one the prophecy required to be sacrificed. Moreover, although Racine asserts that he followed the legend of Phaedra, he retained leeway for creative license: he justifies his inclusion of Aricia in his iteration of the story because he found an obscure passage in Book 7 of Vergil's *Aeneid* that said Aricia was Hippolytus' wife. Given that one should then not assume foreknowledge about a play's plot during composition, the sonnet writers may have a point. An unforgiving or uninformed audience could plausibly sustain their ignorance about Phaedra's pain. Under such conditions, this long, 116-line scene of a sitting and sobbing Phaedra reciting incomprehensible dialogue to evade her nurse, who frantically pesters her ward with questions – this is a theatrical failure. As a gross elaboration of just the situation of the body, it becomes an uncomfortable presence, an assault on the senses that moral reason finds senseless.

In its initial conditions, Racine's play is for an audience, a word that emphasises the aural quality of the Parisian theatre, where sightlines were impeded and where the unruly clamour of its patrons threatened the play's coherence. Racine wrote this scene for star actress Marie Champmeslé, and he was likely trying to leverage the forceful je-ne-sais-quoi that emanated from the body and voice of this star performer to conquer that audience and coerce them into passive spectatorship, preparing them to receive the poetic brilliance of her confession speech.[17] For Racine's critics, however, this moment just doesn't work. They sit and watch Phaedra sit and cry confused and bored. Smith, writing not only in another language and another country but also over a century later – after a period during which the proscenium arch was erected and the boundary between stage and seats began to be policed – may have had this sonnet in mind as he now wonders why the scene succeeds despite this critique. He strives to comprehend how and why it ensnares a more passive and more likely-to-be-seated spectator, who has a fundamentally different relationship to spectacle than the boisterous crowd inside the seventeenth-century parterre. Although eighteenth-century British theatre was still a loud and interactive social venue, and while celebrity remained important, Smith presents a spectator far more interested in moral character than in showmanship. This spectator is not overwhelmed by Champmeslé's sublime presence but absorbed by a curious absence – namely, the same questions that occupy the nurse: what is wrong with Phaedra? What is making her sit and cry? Unlike Racine's rival cabal, who were confused or even repulsed by this absence, Smith deems Phaedra's peculiar situation charming.

Even though Smith's praise of Racine's play as the greatest tragedy ever written aligns with the consensus of eighteenth-century French critics, the substance of his analysis diverges from the traditional defence of Racine's merit. In his Preface to *Hérode et Mariamne* (1724), Voltaire dismisses *Phèdre*'s unfavourable initial reception by contrasting the fleeting qualities of theatre (the situations, the actors, the audience response) with those needed to withstand 'le grand jour de l'impression' ['the great day of printing'] – namely, the 'charme inexprimable de la poésie, que le génie seul peut donner, où l'esprit ne saurait jamais atteindre, et sur lequel on raisonne si mal, et si inutilement depuis la mort de monsieur Despréaux' ['inexpressible charm of poetry that genius alone can give, where the mind can never reach and of which we reason so badly and so uselessly since the death of Monsiuer Despréaux'] (Voltaire 2004: 187). Racine, continues Voltaire, channelled this sublime poetic force in ways Pradon never could, so while it is true that 'les deux *Phèdres* semblèrent d'abord avoir une égale destinée; mais l'impression régla bientôt le rang de l'une et de l'autre' ['the two Phaedra's initially seemed to have an equal destiny, but the publication soon ranked the one and the other'] (Voltaire 2004: 188).[18] Smith admits a version of this sublime in LRBL although he subordinates it to the sympathetic: 'When the sentiment of the speaker is expressed in a neat, clear, plain and clever manner, and the passion or affection he is poss(ess)ed of and intends, *by sympathy*, to communicate to his hearer, is plainly and cleverly hit off, then and then only the expression has all the force and beauty that language can give it' (LRBL i.v.56, original emphasis). This appreciation of rhetoric might hint at Smith's agreement with Voltaire's assessment. But then he never discusses the play in these terms, choosing instead to analyse the play's dramatic situations. While Smith might treasure the sublime beauty of Phaedra's confession speech, he discusses it only to show that curiosity compels us to initially listen.

Syncopated emotional time and the aesthetics of curiosity, suspense, novelty, and nervousness

The aesthetic category of the curious has a long tradition, albeit one overshadowed by the sublime and the beautiful, partly due to long-standing suspicions about its moral value. It was Plato who initiated theoretical interest in the desire to learn when he branded it the 'experience which is characteristic of a philosopher, this wondering: this is where philosophy begins and nowhere else' (Plato 1997: 173). Aristotle later concurred that 'it is because of wondering at things that humans, both now and at first, began to do philosophy' (Aristotle 2016: 5). However, Aristotle then split inquisitiveness into two, specifying that wondering about certain philosophical or scientific principles and causes rather than seeking novel experiences constituted the virtue of wisdom. The Christian tradition seized on this distinction, explicitly characterising the latter as a vice. Saint Augustine, who likely had Aristotle in mind, condemns *curiositas* as a vice of excess that needs to be curbed. He argues that while wonder derives pleasure from 'objects of visual beauty, harmonious sounds, fragrent perfumes, and things that are pleasant to the taste and touch,' curiosity seeks out the opposite: this 'unhealthy curiosity' draws us away from God and towards immoral things like a 'mangled corpose' or other 'freaks and prodigies [that] are put on show in the theatre' (Augustine 1961: 242). In the seventeenth century, René Descartes echoed the ancients by considering this feeling 'la première de toutes les passions' ['the first among the passions'], since unknown objects arouse wonder or curiosity before any other aesthetic judgement (Descartes 1964: 109). Yet, like Augustine, he similarly cautions against letting the pleasures of novelty descend into 'la maladie de ceux qui sont aveuglement curieux' ['the sickness of the blindly curious'], an addiction to wondering at the rarities of the world without consideration for their utility (Descartes 1964: 121).

In his *Enquiry into the Origin of Our Ideas of the Sublime and the Beautiful* (1757), Burke alludes to this tradition when he denigrates curiosity as an important yet juvenile emotion:

> The first and the simplest emotion which we discover in the human mind, is Curiosity. By curiosity, I mean whatever desire we have for, or whatever pleasure we take in novelty. We see children perpetually running from place to place to hunt out something new; they catch with great eagerness, and with very little choice, at whatever comes before them; their attention is engaged by every thing, because every thing has, in that stage of life, the charm of novelty to recommend it. But as those things which engage us merely by their novelty, cannot attach us for any length of time, curiosity is the most superficial of all the affections; it changes its object perpetually; it has an appetite which is very sharp, but easily satisfied; and it has always an appearance of giddiness, restlessness and anxiety.
>
> (Burke 2015: 27)

While curiosity motivates us to seek novelty, Burke's treatise implies that adults with refined tastes abandon it for the superior experiences of beauty and sublimity. Smith reiterates Burke's assessment of curiosity's puerility when he observes that 'One method which most modern historians and all the Romance writers take to render their narration interesting is to keep their event in Suspense' (LRBL ii.28). To appeal to curiosity, a writer needs only to delay resolution, such that

> Whenever the story is beginning to point to the grand event they turn to something else and by this means get us to read thro a number of dull nonsensicall stories, our curiosity prompting us to get at the important event.
>
> (LRBL ii.28)

The successful use of curiosity, continues Smith, compels readers to skip over

> the less important intervening accidents, which if the great event had been intirely concealed, our curiosity would make us hurry over; We would count the pages we had to read to get to the event, as we generally do in a novel.
>
> (LRBL ii.29)

The readers of these sprawling novels and histories are, in this view, like the children from Burke's *Enquiry*, rushing through the narrative, eagerly uncovering the next plot point.

Smith's critique of curiosity contrasts with the perspective of Pierre Corneille (a mentor for Pradon and a figurehead for the cabal that undermined Phèdre's reception), who cultivated curiosity to overthrow Aristotelian *katharsis* as the end of tragedy. For Corneille, *katharsis*, or the purging of pity and fear, was just 'une belle ideé, qui n'ait jamais son effet dans la vérité' ['a nice idea, which never truly works in reality'] (Corneille 1963: 82). Possibly inspired by the popularity of the romance novels Smith disparages, Corneille instead advises playwrights to deploy suspense to please audiences:

> [Q]u'il faut, s'il se peut, lui réserver toute la catastrophe, et même la reculer vers la fin, autant qu'il est possible. Plus on la diffère, plus les esprits demeurent suspendus, et l'impatience qu'ils ont de savoir de quel côté elle tournera est cause qu'ils la reçoivent avec plus de plaisir: ce qui n'arrive pas quand elle commence avec cet acte. L'auditeur qui la sait trop tôt n'a plus de curiosité; et son attention languit durant tout le reste, qui ne lui apprend rien de nouveau. [We must, if possible, delay for him the whole catastrophe, and even, as much as possible, postpone it towards the end. The longer it is deferred, the more spirits are held in suspense, and their impatience to know in which way it will turn causes them to experience it with greater pleasure; this does not occur when the play begins with the act. An audience member that knows it too early loses its curiosity; their attention languishes for the rest of the play, which teaches them nothing new.]
>
> (Corneille 1963: 72)

This description recognises curiosity's immoral characteristic: the pursuit of pleasure for its own sake. Yet, Corneille argues that plays must appeal to and pay off suspense for practical rather than moral reasons – its delights are simply what the audience craves from the theatre.

The Parisian factional politics that organised itself around the rivalry between Racine and Corneille came to a head towards the end of the seventeenth century with a conflict over literary merit known as La Querelle des Anciens et des Modernes. In the aftermath of this debate, and despite what many might now consider his modern interest in moral psychology, Smith decisively sides with the Ancients. He betrays his neoclassical allegiance when he critiques the novel for cultivating this immoral suspense rather than the poetic virtues one finds in ancient literature: 'newness is the only merit in a Novel and curiosity the only motive which induces us to read them'; yet, ancient writers 'never have recourse to this method [of using curiosity]' since 'the importance of the narration they trust to keep us interested' (LRBL ii.30). Hence, both 'Virgil in the beginning of the Æneid and Homer in both his heroic poems inform us in the beginning of the chief events that are told in the whole poem' without fear that the reader will become bored and abandon the text (LRBL ii.30). He similarly celebrates Euripides, who

> often in his Prologues by means of a God or a Ghost makes us acquainted with the Events and puts us on our Guard that we may be free to attend to the Sentiments and Actions of each Scene, some of which he has laboured greatly.
>
> (LRBL ii.30)

In other words, if freedom from curiosity enables the reader to better attend to the text, it also leaves the spectator more open to experiencing a moment of sympathetic engagement with any given scene or character.[19]

Smith's concern about curiosity interfering with the spectator's sympathy anticipates what Gertrude Stein describes as the problem of plays being in 'syncopated time in relation to the emotion of anybody in the audience' (Stein 1995: xxix). This syncopation occurs when 'your emotion concerning [the] play is always either behind or ahead of the play at which you are looking and to which you are listening' (Stein 1995: xxix). Moreover, the disjointed emotional tempo produces in the spectator what she calls a 'nervousness' – or the feeling that one needs 'to go faster or to go slower so as to get together' (Stein 1995: xxx). In Stein's view, real life is exciting because it is something you are doing; similarly, reading a book is exciting because you have 'control over it': you can 'find out the end and so begin over again' (Stein 1995: xxxii). But nervousness is 'on the stage a thing over which you have no real control' because the actor's control the action (Stein 1995: xxxii). Moreover, this nervousness induces a delightful relief rather than pleasurable completion:

> This then is the fundamental difference between excitement in real life and on the stage, in real life it culminates in a sense of completion whether an exciting act or and exciting emotion has been done or not, and on the stage the exciting climax is a relief. And the memory of the two things is different. As you go over the detail that leads to culmination of any scene in real life, you find that each time you cannot get completion, but you can get relief and so already your memory of any exciting scene in which you have taken part turns it into the thing seen or heard not the thing felt. You have as I say as the result relief rather than culmination. Relief from excitement, rather than the climax of excitement.
>
> (Stein 1995: xxxii)

While Stein experiments with ways to tether the spectator's emotion to the present by creating cinematic modernist plays that express the 'standpoint of sight and sound and its relation to emotion and time, rather than in relation to story and action,' Smith proposes repetition as the solution (Stein 1995: xxxv). For Smith,

> The graduall and just development of the Catastrophe constitutes a great beauty in any Tragedy yet is it not a necessary one, otherwise we could never with any pleasure hear or see acted a play for the Second time; yet that pleasure often grows by Repetition.
>
> (LRBL ii.30)

The pleasures of close reading a novel or a play almost always require objectivity or impartiality attained through multiple readings if only to detect how certain expressions allude to or contribute to meanings in the text that have not yet been fully revealed. Despite Smith not being well-known as a theatregoer, he appears to view repetition as a powerful aid to spectacle as well: 'A tragedy can bear to be read again and again tho the incidents be not new to us they are new to the actors and by this means interest us as well as by their own importance' (LRBL ii.30). Although the word 'actor' here comes from student notes rather than Smith's hand, and while 'actor' could refer to an agent or character rather than a stage performer, the passage does suggest that reading a play ahead of time can increase a spectator's sympathetic engagement by realigning their focus from plot to the art of the actor's expression.

Repetition and the consciousness of theatre

Smith's grasp of repetition's capacity to evolve critical and aesthetic judgements challenges one of the bedrock assumptions justifying approbation alone as Smith's solution to the paradox of tragedy, namely the idea that Smith's theory of the sympathetic imagination suspends the distinction between fiction and reality. Since the 1980s, scholars have analysed Smith's TMS by contrasting theatrical spectacle with narrative fiction. David Marshall, for instance, notes that the TMS is so filled with theatrical instances of spectators and spectacles that one must acknowledge the scene of sympathy as an 'inherently theatrical situation' (Marshall 1984: 595). Yet, Smith 'illustrates a discussion of how we enter into the sentiments and actions of others with a description of reading: whether we are confronted with a person or a text, we must face a fiction' (Marshall 1984: 595).[20] Because we sympathise with the poetical situation of the passion rather than the historical or theatrical situation of the body, the distinction between fiction and real life starts to erode such that some conclude that 'the consciousness of fiction and imitation do not account for the pleasure of tragedy, or are at most irrelevant' (Siraki 2010: 219).[21] But if the fictionality of real life erodes the distinction between make-believe and reality, then the objectivity that the sympathetic imagination seeks becomes tenuous: how do we know someone's lamentations are not a sham designed to elicit undeserved sympathy? When we ask what has befallen them, how do we know they are not deceiving us?

By the mid-eighteenth century, these questions had gained urgency partly because of the antitheatrical positions taken by Jean-Jacques Rousseau in his *Lettre à M. d'Alembert sur les spectacles* (1758). In addition to accusing the material theatre of being a hotbed of social and moral corruption, Rousseau raises the ideological problem that the actor poses to a commercial society that depends on trust to manage social exchange. Smith may have been influenced by the arguments presented in Rousseau's *Lettre* when, in the winter of 1762, he joined a committee organised by the University of Glasgow to block the construction of a theatre in the city.[22] Given this connection, it is surprising that Smith supposedly passes over the problem of the false actor in silence.[23] But then his elevation of the man of self-command does indirectly address this issue:

> [W]e reverence that reserved, that silent and majestic sorrow, which discovers itself only in the swelling of the eyes, in the quivering of the lips and cheeks, and in the distant, but affecting, coldness of the whole behavior. It imposes the like silence upon us. We regard it with respectful attention, and

> watch with anxious concern over our whole behaviour, lest by any impropriety we should disturb that concerted tranquillity, which it requires so great an effort to support.
>
> (TMS I.i.5.3)

Outside the theatre, this self-command solves any problems theatricality might pose to the commercial community since the great effort required to maintain a stoic reserve becomes an open pretence whose truth the spectator readily enters. This performance tries to fool the spectator into not sharing the sufferer's pain, and when the spectator recognises that this theatrical deception is for them, they are overcome with admiration.

Theatre historians have observed that the shift in Smith criticism from theatricality to fictionality and narrativity has come at the cost of ignoring the actual theatre, which partially defines itself through repetition.[24] Real-life situations happen but once; the real-life work of professional theatre involves paid performers enacting fictional situations again and again. In real life, scepticism towards an overly emotional performance is warranted even after the sufferer reveals their situation because their narrative is always told from their individual, or even self-interested, perspective. But in the theatre, this suspicion dissipates because the performer has specifically been invited or paid to present a fiction. Moreover, by reading or watching a play multiple times, the spectator can take up a truly impartial perspective because, unlike in real life, where narratives are constructed from an individual's point of view, when watching a play, the spectator can know the whole story and can thus judge the characters with complete objectivity. Smith may have experienced these effects during his visit to Paris in 1766. While he is reported to have frequented the theatre during his stay, it is unknown whether he attended the performance of *Phèdre* starring the esteemed actress Marie-Françoise Dumesnil at the Comédie-Française on 10 March 1766. Dugald Stewart does, however, note that after Smith's trip,

> The admiration with which he regarded the great dramatic authors of France tended to confirm him in these opinions; and this admiration . . . was increased to a great degree, when he saw the beauties that had struck him in the closet, heightened by the utmost perfection of theatrical exhibition.
>
> (Stewart 1858: 49)

If Stewart's recollection is accurate, then any straightforward reading of a context-agnostic approbative pleasure cannot reasonably be Smith's full solution to the paradox of tragedy. For why would seeing the play performed heighten that tragedy's pleasure? Why would potentially seeing Mlle Dumesnil perform an extravagant Phaedra lead to admiration when that feeling is described in TMS as being reserved for a man of self-command? One solution might be that however opposite the sublime man of reserve and the beautiful actress might be, they both project the awareness that what is put on is for the spectator's welfare.

Consider how the awareness of theatre, via repetition, might impact watching the emotional performances in *Phèdre's* scene of inquiry. When Oenone sees the grieving Phaedra, she is so distressed to discover the cause that she, too, collapses. Seeking relief, she lies at Phaedra's feet, clasping the woman's knees, begging to know what's wrong. However, Phaedra refuses to answer her nurse. She says she would rather die than give an 'aveu si funeste' ('so fatal confession') – a phrase that, in a neat, clear, plain, and clever manner, beautifully communicates her sentiments while both echoing Oenone's earlier 'fatal uncertainty' and foreshadowing to those who already know the plot that her words will unleash a catastrophe more deadly than the solitary and secretive death she seeks (*Phèdre* 1.3:226). Offended, Oenone construes Phaedra's repudiation as a cruel, 'silence inhumain' ('inhumane silence') and responds with her own 'juste douleur' ('righteous pain'), effectively breaking the social bond between the two (*Phèdre* 1.3:227; 1.3:232).

Smith rarely raises the issue of curiosity again in TMS, only returning to it towards the end to critique its immorality in terms that mirror the dilemma that now faces Phaedra and Oenone. Just as curiosity about plot can interrupt our sympathies, curiosity about our neighbours, he argues, can destabilise communities forged by the sympathetic imagination:

> This passion to discover the real sentiments of others is naturally so strong that it often degenerates into a troublesome and impertinent curiosity to pry into those secrets of our neighbours which they have very justifiable reasons for concealing; and, upon many occasions, it requires prudence and a strong sense of propriety to govern this, as well as all the other passions of human nature, and to reduce it to that pitch which any impartial spectator can approve of. To disappoint this curiosity, however, when it is kept within the proper bounds, and aims at nothing which there can be any just reason for concealing, is equally disagreeable in its turn. The man who eludes our most innocent questions, who gives no satisfaction to our most inoffensive inquiries, who plainly wraps himself up in impenetrable obscurity, seems, as it were, to build a wall about his breast. We run forward to get within it, with all the eagerness of harmless curiosity; and feel ourselves all at once pushed back with the rudest and most offensive violence.
>
> (TMS VII.iv.28)

When, instead of taking part in the shared pleasures of approbation, individuals prioritise the delight of a gratified curiosity, a moral society can degrade into one of manipulative attention seekers, petty gossipmongers who crave curiosity's satisfaction, and recluses who close themselves to others because they feel violated by what would otherwise bring a community together.

As the relationship between Phaedra and Oenone fractures, specifically along the latter two lines, a new bond forms between her nurse and the audience. Although Smith claims the spectator will eventually sympathise with Phaedra's fear, shame, remorse, horror, and despair, without first knowing about her intrusive desire, it is more likely that they initailly respond to her lamentations with curiosity while also sympathising with her nurse. As Smith elsewhere argues in TMS,

> There is something agreeable even in the weakness of friendship and humanity. The too tender mother, the too indulgent father, the too generous and affectionate friend, may sometimes, perhaps, on account of the softness of their natures, be looked upon with a species of pity, in which, however, there is a mixture of love, but can never be regarded with hatred and aversion, nor even with contempt, unless by the most brutal and worthless of mankind.
>
> (TMS I.ii.4.3)

In other words, the spectator can easily imagine the situation of Oenone's pain because they feel something similar while watching Phaedra, and since they understand the familial love between the two, they can also approve of Oenone's desperation despite not feeling the pain as powerfully as she does. At the same time, Phaedra also watches Oenone. She recognises herself as responsible for her nurse's torment. But while the spectator's sentiments and judgements align with Oenone's, Phaedra believes her refusal to confess is justified, which means Oenone's inquiries become discomforting. She tries to dismiss Oenone – 'Je t'en ai dit assez. Épargne-moi le reste' ['I have told you enough. Spare me the rest'] – but Oenone refuses to leave without satiating her curiosity (*Phèdre* I.iii.225). Eventually, Oenone's pleas overwhelm the already suffering Phaedra's defences, and the latter confesses to the relief of both her nurse and the spectator.

Once both Oenone and the audience learn that Phaedra's agony arises from an unwanted, incestuous passion potentially sparked by a divine curse, and once they hear the torments Phaedra has endured before arriving at her decision to choose death rather than succumb to depravity, they then, according to Smith, relinquish their torturous nervousness for moral approval and sympathy. But this sympathetic identification does not last long. It is soon interrupted by Panope, who enters with word of Theseus' death. This news, claims Oenone, changes the conditions that made Phaedra's love so repulsive: 'Thésée en expirant vient de rompre les nœuds / Qui faisaient tout le crime et l'horreur de vos feux' ['Theseus' death unties the knots / that made your passion a horror and a crime'] (*Phèdre* 1.5.351–2). These lines announce that the narrative is not over. They break the spectator's sympathetic bond with Phaedra by reintroducing nervousness. Oenone performs this change when she starts worrying about the future: what will happen to Phaedra and her son if Hippolytus marries Aricia? Will he arrest or execute his stepmother and stepbrother to take control of Troezen? The solution to this problem is also the solution to Phaedra's no longer disquieting love. Oenone suggests she should marry her stepson and secure the throne, and Phaedra agrees to follow this plan: 'Hé bien! À tes conseils je me laisse entraîner' ['Well! By your counsels, I let myself be swept away'] (*Phèdre* 1.5.363). And so the story continues. The audience reidentifies with Oenone's syncopated emotional time; their sympathy with Phaedra dissolves as they turn their nervous attention towards the continuation of the plot.

In his preface to the play, Racine divulges that he sought to make Phaedra 'un peu moins odieuse' ('a little less odious') than in previous dramatic iterations of this myth by shifting responsibility for the tragic outcome to Oenone (Racine 1999: 817). In his version, Oenone both convinces Phaedra, 'qui a d'ailleurs des sentiments si nobles et si vertueux' ['who otherwise possesses such noble and virtuous sentiments'], to act on her desire and later orchestrates the false accusation of rape against Hippolytus (Racine 1999: 817). But if the scene of inquiry initially aligns the spectator with Oenone, then that sympathetic relationship threatens to contaminate the spectator with her 'inclinations plus serviles' ['more slave-like inclinations'] (Racine 1999: 817). However, when the spectator sees or reads the scene again, they know in advance why Phaedra sits and cries. They are no longer invested in what has or will happen and can instead take up a more objective and impartial position relative to the action, the language, and the performance, one that breaks the spectator's identification with Oenone's desire to satiate her curiosity. Instead, the moral sympathetic connection to Phaedra extends throughout the whole scene (if not the whole play), from her agonised entrance up to and including her fateful and fatal decision to adhere to Oenone's design.

Conclusion

I began this essay by recognising that Smith's praise for *Phèdre* requires rethinking his solution to the paradox of tragedy. By identifying curiosity as a force that both activates and inhibits the sympathetic imagination, I have brought into view several interrelated possibilities – including approbation, admiration, moral edification, formalist appreciation, and relief from suspense. Moreover, I have agreed with the current consensus that, when taken alone, the approbative pleasure that Smith values most might be agnostic towards the difference between the fictional and the real. However, when combined with these other solutions, it becomes clear that the consciousness of fiction or theatre participates in heightening the pleasures of spectatorship. Ultimately, by including and expanding curiosity's overlooked role in producing and maintaining the sympathetic imagination, Smith's moral theory is revealed to be a richer and more complex dynamic capable of entertaining multiple intertwined solutions to the problem of tragic pleasure.

Notes

1 This essay originated as a dissertation chapter and has been substantially revised for publication.

2 According to John Sayer, other possible influences on Racine's retirement from the theatre include his 1679 marriage to the aristocrat Catherine de Romanent, which may have made his theatre career improper; his acceptance of the position of royal historiographer in the same year, which likely occupied much of his time; and his reconciliation with Jansenist religious beliefs that were hostile to the theatre. See Sayer (2006: 266–272)

3 Pradon and his play became what Jennifer Tsien describes as a kind boogeyman or 'ghost,' conjured up 'as if to reassure us that he is really dead' by eighteenth-century

French critics who saw the 'reading public's wayward judgments' as a threat that required a literary elite to correct (Tsien 2012: 94).

4 Vivenza also worries that Racine's play more closely resembles Seneca's Latin interpretation of the myth rather than Euripides' *Hippolytus*, whose sentimental content she claims he may have preferred. See Vivenza (2001: 169). For the influence of Sappho's lyric poem 'fragment 31' on Phaedra's confession, see DeJean (1989: 86–93) and Marcinkowski (2025).

5 For the importance of this note to the pleasure of approbative judgements in Smith, see Rasmussen (2023) and Brown (2016: 235).

6 For the conclusion that using the pleasure of approbative judgement to resolve the paradox of tragedy leads to the view that stoic performance (and, therefore, the character of Cato) ought to be the tragic ideal, see Siraki (2010: 214) and Ellison (1999: 69–71)

7 Critics have noted that 'Addison's play does not offer Cato himself as an unqualified ideal, or even as an ideal all'; it instead positions the Numidian prince Juba as 'the drama's hopeful alternative to Cato's stubborn, suicidal despair' (Rosenthal 1999: 63). See also Freeman (1999). Although it is possible this ambivalence towards Cato might explain why Smith generally ignores Addison's play, it is unlikely that Smith would have interpreted *Cato* this way since, as David Taylor points out, this modern reading 'runs up against the fact that most of Addison's immediate contemporaries – that is, *Cato*'s first audiences – simply did not experience the play in such terms' (Taylor 2022: 57).

8 Charles Griswold argues that 'Smith's choice of high literature is telling, for it points to a conviction that the distortion of sound judgment and sympathy . . . poses a particular danger to moral education,' and he believes Smith elevates Racine's play 'presumably because it depicts so movingly the phenomenon of remorse, thus showing us how the voice of the internalized impartial spectator cannot be entirely extirpated' (Griswold 1999: 216–217). Vanessa Michel concurs that Smith approves of this play because 'les concepts de sympathie et de spectatuer impartial' ['the concepts of sympathy and the impartial spectator'] are 'illustrés par cette héroïne tragique' ['illustrated by this tragic heroine'] (Michel 2023/2: 28).

9 See also Rosenthal (2016: 122–141).

10 As I discuss below, although Racine closely follows Euripides' *Hippolytus*, he does remove the prologue spoken by the goddess Aphrodite. Phillipson may have in mind the Preface that Racine added to the published version of his play.

11 For a description of how 'sympathetic engagement was a function of a seemingly natural curiosity which all human beings have in the future of others' in both Hutcheson and Smith, see Phillipson (2010: 150–151).

12 All French translations throughout this essay are my own.

13 The author of the *Dissertation sur les tragedies de Phèdre et Hippolyte* points out that right up until her confession speech, 'Cette languissante conversation de Phedre, et d'Henone, est prise toute entiere & mot pour mot d'Euripide' ['this languid conversation of Phaedra and Oenone is taken entirely and word for word from Euripides'] (1677: 23).

14 Lauren Kopajtic connects this distinction between primary and secondary passions to the narrative structure of the novel (Kopajtic 2023: 202–204).

15 For a review of the connections between Smith's TMS and neoclassical dramaturgy, see Camp (2020). For an account of this conspiracy, see Bussom (1922).

16 Aricia was originally played by the purportedly overweight Mlle d'Ennebaut. It is unclear why she is the target of such vitriol in this poem, which riffs on Hippolytus' traditional association with horses to depict her as horse-like.

17 For more on this likelihood, as well as the metatheatricality of Phaedra's confession speech, see Marcinkowski (2025).

18 Hume presents a similar idea as his solution to the paradox of tragedy in his 1757 essay 'Of Tragedy.' There, Hume appeals to the pleasures of the rhetorical sublime by arguing that the

'melancholy passions' of tragedy are 'converted into pleasure' through 'noble talents, along with the force of expressions, and beauty of oratorial numbers' that 'diffuse the highest satisfaction on the audience, and excite the most delightful movements' (Hume 1964: 261).

19 Smith's model of normative, sympathetic responses to tragic circumstances implicitly redefines the meaning of *katharsis*, transforming the effect of tragedy from the purgation Cornielle dismisses into what Thomas Twining would later describe in his translation of Aristotle's *Poetics* as a 'correction or refinement' initiated by a sympathetic engagement with the characters (Twining 1789: 75). While Twining did not cite Smith when he translated Aristotle, his work manifests a late eighteenth-century intellectual culture fascinated by the sympathetic imagination's transformative power, one that Smith's philosophy had likely influenced.

20 For a review of this direction of scholarship on Adam Smith, see Karen Valihora (2016) and Kopajtic (2023).

21 Siraki argues that Smith 'attenuates or dissolves the distinction between real and feigned spectacles' to discount rival eighteenth-century solutions to the paradox of tragedy, specifically Joseph Addison's Aristotelian belief in the inherent pleasure of imitation (Siraki 2010: 216).

22 According to Ryan Patrick Hanley, it is entirely possible that Smith turned to the French philosopher to stake out an antitheatrical position while on this committee given that 'the Rousseau of the *Letter* and the Smith of *The Theory of Moral Sentiments* share a common understanding of the nature of modern morality and also propose a similar remedy for modernity's corruptions of that morality' (2006: 178).

23 Ellwood Wiggins observes that 'Smith's understanding of the mechanics of sympathy is profoundly theatrical, but he never engages seriously with the theater or the actor's craft' (Wiggins 2015: 86).

24 For critiques of the theatricality/narrativity distinction in readings of Smith, see Rosenthal (2016: 126); and Marsden (2019: 25). For theatre as repetition and as work, see Ridout (2006: 19–20).

Bibliography

Anon. (1677) *Dissertation sur les tragedies de Phèdre et Hippolyte*, Paris: C. de Sercy.

Aristotle (2013) *Poetics*, (trans.) A. Kenny, Oxford: Oxford University Press.

Aristotle (2016) *Metaphysics*, (trans.) C. D. C. Reeve, Cambridge: Hackett.

Augustine (1961) *Confessions*, (trans.) R. S. Pine-Coffin, London: Penguin.

Brown, V. (2016) 'The Impartial Spectator and Moral Judgment', *Econ Journal Watch*, 13(4): 232–248.

Burke, E. (2015) *A Philosophical Enquiry into the Origin of Our Ideas of the Sublime and Beautiful*, (ed.) P. Guyer, Oxford: Oxford University Press.

Bussom, T. (1922) *A Rival of Racine: Pradon, His Life and Dramatic Works*, Paris: Édouard Champion.

Camp, P. (2020) 'The Theatre of Moral Sentiments: Neoclassical Dramaturgy and Adam Smith's Impartial Spectator', *Journal of the History of Ideas*, 81(4): 555–576.

Corneille, P. (1963) *Trois discours sur le Poème dramatique*, (ed.) L. Forestier, Paris: Société d'Édition d'Enseignement Supérieur.

DeJean, J. (1989) *Fictions of Sappho, 1546–1937*, Chicago: University of Chicago University Press.

Descartes, R. (1964) *Les passions de l'âme*, (ed.) G. Rodis-Lewis, Paris: J. Vrin.

Deshoulières, A. and Deshoulières A. T. (1764) *Œuvres de madame et de mademoiselle Deshoulieres*, vol. 1, Paris: Libraires associés.

Ellison, J. (1999) *Cato's Tears and the Making of Anglo-American Emotion,* Chicago: University of Chicago Press.

Freeman, L. (1999) 'What's Love Got to Do with Addison's "Cato"', *Studies in English Literature, 1500–1900*, 39(3): 463–482.
Griswold, C. (1999) *Adam Smith and the Virtues of Enlightenment,* Cambridge: Cambridge University Press.
Hanley, R. P. (2006) 'From Geneva to Glasgow: Rousseau, and Adam Smith on the Theater and Commercial Society', *Studies in Eighteenth-Century Culture*, 35(1): 177–202.
Hume, D. (1882) *The Complete Philosophical Works of David Hume*, vol. 3, (eds.) T. H. Green and T. H. Grose, London: Longmans, Green, and co. Reprinted, Scientia Verlag (1964).
Kopajtic, L. (2020) 'Adam Smith's Sentimentalist Conception of Self-Command', *Adam Smith Review*, 12: 7–27.
Kopajtic, L. (2023) '"Much Better Instructors": Adam Smith and the Role of Literature in Moral Education', in P. Sanger (ed) *Interpreting Adam Smith: Critical Essays*, Cambridge: Cambridge University Press, pp. 194–213.
Kovacs, D. (1980) 'Shame, Pleasure, and Honor in Phaedra's Great Speech (Euripides, Hippolytus 375–87)', *The American Journal of Philology*, 101(3): 287–303.
Marcinkowski, A. (2025) 'Phèdre's Sapphic Speech: Racine's *Phèdre*, Sappho's "Fragment 31," and the Theatrical Sublime', *French Studies*, 79(3): 368–385.
Marsden, J. (2019) *Theatres of Feeling: Affect, Performance, and the Eighteenth-Century Stage*, Cambridge: Cambridge University Press.
Marshall, D. (1984) 'Adam Smith and the Theatricality of Moral Sentiments', *Critical Inquiry*, 10(4): 592–613.
Michel, V. (2023/2) '*Phèdre* et la *Théorie des sentiments moraux* d'Adam Smith. Quelles heuristiques pour une économie morale des comportements?', *Cahiers d'économie politique*, 83: 23–51.
Phillipson, N. (2010) *Adam Smith: An Enlightened Life*, London: Allen Lane.
Plato (1997) '*Theaetetus*', (trans.) M. J. Levett and M. Burnyeat, in J. M. Cooper and D. S. Hutchinson (eds.), *Plato: Complete Works*. Indianapolis: Hackett.
Racine, J. (1999) *Phèdre et Hippolyte*, in G. Forestier (ed.), *Œvres complètes*, vol. 1, Paris: Gallimard.
Rasmussen, D. C. (2023) 'Mutual Sympathy, Hospitals, and Balls: David Hume's Objection to the "Hinge" of Adam Smith's Moral Theory', *The Adam Smith Review*, 13: 46–60.
Reisman, D. (1976) *Adam Smith's Sociological Economics*, New York: Barnes and Noble.
Ridout, N. (2006) *Stage Fright, Animals and Other Theatrical Problems*, Cambridge: Cambridge University Press.
Rosenthal, L. (1999) 'Juba's Roman Soul: Addison's *Cato* and Enlightenment Cosmopolitanism', *Studies in the Literary Imagination*, 32(2): 63–76.
Rosenthal, L. (2016) 'Adam Smith and the Theatre in Moral Sentiments', in H. Kerr, D. Lemmings and R. Phiddian (eds.), *Passions, Sympathy, and Print Culture: Public Opinion and Emotional Authenticity in Eighteenth-Century Britain*, London: Palgrave Macmillan, pp. 122–141.
Sayer, J. (2006) *Jean Racine: Life and Legend*, Bern: Peter Lang.
Siraki, A. (2010) 'Adam Smith's Solution to the Paradox of Tragedy', *The Adam Smith Review*, 5: 213–230.
Smith, A. (1976) *The Theory of Moral Sentiments*, Glasgow Edition, (eds.) D. D. Raphael and A. L Macfie, Oxford: Oxford University Press. Reprinted, Liberty Press (1982).
Smith, A. (1983) *Lectures on Rhetoric and Belles Lettres*, Glasgow Edition, (ed.) J. C. Bryce, Oxford: Oxford University Press. Reprinted, Liberty Press (1985).
Smith, A. (1977) *Correspondence of Adam Smith*, Glasgow Edition, (eds.) E. C. Mossner and I. S. Ross, Oxford: Oxford University Press. Reprinted, Liberty Press (1987).
Stein, G. (1995) *Last Operas and Plays*, (ed.) C. Vechten, London: John Hopkins University Press.
Stewart, D. (1858) *The Collected Works of Dugald Stewart*, vol. 10, (ed.) W. Hamilton, Edinburgh: Thomas Constable and Co.

Taylor, D. F. (2022) 'What Cato Did: Suicide, Sentimentalism, and the Drama of Emulation', *Eighteenth-Century Life*, 46(1): 56–78.

Tsien, J. (2012) *The Bad Taste of Others: Judging Literary Value in Eighteenth-Century France*, Philadelphia: University of Pennsylvania Press.

Twining, T. (1789) *Aristotle's Treatise on Poetry, Translated: with Notes on the Translation, and on the Original; and Two Dissertations, on Poetical, and Musical, Imitation*, (trans.), London: Payne and Son et al.

Valihora, K. (2016) 'Adam Smith's Narrative Line', in R. P. Hanley (ed.), *Adam Smith: His Life, Thought, and Legacy*, Princeton: Princeton University Press, pp. 405–421.

Vivenza G. (2001) *Adam Smith and the Classics: The Classical Heritage in Adam Smith's Thought*, Oxford: Oxford University Press.

Voltaire. (2004) *Les œuvres complètes de Voltaire*, vol. 3C, (ed.) M. Frayne, Oxford: Voltaire Foundation.

Wiggins, E. (2015) 'Pity Play: Sympathy and Spectatorship in Lessing's Miss Sara Sampson and Adam Smith's Theory of Moral Sentiments', in M. H. Dupree and S. B. Franzel (eds.), *Performing Knowledge, 1750–1850*, Boston: De Gruyter, pp. 85–112.

8 Looking glasses, spectators, and strangers

Individual and social identity in Shaftesbury, Montesquieu, and Adam Smith

Stefano Fiori

Introduction

In the eighteenth century, the notion of individual and social identity was often developed through philosophical metaphors, including those of the 'spectator,' who observes her own and others' behaviours, and of the 'looking glass,' through which such behaviours could be evaluated. Usually, these images were presented in connection with other conceptual metaphors that added new meanings and greater detail to investigations into the psychological, cultural, and social features of the individual. Some of the implicit metaphors include the 'gaze' of an external and/or impartial spectator, of the 'division of self,' and of the 'stranger,' as a spectator who observes, understands and learns the social and cultural habits of other countries. These metaphors are 'implicit' because, although eighteenth-century authors did not explicitly formulate them, they reflect concepts expressed with other terms. Lastly, legal metaphors, such as those of the 'judge' and of the 'tribunal,' identify the spectator as an evaluator of behaviour and the symbolic place where relationships between spectator and actor take shape.

Shaftesbury, Montesquieu, and Smith – the philosophers discussed in this chapter – and, to varying degrees, Addison, Hutcheson, Hume, and Kant all used these figures to conceptualise individual identity.

The idea that metaphors play a conceptual function has been explored in many disciplines, from analytic philosophy to the philosophy of science, from cognitive sciences to neurosciences, and even in economic methodology. Research in this area has been spearheaded by scholars such as Pepper, Richards, Black, Hesse, Boyd, Kuhn, Lakoff, Johnson, and many others. However, in this chapter, I will limit myself to the notion of conceptual metaphor, by which I mean that the development of philosophical concepts can depend on the representation of phenomena provided in the first instance by metaphors.[1] From this perspective, metaphors are used to explore potential theoretical explanations when phenomena are not theoretically defined. This does not mean that they disappear when a theory replaces them, because in many circumstances theories, despite their non-metaphorical language, are a development of underlying (implicit or explicit) metaphors. From this, it follows that metaphors and non-figurative philosophical discourses continuously

DOI: 10.4324/9781003767824-11

and mutually influence each other (see Fiori 2021). This is the case of the concept of the individual and social identity in Shaftesbury, Montesquieu, and Smith.

These topics are organised as follows. The second and third sections show how in Shaftesbury the idea of the division of the self was conveyed through a series of metaphors. The objective of conceiving the unity of the individual's personality paradoxically requires awareness of its division, a condition which denotes an asymmetry between the different components of individual identity. The means of achieving this result, that is, self-recognition by the individual, is metaphorically called 'mirror writing.' The fourth and fifth sections discuss the role of the metaphor of (cultural) distance and of the spectator-stranger in Montesquieu. Moreover, these sections explore how the system of gazes influences the behaviour of some characters and produces a sort of masking. The sixth section compares the mirror metaphor in Hume and Smith and argues that, while Hume emphasises the emotional continuity between the external spectator and the observed person, in Smith the metaphorical argument of discontinuity and distance in moral relationships prevails. The seventh section argues that, according to Smith, discontinuity can also be found in the relationship between the impartial spectator and the agent. The last section provides some concluding remarks.

Metaphors of the divided identity in Shaftesbury[2]

The maxim that Shaftesbury (2000 [1711]: 77) suggested as a rule for self-analysis was 'Recognize yourself!,' the 'celebrated Delphic inscription' that in his view meant 'Divide yourself!' or 'Be two!'[3] To the question 'who can . . . multiply himself into two persons and be his own subject?' he answered:

> Go to the poets. . . . Nothing is more common with them than this sort of *soliloquy*. A person of profound parts . . . *comes alone upon the stage*, looks about him to see if anybody be near, then takes himself to task without sparing himself in the least. You would wonder to hear how close he pushes matters and how thoroughly he carries on the business of *self-dissection*. By virtue of this soliloquy, he becomes *two distinct persons*. He is *pupil and preceptor*.
>
> (Shaftesbury 2000 [1711]: 72, emphasis added)

Shaftesbury (2000 [1711]: 71) implicitly linked the image of psychological 'self-dissection' to 'a case of surgery.' This conveyed the traditional idea that truth is hidden, and to make it visible we must go beyond the surface of things. If our complex identity can be revealed, this 'surgery' can be described as a 'self-dissection' in which an imaginary – but not mentioned – scalpel psychologically divides the individual into 'two distinct persons.' In turn, the imaginary scalpel is identified with 'soliloquy,' a tool whereby the two components of our personality acquire a voice. But, if the two selves present in an individual communicate with each other, then the 'soliloquy' is at the same time a 'dialogue' (see Brown 1994: Chapter 3). Lastly, a further element that connects these images is that the soliloquy ideally is a medical treatment for the *care* of the soul.

The cognitive strategy, expressed by this bundle of metaphors,[4] puts forward the only apparently contradictory idea that splitting the individual is an indispensable step to bring the individual's *divided identity* back to a fully conscious *unity*, as a result of which a person recognises themselves. Identity should be stable, but this condition may be threatened because 'humor and fancy' inconsistently govern the 'will' (Shaftesbury 2000 [1711]: 83). Therefore, there must be a 'formidable' court 'erected in ourselves, if we would pretend to that uniformity of opinion which is necessary to hold us to one will and preserve us in the same mind from one day to another' (Shaftesbury 2000 [1711]: 83–84).

This splitting of the individual also involves two different aspects of the theatrical dimension. One is that self-discovery requires that the individual 'comes alone upon the stage,' where spectators are virtually present. The other is that poets and writers frequently stage self-analysis. With caution, Shaftesbury conceives his role as the author of the *Soliloquy* in these terms:

> Are we to go therefore to the *stage for edification*? Must we learn our catechism from the poets and, like the players, speak aloud what we debate at any time with ourselves alone?' Not absolutely so, perhaps, though where the harm would be of spending some discourse and bestowing a little breath and clear voice purely upon ourselves, I cannot see.
>
> (Shaftesbury 2000 [1711]: 73, emphasis added)

The relationships between the poet and the reader, and between the player and the spectator, span a dual dimension in both the real and psychological spheres.

As for the real dimension, the medical treatment mentioned earlier reflects a relationship between author and reader. Introspective learning represents the care of the soul, where the 'reader' is a 'patient,' and the author is metaphorically a physician (Shaftesbury 2000 [1711]: 84).

As for the psychological dimension, Shaftesbury (2000 [1711]: 73) describes the two components of our personality through metaphorical pairs (see next section). One of them, mentioned earlier, is that of 'pupil and preceptor,' but it is not the only one:

> we could discover a certain duplicity of soul and divide ourselves into two parties.' One of these . . . would immediately approve himself a *venerable sage* and, with an air of *authority*, erect himself *our counsellor and governor* while the other party, who had nothing in him besides what was base and *servile*, would be contented to follow and obey.
>
> (2000 [1711]: 77, emphasis added)

Furthermore, the wise part of our personality plays the role of an 'inspector and auditor,' as a figure 'established within us,' who examines and controls, given their volatility, 'opinions and fantasies' to give stability to the self (Shaftesbury 2000 [1711]: 83). In short, the person's splitting is played out seamlessly on the internal level, that of the divided individual, and on the external level, the one in which the doctor and the author address the patient and the reader.

The looking glass as a tool for 'self-inspection' in Shaftesbury

The idea of individual duality is further developed by the metaphor of writing as a looking glass. Speaking of classical poems and quoting Horace, Shaftesbury (2000 [1711]: 87, emphasis added) maintained: 'We might here, therefore, as in a looking-glass, discover ourselves and *see our minutest features nicely delineated* and suited to our own apprehension and cognizance.'

Once again, writing (exemplarily expressed by classical literature) establishes a relationship between two separate individuals, the writer and the reader, and provides the reader with the tools to discover their dual identity. In this type of text, along with the 'principal character,' 'second characters showed human nature more distinctly' (2000 [1711]: 87). The mirror-work shows the reader (and possibly the spectator) their duality through a realistic representation of human nature. In it

> there were *two faces* which would naturally present themselves to our view: one of them, like the commanding genius, the *leader and chief* above-mentioned; the other like that *rude, undisciplined and headstrong creature* whom we ourselves in our natural capacity most exactly resembled. Whatever we were employed in, whatever we set about, if once we had acquired the *habit of this mirror*, we should, by virtue of the double reflection, distinguish ourselves into two different parties. And in this dramatic method, the work of *self-inspection* would proceed with admirable success.
>
> (2000 [1711]: 87–88, emphasis added)

In the relationships between 'pupil and preceptor,' and between the 'servile' person and the 'counsellor and governor,' the relationship between a 'rude, undisciplined and headstrong creature' and a 'leader and chief' shows an asymmetry between the pairs of figures that constitute the self. This asymmetry has two related features. One is pedagogical, as one component of individual identity (the 'leader and chief' and 'preceptor') suggests, orients, and teaches the other part (the 'servile' component and the 'pupil'). The other is hierarchical, as it represents a leadership with command power over a subordinate party (see Boeker 2018; Kisner 2023). This perspective shows that, with the 'method of soliloquy,' 'the mind [our rational part] apostrophizes its own fancies, raises them in their proper shapes and personages.' It is in accordance with this conceptualisation that the metaphors of the 'court' 'erected within ourselves,' and the 'supreme judge' who goes 'against the heart' are introduced (Shaftesbury 2000 [1711]: 83–84). The self is well organised when a precise hierarchy between its components is established, and an enforcement power is exercised by one (the more rational and informed part) of them. The 'doctrine of two persons' can even be 'thought perhaps little better than persecution' (Shaftesbury 2000 [1711]: 84). However, it is to be hoped that 'this regimen or discipline of the fancies may not in the end prove so severe or mortifying as is imagined' (Shaftesbury 2000 [1711]: 84). Therefore, the metaphors of the 'court' and 'supreme judge' point out a disciplinary attitude of the self. The person must recognise the composite nature of individual identity, but without giving up a control regime that preserves its unity. As will be discussed later, these meanings do not coincide with those that Smith ascribes to the terms 'tribunal' and 'judge.' In Smith's *The Theory of Moral Sentiments* (TMS), both the impartial spectator and external spectator are 'judges,' in that they are more 'examiners' and 'arbiters' (TMS III.i.6: 113, and III.3.5:137) of our own and others' behaviours rather than authorities who impose discipline on the self, although their pedagogical function aims to direct individual behaviours appropriately. Furthermore, while in Shaftesbury the recognition of one's identity is an act of discovering our psychological complexity, self-referentially achieved by the individual, in Smith the individual's self-recognition is chiefly linked to relationships with other individuals. This perspective also emerges in Smith's impartial spectator, the ideal figure present in the agent, who, embodying society's point of view, helps the individual in the process of self-evaluation (see Marshall 1986: 178).

In relation to Shaftesbury, one might ask why we should turn to a moral, literary, and philosophical mirror to perceive the complexity of our identity. Why shouldn't an investigative, direct, slightly more in-depth look be enough? The answer is that the looking glass objectively reproduces all aspects of human personality, without narcissistic distortions. By contrast, direct observation can be distorting. Shaftesbury develops these concepts starting from an analysis of the differing characteristics of ancient and modern literature.

In ancient times, poets were considered wise men and 'well-practised dialogists.' Poetry 'was defined an imitation chiefly of men and manners.' The most representative poet, Homer, portrayed his characters with 'a likeness beyond what any succeeding masters were ever able to describe':

> He describes no qualities or virtues, censures no manners, makes no encomiums nor gives characters himself, but brings his actors still in view. It is they who show themselves.
>
> (Shaftesbury 2000 [1711]: 88)

But this way of proceeding has been abandoned in modern literature. The modern author who 'writes in his own person has the advantage of being who or what he pleases.' He 'suits himself on every occasion to the fancy of his reader.' The adaptation of the modern writer to the taste of the audience reveals a narcissistic attitude of the author and reader/spectator, because '[a]ll turns upon their two persons' (Shaftesbury 2000 [1711]: 89). In particular, 'the coquetry of a modern author' draws 'attention from the subject towards himself' (Shaftesbury 2000 [1711]: 90). By contrast, in classical writings 'there was neither the "I" nor "thou"' (Shaftesbury 2000 [1711]: 90).

The writing of the classics is not self-referential because is a fully imitative 'mirror writing.' This mirror faithfully reproduces, and consequently imitates, the variety of human characteristics, even contradictory ones. There is thus no room for unilateral representations of the individual. In classic dialogue 'the author is annihilated, and the reader, being no way applied to, stands for nobody. The self-interesting parties both vanish at once. The scene presents itself as by chance and undesigned' (Shaftesbury 2000 [1711]: 90). The poet who follows these teachings, as a 'real master,' 'notes the boundaries of the passions and knows their exact tones and measures,' and as a 'moral artist' 'imitate[s] the Creator and is thus knowing in the inward form and structure of his fellow creature' (Shaftesbury 2000 [1711]: 93).

Mirror writing, then, is a tool that makes realistic imitation possible. While modern literature distorts the multiple traits of the human character, the mirror writing of classical works, from which we must draw inspiration, reflects these traits in a realistic, objective way. This aspect is noteworthy in regard to later uses of the mirror metaphor. In Shaftesbury, awareness of subjective identity is achieved by acquiring the complete image of the many aspects of the self. The mirror (i.e. mirror writing) makes visible what, on the contrary, is hidden in the self-referential writing of modern authors. It makes human nature visible in all its facets because, by dissecting it, it enables us to 'discover ourselves and see our minutest feature.' Mirror writing thus correctly reflects the image of how we are. For this reason, it is a non-distortive imitation of reality. In Smith, on the contrary, the mirror that the individual should turn to does not reflect what we are, but what we should be if we looked at ourselves with the eyes of an 'impartial spectator,' that is, with a mirror that represents society's point of view, which helps us evaluate our behaviours. While Shaftesbury investigates self-recognition as a process that occurs internally within the individual, Adam Smith analyses both the mutual, intersubjective recognition between external spectator and agent, and recognition of the agent through the figure of the impartial spectator. From this perspective, Shaftesbury's view of the self, circumscribed within the private dimension, and Smith's view of the self, related to a social dimension, differ significantly (Kisner 2023).

Strangers, spectators, and gazes in Montesquieu's *Persian Letters*

Montesquieu's *Persian Letters* tells the story of two Persians, Usbek and Rica, who, during their visit to Paris and other European towns, maintain an epistolary relationship with people from their world of origin. Through Usbek's and Rica's naïve gazes, Western readers are invited to view the institutions and beliefs of their culture from a distance. The book also explores how the two protagonists relate to their world as they embark on their journey to Europe. If we set aside the effect that the text should have on the reader, the story stages three kinds of gaze. The first is that of the spectator-stranger directed towards the Western life he is experiencing. Here, *physical distance* acts as *cognitive distance*, in that the spectator-stranger, far from his native land and culturally distant from the country in which he is temporarily living, relates to habits and customs that are unusual to him. The second is the perspective that the Persians adopt towards their own country's customs and practices (see next section). This is not the gaze of the spectator-stranger because it does not involve estrangement. The third is the gaze of Westerners as described through the Persians' narrative (see next section).

As for the first perspective, Montesquieu notes that the psychological attitude with which the spectator-stranger classifies other cultures is subject to a general distortion. In a different context, this distortion was highlighted by Montaigne, who described the attitude that civilised societies take towards savages in his *Essays* (Chapter 31, 'On cannibals'):

> [E]very man calls barbarous anything he is not accustomed to; it is indeed the case that we have no other *criterion of truth* or right-reason ['mire de la verité e de la raison'] than the example and form of the opinions and customs of our own country.
>
> (Montaigne 1991: 231, emphasis added)

The origin and error of this judgement are that Western societies project their image, conceptions, and criteria of relevance onto non-Western societies, thus abandoning any attempt to understand these cultures' distinctive features. In the resulting reductionist approach, the known becomes the key (the 'criterion of truth') to understanding the unknown.

Montesquieu reformulates this perspective when he has Rica say in a letter to Usbek: 'It seems to me . . . that we never judge anything without secretly considering it in relation to our own self' (Montesquieu 2008: 78). This behaviour emerges, for example, when 'black men depict the devil as brilliantly white, and their own gods as coal-black' (Montesquieu 2008: 78). Despite the different contexts, both Montaigne (in more negative terms) and Montesquieu describe the human tendency to start from oneself to identify the other and form ideas about unknown, or relatively unknown, objects.[5] This practice is followed, according to Montaigne, by civilised societies and, according to Montesquieu, by 'black men' and 'idolaters,' who attribute to their gods 'their own propensities' (Montesquieu 2008: 78). Lastly, although this approach seems an inevitable way to conceptualise the new, both authors highlight its conceptually misleading consequences in different ways.

The point of view of the spectator-stranger is partial and, as Todorov remarks, Montesquieu seems to adhere to the idea that spectators-strangers formulate 'only particular points of view about truth . . ., not truth as such' (Todorov 1994: 358, see also Harari 1987: 69). The gaze of the Persians serves the *reader* to appropriately observe and judge Western society from a distance, but not the protagonists of the story, as they continue to use their beliefs and opinions to interpret European customs.[6] Therefore, Usbek and Rica remain *partial spectators*, despite the 'epistemological privilege' of being strangers (Todorov 1994: 353). This partiality is related to the fact that Usbek and Rica do not acquire a more comprehensive awareness of themselves from their privileged condition as external observers. Usbek does not cease to be a character whose psychology is embedded in Persian culture, as his relationships with friends, eunuchs, and women of his harem show. This condition leads to the second type of gaze: the gaze that lacks estrangement and, in certain circumstances takes on the character of surveillance.

Rica seems more involved in Western customs than Usbek. This involvement leads to a replacement of the old point of view with a new one, rather than an awareness that would enable him to make a balanced assessment of Eastern and Western cultures. As he confesses to Usbek: 'my mind is gradually shedding what little it still retained of the Oriental' (Montesquieu 2008: 82). Rica's criticism of Persian culture proceeds hand in hand with an appreciation of European customs:

> In Persia, all characters are identical because they are forced; we never see people as they are, but as they are constrained to be; in that enslavement of the heart and mind you hear nothing but the voice of fear. . . . Dissimulation, among us so widespread and so essential an art, is here unknown; all is said, all is seen, all is heard; the heart, like the face, reveals itself; in customs, in virtue, and even in vice, you are always conscious of something artless.
>
> (Montesquieu 2008: 82–83)

However, the transparency of European behaviour is not always perceived. Usbek, unlike Rica, finds European customs obscure:

> my mind has been hard at work for two days, there isn't a single one of these men over whom I haven't been in torment countless times, yet not in a thousand years shall I be able to fathom them; they are more invisible to me than the wives of our great monarch.
>
> (Montesquieu 2008: 59)

The characters in the *Persian Letters* use their journey to gradually familiarise themselves with European culture. In this sense, travel functions as an accelerator of experience. However, Rica and Usbek are different types of travellers: the former integrates more into Western society, while the latter remains more tied to his origins (Romanowski 2005: 49–52). This means that 'the possibility of a unitary subject [is] left behind with the exile' (Romanowski 2005: 50). The '"nous" is also split mainly into [these two figures], . . . but occasionally "nous" refers to several other writers as well' (Romanowski 2005: 50, see also Lloyd 2012).

Cultural distance appears as a necessary but not sufficient condition to formulate a judgement about the other. Rica's point of view tends to become closer to that of Western culture, but this means that the more this process continues, the more the material condition – the strangeness – that engendered his effort to understand the other, tends to disappear. Within certain limits, Montesquieu's idea of *cultural distance* can be compared to the *moral distance* between spectators and actors described by Smith in *The Theory of Moral Sentiments*. Both Montesquieu and Smith, although in different frameworks, respectively suggest that cultural and moral distance among individuals can be reduced. Cultural distance in Montesquieu concerns the differences between individuals that depend on the ways of life, habits and beliefs of their countries of origin. Moral distance in Smith concerns the differences between individuals living in the same society, attributable to their different experiences and positions. Both Smith's spectator and Montesquieu's spectator-stranger show a certain ability to reduce the distance from the observed person. In Smith, this is what spectators and observed persons do when they cooperate to make their sympathetic relationship effective (TMS I.i.4.6: 21, I.i.4.8: 22); in Montesquieu, this is what Rica does.

Camouflage, kinds of gaze, and spectators

Gazes of others can be blocked, diverted, or redirected if the actors disguise themselves. This technique, adopted by Rica, Usbek, and Roxane – one of Usbek's harem wives – reveals much about the functions of gaze.

In letter 28, Rica describes himself not as the one who looks, but as the one who is looked at: 'When I first arrived I was stared at ["regardé"] as if I had been sent from heaven . . . no man has ever been seen as much as me' (Montesquieu 2008: 40). Such attention, resulting from Parisians' superficial curiosity, induced Rica to change his behaviour.

> I . . . resolved to set aside my Persian clothing and dress instead as a European, to see whether anything in my appearance would still astonish. From this test I learnt my true worth: stripped of my exotic finery, I found myself appraised at my real value.
>
> (Montesquieu 2008: 40)

Rica is forced to disguise himself as a European to be 'appraised at [his] real value' ('je me vis apprécié au plus juste'). The Western gaze turned to the Persian is partial and distorted as it does not correctly evaluate a person's qualities. Since being looked at as a stranger has negative implications, Rica disguises himself so that the part of his personality that he deems most worthy of being appreciated is visible. In this game of glances and constructed images, what apparently conceals, that is, disguising oneself as someone one is not, paradoxically reveals what is invisible to Western eyes and, in some respects, even to his own eyes since Rica thereby 'learnt [his] true worth' ('Cet essai me fit connaître ce que je valais réellement').

In another circumstance, changing one's public image can be useful, while showing oneself as we are can be harmful. We can take Usbek's account of his failed attempt to expose vice in his home country as an example: 'I brought truth to the very foot of the throne . . . But when I saw that my sincerity had made me enemies, . . . I determined to leave' (Montesquieu 2008: 11). The metaphorical disguising consists in the fact that, he maintains, 'I *feigned* a deep devotion to the sciences and, by dint of *feigning* it, in fact grew to feel this devotion' (Montesquieu 2008: 11, emphasis added, see also Romanowski 2005: 48–49).[7] From this experience, which initially led him to live in the countryside, the plan to travel to learn 'the sciences of the West' took shape (Romanowski 2005: 48–49).

The case of Roxane is the last example of how to hide from the eyes of others by projecting another image of oneself[8] This behaviour is motivated by the need for self-protection. In this respect, Usbek's initially deceptive behaviour of feigning interest in science is similar to that of Roxane. He protects himself from the envy of ministers and enemies, and Roxane protects herself from repression in the harem. In both situations the two characters hide the real reasons for their public behaviour. Compared to Rica's change in public image, however, there are both analogies and differences. On the one hand, Usbek and Roxane are similar to Rica because, like him, they present themselves as different from what, deep down, they are. On the other hand, while Rica hides his Persian identity to make people appreciate his qualities, Usbek and Roxane project their deceptive image *not to highlight* a particular quality of their personhood, but *to hide* something about themselves. In short, in one case masking hides, and in the other, it brings out our fundamental characteristics.

The nature of gazes can be considered from another perspective, which includes two types of gaze. The first is the cognitive gaze of Usbek and Rica, which compares aspects of Western and Persian civilisations. The second is the surveillance gaze, used by the eunuch, for example, from which one must defend oneself (see Durand-Sendrail 1988: 75). Lastly, unlike Smith, who saw the gaze as favouring a process of mutual attunement among individuals' behaviours as a consequence of being judged with approval or disapproval, in Montesquieu the types of gaze do not produce such a result. They are unidirectional in the sense that Rica and Usbek's cognitive-comparative gaze has effects on them, but not on Westerners, while the eunuch's gaze on Roxane and the other women serves only to exercise power and control over them.[9]

In Montesquieu's, 'Persian Letters,' the readers can aspire to self-recognition, but not the characters in the novel. It is the (Western) reader who becomes aware of Western oddities and, at the same time, the unattractive features of the Persian system. This awareness is not achieved by the protagonists of the *Persian Letters*. Usbek sees himself as a *stranger in a strange land*, but when he governs his harem through eunuchs he is a Persian in his own home. He does not use the estrangement of the journey to reshape his behaviour in the harem. In Montesquieu, there is no division of the self that leads to self-recognition, as there is in Shaftesbury. Although Montesquieu's discourse narrates the stories of Rica and Usbek, it focuses on the comparison between different cultures. Therefore, unlike Shaftesbury, there is no analysis of the divided self. Despite these differences, the two dimensions treated by Shaftesbury and Montesquieu achieve a certain synthesis in Smith. The self is divided, as in Shaftesbury, and analysed in its social dimension, like Montesquieu. However, unlike Montesquieu, Smith does not consider individuals' cultural differences.

Mirrors, real spectators, and actors in Adam Smith and David Hume

Although with different meanings, the mirror and spectator metaphors play a role not only in Shaftesbury but also in David Hume and especially in Adam Smith.

In the *Treatise*, Hume argued that

> the minds of men are *mirrors* to one another, not only because they reflect each other's emotions, but also because those rays of passions, sentiments and opinions may be often reverberated, and may *decay away by insensible degrees*. Thus the pleasure, which a rich man receives from his possessions, being thrown upon the *beholder*, causes a pleasure and esteem; which sentiments again, being perceiv'd and *sympathiz'd* with, encrease the pleasure of the possessor; and being once more reflected, become a new foundation for pleasure and esteem in the beholder.
>
> (Hume 2007 [2.2.6.21]: 236, emphasis added)

These statements are based on a mix of conceptual metaphors. With the metaphor of minds as mirrors, Hume argues that in relating to each other, minds increase the communication of passions. This image develops into the visual metaphor of the reverberating 'rays of passion and feelings.' In turn, the latter tacitly evokes the metaphor of the echo, since the sounds transmitted by the echo, like the rays of light, 'decay away by insensible degrees.' Therefore, the reflection of the other person's emotions not only realises but also enhances the mutual sympathy between the spectator and actor through a chain of effects, where it is 'difficult to distinguish the [original] images and reflections [of the original images], by reason of their faintness and confusion' (Hume 2007 [2.2.6.21]: 236). Lastly, these effects are explained with the metaphorical idea of communication because the transmission that Hume speaks of concerns not only 'passions [and] sentiments' but also 'opinions' (see Broadie 2006: 162).

This sympathetic situation denotes an emotional continuity between the spectator and the agent that Hume conceptualised as a contagious spread of mental states (see, among others, Mercer 1972: 36 and Lenz 2022: 158). This view applies to some 'mental qualities,' like cheerfulness, which 'diffuse a satisfaction on the beholders' and stimulate imitative behaviours in consequence of which 'Others enter into the same humour, and catch the sentiment, by a contagion or natural sympathy' (Hume 1983: 61).

By contrast, in Smith, the relationship between the (real or impartial) spectator and the agent is characterised by *discontinuity*. Regarding the real spectator and the agent, the discontinuity stems from the fact that the real spectator does not have access to the 'immediate experience of what other men feel' (TMS, I.i.x.2: 9) and, for this reason, projects themselves into another person's situation.[10]

Placing ourselves in the other's situation implies that we can only imagine the emotional situation of another person. We can represent and evaluate the passions of the other according to our criteria, but not be the other (see Otteson 2002: 20 and 33–34). The mental state of the other is not communicated immediately by 'contagion,' but is cognitively reconstructed by putting ourselves in the other's shoes and having 'knowledge' of the causes of her psychological situation. Emotions such as 'grief' and 'joy' can be shared if the spectator knows the causes of the emotional condition experienced by the person observed. If we do not possess this knowledge, we have only a 'vague idea of [agent's] misfortune' and 'our fellow-feeling is not very considerable' (TMS, I.i.10.9: 11–12). While Hume seems to maintain that individuals' passions 'reverberate' as an effect of emotional contagion, Smith remarks that the

> passions, upon some occasions, may *seem to be transfused* from one man to another, instantaneously and antecedent to any *knowledge* of what excited them in the person principally concerned. . . . This, however, does not hold universally, or with regard to every passion.
>
> (TMSI.i.x.6–7: 11, emphasis added)

Smith remarks that individuals should communicate and harmonise their mental states through a cognitive process, reducing their moral and emotional discontinuity, a concept that can be interpreted as a reduction of moral 'distance.' He describes the creation of a common ground between the spectator and the agent as follows: 'In order to produce this concord, as nature teaches the spectators to assume the circumstances of the person principally concerned [that is, the agent], so she teaches this last in some measure to assume those of the spectators' (TMS, I.i.4.8: 22, see also I.i.5.1: 23).

The distance metaphor is a metaphor in which the cognitive dimension is conceptualised as a physical dimension. In the fourth section, I noted that Smith's concept of moral distance and Montesquieu's concept of cultural distance are comparable because they both highlight cognitive issues and provide theoretical arguments for a moral and cultural uniformity of individuals who should make an effort to reduce the distances (or discontinuities) between them. But this metaphor also has other theoretical implications. Paradoxically, if the cognitive distance is not only reduced but also finally cancelled, then the condition that allows both self-recognition and recognition of the other is also cancelled. The initial condition of distancing between individuals sets in motion a process that reduces differences. But if this process were fully realised, the requirement that triggered it would disappear. Cognitive distance invites us to look at ourselves from the outside and to be alert, wary of perspectives that are both self-referential (Smith) and based exclusively on one's own culture (Montesquieu). Smith's 'impartial spectator' and Montesquieu's invitation to readers to look at themselves with the Persians' gaze seem to indicate that cognitive distance must always be preserved in order to evaluate others and oneself appropriately. But if differences are reduced to the point of disappearing, and people cease to be spectators and strangers, doesn't cognitive distance itself also disappear? In truth, Smith denies that this happens completely, while Montesquieu is more ambiguous on this point.

Looking glasses, impartial spectators, and judges in Adam Smith

Distance and discontinuity are detectable not only between the agent and the real spectator but also between the agent and the impartial spectator, that is, the 'man within' imaginatively created in the individual mind. Since Smith is clear in establishing a close analogy between the real spectator and the impartial spectator (TMS, III.I.2: 109–110), it comes as no surprise that the cognitive distance also appears in the process of moral self-evaluation, albeit with a difference.[11] In the relationship between the real spectator and the agent, cognitive distance is a consequence of the factual separation of these two distinct figures. However, in the relationship between the impartial spectator and the agent, cognitive distance is not present at the outset. It is mentally constructed through an ideal splitting of the self, where the impartial spectator evaluates the agent's behaviour. In particular, regarding the argument of distance, Smith maintains:

> We can never survey our own sentiments and motives, we can never form any judgment concerning them; unless we remove ourselves, as it were, from our own natural station, and endeavour to view them as at a certain *distance* from us.
>
> (TMS, III.I.1: 110, emphasis added)

As for the topic of the division of the self, he states that in the process of moral self-evaluation: '*I divide myself, as it were, into two persons*; and that I, the *examiner* and *judge*, represent a different character from that other I, the person whose conduct is examined into and judged of' (TMS, III.I.6: 113; emphasis added).

In the second and third sections, I noted that for Shaftesbury, the concept of divided identity is a strategy for the individual to recognise themselves as a composite unit. In Smith, by contrast, the argument of the division of the self serves not to recognise and reconcile the various components of the individual personality in a unitary dimension, but to favour the harmonious relationship between the agent and others. Dividing one's self consists of 'placing ourselves before a looking-glass, or . . . endeavour, as much as possible, to view ourselves at the distance and with the eyes of other people' (TMS, III.I. 4: 112). The figure of the Smithian looking glass is interesting because, unlike a real mirror, the moral mirror does not reproduce an image identical to the original, so the individual does not recognise herself perfectly. It is not the Shaftesburian mirror that faithfully reproduces nuances of our personality, and reflects a correct image of ourselves. Rather, its function is to project an image of ourselves that differs from the one we perceive in its absence, not simply because the mirror reveals details that had escaped our gaze. The problem does not consist in discovering that our identity has a composite structure, as in Shaftesbury, but in observing ourselves with the 'eyes of other people.'[12] Shaftesbury focuses on the process that leads us to become aware of our articulated identity, enabling us to recognise ourselves as we really are. Smith, on the other hand, describes how we relate to others and how this influences our personality by helping us evaluate our behaviour. However, both authors deal with the metaphorical looking glass as a cognitive instrument that allows us to see and, therefore, identify ourselves from a (metaphorical) distance.

Another anomaly arises in the relationship between the impartial spectator and the agent's self in comparison to the relationship between the real spectator and the agent. This can be seen when Smith identifies the 'two persons' who constitute the self:

> The first is the spectator, whose sentiments with regard to my own conduct I endeavour to enter into. . . . The second is the agent, the person whom I properly call myself, and of whose conduct, under the character of a spectator, I was endeavouring to form some opinion.
>
> (TMS, III.I.6: 113)

On the one hand, the self-agent's effort to conform her behaviour to the expectations of an impartial spectator who represents the internalisation of society's point of view is evident. An implication is that, while the real spectator is an individual, the impartial spectator represents a collective rather than an individual point of view. As a consequence, through the impartial spectator, the agent seeks broader recognition than she can obtain from the judgement of a single, real spectator. On the other hand, it is not clear why the impartial spectator, as an expression of the self, should 'endeavour' to identify with the self-agent. The self-agent must already be known to the impartial spectator, as both figures are constitutive elements of the individual mind.[13]

In turn, this has implications for the concept of discontinuity. The discontinuity among real individuals depends on the fact that we have no experience of the feelings of others (TMS, I.i.x.2: 9). But this condition does not apply to processes of self-evaluation, where the impartial spectator, as a projection of the self, is not something different from the agent. Despite this, a discontinuity is also observed in moral self-evaluation processes, which depends on the fact that there is a gap between society's point of view, represented by the impartial spectator, and the agent's point of view about herself that she tries to fill.

This perspective is connected to the metaphor of the spectator-judge. As discussed in the third section, the Smithian spectator (both empirical and impartial) is a peculiar 'judge.' He does not impose punishments, but evaluates and examines behaviours. As such, his function for the agent is more pedagogical than sanctioning. This happens, for example, when a child is induced to correct his behaviour by the reaction of his peers (TMS, III.3.22: 145). However, the judge is a metaphor that, in Smith, reveals an asymmetry. It denotes a power of the spectator over the person observed or over one's identity as an observed agent, although these figures cannot be said to be defendants. While Shaftesbury describes the asymmetry between the components of the personality as a hierarchy in which the rational part of the self should exercise command over the other parts, Smith's asymmetry consists of the fact that the spectator can play the role of examiner of the agent's behaviour. But exercising moral evaluation and, in the case of the impartial spectator, providing a tool whereby the agent's behaviour can be reoriented, are not the same as exercising command.[14]

Conclusion

According to Mark Johnson (2008: 44), 'our abstract concepts are defined by conceptual metaphor and metonymy.' This view seems applicable to the works of Shaftesbury, Montesquieu and Adam Smith, where some crucial concepts show a metaphorical origin. Terms used explicitly, such as 'mirror,' 'distance,' 'spectator,' or used implicitly, such as 'division of the self,' 'stranger,' and 'gaze,' are conceptual metaphors that determine a network of meanings in each of these authors' theories.

Smith is the most philosophically refined of the three authors. Shaftesbury's text is mostly evocative, while Montesquieu's, partly because of its epistolary form, does not extract explicit theoretical statements from the storytelling. Furthermore, there are theoretical views in *The Theory of Moral Sentiments* that make a comparison with the approaches of Shaftesbury and Montesquieu pertinent, although the latter two authors have little in common. Despite analytical differences, the metaphors of the division of the self, the mirror, and the court are used by Smith and Shaftesbury, while the metaphors of the mirror, the spectator and the gaze are used by Smith and Montesquieu. Lastly, Smith's approach has another merit. Within a unitary conception, it analyses the dimensions of both individual identity, as Shaftesbury does, and the relationship between individuals, as Montesquieu does, although Smith does not investigate how cultural differences influence personal identities.

Notes

1 Lakoff and Johnson give the expression 'conceptual metaphor' a broader meaning than I do in this work, which examines only philosophical texts. The two authors consider the multiple manifestations of metaphor as categorisations (which may also be non-linguistic) of reality, resulting from the fact that the mind is 'embodied.'

2 Some scholars have examined the problem of personal identity in Shaftesbury from other perspectives than that taken here. Purviance (2004) argued that Shaftesbury conceives of the self as a 'set of practices.' Jaffro (2008), considering the public and private sides of the self, showed the relevance of the Stoic model in Shaftesbury. According to Winkler (2000), Shaftesbury was a critic of Locke. In dealing with this topic he renounced a metaphysical approach in favor of an appeal to ethics or practice. Ruth Boeker (2018) has argued that the 'metaphysical' problem of personal identity in Shaftesbury is closely related to the problem of 'necessary and sufficient conditions' that 'make a person the same over time.' Therefore, his 'approach to persons has a developmental dimension.'

3 For a helpful general analysis of Shaftesbury's views, particularly on sympathy, see Lobis (2015: Chapter 5). See also Barton (2020: Chapter 2) and Maurer (2020: Chapter 2).

4 Adam Smith, in the *Lectures on Rhetoric and Belles Lettres* (LRBL i.13: 8), maintained that Shaftesbury made excessive use of metaphors and that this greatly limited the clarity of his discourse.

5 This argument is taken up by Smith, who maintains 'Every faculty in one man is the measure by which he judges of the like faculty in another. I judge of your sight by my sight, of your ear by my ear, of your reason by my reason, of your resentment by my resentment, of your love by my love. I neither have, nor can have, any other way of judging about them' (TMS, I.i.3.10: 19).

6 Todorov (1994: 353) points out that this occurs in many circumstances, for example, when the Persians conceive of priests as dervishes.

7 I replaced the words 'affected' and 'affecting' used by the English translator with the words 'feign' and 'feigning,' which more effectively convey the idea of disguising and self-concealment. The French text is as follows: 'Je feignis un grand attachement pour le sciences; et, à force de le feindre, il me vint réellement' (Montesquieu 1973: 60–61). Usbek states that initially he wanted to unmask vice (Montesquieu 2008: 11), and Starobinski (1973: 27) argues that Usbek is an enemy of disguising but, as we have seen, he disguises himself, even if only to defend himself.

8 Solim, the last eunuch who surveils and punishes the women of Usbek's harem, initially writes 'Roxane alone remains dutiful and behaves with decorum' (Starobinski 1973: 208). But Roxane will reveal in her last letter that she has deceived Usbek and 'seduit' the eunuchs.

9 Lefter (2008) observes that games of looks in the *Persian Letters* are included in the theatrical framework of the actor-spectator relationship.

10 On this topic, see Darwall (1998), Fleischacker (2019: Chapters 1 and 2); Frazer (2010: 97–100), Lecaldano (2013).

11 For a reconstruction of the concept of impartial spectator through the different editions of *The Theory of Moral Sentiments*, see Raphael (2007: Chapter 5).

12 The recurring concept of the gaze introduces the metaphor of the spectator and the spectacle. In this respect, by following Marshall (1986), Griswold (1999: 64) examines the spectator/agent relationship in light of the metaphor of the theater: 'Smith compares human life to spectacles represented in plays, and the phenomenology of the book is oriented around a spectator-actor dichotomy.'

13 As Broadie (2006: 182) points out: 'The impartial spectator as a creature of a person's imagination has no more (nor less) information about what is to be judged than the agent, for the creature cannot be better informed than its creator.'

14 Forman-Barzilai (2010: 171–175) disagrees with Griswold's argument that an asymmetry between spectator and agent is present in Smith, because the spectator's standpoint has 'normative superiority.' However, she recognizes that spectators 'have extraordinary

power in Smith's theory to motivate conformity' (Forman-Barzilai 2010: 173, note 160). In my opinion, the distinction between the power to exercise command and the power to evaluate morally explains how the latter highlights the asymmetry between spectator and agent in Smith.

References

Barton, R. A. (2020) *The Making of the Sympathetic Imagination. Transformations of Sympathy in British Eighteenth-Century Philosophy and Fiction*. Berlin: De Gruyter.

Boeker, R. (2018) 'Shaftesbury on Persons, Personal Identity and Character Development', *Philosophy Compass*, 13(1): e12471. https://doi.org/10.1111/phc3.12471

Broadie, A. (2006) 'Sympathy and the Impartial Spectator', in K. Haakonssen (ed.) *The Cambridge Companion to Adam Smith*. Cambridge: Cambridge University Press, pp. 112–135.

Brown, V. (1994) *Adam Smith's Discourse: Canonicity, Commerce and Conscience*. London and New York: Routledge.

Darwall, S. (1998) 'Empathy, Sympathy, Care', *Philosophical Studies*, 89(2–3): 261–282.

Durand-Sendrail, B. (1988) '*Mirage des Lumières: politique du regard dans les* Lettres persanes', *L'Esprit Créateur*, 28(4): 69–81.

Fiori, S. (2021) *Machines, Bodies and Invisible Hands: Metaphors of Order and Economic Theory in Adam Smith*. Palgrave Macmillan.

Fleischacker, S. (2019) *Being Me Being You: Adam Smith and Empathy*. Chicago and London: The University of Chicago Press.

Forman-Barzilai, F. (2010) *Adam Smith and the Circles of Sympathy: Cosmopolitanism and Moral Theory*. Cambridge: Cambridge University Press.

Frazer, M. L. (2010) *The Enlightenment of Sympathy: Justice and the Moral Sentiments in the Eighteenth Century and Today*. Oxford: Oxford University Press.

Griswold, C. L. Jr. (1999) *Adam Smith and the Virtues of Enlightenment*. Cambridge: Cambridge University Press.

Harari, J. V. (1987) *Scenarios of the Imaginary: Theorizing the French Enlightenment*. Ithaca and London: Cornell University Press.

Hume, D. (1983) *An Enquiry Concerning the Principles of Morals*. Cambridge: Hackett Publishing.

Hume, D. (2007) *A Treatise of Human Nature*, (eds.) D. F. Norton and M. J. Norton, Vol. 1. Oxford: Clarendon Press.

Jaffro, L. (2008) 'Shaftesbury on the "Natural Secretion" and Philosophical Personae', *Intellectual History Review*, 18(3): 349–359.

Johnson, M. (2008) 'Philosophy's Debt to Metaphor', in R. W. Gibbs Jr. (ed.) *The Cambridge Handbook of Metaphor and Thought*. Cambridge: Cambridge University Press, pp. 39–52.

Kisner, M. J. (2023) 'Shaftesbury's Distinctive Sentiments: Moral Sentiments and Self-Governance', *Archiv für Geschichte der Philosophie*. https://doi.org/10.1515/agph-2022-0061

Lecaldano, E. (2013) *Simpatia*. Milano: Raffaello Cortina.

Lefter, D-A. (2008) 'Spectateur vs. acteur. La séduction de l'ethnocentrisme ou de l'exotisme? La lettre xxx des Lettres Persanes de Montesquieu', *Studii şi cercetari filologice. Seria limbi romanice*, 3: 20–30.

Lenz, M. (2022) *Socializing Minds. Intersubjectivity in Early Modern Philosophy*. Oxford: Oxford University Press.

Lloyd, G. (2012) 'Imagining Difference: Cosmopolitanism in Montesquieu's Persian Letters', *Constellation,* 19(3): 480–493.

Lobis, S. (2015) *The Virtue of Sympathy: Magic, Philosophy, and Literature in Seventeenth-Century England*. London: Yale University Press.

Marshall, D. (1986) *The Figure of Theatre: Shaftesbury, Defoe, Adam Smith and George Eliot*. New York: Columbia University Press.

Maurer, C. (2020) *Self-Love, Egoism and the Selfish Hypothesis: Key Debates from Eighteenth-Century British Moral Philosophy*. Edinburgh: Edinburgh University Press.

Mercer, P. (1972) *Sympathy and Ethics: A Study of the Relationship between Sympathy and Morality with Special Reference to Hume's Treatise*. Oxford: Clarendon Press.

Montaigne, M. (1991) *Complete Essays*, (ed.) M. A. Screech. London: Penguin.

Montesquieu. (1973) *Lettres persanes*, Préface de Jean Starobinski. Paris: Gallimard.

Montesquieu. (2008) *Persian Letters*, (ed.) A. Kahn. Oxford: Oxford University Press.

Otteson, J. R. (2002) *Adam Smith's Marketplace of Life*. Cambridge: Cambridge University Press.

Purviance, S. M. (2004) 'Shaftesbury on Self as a Practice', *Journal of Scottish Philosophy*, 2(2): 154–163. https://doi.org/10.3366/jsp.2004.2.2.154

Raphael, D. D. (2007) *The Impartial Spectator: Adam Smith's Moral Philosophy*. Oxford: Clarendon Press.

Romanowski, S. (2005) *Through Strangers' Eyes: Fictional Foreigners in Old Regime France*, West Lafayette, IN: Purdue University Press.

Shaftesbury, Third Earl of. (2000 [1711]) 'Soliloquy, or Advice to an Author', in L. E. Klein (ed.) *Characteristics of Men, Manners, Opinions, Times*. Cambridge: Cambridge University Press, pp. 70–162.

Smith, A. (1984) *The Theory of Moral Sentiments*, (eds.) D. D. Raphael and A. L. Macfie. Indianapolis: Liberty Fund.

Smith, A. (1985) 'Lectures on Rhetoric and Belles Lettres', in J. C. Bryce (ed.) *The Glasgow Edition of the Works and Correspondence of Adam Smith*, Vol. IV. Indianapolis: Liberty Fund.

Starobinski, J. (1973) *Préface to Montesquieu, Lettres persanes*. Paris: Gallimard, pp. 7–40.

Todorov, T. (1994) *On Human Diversity: Nationalism, Racism, and Exoticism in French Thought*. Cambridge, MA: Harvard University Press.

Winkler, K. P. (2000) '"All Is Revolution in Us": Personal Identity in Shaftesbury and Hume', *Hume Studies*, 26(1): 3–40. https://doi.org/10.1353/hms.2011.0311

9 Aspiration in Adam Smith's virtue ethics

Brennan McDavid

> The wise seek the virtues with nature's guidance, while people who are imperfect but endowed with outstanding abilities are often motivated by honour, which has the appearance and image of morality. Morality itself, though, is in every way perfect and complete, a single object of absolute splendour, the most glorious of all things. If only they could gaze upon it directly, how joyously these people would embrace it, given the delight they take in a shadowy impression!
>
> Cicero, *On Moral Ends* V.69[1]

Introduction

The characterisation of Adam Smith as a virtue ethicist is not without controversy. Though virtue is undeniably present and prominent in the *Theory of Moral Sentiments*, the part that examines virtue most closely – Part VI, entitled 'Of the Character of Virtue' – was added by Smith only in the final version and, so it may be thought, as a remnant of his moral theory rather than its starting point. Many scholars embrace Smith's preoccupation with clarifying his conception of virtue in that part of the text as a sign that he is consciously perpetuating the virtue ethical programme of the ancients.[2] Others take the account of virtue to be sufficiently peripheral to his moral theory that they can reconstruct his view with little reference to it at all.[3] Still others argue that Smith self-consciously seeks to reconcile ancient and modern ethical sensibilities, with the result that he cannot be neatly categorised.[4]

What determines whether a moral theory is virtuous or ethical? This is the question that stands prior to any effort at categorising Smith's theory, and it is nearly intractable due to the variations observed in virtue ethical theories both ancient and modern. Even though the ancient philosophical schools agreed about the centrality of virtue in the good life, they disagreed about both the nature of virtue and how many virtues there are. Plato thought there were four cardinal virtues (at least, that is the view presented in the *Republic*, but we should wonder at the importance of piety in *Euthyphro*), while Aristotle generates a taxonomy of intellectual and character virtues that enumerates perhaps 12 character virtues, or maybe 11, and five intellectual virtues, but maybe only two really count.[5] The Stoics introduced further variation when they reduced all excellence to a single virtue: the perfection of reason.[6] Perhaps surprisingly, even those hedonistic Epicureans were committed

DOI: 10.4324/9781003767824-12

virtue ethicists, differing from the other philosophical schools only by way of conceiving of virtue as a *means* rather than an end of the good life.[7] These few examples demonstrate that we cannot look to the list of virtues in a given moral theory to determine its virtue ethical bonafides, nor to the way virtue figures as a means or end, or as necessary or otherwise.

What all virtue ethical theories do have in common, however, is a special kind of aspiration that marks the virtuous world view. That is, virtue ethics is premised on the idea that virtue endows individuals with a particular way of understanding and valuing the world and their relationship to it. It is the perspective marked by Cicero in the epigraph to this chapter: the joyous direct gaze upon morality and corresponding seeking of virtue with nature as a guide.[8] This value orientation varies from one system to the next in its substance – certainly the virtuous Epicurean does not value what the Stoic Sage values – but what is common to all is that it fundamentally involves aspiring to something distinct from and better than one's existing moral dispositions and circumstances. Virtue makes people desire what is really good and to be it, and any system of ethics that does not or cannot hold space for this special kind of aspiration ought not to be considered virtue ethical. Without it, Adam Smith's moral theory will not be a virtue ethics either.

Prima facie, it is easy to locate this desire in Smith's theory. When he says that 'man naturally desires, not only to be loved, but to be lovely,' Smith identifies a psychological mechanism by which we seek real moral correctness, beyond mere appearance (TMS III.ii.1). 'He desires,' Smith continues, 'not only praise, but praise-worthiness; or to be that thing which, though it should be praised by nobody, is, however, the natural and proper object of praise' (TMS III.ii.1). Many scholars have considered the notion of loving praiseworthiness as the touchstone of aspiration in Smith's work.[9] But others have doubted the power of a desire 'to be really fit' to propel individuals beyond parochial moral values and viewpoints (TMS III.ii.6; 117). This suspicion is stirred by the fact that Smith anchors our desire to be good to the examples of excellence that we directly observe in our communities.

> The love and admiration which we naturally conceive for those whose character and conduct we approve of, necessarily dispose us to desire to become ourselves the objects of the like agreeable sentiments, and to be as amiable and as admirable as those whom we love and admire the most. Emulation, the anxious desire that we ourselves should excel, is originally found in our admiration of the excellence of others. We must at least believe ourselves to be admirable for what they are admirable.
>
> (III.ii.3; 114)

If the living embodiment of moral excellence fully informs our conception of virtue and its desirability, then we will be limited in our moral aspirations to the degree of excellence exhibited in the examples we admire.[10]

This complaint is both well-founded and serious. The former because Smith does conceive of morality as being generated by a process of reciprocal sympathetic responses that is intersubjective and renders morality 'a matter of socialization.'[11]

And the latter because Smith's theory of virtue and concomitant virtue ethics suffers from an underpowered account of aspiration.

The task of defending Smith's program against the charge of parochialism has rightly sustained attention among scholars, then.[12] In my view, showing that his moral theory, inclusive of sentimentalist psychology, can accommodate a kind of moral aspiration that escapes parochialism is essential to rescuing the moral theory. That rescue has been adequately executed, I think, and a rest from the contest is well-deserved by the defenders. However, also in my view, a different spectre of inadequate aspiration has been looming just beyond the gaze of scholars. Smith's fully developed moral agent may rise to a 'transethical horizon' unbound by the parochial sentiments of his fellows, but can he find himself reoriented specifically by the values proper to the virtuous world view? That is, can Smith's moral theory make sense of the distinctively virtue ethical kind of aspiration?

This study proposes to conduct a test to determine Smith's virtue ethical commitments. The test is perhaps simple in scope: to discern a particular type of aspiration in his work, namely the aspiration characteristic of virtue. But first the test itself must be shown to be revelatory. Thus, in the second section, I begin by documenting that this 'aspiration of virtue' is indispensable to any program in virtue ethics that is worth the name. In the third section, I turn to the hard work of looking into Smith's texts for the purpose of carrying out the test. Many scholars have denied that aspiration can be accommodated by a theory that describes human beings as bound by sympathy, desire for approval, and an imaginative power that is itself limited to the finite range of our experiences. Smith's moral theory seems to be poor soil for the aspiration of virtue, then, and a poor candidate for a virtue ethics. In the fourth section, I argue that the very particular brand of longing for something greater that marks the moral exemplars of ancient ethics is discernible in Smith, and in the fifth section I briefly consider an objection. My verdict is that his ethics is a virtue ethics.

Aspiration in virtue ethics

Virtue ethical theories posit a particular kind of aspiration that is the exclusive province of virtue. It bears a likeness to Smith's concept of the desire 'to be really fit,' but whereas that desire is common, virtue ethical aspiration is exceptional. Only individuals possessed of some genuine understanding of what it is to be really fit are in a position to aspire to fitness in the virtuous way, that is, to desire it for what it is. It is one thing to have a raw – that is, uneducated – and perhaps innate impulse to be an authentic version of what wins praise, but it is quite another to set clear eyes on that object, to understand the difficulties and costs of achieving it, and to strive for it with not less, but greater passion. It is this informed, purposive, and more inflamed drive to attain virtue that constitutes moral aspiration in history's great virtue ethical programmes.

For Aristotle, individuals are ready for serious ethical reasoning only once they have acquired what he calls the 'starting points' of ethics (*NE* 1.3). These are 'good habits,' the propensities to take pleasure in the right things, pain in the wrong, and basically to believe that good things are good and bad things are bad.[13] These beliefs and dispositions are not inborn but are acquired via habituation, as Aristotle explains (*NE* 2.1). Moral development requires not just an initial dispositional orientation to the good but a trained and acquired orientation that transforms our basic desires and becomes the compelling reason to make further progress.

In Stoicism, motivation to pursue virtue and mould oneself in likeness to the Sage is derived from a rational understanding of what is good, bad, and indifferent to our flourishing. We develop, the Stoics argue, via a process called *oikeiosis,* which naturally orients us, from birth through to adulthood, towards what is proper to us and necessary for our self-preservation.[14] Orientation to virtue is not set at birth. It requires the development of rational capacities that, once possessed, enable us to make purposeful movements towards wisdom and virtue. Reason endows us with the ability to aspire, and as we exercise reason and increase our understanding, we aspire even more.

Modern iterations of virtue ethics, indebted as they are to the Aristotelian and Stoic models, prominently feature this specifically virtue ethical aspiration. McDowell, in arguing that moral development delivers us to a special appreciation of what is salient in ethical situations, proposes that 'it is highly implausible that all the concerns which motivate virtuous actions are intelligible, one by one, independently of appreciating a virtuous person's distinctive way of seeing situations.'[15] The motivations of virtuous individuals are inaccessible from outside the virtuous perspective. For McDowell, the 'concerns which motivate' are primarily derived from 'perceptions of saliences,' that is, the recognition that specific details of a situation are considered reasons for acting in a certain way in response.[16] If virtue consists primarily in being sensitive to saliences as reasons, then virtue fosters a unique aspiration by giving the virtuous person unique insight into why such sensitivity is desirable. She desires it strongly because she understands the value of desiring it.

Julia Annas, in building her profile of the virtuous person, conveys a similar notion of global transformation when she says of her conception of virtue that it 'gives a life what we can call a positive directionality.'[17]

> The life is pointed in a positive direction by the fact that the aims and values the person pursues form a whole which is marked by absence of conflict and increasing cooperation of the sources of energy. This is not like the kind of direction given to a life by the exclusive pursuit of money, say, or of fame. The kind of direction given to a life by virtue is a direction of overall aim in the *way the life is lived* – in the aim to live well, to live a good life – not a direction given by a specific objective such as wealth or fame, which can be pursued either virtuously or viciously.[18]

What makes the virtuous person proceed along this positive direction is what Annas calls the 'drive to aspire,' which comprises three desires: (i) the need to understand, (ii) the desire to be self-directing, and (iii) the eagerness to improve.[19] The drive to aspire belongs to the 'learner,' Annas says. But it is clear also that the person possessed of these elements of aspiration is someone already meaningfully on the road, not the person who is deciding whether to pursue wealth or fame or the life of virtue. The drive to aspire is a uniquely virtuous aspiration.[20]

With these examples from the history of virtue ethics in mind, I propose that we should investigate Adam Smith for signs of a similar commitment to virtue's transformational power. Does Smith conceive of virtue as the virtue ethicists do, not only as a disposition to be good but also as founding a unique value orientation and aspiration to become better?

Identifying aspiration in the *Theory of Moral Sentiments*

We see the materials of an account of aspiration in multiple and disjoint passages in Smith's *Theory of Moral Sentiments*. The *locus classicus,* and by far most often appealed to, is the TMS III distinction, referred to in my introduction above, between the 'love of praise' and the 'love of praiseworthiness.'

> Man naturally desires, not only to be loved, but to be lovely; or to be that thing which is the natural and proper object of love. He naturally dreads, not only to be hated, but to be hateful; or to be that thing which is the natural and proper object of hatred. He desires, not only praise, but praiseworthiness; or to be that thing which, though it should be praised by nobody, is, however, the natural and proper object of praise. He dreads, not only blame, but blameworthiness; or to be that thing which, though it should be blamed by nobody, is, however, the natural and proper object of blame.
>
> (TMS III.ii.1; 113)

Scholars have recognised that Smith appears to be responding to Mandeville with this observation.[21] Where Mandeville had provocatively and cynically asserted that human beings are motivated in all their actions by either vanity or a desire to win approval and praise, Smith counters that people are sensitive to the distinction between mere praise and praiseworthiness and that the 'love of praise seems, at least in a great measure, to be derived from that of praiseworthiness' (TMS III.ii.3; 114). By endowing human beings with this 'distinct and independent' principle of action, nature has equipped us with the capacity to pursue virtue for its own sake, rather than as a means to other ends.[22]

This love of praiseworthiness is recognised by Smith as belonging to us by nature. He must have in mind that we are possessed of an innate or at least intuitive sense of the difference between the condition of receiving praise and the condition of being worthy. This is not yet to say that we possess any innate conception of the substance of such conditions, however. We arrive at moral beliefs, on Smith's view, through social interactions.[23] But the desires that direct us through those interactions are nevertheless minted in two kinds: the desire to secure approval, which comes to be informed by an understanding of what in fact secures such approval, and the desire to be worthy of approval, which will – or *can* – also come to be informed by an understanding of what *in fact* is so worthy.

In distinguishing these two fundamental desires, Smith has not yet isolated a uniquely virtue ethical form of aspiration for two reasons, then: (1) the love of praiseworthiness belongs to everyone by nature, which precludes the possibility that it is a characteristic of excellence, and (2) the love of praiseworthiness itself lacks the content that is definitive of virtue ethical aspiration, namely, the accounts of what is and what is not in fact worthy.[24] Nonetheless, the love of praiseworthiness must be the psychological capacity upon which aspiration is built. Specifically, this desire is a match for Aristotle's conception of a natural orientation to the good (a potentiality) that stands in need of actualisation before it can be correctly described as good in itself.[25] The aspiration we are looking for is the informed and transformed capacity for desiring to be worthy, for that is the virtue ethical aspiration shaped by a value orientation accessible only from *inside* the virtuous condition. These other desires are available outside of that condition.

There are two other passages in which Smith asserts distinctions that are *prima facie* similar to the love of praise and of praiseworthiness distinction. The first is in TMS I, where he identifies 'two different characters' of success:

> To deserve, to acquire, and to enjoy the respect and admiration of mankind, are the great objects of ambition and emulation. Two different roads are presented to us, equally leading to the attainment of this so much desired object; the one, by the study of wisdom and the practice of virtue; the other, by the acquisition of wealth and greatness. Two different characters are presented to our emulation; the one, of proud ambition and ostentatious avidity. the other, of humble modesty and equitable justice. Two different models, two different pictures, are held out to us, according to which we may fashion our own character and behaviour.
>
> (TMS I.iii.3.2)

These 'two different models, two different pictures' are, unlike the two fundamental desires discussed earlier, substantial and content-filled. The two models perform the same function as one another: presenting somewhat determinate 'models' according to which we can 'fashion our own character.' They are distinct insofar as they aspire to widely different values, one to wisdom and virtue and the other to worldly success.

The second passage asserting a similar distinction occurs in TMS VI, which is understood to contain and represent Smith's final reflections on moral theory and, therefore, to represent his considered view.[26]

> In estimating our own merit, in judging of our own character and conduct, there are two different standards to which we naturally compare them. The one is the idea of exact propriety and perfection, so far as we are each of us capable of comprehending that idea. The other is that degree of approximation to this idea which is commonly attained in the world, and which the greater part of our friends and companions, of our rivals and competitors, may have actually arrived at. We very seldom (I am disposed to think, we

> never) attempt to judge of ourselves without giving more or less attention to both these different standards. But the attention of different men, and even of the same man at different times, is often very unequally divided between them; and is sometimes principally directed towards the one, and sometimes towards the other.
>
> (TMS VI.iii.23; 247)

Here Smith outlines 'two different standards' for self-assessment. Perhaps these are also 'models' for fashioning our character and conduct, as the 'two different characters' of TMS I are, but Smith is interested here in accounting for the process of exercising 'judg[ment] of ourselves' much more than in the process of forming our characters.[27]

Now, when we consider all three of these distinctions together – the two fundamental desires (TMS III), the two different characters (TMS I), and two different standards (TMS VI) – we might initially think that they offer pairwise comparisons reducible to one another. Because all three mark out a propensity to reach for moral excellence, it might seem that an orientation towards moral excellence – conceived as moral aspiration – is being contrasted with a non-aspirational orientation or at least a non-moral aspiration. After all, the love of praiseworthiness, the pursuit of wisdom and virtue, and the comparison of self to 'exact propriety and perfection' appear to coincide.

But the claims of these texts defy reduction for two reasons: first, the 'two different models, two different pictures' of TMS I and the 'two different standards' of TMS VI are each and all considered praiseworthy. The model of wisdom and virtue contrasts with the model of worldly riches not because the former is praiseworthy while the latter is merely praised, but because they are 'equal' by quite 'different roads' to deserving – and acquiring, and enjoying – the admiration of our fellows. Likewise, the standard of perfect propriety contrasts with the 'degree of approximation . . . commonly attained in the world' not because the former is praiseworthy while the latter is merely praised, but because one is an unachievable – by Smith's lights – ideal while the other is an achievable – and commonly achieved – non-ideal. These distinctions cannot be reduced to the distinction between love of praise and praiseworthiness, then.

Second, pertaining particularly to the TMS VI distinction, Smith recognises that 'we very seldom (I am disposed to think, we never) attempt to judge of ourselves without giving more or less attention to both these different standards,' but 'the wise and virtuous man directs his principal attention to the first standard' (VI.iii.23 and 25).[28] Smith here is saying that we consult both standards in each instance of judgement, which entails that they are not appealed to one at a time, dependent upon the dimension of life – whether moral or worldly – that is under scrutiny. Rather, he sets out two standards that are consulted in judgement of ourselves in relation to the same dimension, and it is clear from the mention of perfect propriety and the wise man's inclination to prioritise that standard, that the dimension in question is moral. There is complexity in our conception of success in the moral domain, Smith observes. We consult two different standards, in accordance with ideal and non-ideal expectations. But both standards are moral standards, and both standards are informed by models of moral excellence, that is, the first of the 'two different characters' in the TMS I distinction.

This reveals that it is moral aspiration itself that is differentiated in TMS VI rather than only *aspirational* motivation from *nonaspirational* motivation. Indeed, we can see now that there are three very different distinctions being made across these passages: the first alone marks out *nonaspirational* desire from aspirational desire; the second distinguishes moral aspiration from secular or worldly aspiration; and the third dissects moral aspiration itself and differentiates it. For this reason, I believe the TMS VI passage is the choicest of these texts for considering Smith's conception of aspiration and his theory's ability to accommodate a particularly virtue ethical aspiration. If virtuous aspiration is to be found anywhere, it is here in the longing for perfect propriety.

Standards of moral aspiration

I have argued that there are several kinds of aspiration on display in Smith's moral theory, but the aspiration to perfect propriety is the most likely site of virtue ethical aspiration. After all, Smith does say that 'the wise and virtuous man directs his principal attention to the first standard' (VI.iii.25). However, isolating the particular aspiration of virtue ethics is not a simple matter of picking out the target that is ('principally') aimed at by the virtuous person. The aiming must also take a certain form: the standard of perfect propriety must be desired in a way that motivates deeply transformative self-improvement. It must shift the value orientation of the aspirant and give her access to moral reasons and understanding that are unavailable to her from outside that perspective. Recall that Annas analyses the relevant motivation – what she calls the 'drive to aspire' – into three elements: (i) the need to understand, (ii) the desire to be self-directing, and (iii) the eagerness to improve. If Smith's wise and virtuous person is possessed of this kind of motivation, then we will have located virtue ethical aspiration in his theory.

The issue is not straightforward. We may infer that Smith's 'wise and virtuous man' exhibits these characteristics of aspiration through the direction of attention to perfect propriety, as such direction of attention would seem to constitute all dimensions of a drive to aspire. But we must make this picture of directed attention comply with the dimension of Smith's ethics that tethers moral motivation to the judgement of the impartial spectator. Smith introduces the concept of the impartial spectator in Part III of the TMS, where he aims to account for the 'origin and foundation' of our judgements of our own conduct and sentiments (III.1.1). We judge the conduct of others in accordance with our ability to sympathise with the sentiments we imagine motivated the conduct, so we judge our own conduct by imaginatively positing an observer of ourselves and consulting their sympathy or lack of sympathy with our sentiments (III.1.2). This imagined judge is 'impartial' in the sense that he does not have any personal stake in the sentiments or conduct under judgement, but we ourselves are scarcely impartial about being judged favourably. We are anxious to win his approval – even more than we are anxious to win the approval of our peers, for we imagine this impartial spectator to be fair and just, so our desire to be praiseworthy is inflamed through consulting his judgement. Thus, through the mechanism of imagining the judgement of this impartial spectator, we are able to abstract away from our personal stake in an issue in order to exercise disinterested self-evaluation even while being motivated to win a favourable evaluation.[29]

These two dimensions of Smith's theory – the standard of perfect propriety and the judgement of the impartial spectator – are difficult to reconcile. The first is a normative ideal that Smith represents as being desirable for its own sake, not for the sake of winning approval. The latter incentivises modifying conduct and sentiment towards virtue for the sake of winning the impartial spectator's approval, which means that it does not call upon us to desire virtue for its own sake. In other words, they differ precisely in how they motivate us towards virtue, and this difference matters to the project of discerning virtual ethical aspiration in Smith's theory because such aspiration is definitively powered by a 'for its own sake' motivation. The person on the path to virtue has unique access to reasons that cast virtue as a final good.

Den Uyl and Griswold (1996) envision reconciliation of approval-seeking and 'for its own sake' valuing when they argue that it is through imagining the judgement of an impartial spectator that we can conceive of virtue as an end in itself. 'If we are moved by the desire to be praiseworthy, and praiseworthiness is determined by the motives or forms of conduct sanctioned by the impartial spectator, then we can pursue moral virtue for its own sake' (Den Uyl and Griswold 1996: 619). In desiring to be lovely and genuinely *worthy* of praise, we are desiring something distinct from actual praise. But it is through the idea of an impartial spectator, generated from the desire for approval, that we are able to conceive any praiseworthiness distinct from actual praise in the first place. So 'for its own sake' valuing is derived from approval-seeking in our moral development.

This solution merits consideration for many reasons, not least that it traces a developmental account that sits well with Smith's moral theorising. But it falters by locating the 'for its own sake' valuing in the desire for praiseworthiness. If the argument in my previous section is right, then the desire for praiseworthiness is both too common and too contentless to be the locus of virtue ethical aspiration. The content supplied by the exercise of positing and consulting the impartial spectator is distinct from the bare desire for praiseworthiness that belongs 'naturally' to all people (TMS III.2.1). We cannot depend on it to carve out a desire belonging uniquely to the excellent outlook, that is, the virtuous outlook. Thus, if we grant that Den Uyl and Griswold are right that the desire for praiseworthiness delivers us to a 'for its own sake' valuing of virtue, it must be through the downstream activities of actualising the natural desire and supplying it with content. The desire itself is not yet the aspirational kind of valuing.

Virtue ethical aspiration requires at least the possibility of a pure motivation to be virtuous, unmixed with approval-seeking. But Smith seems at moments to preclude this possibility when he asserts that we are psychologically incapable of engaging in moral judgement in the absence of considering the approbation or disapprobation of other judges. 'We can never survey our own sentiments and motives, we can never form any judgment concerning them,' he says, without consulting what we imagine to be the judgements of others. 'Whatever judgment we can form concerning them, accordingly, must always bear some secret reference, either to what are, or to what, upon certain condition, would be, or to what, we imagine, ought to be the judgment of others' (TMS III.1.2). The wise and virtuous person is no exception to this rule.

> He has never dared to suffer the man within the breast to be absent one moment from his attention. With the eyes of this great inmate he has always been accustomed to regard whatever relates to himself. This habit has become perfectly familiar to him. He has been in the constant practice, and, indeed, under the constant necessity, of modelling, or of endeavouring to model, not only his outward conduct and behaviour, but, as much as he can, even his inward sentiments and feelings, according to those of this awful and respectable judge.
>
> (TMS III.3.25)

Even though the wise and virtuous person is depicted as depending on his imagination of a fair and impartial judge, not an actual judge, it is nevertheless approbation that is accepted as the moral standard of self-evaluation.

We should observe, of course, that the determination of what a wise and just person would approve of and the discovery of moral motivation in that determination do not amount to approval-seeking. Smith need not intend an equivocation like that anymore than Aristotle did when he suggested that 'an excellent person is distinguished most by his seeing what is true in each case, since he is like a standard and measure' (Aristotle *NE* 3.4). We consult what a virtuous person would do in these circumstances – or imagine how they would judge someone behaving in a given way – and feel motivated to act in accordance with what we discover in the consultation not because we want their approval but because theirs is the virtuous action.[30] To consult the judgements of an imagined wise and fair judge *qua* exemplar of virtue is consistent with pure motivation, unmixed with approval-seeking. To the extent that Smith might conceive of the approbation of the impartial spectator – or 'man within the breast' and 'great inmate' – as valued by some people because it particularly indicates the way to virtue, he may have in mind that consultation of moral exemplars stirs aspiration. Indeed, Smith indicates that he is an exemplarist when he says, in the III.3.25 passage quoted at length above, that the wise and virtuous man engages in constant practice of 'modelling, or of endeavouring to model, not only his outward conduct and behaviour, but, as much as he can, even his inward sentiments and feelings, according to those of this awful and respectable judge.'[31]

The problem remains, though, that it is unclear how this moral exemplar fits with the standard of perfect propriety. Consider how Smith describes the standard as an idea whose outlines are 'in every man more or less accurately drawn,' in accordance with the attentiveness of each individual in sketching them. He exalts the virtuous person for their extraordinary execution of this work.

> In the wise and virtuous man they [the outlines] have been made with the most acute and delicate sensibility, and the utmost care and attention have been employed in making them. Every day some feature is improved; every

> day some blemish is corrected. He has studied this idea more than other people, he comprehends it more distinctly, he has formed a much more correct image of it, and is much more deeply enamoured of its exquisite and divine beauty.
>
> He endeavours as well as he can, to assimilate his own character to this archetype of perfection. But he imitates the work of a divine artist, which can never be equalled. He feels the imperfect success of all his best endeavours, and sees, with grief and affliction, in how many different features the mortal copy falls short of the immortal original. He remembers, with concern and humiliation, how often, from want of attention, from want of judgment, from want of temper, he has, both in words and actions, both in conduct and conversation, violated the exact rules of perfect propriety; and has so far departed from that model, according to which he wished to fashion his own character and conduct.
>
> (VI.iii.25)

Smith represents the wise and virtuous person as engaged in direct contemplation of the idea of perfect propriety. He mentions neither the judgement nor the exemplarity that is generated from imagining a fair and impartial spectator. Interestingly, the standard is – at least as the wise and virtuous man posits it through his 'acute and delicate sensibility' – unattainable.[32] Smith walks back and forth a bit between portraying this judgement of unattainability as, on one hand, simply a perception of the virtuous person who is sensitive to his 'imperfect success' and, on the other, as a fact derived from the inevitable gap between a 'mortal copy' and an 'immortal original.' But he suggests, in characterising the virtuous person's daily work here as 'improving' and forming 'a much more correct image,' that he considers the virtuous person to be truth-tracking in their ideation about propriety.

There is a solution to our puzzle in this depiction of the wise and virtuous person's work of drawing the outlines of propriety. The activity is reminiscent of Den Uyl and Griswold's model of the love of virtue for its own sake being generated from the exercise of imagining a wise and impartial judge. The virtuous person revises and improves his conception of perfect propriety in the same way: by consulting his own – more perfect – iteration of such a judge. Thus, the standard of perfect propriety and the judgement of the impartial spectator coincide completely through all the stages of drawing clearer and more accurate outlines of propriety. The more mature moral agent will imagine an impartial spectator who exercises greater scrutiny and discrimination in judging conduct and sentiments. As a result, their standard of perfect propriety will bear the marks of scrutiny and discrimination accordingly.

An objection

An objection to this vision of complete coincidence of the standard of perfect propriety and the judgement of the impartial spectator might be raised in the following way: the impartial spectator is disinclined to hold us to the standard of perfect propriety because that standard leaves even the virtuous person disappointed and unhappy.[33] Speaking of even 'the wisest and best of us all,' Smith says that they 'see nothing but weakness and imperfection' when they compare themselves with the standard of perfection (TMS III.iii.24).[34] Though superlatively good, this moral agent 'can discover no ground for arrogance and presumption, but a great deal for humility, regret and repentance' (TMS VI.iii.24). The impartial spectator does not want us to be unhappy, though. Smith says, 'That degree of self-estimation, therefore, which contributes most to the happiness and contentment of the person himself, seems likewise most agreeable to the impartial spectator' (TMS VI.iii.50). The impartial spectator wants us to attain happiness and therefore approves of the self-approbation that is productive of happiness and contentment. Insofar as clinging to a standard of perfect propriety generates feelings of regret and repentance inconsistent with happiness and contentment, the impartial spectator will disapprove, or perhaps only withhold approval, of such adherence to the standard.[35] It is as if Smith took to heart the lesson of Horace's *Epistles* 1.6: *insani sapiens nomen ferat, aequus iniqui/ultra quam satis est Virtutem si petat ipsam.*[36]

This worry is well-founded insofar as there is a *prima facie* tension between, on one side, the fact that our desire to attain perfect propriety generates disappointments and, on the other side, the impartial spectator's inclination to find agreeable what contributes to our flourishing. Indeed, if the desire to attain the standard is constitutive of aspiration, then we would see in this tension an ultimate disapproval of aspiration by the impartial spectator. The complete coincidence in the exemplarist account would be undone.

But the tension is superficial. The wise and virtuous person who principally attends to the standard of perfect propriety is not robbed of happiness by the regret and repentance that he endures in reflecting on his moral shortcomings. For one thing, he is exceptionally aware and sensitive to the moral sensibilities of his fellows, and so has a gladdening (but not insolent) conception of his own moral achievement (TMS VI.iii.25). And, second, precisely because of his understanding of the difficulty in achieving moral excellence, he is in a unique epistemic position to recognise and rejoice in the moral achievements of others. 'He, who knows how difficult it is to excel, esteems and honours their excellence, and never fails to bestow upon it the full measure of applause which it deserves' (TMS VI.iii.25). All the pleasures that come with sympathising with our fellows are magnified for the virtuous man who sympathises with the good, knowing it is good.[37]

The exemplarist interpretation of how the virtuous person engages the idea of an impartial spectator remains viable. When this reading is applied to particular passages in TMS, a vision of aspiration readily emerges. Consider the application to Smith's account of the stages of natural development of self-command.[38] The young child reflects not at all upon the judgements of others and so has no reflective ability to equilibrate their emotions and conduct with the expectations of those upon whom they are making demands. As the child matures, a 'natural wish' to win the approbation of his peers drives the youth to act in ways that gain their favour (TMS III.3.22). Even in the 'weakest man,' a brief and cursory consideration of how a fellow will observe his situation 'calls off his attention from his own view;

and his breast is, in some measure, becalmed the moment they come into his presence' (TMS III.3.23). The pleasure of fellow-feeling can elevate the weak man to firmness since 'the pleasure which he derives from this sentiment supports and enables him more easily to continue this generous effort' (TMS III.3.24). Finally, 'the man of real constancy and firmness, the wise and just man' will bear self-command as a habit. 'He does not merely affect the sentiments of the impartial spectator. He really adopts them. He almost identifies himself with, he almost becomes himself that impartial spectator, and scarce even feels but as that great arbiter of his conduct directs him to feel' (TMS II.3.25).

These passages describe the development of self-command, which is the virtue Smith considered foundational to all others.[39] What drives the development, I am contending, is an initial 'natural wish' that gives way to virtue ethical aspiration. After firmness and constancy have become habits, individuals are released from 'merely affect[ing] the sentiments of the impartial spectator.' They are able to *adopt* them, *identify* with them, and *almost become* the impartial spectator itself. These dimensions of post-habituation conceptualising of the impartial spectator match the elements of the drive to aspire. The man of self-command (i) has the need to understand the impartial spectator's sentiments, not merely to imitate them; (ii) desires to be self-directing by identifying with the impartial spectator; and (iii) is eager to improve by (almost) becoming an impartial spectator – the 'almost' emphasises the perpetuity of the eagerness.

Not only do these attributes of the firm and constant man match the elements of the drive to aspire, but they also echo particularly the ancient models of virtue ethics that depict aspiration as a value orientation that is available only to those who are already on the path to virtue. Recall that for Aristotle, ethical theorising is reserved for those who have already been brought up well, and for the Stoics, virtue has the advent of reason as a prerequisite. Smith establishes the habit of self-command as the disposition from which we can look upon the impartial spectator and, with firmness and constancy already established, desire to better ourselves even more.

Conclusion

I have argued that a uniquely virtue ethical mode of aspiration can be located in Adam Smith's moral theory particularly in his description of the way in which wise and virtuous people are motivated to pursue perfect propriety. Locating aspiration in his theory is vital to understanding his theory as virtue ethical in its conception. Without virtue ethical aspiration, the theory departs from a central tenet of virtue ethical programs, both ancient and modern.

In uncovering this mode of aspiration, two aspects of Smith's work are brought to light. First, we can see that there is more involved in the motivation for virtue than just the inborn disposition to desire praiseworthiness. In addition, we may acquire a motivation that is informed, educated, and more purposefully trained on the goal of being good. To aspire in the virtue ethical mode is not merely to desire generally 'to be really fit,' but to desire particularly to realise the exact and exacting details of perfect propriety and adopt, not merely imitate, all the sentiments of an ideal judge. That is, we can see that moral motivation is thought by Smith to have its untrained and innate iteration, but also its developed and mature iteration. The latter is the site of aspiration.

Second, by considering the shape of aspiration – its recruitment of desires for understanding and self-direction and improvement – we can more readily appreciate the complexity of the virtuous person's motivation. He imitates the judgements of the impartial spectator, but not merely for the sake of imitation. His goal is to become self-determining and independent in his judgements, and so he wants to think as the impartial spectator thinks, act as the standard of perfect propriety demands. He consults external standards, but only in his effort to embody the standard. Understanding the difference between adhering to a standard and becoming the standard is a mark of aspiration, and Adam Smith has equipped his wise and virtuous agent with exactly that.

Notes

1 This translation of Cicero is from Raphael Woolf, edited by Julia Annas (Cicero 2017). As this paper will show, I owe much of my thinking about virtue ethics to Julia Annas. I am grateful for her mentorship and for her encouragement of this project. Thanks also to Emily Hulme and Jeremy Reid, and to a particularly rousing audience at the 2023 International Adam Smith Society meeting in St. Andrews. Nir Ben-Moshe, Chapin Cimino, and Christel Fricke were especially helpful in that session. Most of all, thanks to Doug Den Uyl for multiple rounds of constructive feedback.

2 See McCloskey (2008: 52), who argues that Smith 'was building an ethic for a commercial society, but on the foundation of ethical thought in the West.' Similarly, Smith (2020: 67) accounts for how the TMS represents a 'reordering of the classical virtues for a modern society.' Montes (2003: 57) recognises that Smith does not merely rely on the tradition to fill out the centre of his moral theory, but that he develops a virtue theory his own. See Hanley (2009: 6) for an account of Smith's 'synthesis' of ancient and Christian virtue traditions under the principal concept of self-love.

3 See, for example, Fleischacker (2021), who rejects the scholarly view that the normative project of TMS VI is the centre of the moral theory, arguing that it is subordinate to the theory of the impartial spectator. Indeed, Fleischacker (2020) is emphatic that Smith is, on balance, more virtue ethical than rule-based or consequentialist, but 'nevertheless, he tries to incorporate some of the intuitions that generated these other systems.' Schliesser (2017: 225–234) also devotes scant space to discussion of virtue in his treatment of Smith's expansive 'systematicity' and draws the conclusion that 'realistic' exemplars are described all along in the TMS, rendering Part VI a continuation rather than a special insight of the text.

4 Carrasco (2014: 225), for example, argues that Smith 'configures an ethical framework that makes space for both ideals of excellence and Modern imperatives.' Many have observed Smith's ambition to update ancient theories of virtue to fit his modern, commercial world and to accommodate the ideals of liberalism, for example, Darwall (1999), Griswold (1999), Vivenza (2001), Winch (1978).

5 The intellectual virtues might be identified with the five 'states by which the soul tracks truth' enumerated in *Nicomachean Ethics* (*NE*) 6.3, but among those *phronesis* and *sophia* are identified as the exclusive province of happiness (*NE* 10.7–8). The character virtues are discussed across *NE* Books 2–5. Doris (1998: 508) counts 12 of them and, strangely, eight intellectual ones. Alighieri (1909: IV, xvii, 4–8) had counted only 11 character virtues.

6 Brennan (2015: 37–38) presents the textual evidence for this interpretation.

7 Shaw and Robitzsch (2024) show that, for Epicurus, 'the pleasant life requires virtue, and indeed is guaranteed by it.' So virtue is not only a means but also a *necessary* means to the good life.

8 It is worth noting Smith's familiarity with Cicero's *De Finibus*, as attested by Vivenza (2001: 1–7).

9 Hanley (2009: 146), for example, describes praiseworthiness as the natural psychological mechanism by which a 'transethical horizon' is conceived. See also Carrasco (2014: 229–230), Griswold (1999: 132), Forman-Barzilai (2010: 99), and McHugh (2022: 113–117).

10 Forman-Barzilai (2010) wages the most sophisticated version of this argument. Arguments to this conclusion often appeal to Smith's conception of the impartial spectator, charging that the impartial spectator is necessarily 'closed' (Golemboski 2020: 9) or equilibrated to a local standard of common sense (Fleischacker 2011: 27), or else that for any moral agent – even the 'wise and virtuous' – 'absolute certainty in moral matters is not possible' so that even a cosmopolitan achievement must be tempered with humility (Fricke 2013:198). Additionally, Smith adopts a Humean conception of imagination, according to which we are limited, in both our scientific and moral exercise of imagination, to the simple ideas and sense perceptions with which we are already familiar (Harrison 1995; Haakonssen 2002; Hankins and McDavid 2023). This means our moral imagination is limited.

11 Berry (1992: 80). This intersubjectivity is what Hanley (2009: 145–146) conceives facilitating that love of praiseworthiness and magnanimity that gives rise to the 'transethical horizon,' mentioned earlier, rather than towards ever worsening corruption in a pursuit of unenlightened praise. In other words, moral development conceived as a process of socialisation need not tether the individual to local norms and expectations. But Hanley's treatment itself discloses the work to be done in showing how the transcendence is possible.

12 McHugh (2020) offers a persuasive defense in this vein and nicely summarizes the development of the debate in scholarship.

13 Aristotle (2014: 1.4). See Burnyeat (1980) for examination of Aristotle's reasons for setting this pre-requisite.

14 Klein (2016: 149) translates *oikeiosis* as 'appropriation' and explains that 'appropriate action,' for the Stoics, is 'achieved by human agents through a cognitive grasp of one's own constitution and through the perfection of the faculty on which this grasp depends.' There are many difficulties of interpretation surrounding the Stoic theory of *oikeiosis*, as surveyed and navigated thoroughly by Klein, but I agree with Klein's understanding that 'in rational agents the character of impulse is conditioned by the discursive and inferential abilities that underwrite higher-order modes of phantasia and, crucially, by the capacity to pass judgment on phantasiai' (194). The advent of reason subordinates impulse and enables the individual to lead their life rationally. Cooper (1995: 593) states this elegantly: 'The final state is reached when, reflecting upon what one has been doing while acting for these earlier reasons, one comes to realize that merely acting that way has tremendous appeal, that it is a mistake to think of the value of so acting in any given instance as derivative from – needed because of its presumed efficacy in achieving – the assumed value to oneself of the continuance of one's constitution or of getting whatever it was one was then acting appropriately so as to get. Such action is then seen as having an intrinsic value of its own, consisting in the fact that it is reason-directed action, where what is done is "appropriate" because it fits in with one's natural needs.'

15 McDowell (1979: 346).

16 McDowell (1979: 346). Lacking an economical expression for these ideas in English, he says in *Mind and World* that the German *Bildung* captures the idea (McDowell 1996: 84).

17 Annas (2011: 117)

18 Annas (2011: 117), emphasis is hers. She concedes that this positive directionality is a feature of her account of virtue, but 'not all accounts, nor even . . . all the ones in which virtue is committed to goodness' (117). But hers is a compelling and attractive account that returns virtue ethics to its more ancient form through emphasis on virtue's likeness to skill and its cognitive resources in understanding not only that something is good, but also why.

19 Annas (2011: 17–18)

20 Callard (2018: 8) offers a complex analysis of aspiration as 'rational, purposive value acquisition.' The process requires work, Callard argues. 'The aspirant sees that she does not have the values that she would like to have, and therefore seeks to move herself towards a better valuational condition' (5). Callard is motivated by the version of Meno's paradox that resides at the heart of this situation: how can we desire to value what we do not value? And, interestingly, she does not engage with virtue ethics as a special iteration of the phenomenon. It is unclear how she would apply her model. Because she places aspiration prior to value acquisition, she could deny that aspiration belongs to the person who has already acquired virtue. But I think her puzzle persists throughout the life of the virtuous person, for virtue is excellence in one's condition (cognitive or emotional or both), and the virtuous person goes on desiring always to be more excellent, assuming that the virtuous person is always in some sense a learner.

21 For example, Den Uyl and Griswold (1996: 619) and Hanley (2009: 99).

22 Den Uyl and Griswold (1996: 619) show that valuing virtue 'for its own sake' is possible only through seeking the approval of the impartial spectator since worthiness must be measured not against what is actually praised but only against what we imagine could be approved by well-informed and just judge. I will return to this idea of 'for its own sake' striving in the fourth section, where I raise the issue that Smith's emphasis on the impartial spectator as a tool for self-assessment presents a difficulty for locating a pure for-its-own-sake motivation even in the people he identifies as 'wise and virtuous.'

23 McHugh (2022) explores the workings of the natural insight.

24 Brown (2012) examines the 'intersubjectivity' and dependency on social interactions in Smith's theory of moral belief, referred to also in Berry (1992) and Hanley (2009).

25 For the first of these points, see Smith's declaration that 'virtue is excellence, something uncommonly great and beautiful, which rises far above what is vulgar and ordinary' (TMS I.i.5.6). See Forman-Barzilai (2010: 111–112) for discussion of this passage in particular, and Darwall (1999) and Fleischacker (2004: 141) for discussion of an egalitarianism in Smith, which egalitarianism describes the universal predication of the desire for praiseworthiness and capacity for virtue, but not of realized virtue.

26 Aristotle distinguishes potentiality from actuality in the Metaphysics: 'the excellent activity is better and more honorable than the potentiality' (Met. 1051a). See Baker (2017) for discussion of Aristotle's conception of human orientation to goodness. Human beings have a natural or inborn potential for goodness insofar as we are capable of becoming good, but we are not good by nature in actuality (see NE 2.1).

27 Of course, these two processes are only conceptually distinct in Smith's theory, for the process by which we fine-tune our judgements just is the process by which we sculpt our character and conduct. But it is worthwhile to avoid collapsing the conceptual distinctions in the text in order to avoid unwarranted reductions.

28 See Carrasco (2004: 109), who analyses the first standard by taking up the question 'what is this 'archetype of perfection' that the moral elite tend to emulate?' Carrasco argues persuasively that the standard attracts the virtuous person 'as a final cause' (in the Aristotelian sense) and grounds their pursuit of happiness (2004: 109).

29 Hanley (2009: 136), in introducing the impartial spectator, says that 'the intention of this mechanism is to enable the person concerned to become a self-spectator and thereby promote the development of conscience.' The 'self-spectator' notion may seem at odds

with the objective of impartiality, but Hanley explains that the development is one in learning to 'transcend self-preference' (Hanley 2009: 136). Forman-Barzilai (2010: 166) says that Smith invokes the faculty to 'overcome the near-sightedness of our passive sentiments.' Griswold (1999: 144, emphasis in the original) says that it '*defines* the moral point of view already latent in ordinary life.' The tethering of moral motivation to the spectator can be observed even among these subtle differences of emphasis.

30 Zagzebski (2004: 160) makes the case for this motivational schema in relation to right acts, wrong acts, virtuous acts, and duties. This is a common commitment among exemplarist virtue ethical theories. See Brennan (2015: 44–45) for discussion of the Sage as exemplar in Stoicism.

31 He reinforces this impression when he calls the standard of perfect propriety a 'standard of ideal' at TMS III.iii.27. See Sayre-McCord (2010) for examination of how ideal or otherwise Smith conceives of the impartial spectator. I concede to Sayre-McCord that Smith's preoccupation with the narrow circumstances of behaviour can diminish the ideality of the spectator. My present discussion will focus more on the power of consulting the impartial spectator for holding us to a high standard rather than an analysis of the standard itself.

32 In this, Smith echoes the Stoic denial that anyone can actually achieve the moral status of the Sage. See Brennan (2015). Of course, he evidently disagrees with them in his choice to predicate wisdom and virtue of high achievers nonetheless.

33 I am grateful to an anonymous referee for directing my attention to Smith's characterisation of the standard as particularly onerous.

34 Note Smith's use of the superlative (wisest and best) rather than only the positive here. He means to emphasize that the achievement of the greatest moral progress is no release from the humiliation of self-evaluation.

35 I will ultimately reject this counterargument, but it is worth noting that something like this might be at play in I.i.5.8. Smith says there that life sometimes serves up unbearably difficult situations, and though our conduct and sentiments in those situations may 'fall short of the most perfect propriety, it may still deserve some applause, and even in a certain sense, may be denominated virtuous.' However, he explicitly says in this same passage that these are situations in which we cannot moderate our sentiments to a level 'in which the impartial spectator can enter into them,' suggesting that the impartial spectator does hold the bar at the standard of perfect propriety.

36 'Let the wise man bear the name of madman, the just of unjust, should he pursue Virtue herself beyond due bounds' (1.6.15–16).

37 Further, against the interpretation that the impartial spectator aims at happiness rather than a high standard, Smith says in TMS VI.iii.53 that the degree of emotion and habit 'that is most agreeable to the impartial spectator is likewise most agreeable to the person himself.' This passage presents the same likeness that is articulated at TMS VI.iii.50, but it reverses the items that are identified as alike. In presenting the self-estimation 'which contributes most to the happiness and contentment of the person himself' as 'seem[ing] likewise most agreeable to the impartial spectator,' it seemed as though Smith meant that the fact of the contribution to the person's happiness is what grounds or causes the impartial spectator's approval. But in reversing the items at TMS VI.iii.53, we can see that the causal claim was not intended. The impartial spectator and the wisest and best person himself most likely coincide in their judgements, I think, because they are both correct.

38 Strictly, he says that these are 'the different shades and gradations of weakness and self-command,' but because he begins with the account of a young child and ends with a fully actualised wise person, it is difficult to read the passage as offering no developmental theory (TMS III.3.21–25). Smith's fondness of the Stoic theory of *oikeiosis*, see n. 14, lends itself to this interpretation. See Forman-Barzilai (2010) for the most thorough examination of Smith's thought about *oikeiosis*.

39 See TMS VI.3.11: 'Self-command is not only itself a great virtue, but from it all the other virtues seem to derive their principal lustre.'

References

Alighieri, D. (1909) *Convivio*, (ed. and trans.) Philip H. Wicksteed. Originally written c. 1304–1307. Oxford, UK: Oxford University Press.

Annas, J. (2011) *Intelligent Virtue*. Oxford, UK: Oxford University Press.

Aristotle. (2014) *Nicomachean Ethics*, (ed. and trans.) C. D. C. Reeve, 2nd edition. Abbreviation: *NE*. Indianapolis, IN: Hackett Publishing.

Baker, S. (2017) 'The Metaphysics of Goodness in the Ethics of Aristotle', *Philosophical Studies*, 174: 1839–1856.

Berry, C. (1992) 'Adam Smith and the Virtues of Commerce', *Nomos*, 34: 69–88.

Brennan, T. (2015) 'The Stoic Theory of Virtue', in L. Besser-Jones and M. Slote (eds.) *The Routledge Companion to Virtue Ethics*, 1st edition. New York, NY: Routledge, pp. 31–49.

Brown, V. (2012) 'Intersubjectivity and Moral Judgment in Adam Smith's Theory of Moral Sentiments', in C. Fricke and D. Føllesdal (eds.) *Intersubjectivity and Objectivity in Adam Smith and Edmund Husserl*. Ontos-Verlag, pp. 243–272.

Burnyeat, M. (1980) 'Aristotle on Learning to Be Good', in A. O. Rorty (ed.) *Essays on Aristotle's Ethics*. Berkeley: University of California Press, pp. 69–92.

Callard, A. (2018) *Aspiration: The Agency of Becoming*. Oxford University Press.

Carrasco, M. A. (2004) 'Adam Smith's Reconstruction of Practical Reason', *The Review of Metaphysics*, 58: 81–116.

Carrasco, M. A. (2014) 'Adam Smith: Virtues and Universal Principles', *Revue Internationale de Philosophie*, 68(3): 223–250.

Cicero. (2017) *On Moral Ends*, (ed.) J. Annas, (trans.) R. Woolf. Cambridge: Cambridge University Press.

Cooper, J. (1995) 'Eudaimonism and the Appeal to Nature in the Morality of Happiness: Comments on Julia Annas, the Morality of Happiness', *Philosophy and Phenomenological Research*, 55(3): 587–598.

Darwall, S. (1999) 'Sympathetic Liberalism: Recent Work on Adam Smith', *Philosophy & Public Affairs*, 28(2): 139–164.

Den Uyl, D. and Griswold, C. (1996) 'Adam Smith on Friendship and Love', *The Review of Metaphysics*, 49(3): 609–637.

Doris, J. M. (1998) 'Persons, Situations, and Virtue Ethics', *Nouˆs*, 32(4): 504–530.

Fleischacker, S. (2004) *On Adam Smith's Wealth of Nations*. Princeton, NJ: Princeton University Press.

Fleischacker, S. (2011) 'Adam Smith and Cultural Relativism', *Erasmus Journal for Philosophy and Economics*, 4: 20–41.

Fleischacker, S. (2020) 'Adam Smith's Moral and Political Philosophy', in N. E. Zalta (ed.) *The Stanford Encyclopedia of Philosophy*. https://plato.stanford.edu/archives/win2020/entries/smith-moral-political/

Fleischacker, S. (2021) *Adam Smith*. The Routledge Philosophers. New York, NY: Routledge.

Forman-Barzilai, F. (2010) *Adam Smith and the Circles of Sympathy: Cosmopolitanism and Moral Theory*. Cambridge: Cambridge University Press.

Fricke, C. (2013) 'Adam Smith: The Sympathetic Process and the Origin and Function of Conscience', in C. Berry, M. P. Paganelli and C. Smith (eds.) *The Oxford Handbook of Adam Smith*. Oxford: Oxford University Press.

Golemboski, D. (2020) 'The Impartiality of Smith's Spectator: The Problem of Parochialism and the Possibility of Social Critique', *Journal of Scottish Philosophy*, 17(2): 111–125.

Griswold, C. (1999) *Adam Smith and the Virtues of Enlightenment*. Cambridge: Cambridge University Press.

Haakonssen, K. (ed.) (2002) *Adam Smith: The Theory of Moral Sentiments*. New York: Cambridge University Press.

Hankins, K. and McDavid, B. (2023) 'Adam Smith and the Creative Role of Imagination', in A. Burgio (ed.) *Adam Smith and Modernity*. London: Routledge.

Hanley, R. (2009) *Adam Smith and the Character of Virtue*. Cambridge: Cambridge University Press.

Harrison, J. (1995) 'Imagination and Aesthetics in Adam Smith's Epistemology and Moral Philosophy', *Contributions to Political Economy*, 14: 91–112.
Klein, J. (2016) 'The Stoic Argument from *oikeiosis*', *Oxford Studies in Ancient Philosophy*, 50: 143–200.
McCloskey, D. (2008) 'Adam Smith, the Last of the Former Virtue Ethicists', *History of Political Economy*, 40: 43–71.
McDowell, J. (1979) 'Virtue and Reason', *The Monist*, 62: 331–350.
McDowell, J. (1996) *Mind and World*. Cambridge, MA: Harvard University Press.
McHugh, J. (2020) 'Hume's General Point of View, Smith's Impartial Spectator, and the Moral Value of Interacting with Outsiders', *Journal of Scottish Philosophy*, 19: 19–37.
McHugh, J. (2022) *Adam Smith's The Theory of Moral Sentiments: A Critical Introduction*. Cambridge, UK: Cambridge University Press.
Montes, L. (2003) *Adam Smith in Context: A Critical Reassessment of Some Central Components of His Thought*. Palgrave Macmillan.
Sayre-McCord, G. (2010) 'Sentiments and Spectators: Adam Smith's Theory of Moral Judgment', in V. Brown and S. Fleischacker (ed.) *The Philosophy of Adam Smith: Essays Commemorating the 250th Anniversary of the Theory of Moral Sentiments*. Routledge, pp. 124–144.
Schliesser, E. (2017) *Adam Smith: Systematic Philosopher and Public Thinker*. Oxford, UK: Oxford University Press.
Shaw, J. C. and Robitzsch, J. M. (2024) *Epicurean Ethics*. https://www.oxfordbibliographies.com/display/document/obo-9780195389661/obo-9780195389661-0367.xml
Smith, C. (2020) *Adam Smith*. Cambridge: Polity Press.
Vivenza, G. (2001) *Adam Smith and the Classics: The Classical Heritage in Adam Smith's Thought*. Oxford, UK: Oxford University Press.
Winch, D. (1978) *Adam Smith's Politics: An Essay in Historiographic Revision*. Cambridge, UK: Cambridge University Press.
Zagzebski, L. T. (2004) *Divine Motivation Theory*. New York: Cambridge University Press.

10 'If i was really you . . .'

Adam Smith on imagination, education, and as an antidote to identity politics

Trevor Shelley

Introduction

Contemporary culture has become obsessed with the language of 'identity.' Civic and political discourse is consumed by an identitarian perspective, on both the left and right sides of the political divide. Thus, the phrase 'identity politics' has become part of common parlance. According to Google's Ngram Viewer, there was a 249% increase in the usage of the expression across publications from 1985 to 2019.[1] However, despite the rise in frequency of use, there is little agreement on the meaning of the phrase 'identity politics,' and commentators likewise dispute its origins and genesis. This is not the place to provide yet another genealogical account of identity politics.[2] However, it is necessary to delve into the identity discourse from the outset to substantiate the following claim: certain elements or facets that fall under the category of identity politics risk constricting or cordoning off the human faculty of imagination. This tendency is bound up with ideas and positions that set limits to the emotional accessibility and intelligibility of various human experiences for observers due to the specific identities or identity claims of the subject – that is, parts of experience are claimed as impenetrable to the minds and imaginations of others who do not possess similar identity traits to the self in question.

Not all advocates, activists, or scholars of identity politics go so far as to make these kinds of arguments; moreover, such claims are not always explicit but are sometimes implied or are the logical consequence of the position defended. However, it is a sufficiently pervasive, if underlying, suggestion that it should be considered more directly. The narrowing or closing of the imagination is not without significant social consequences. This aspect of identity politics is rarely discussed but comes to light when reflecting on the phenomenon through the work of Adam Smith. This essay argues that in considering identity politics through a Smithian lens, we come to see it *as a problem of imagination* and a consequent threat to our contemporary social order. For, on Smith's view, imagination is not merely associated with creativity, aesthetics, or human ideals. Rather, it is *the* faculty crucial to social, moral, and economic life; and especially so in modern, diverse, commercial societies like our own. Thus, correctly educating the imagination is, for Smith, an important means towards cultivating and maintaining the moral and social bonds

DOI: 10.4324/9781003767824-13

that are conducive to individual and collective human flourishing. Consequently, any truncation or restriction of the imagination serves the opposite purpose. Seen from a Smithian perspective, certain strands of identity politics that have gained broad currency threaten just such a closing of the imagination. And by imposing constraints on the kinds of individuals or experiences with which one may imaginatively engage, this view – increasingly widespread in pedagogical theory and practice, as well as elsewhere[3] – risks undermining the very thing that Adam Smith saw as the basis of social cohesion and a shared morality. For, as Smith himself foresaw, modern commercial societies depend on widespread moral and economic exchange among individuals of varying backgrounds and varied experiences, the precursor for which was an ability to see one another as sufficiently equal – or, as we might say today, as individuals with whom we could sufficiently identify to understand them and their lived experience. In sum, recalling Smith's insight into the centrality of imagination illuminates an important dimension of identity politics, helps us to see why, in its extreme form, it is a potential threat to morality and social cohesion, and thereby provides intellectual and moral resources to contribute to contemporary debates concerning identity.

In the next section, I continue the discussion of identity politics and consider one of its underlying epistemological theories that argue for a sort of radical particularity to experience and understanding. I then turn to briefly examine the debate around 'cultural appropriation,' which is firmly rooted in strong identity claims and demonstrates this epistemology in practice. This debate reveals how culture and experience become akin to possessions accessible only to limited individuals and groups, rather than to human beings or humanity at large. Weaving a thread through these issues connecting concerns about culture and its appropriation with the experience of individuals and their identity claims we get a sense of the place – or displacement – of the imagination. Following this section, I then turn to Adam Smith's account of the imagination, and discuss its key role in his thought and his view on how crucial it is to all of our lives. Smith's project is inconceivable without the unique capacities of imagination, and, according to him, our sociality and morality lose their very foundation without imagination's powerful presence and continued cultivation. Imagination is precisely what allows us to go beyond our selves and the contours of our own individual – even selfish or self-oriented – experience, and is key to widening our understanding and moral disposition towards others. I discuss how narrowing and confining the imagination by delineating and circumscribing in advance the kinds or parts of experience with which one might identify constrains intellectual wonder and curiosity and is antithetical to desires basic to the human mind. Furthermore, I elaborate on why limits and impositions on imagination's sympathetic endeavour and its consequent closure threaten the moral and social fabric of our shared life with others, inhibiting individuals' ability to relate to others through our natural sentiments or passions, as Smith outlines. Thus, while identity politics may, in many cases, be motivated by a positive desire for justice, we must be wary of strands that tend towards imaginative closure, for the consequences could be significant privation in education and impoverishment in the moral and social capacities of individuals.

Identity politics and the closing of the imagination

The philosopher Kwame Anthony Appiah once remarked:

> I am never quite sure what people mean when they talk about "identity politics." Usually, though, they bring it up to complain about someone else. One's own political preoccupations are just, well, politics. Identity politics is what other people do.[4]

While there is some truth to his claim that reflects confusion and partisan use or abuse of the term, nevertheless, 'identity is today a growth industry in the academy, across the humanities and social sciences, influencing even law and communication studies. The constitutive power of gender, race, ethnicity, sexuality, and other forms of identity has,' argues one of its advocates, 'finally, suddenly, been recognized as a relevant aspect of almost all projects of inquiry.'[5] Thus, 'Claims for the recognition of difference now drive many of the world's social conflicts.'[6] Identity politics has 'both an activist and an academic existence' insofar as the concept of identity has been evoked in activists' 'struggles for social justice' and has likewise served as a 'grounding assumption of the new identity-based scholarly programs' that have sprung up and multiplied at most American universities and colleges.[7]

However, there is underlying disagreement about some important ontological and epistemological assumptions regarding identity and its politicisation. A crucial element in these debates includes differing views on the role of contingency and the degree to which it is significant in both constituting and accessing knowledge – that is, whether differences in experience and accidents of life shape alternate, even irreconcilable patterns of meaning and knowing.[8] Theorists vary on whether and how identity is socially and historically based or is rather something more stable and inherent. At one extreme are some post-structuralists who believe identity is altogether contingent and therefore constructed by the subject and circumstances, and at the other are essentialists who conceive identity as ahistorical and fixed.[9] For our purposes, a particular group of theorists is most relevant, namely, those who hold to what is called 'standpoint epistemology,' or variations of this theory.

Writing in defence of identity politics, the feminist, Suzanna Danuta Walters, argues, 'One's embodied, experienced, and structural location in the world matters,' and such a view 'has always been an important corrective to the Enlightenment fantasy of a view from nowhere that was always a view from a dude.'[10] In correcting this 'Enlightenment fantasy,' standpoint epistemologists argue that 'subject positions' or 'social locations' of individuals and groups are of great significance in both constituting and understanding identity. Therefore, all forms of knowing ought to be qualified as 'situated knowledges.'[11] As Nancy Hartsock writes, 'the position of women is structurally different from that of men, and the lived realities of women's lives are profoundly different from those of men.' Thus, she encourages feminist scholars to draw out the epistemological implications of these facts, which she herself begins to do. One such consequence is that there is a deeply 'rooted . . . opposition between feminist and masculinist experience' that begets 'a series of boundary challenges' on both physiological and social grounds. For Hartsock, nothing short of a revolutionary reconfiguring of social order and relations can overcome these challenges.[12] Thus, human imagination is severely limited in its capacity to follow and recreate, to a satisfying point of replicability and intelligibility, the experience of another based on linguistic and other signs or symbols provided by the subject of the original experience.[13] As Francis Fukuyama observes, 'The idea that each group has its own identity that was not accessible to outsiders was reflected in the use of the term *lived experience*, which has seen explosive growth in the popular culture since the 1970s,' that has, in turn, 'erode[d] . . . the possibility of . . . perspectives and feelings that can be shared across group boundaries.'[14] Again, 'positions' or 'structures' (such as class, sex, and gender, as well as race, ethnicity, and other markers) pose sufficient barriers for imagination's penetration.

Standpoint epistemology originated in feminist theory as an effort to define and defend 'the feminine standpoint' as 'women's unique standpoint in society' providing 'justification for the truth claims of feminism while also providing it with a method with which to analyze reality.'[15] Women's experiences, in other words, were deemed sufficiently different or unique to require a distinct methodology and epistemological apparatus for proper understanding. Men's imaginations, so the argument goes, do not share a compatible or equivalent capability due to distinctions of embodiment and location in human and social reality. While at one time a staple of feminist theory, the theory is not without its critics.[16] The complex history and development of feminism are beyond the purview of this essay, but the central claims of standpoint epistemology remain salient: 'that knowledge is situated and perspectival and that there are multiple standpoints from which knowledge is produced.'[17] Moreover, this epistemological theory now extends beyond feminist thought, as 'knowledge is socially situated and is influenced by "noncognitive" factors' including 'one's gender' but no longer limited to it. Instead, it includes other 'noncognitive' markers of identity that frame lived experience, such as race and sexual orientation.[18] Given the broad basis of women and female experience, some argue that 'standpoint theory might be better suited to black women than to women in general.'[19] As Patricia Hill Collins argues, there are elements of the Afro-American female experience that white males or nonwhite and/or females 'are certainly in no position to notice' given their 'positionality.'[20] Popular writers like Ta-Nehisi Coates have built on such scholarship to argue that there is often an insurmountable 'epistemic gap' between whites and blacks. Thus, standpoint epistemology has proliferated a multitude of positions, in some cases to be found at different 'intersections' of identities. It is one thing to suggest that knowledge is perspectival and benefits from multiple standpoints to form a larger whole; however, it is quite another thing altogether to suggest that there is no whole and the variegated parts – perspectives, standpoints, or identities – are incommensurate and irreconcilable. The latter view is found among some of the most vocal opponents of cultural appropriation, which I will now discuss.[21] Underlying concerns about cultural appropriation are claims that lived experience is proprietary and off-limits to those who do not share the same identity, or 'structural location,' in the world – a more vehement extension of the claims made by standpoint epistemologists.

Discussions involving cultural appropriation vary in their charges and concerns, from the taking or theft of artifacts by one government or people from another culture, to the adoption or incorporation by an artist of elements from a culture other than their own in their artwork.[22] It is especially in instances like the latter that one perceives something akin to standpoint epistemology at play, and the curtailing of imagination to limit such appropriation. Claims regarding what scholars refer to as 'literary appropriation' or 'voice appropriation' consist of arguments chastising authors for including characters of different identities from themselves in their fiction, leading some to argue, 'there is something to be said about controlling the process of creating that [constructed] world, of imposing some control over who can or should hold the pen.'[23] Reasons for this vary, but the underlying suggestion is that the creative imagination has limits insofar as the particularities of human experience are not equally open to all for imaginative exploration. One of the earliest such situations that attracted debate transpired in the 1990s in Canada regarding white novelists who wrote about indigenous culture or otherwise adopted the perspective of native characters in their novels. Various responses ensued, from those actively seeking to support minority voices in the literary world, to those who decried the acts and claimed the artists should be penalised, for example, by having their government funding revoked. Some defending this more stringent view took the tact of demanding that property laws ought to protect against individuals speaking on behalf of cultures, ethnicities, or related identities in which authors did not share.[24]

The Writers' Union of Canada entered the fray and left its membership divided by penning a resolution that encouraged 'the responsibility and accountability that attend the freedom of imagination and the freedom of expression.'[25] This view of freedom, however, is not shared by all, and the Union later recanted. Similar arguments and debates erupted around the Canada Council for the Arts and in other spheres of Canadian society.[26] The two sides of the polarised Canadian debate have been characterised as 'Romanticism and Orientalism,' the former of which upholds 'the transcendent genius of the Romantic author and his unfettered imagination' while affirming 'possessive individualism and liberal democracy' and the latter that is espoused by critical theorists who defend 'the cultural construction of the self and discursive formations of subjectivity to counter the universalising rational individualism that dominates' in liberal societies.[27] The issue resurfaced again in 2017 in Canada when an editor of the Writers' Union journal suggested that appropriation was not only inevitable but also to be celebrated and ought to be honoured with an 'Appropriation Prize' – the backlash was severe, the editor was fired, and various artists made proprietary defences of their cultural experiences and identities. The situation is by no means isolated to Canada, as similar instances have arisen in the United States and in other liberal democracies as well.[28] In March 2017, for example, the black female artist Hannah Black protested and penned an open letter excoriating the white female artist Dana Schutz. Schutz's painting, 'Open Casket,' displayed at the Whitney Biennial in New York in 2017, depicted an abstract version of a widely reproduced photo of Emmett Till's open-casket funeral. Black remarked that '[Schutz] has nothing to say to the black community about trauma.'

In her letter, co-signed by 30 other artists, Black demanded that the painting be destroyed and prevented from being sold or hung in any museum. She reminded readers that 'Non-Black people must accept that they will never embody and cannot understand' the suffering and traumatic experiences of African-Americans.[29] The incident is just one of many that have been labelled 'identity aesthetics' where 'the ethos and dynamics of identity politics into the arts,' the 'central tenet' of which is that 'we are unable to understand the experiences and *mentalité* of any identity group other than our own.'[30]

Another occasion that drew international attention was Lionel Shriver's keynote address at the Brisbane Writer's Festival in 2016. Shriver expressed grave concern that, 'Taken to their logical conclusions, ideologies recently come into vogue challenge our right to write fiction at all.'[31] The ideologies she has in mind include various forms of 'identity politics,' and for Shriver, the effects are by no means restricted to novelists, or, for that matter, to readers of novels. As she writes:

> In the latest ethos, which has spun well beyond campuses in short order, any tradition, any experience, any costume, any way of doing and saying things, that is associated with a minority or disadvantaged group is ring-fenced: look-but-don't-touch. Those who embrace a vast range of 'identities' – ethnicities, nationalities, races, sexual and gender categories, classes of economic underprivilege and disability – are now encouraged to be *possessive of their experience* and to *regard other peoples' attempts to participate in their lives and traditions, either actively or imaginatively, as a form of theft.*
>
> (emphasis added)

Shriver's account of this 'latest ethos' captures its startling claim that experience is something possessed by the individual that ought to be quarantined from entrance or intrusion by another. Each self and the range of experiences it has undergone is hermetically sealed from the participation of others, 'either actively or imaginatively.' Human experience is made akin to real estate, demarcated and fenced off from neighbours and passersby, thereby imploring each of us to retreat into our own individual, constricted selves.

Reflecting on the implications of the above discussion, we find ourselves not merely in the realm of restricted speech, as various observers have argued, but in a world that goes deeper by mandating the constriction of imagination. We are helped in seeing this by thinking with Adam Smith, whose work demonstrates that the faculty of imagination underlies our capacity to enter into lives and worlds beyond our own, plays a role in coordinating and ordering our actions, and facilitates proper judgement and evaluation of the arguments and actions of others.

Enter Adam Smith

Adam Smith was deeply interested in the origins of social cohesion and worried about the danger of factionalism to social stability.[32] It is here that I argue we see the true significance and relevance of Smith to matters of identity. It is found in his anthropology, which serves to underpin his view of sociability or human sociality. This, in turn, is foundational to his entire enterprise – one rightly characterised by 'a way of looking at the social world that balances moral concern with a realistic appraisal of human nature and human institutions.'[33] Central to his account of human nature is the faculty of imagination, and it is, according to his view, this rather elusive force and function that makes human community as well as morality possible at all.[34] It is therefore the basis of ordering individual and communal life, and important for appreciating the connection between the two.[35] For Smith, the very 'ground' of sociality or sociability is found in the imagination; therefore, a failure to form, cultivate, and properly educate our imaginative faculties cannot but have implications for human relations and for the fabric of a commercial republic more broadly.[36] Thus, the closing of the imagination induced by some forms of identitarianism, as limned above, is better appreciated for the challenge it is when seen from this Smithian perspective.

Inasmuch as imagination does not come fully formed, it is likewise susceptible to corruption. For we often don what Smith calls 'the mysterious veil of self-delusion,' whereby we hide ourselves from our own view, precluding moral clarity in thought and action, in no small part by allowing imagination to compound our love of self.[37] Indeed, vanity itself arises, Smith argues, from an 'illusion of the imagination.'[38] Its ambivalence is something about which Smith understood well, even if he often speaks indirectly about the imagination.[39] Following some of Smith's brief but weighty passages on this significant faculty, particularly as he describes its manifest operations, provides an opportunity to reflect on the imagination's continued importance today for shaping and cultivating a common moral life. Such reflection in turn helps us appreciate why identity politics that constricts the imagination, as limned above, poses such a risk to our moral and social life.

In so doing, we are led to see that the present crisis of polarisation, fragmentation, and social unrest bears some relation to debates over identity politics and restrictions on the imagination in the arts and beyond. The concerned and cautionary remarks by Shriver suggest that tendencies in the literary world are by no means confined there. Not by coincidence, Smith himself happened to be keenly interested in literature, both modern and ancient, and in rhetoric and *belles-lettres* more broadly. He well understood its formative role for the imagination and for modern commercial individuals and would have been worried about claims to limit its activity.

Imagination, sympathy, and sociality

In a remarkable passage in *The Theory of Moral Sentiments*, Smith examines 'the Foundation concerning our own Sentiments and Conduct,' which begins with a notable thought experiment. He asks us to imagine the situation of 'a human creature' who grows up in isolation from others. Smith suggests this individual would be blind in certain important respects: 'he could no more think of his own character, of the propriety or demerit of his own sentiments and conduct, of the beauty or deformity of his own mind, than of the beauty or deformity of his own face' (TMS

III.i.3, 110). His inability to see or perceive and judge himself – his character, his motives, his intellect, and his countenance – follows from his being 'provided with no mirror which can present them to his view.' For, 'society' alone provides 'the mirror which he wanted before' (TMS III.i.3, 110). Only through interaction with others does this 'creature' come to a clearer, reflective grasp of himself, by experiencing 'the countenance and behaviour of those he lives with, which always mark when they enter into, and when they disapprove of his sentiments.' Thus, 'it is here that he first views the propriety and impropriety of his own passions, the beauty and deformity of his own mind' (TMS III.i.3, 110).

The 'mirror' of society has a double effect of turning attention towards oneself in a new and significant way – by seeing things refracted through others – while furthermore enhancing and compounding the possibilities of what is sensed among others. By way of both comparison and complexity, moral judgement becomes possible. Smith writes,

> We can never survey our own sentiments and motives, we can never form any judgment concerning them; unless we remove ourselves, as it were, from our own natural station, and endeavor to view them as at a certain distance from us. But we can do this in no other way than by endeavouring to view them with the eyes of other people, or as other people are likely to view them.
> (TMS III.i.2, 110)

Thus, for the theoretical pre- or a-social creature of Smith's imagination, his whole attention would be preoccupied by 'the objects of his [own] passions,' as he would have no distance from them: 'The passions themselves . . . could scarce ever be the objects of his thoughts. The idea of them could never interest him so much as to call upon his attentive consideration' (TMS III.i.3, 110–111). As Griswold writes, for Smith, 'We are not transparent to our own consciousness; indeed, without the mediation of the other, we have no determinate moral selves 'there' waiting to be made transparent.'[40]

The faculty latent in this mirroring potential and realisation is that of the imagination, which must be awakened and is only stimulated to this level of vibrancy through social interaction – through 'the mediation of the other.'[41] Our imaginative capacity detaches the sensation of a thing's presence from the brute factuality of its existence, which makes possible the creation of an image that can thereafter be both altered and assessed. Once such forms are perceived, they can likewise be transformed by the imagination and so too reproduced as objects of perception that may be communicated to others, for example, through myths, stories, rituals, and the like. The images and productions may serve as guiding models, ideas, or principles, and so the artifacts of the imagination as much express the reality of sociality (and therefore morality) as they constitute or shape the mores and morality of society. Therefore, the operation and development of the imagination is the central component of Smith's oeuvre, for it underlies morality and sociality, as well as language, which in turn is requisite for persuasion, that is the basis of his political economy.[42] A theory that denies the possibility of imaginative reach and uses this as a basis to insist that the community pressure individuals into curtailing imagination's cultivation and use will find itself morally and socially impoverished.

To underscore the hypothetical or experimental nature of Smith's thought about the 'human creature' found in Part III of his work, and to clarify imagination's operative role, we must return to the famous words with which Smith opens his text:

> How selfish soever man may be supposed, there are evidently some principles in his nature, which interest him in the fortune of others, and render their happiness necessary to him, though he derives nothing from it except the pleasure of seeing it.
>
> (TMS I.i.1.1, 9)

As many readers have noted, Smith begins on a polemical note directed against the likes of Hobbes and Mandeville and their 'egoist' anthropologies.[43] But he also begins '*the* theory of moral sentiments' with humans as *already* social. He supposes some degree of selfishness but suggests that interest in others makes evident some natural principles that qualify our selfishness, the proof of this being that we take pleasure in even just the *sight* of others' happiness. Thus, man's other-directedness and tie to his fellows is a consequence of his ocular organ and faculties. Recalling the aforementioned mirror metaphor, it would indeed be an inappropriate and ineffective instrument for the blind. However, seeing alone does not beget understanding. For pleasure to be derived at the sight of another's fortune or happiness, one must be able to grasp it – that is, relate to, or identify with it, in some deeper way.

Smith speaks of being able to 'enter into' the fortune, the sentiments, or more broadly, the experience of another. However, Smith here proceeds by acknowledging a major challenge: 'As we have no immediate experience of what other men feel, we can form no idea of the manner in which they are affected, but by conceiving what we ourselves should feel in the like situation.' Smith intensifies the situation for the reader:

> Though our brother is upon the rack, as long as we ourselves are at our ease, our senses will never inform us of what he suffers. They never did, and never can, carry us beyond our own person, and it is *by the imagination only* that we can form any conception of what are his sensations.
>
> (TMS I.i.1.2, 9)

By way of our senses alone, we are effectively like the 'human creature' whose whole attention is preoccupied by the 'objects of his passions,' where each other 'creature' would remain but an 'object' (something less than a fellow human being, and so indeed, *creature*-like) to be sensed – seen, heard, smelled, touched, or even tasted. But thanks to the imagination – and by the imagination *alone* – are we carried beyond 'our own person' and thereby able to form a 'conception' – something more than a mere sensation – of the sensations of another. Sensations become a conception because of the imagination's power of representation:

> Neither can that faculty help us to this [i.e., to carry us beyond ourselves] any other way, than by *representing to us what would be our own, if we were* in

> *his case*. It is the impressions of our own senses only, not those of his, which our imaginations copy.
>
> (emphasis added)

Thus, we do not directly sense the senses of another, but in a mediated form; how could it be otherwise? (cf., TMS I.i.4.7, 21).[44] Our own sensations are transformed by way of representation – we are not only presented with our own sensations *per simpliciter,* but sensations can also be re-presented to us *as though* they were our own, even when they are the (apparent) senses of another.

> By the imagination we place ourselves in his situation, we conceive ourselves enduring all the same torments, we enter as it were into his body, and become in some measure the same person with him, and thence form some idea of his sensations, and even feel something which, though weaker in degree, is not altogether unlike them. His agonies, when they are thus brought home to ourselves, when we have thus adopted and made them our own, begin at last to affect us, and we then tremble and shudder at the thought of what he feels.
>
> (TMS I.i.1.2, 9)[45]

No wonder then that insofar as we can 'br[ing] home to ourselves' the sensations of others, we find ourselves interested 'in the fortune of others.'

For Smith, this 'fellow-feeling' and the capacity to 'chang[e] places' with another is what he calls 'sympathy,' which David Hume once referred to in a letter to Smith as 'the Hinge of your System.'[46] Smith broadens the typical definition beyond an identification with the sorrow or pain of others, however, 'to denote our fellow-feeling with *any passion whatever*' (TMS I.i.i.5, 10; emphasis added). We have the capacity to share passions or emotions with another; this seemingly obvious but upon reflection truly remarkable fact forms the basis of moral judgement for Smith. By virtue of the fact that we can enter into the emotional lives of others, we are able to judge the propriety and merit of a whole range of sentiments that move us and our fellows to act and behave in one or another manner in any given situation. This capacity to participate in the emotions of others, or to sympathise (which Smith likewise refers to as 'fellow-feeling'), does not, however, imply we necessarily approve of all passions or responses of others; far from it. Getting inside another's experience, for Smith, means yet retaining the distance for moral evaluation. We enter into, in order to retreat; we depart from ourselves in order to return. This imaginative travelling to and fro creates the space in which judgment becomes possible, and likewise makes possible its improvement. Notably, Smith writes, in the 'imaginary change of situations . . . I consider what I should suffer *if I was really you*, and I not only change circumstances with you, but *I change persons and characters*' (TMS VII.iii.1.4, 317, emphasis added).[47] But again, there is a return, insofar as we transpose by way of the imagination, yet we do not live according to imagination alone, embodied beings that we are. This displacement and transposition of persons and even characters – what some aptly refer to as Smith's 'simulation' theory of sympathy[48] – evince the potency and importance of imagination for our social and moral life. It also suggests, as Phillipson writes, that on Smith's account, 'we exercise our imaginative curiosity quite hard in order to achieve what we judge to be a critical detachment in our understanding of another man's behaviour.'[49] What I have referred to above as identitarianism's closing of the imagination is, on Smithian grounds, a form of dehumanisation for both the actor and the observer – it constricts the fundamentally human means by which we grant access to one another's experience and thereby form relations with each other.

That said, we enter more or less readily into different passions. Smith argues that the 'general idea of good or bad fortune' allows us to identify with grief or joy even by their 'very appearances,' while on the other hand, anger is something that demands knowing more details: 'Nature, it seems, teaches us to be more averse to enter into this passion, and, till informed of its cause, to be disposed rather to take part against it' (TMS I.i.i.8, 11). Overall: 'Sympathy, therefore, does not arise so much from the view of the passion, as from that of the *situation* which excites it' (TMS I.i.i.10, 12; emphasis added). The imaginative capacity to represent sensations is only a necessary condition, but not altogether sufficient for sympathy, as we often need more knowledge about the circumstances.[50] However, it is likewise imagination that helps to provide certain details. In other words, imagination is able to transcend the particularities of an individual's 'standpoint' or 'structure' – to adopt the language used earlier – in order to bridge or fuse the differences for the sake of entering into another's experience. As Griswold compellingly argues, the imagination is 'primarily narrative, seeking to flow into and fill up another situation, and to draw things together into a coherent story.'[51] Indeed, Smith elaborates on the way in which the imagination seeks to order our perceptions and the objects of experience, not least in its desire for 'tranquility.' This is true in theoretical activity – at the highest level in philosophy, which Smith says is an art that addresses itself to the imagination – as Smith recounts in his *History of Astronomy* (or, on the 'different systems of nature'). But the desire for equilibrium or rest is likewise true in social activity, for the mind finds in this repose a degree of pleasure.[52] The motive behind the act of sympathising, as indicated by the opening words of *TMS*, is a kind of 'pleasure,' which results from a concordance of sentiments among the observer and the observed, or the spectator and the agent. For Smith, reaching a situation of concord or harmony requires coordination on the part of both the observer and the observed, as well as the filling in of what might otherwise be missing by the imagination. Social interaction and human relations for Smith involve a constant endeavor of sensing the sentiments of others through imaginative reflection, and both parties adjusting accordingly.

Smith builds on the distinction between that of the spectator and that of the one observed to speak of 'two different *efforts*' upon which 'are founded two different sets of virtues,' the first being the 'soft, the gentle, the amiable virtues, the virtues of candid condescension and indulgent humanity' and the second that of 'the great, the awful and respectable, the virtues of self-denial, of self-government, of that command of the passions' (TMS I.i.5.1, 23; emphasis added). The very prospect of virtue then rests on the self-reflective ability to see ourselves and our deeds through the eyes of others who, in principle, remain removed from it; their interest in our situation is necessarily less than our own, though they derive some pleasure from sympathising with it to the extent that they do (insofar as we act with propriety). The sympathetic process, however, is not always 'well-functioning,' for the 'effort' on the part of all is not always manifest and varies by degrees, requiring as it does buttressing by forms of encouragement and uplift, not least that of education and inspiring models. Imagination is likewise an ambivalent faculty, for, as Smith indicates on numerous occasions, it can have corrupting effects. The higher standard to which he seeks to draw readers – the pedagogical component of his own work – is towards a measure that transcends particular observers and actors to one of impartiality, so as to align one's sympathy with an imagined individual he calls the 'impartial spectator.'[53] Achieving this degree of impartiality is the objective of educating the moral imagination – an education that can be both informal and formal.

It is precisely this achievement that the previously discussed forms of identity politics deny. According to some of the previously discussed standpoint epistemologists, impartiality is not only an impossibility but the imagination's aspiration to the status of an impartial spectator is also a fraud.[54] Focusing attention instead on radical particularity for Smith would only cater to individual self-love and indulge in a sort of corruption of the imagination that he would have likewise found troubling. Denying or decrying the entering into the experiences of others from different cultures or identities risks endorsing egoism or self-centredness. For Smith, this would be not only a moral lapse or error but also a form of egoism that would threaten the very dissolution of society. Its unfolding logic is tantamount to a Hobbesian state of nature where each becomes an enemy to every other.[55] Short of such a dire situation, it certainly conduces to a form of zero-sum politics of which Smith was highly critical.[56] Impartiality, according to Smith, is an achievement that can only be cultivated through repeated engagement in the sympathetic process; it is akin to a virtue developed by way of habit.[57] It is this habituation that allows for the widening and growing concentric circles of sympathy an individual casts towards others of increasingly distant positions and varying identities – the broader the sympathetic rings, the more they conduce to moral maturity, according to Smith.[58] Thus, Smith's combined analytical and phenomenological account demonstrates that the pursuit of a higher, impartial standard is part of genuinely lived human experience and that we are not simply doomed to our limited identities or partial selves.[59] However imperfect or limited, it is absolutely necessary for us to develop a sense of self and others, and the moral maturity to control our partial passions.

Impartiality and educating the moral imagination

While the phrase is initially mentioned in passing (TMS I.i.5.4, 24), and then employed on a number of occasions later in the work (albeit in a surprisingly discreet or subtle manner given its importance), the notion of impartiality is itself first hinted at when Smith elaborately describes the situation of sentimental and moral calibration:

> In order to produce this concord, as nature teaches the spectators to assume the circumstances of the person principally concerned, so she teaches this last in some measure to assume those of the spectators. As they are continually placing themselves in his situation, and thence conceiving emotions similar to what he feels; so he is as constantly placing himself in theirs, and thence conceiving some degree of that coolness about his own fortune, with which he is sensible that they will view it. As they are constantly considering what they themselves would feel, if they actually were the sufferers, so he is as constantly led to imagine in what manner he would be affected if he was only one of the spectators of his own situation. As their sympathy makes them look at it, in some measure, with his eyes, so his sympathy makes him look at it, in some measure, with theirs, especially when in their presence and acting under their observation: and as the reflected passion, which he thus conceives, is much weaker than the original one, it necessarily abates the violence of what he felt before he came into their presence, before he began to recollect in what manner they would be affected by it, and to view his situation in this candid and impartial light.
>
> (TMS I.i.4.8, 22)

The passage not only highlights the degree of approximation (i.e. 'some degree,' 'in some measure') and the strong element of conditionality but also illustrates that mutual emotional and situational interchange creates the possibility of rising above one's own self and position – of transcending our natural partiality and our original prejudices. A new 'impartial light' becomes possible through reflective imagination, which has the important result of 'neutraliz[ing] the individual's self-centeredness.'[60] Innate principles that turn us away from ourselves, or mitigate and moderate our self-love, must be cultivated and exercised, which the imagination both invites and undergirds. After all, 'Every man . . . is much more deeply interested in whatever immediately concerns himself, than in what concerns any other man' (TMS II.ii.2.1, 82–83). It is one thing to enter into the situation and sentiments of *one* other, and reflect back upon *one*-self – two parts, as it were, of a situational whole – it is another and morally superior thing to rise above this whole to see it without partiality or the tug of interest; or, for that matter, of one's identity. This, for Smith, is nothing short of imagination's great achievement. Cultivating this habit, we further elevate our faculty of moral judgement and our capacity for genuine virtue.

When Smith elaborates on 'the supposed impartial and well-informed spectator' he speaks of 'two tribunals' that resemble one another but are 'in reality different and distinct.' The first 'tribunal' is that of 'the man without,' which he argues is 'founded altogether in the desire of actual praise, and in the aversion to actual blame.' By contrast, that of 'the man within, is founded altogether in the desire of praise-worthiness, and in the aversion to blame-worthiness' (TMS III.2.32–33, 130–131). This distinction between praise and praiseworthiness is crucial to Smith's thinking, insofar as love of the former is a matter of appearances, or the external appearance of value, while the latter is a matter of substance, or the internal reality of value. Ideally, individuals pursue both, and for Smith, 'Man naturally desires, not only to be loved, but to be lovely; or to be that thing which is the natural and proper object of love' (TMS III.ii.1, 113). Indeed, on his view, 'the chief part of human happiness arises from the consciousness of being beloved' (TMS I.ii.5.1, 41; cf. III.i.7, 113). To be clear, while both may be desired, they may readily part ways, for, 'the desire of praise and that of praise-worthiness, though very much a-kin, are yet distinct and separate desires' (TMS VII.iv.24, 336; cf. III.ii.3, 114). This twofold set of desires corresponds to the two sides of the self, our internal and external selves – to 'the man within' and 'the man without' – and thus, on the one hand, to ourselves as actors acting according to our own motivations and, on the other hand, being observed by others in our deeds. Smith even speaks at one point of the splitting of the self into two:

> When I endeavour to examine my own conduct, when I endeavour to pass sentence upon it, and either to approve or condemn it, it is evident that, in all such cases, I divide myself, as it were, into two persons; and that I, the examiner and judge, represent in a different character from that other I, the person whose conduct is examined into and judged of.
>
> (TMS III.i.6, 113)

Again, we become mirrors to ourselves and to others by the power of the imagination to enter into the experiences of others as actors, as well as by reflecting on our own actions and sentiments as observers – for the sake of judging both others and ourselves and reaching moral calibration.

'In solitude,' Smith writes, our sentiments may be obscured or exaggerated; consequently, the impartial spectator needs to be sometimes 'awakened . . . by the presence of the real spectator.' To this, Smith adds, '[I]t is always from that spectator, from whom we can expect the least sympathy and indulgence, that we are likely to learn the most complete lesson of self-command' (TMS III.3.38, 153–154). And self-command, for Smith, 'is not only itself a great virtue, but from it all the other virtues seem to derive their principal lustre' (TMS VI.iii.2.11, 241). Thus, its cultivation is among the greatest moral achievements of the sympathetic imagination, which develops through imaginative restraint that mitigates any excessive impulse towards praise at the expense of praiseworthiness. An habitual consultation with both 'tribunals,' as it were, is necessary. Therefore, Smith argues, 'The great secret of education is to direct vanity to proper objects' (TMS VI.iii.46, 259), by which Smith implies objects of both a literal and metaphorical variety. Given the potency of both the eyes and the imagination in his moral theory, he is explicit about the role of imitation and emulation in human action and character formation. The 'awaken[ing]' of the impartial by 'the presence of the real spectator' who is less than indulgent and beckons from us a degree of self-command may very well follow from our encounter with exemplary individuals. Their presence, overall character, or way of life, through our sense of admiration, may inspire us to aspire to their pursuit. They may very well become objects of our vanity and lead us away from the desire for praise towards praiseworthiness. Stated otherwise, the imagination as an instrument of order, is also one of rule – not simply with respect to ruling passions or emotions, but regarding admirable individuals we wish to mimic or follow, both for better and for worse, to be sure. So much is, to reiterate, part of the ambivalence of the imagination, which underscores the crucial – even 'secret' – role of education in ennobling the desires and aspirations of individuals. That said, as Phillipson rightly claims, 'Smith never discusses systematically when and how we acquire our moral education.'[61] Nevertheless, Smith offers a variety of clues about the mimetic component that involves, as much as it shapes in turn, our imagination. Smith refers to '[e]mulation' as 'the anxious desire that we ourselves should excel' and argues that it 'is originally founded in our admiration of the excellence of others' (TMS III.ii.3, 114). Thus, we are anxious to be like those we admire, insofar as we imagine that we may likewise become excellent; imagination draws us out of ourselves towards others by providing the capacity to see ourselves in their place and consequently be moved to become like them.

In an important chapter devoted to 'the corruption of our moral sentiments,' Smith discusses the 'disposition to admire, and almost to worship, the rich and the powerful, and to despise, or, at least, to neglect persons of poor and mean condition' (TMS I.ii.3.1, 61). While this disposition is 'necessary both to establish and to maintain the distinction of ranks and the order of society,' he says that it is, 'at the same time, the great and most universal cause of the corruption of our moral sentiments.' The manifest ambivalence of our imaginative capacity to admire is such that it may beget positive collective benefits alongside negative individual repercussions. The visibility of power and wealth, its conspicuous nature, grants it greater immediacy and allure – it quite literally affects the senses, not least that of sight, for it cannot but be noticed. We may not readily admit it, but, Smith writes, the reality is that the rich and powerful do receive the respect and admiration of many, who dream of being like them, even as they fall well short of their status and riches. They are, Smith reluctantly suggests, 'in some respects, the *natural* objects' of our admiration (TMS I.iii.3.4, 62; emphasis added). To highlight the point he introduces an important contrast between a cast of additional alternate characters. 'The external graces, the frivolous accomplishments of that impertinent and foolish thing called a man of fashion, are commonly more admired than the solid and masculine virtues of a warrior, a statesman, a philosopher, or a legislator' (TMS I.iii.3.6, 63). Fashion and the fashionable rise to the level of an important theme in Smith's text, for it speaks to the way that desire and taste both change and are regulated through the imagination's attraction to images and individuals believed worth imitating. There is an element of rule by fashion, from a style of dress to the ideas and opinions that dominate, to the way of life that becomes representative and overwhelmingly sought after.[62] And as Smith reiterates: 'It is from our disposition to admire, and consequently to imitate, the rich and the great, that they are enabled to set, or to lead what is called the fashion' (TMS I.iii.3.7, 64). The warrior, statesman, philosopher, and legislator, are significantly less likely to serve as models of emulation when the many are drawn to the 'man of fashion.'[63] However, steering natural human tendencies towards nobler ones is precisely the aim of education.

In addition to focusing on exemplary individuals – what we may call an education in quality – Smith also underlines the importance of encountering a diversity of individuals and experiences – what we might refer to as an education in quantity. The division of labour, for Smith, is responsible for a proliferation of trades and activities and commerce itself brings increasing encounters between individuals – across erstwhile barriers of sex, race, and culture. Commercial societies, which are often more pluralistic, open up possibilities for informal modes of educating the imagination that may be reinforced by formal means of educating individuals as well. As Weinstein argues, 'who one is and associates with heavily influences the imaginative framework that cultivates sympathy,' and so Smith 'develops a philosophy of education that presumes that the more variety a person is exposed to, the more capable he or she is of seeing others.'[64] For Smith, as Court adds, 'education was neither a luxury for the privileged few, as so many educators before him had advocated, particularly during the Renaissance, nor a charity to be bestowed upon the many,' rather, 'it was instead a necessary organic process of development without which humanity could not advance in its pursuit of the perfection of nature and the improvement of the social order.'[65] And literature played a significant role in positively shaping and refining the moral sensibilities and sentiments of individuals, according to Smith's view. Education through literature 'can provide the formative structures that will determine the development of [the] spectator within.'[66] This is especially important in commercial societies that tend towards higher degrees of individualism, whereby individuals turn increasingly inward to focus on themselves. It may likewise serve as a remedy against present proclivities to dwell on personal and particularist identity traits that divide one from others; restrictions on authors and audiences would inhibit the exercising of important muscles of the imagination. Rather than overemphasising differences to the point of insurmountability or gainsaying appropriation of content and experience, education and society at large ought to encourage imagination along routes towards appreciating commonality amidst diversity. 'Education must be geared toward encouraging a diversity of shared experiences that allow for commonality between those whose own experiences seem farther from those of others. In a mosaic pluralism, Smith asks people to imagine a melting pot.'[67] An education that invites individuals to imaginatively explore the lives of truly virtuous individuals, not least of all warriors and statesmen, philosophers and legislators – that is to say, a classical education – as well as one that remains open to the study of all things human and to experience most broadly – that is to say, a liberal education – remain key pedagogical forms for cultivating our sympathetic and moral imaginations and for steering minds away from the latest corruptive intellectual fads.

Conclusion

Smith's work draws our attention to the importance of the imagination in ordering our individual and collective lives. Thinking with him encourages us to develop our imaginative capacities and abilities to sympathise with others – both real and imaginative, as well as present and past. He would be surprised – and concerned – at any effort to constrict the imagination, for it was his belief that, '[o]ur imagination . . . expands itself to every thing around us,' especially in times of prosperity such as ours (TMS IV.i.9, 183). However, Smith was also aware of the possibility of distortion and corruption of our imaginations and moral sentiments; hence, the importance of education in cultivating imaginative openness. Whether or not Smith's work provides us with sufficient diagnostic tools for understanding the origins and emergence of identity politics, he helps draw our attention to the risks of limiting or closing the imagination that are associated with some of the more extreme versions of identitarianism. Thus, his instructive approach to educating the imagination continuously engaging with, and entering into, the lives of others, including proper and deserving models for imitation, suggests that we may live with the guidance offered by an imagined impartial spectator; we need not remain confined to the particulars of our identity – any 'position' or 'standing' – or any intractable partisanships. 'Conversation with self and others on the great stage of human life is part and parcel of education [toward virtue],' as Griswold writes, and for Smith: 'Much of moral education consists in training the imagination rightly.'[68] We *really* can take on something of the lives of others – the conditional *if* of Smith's statement, 'if I was really you' is made possible by the imagination and thereby opens us to one another in significant and deeply human ways. The recent denial that this sort of imaginative reach is possible, and the subsequent extension of that view into advocacy that specifically restricts the scope of the imagination on the basis of identity, are deeply at odds with Adam Smith's central claims about what it means to be human.

Notes

1 https://books.google.com/ngrams/graph?content=identity+politics&year_start=1980&year_end=2019&corpus=en-2019&smoothing=3

2 For an overview of various definitions and uses of the term, largely prior to the turn of the century, see Mary Bernstein (2005). For some recent observers, identity politics is a form of religiosity, possibly due to Christianity's retreat in the West; the consequence of a natural religious sentiment that must find outlet; or, for political purposes to bind individuals to one another by way of new rituals, rites, and language. See McWhorter (2021) and Mitchell (2020). For others, it is an offshoot of liberalism gone astray Lilla (2017); Fukuyama (2018); Mounk (2023). For others yet, it is a product of Marxism in new garb. Rufo (2023). For some who are supportive, it is the next step in the civil rights movement, or a successive stage in the progress of justice to rectify historical wrongs and beget greater equality Freeman (1995); Davis (1989); Táíwò (2022); Crenshaw (1991); Wildman and Davis (1995). The aforementioned are but a sample of some of the literature. A comprehensive genealogical account of identity politics would also consider the development from earlier expressions and ideas of multiculturalism, recognition, political correctness, critical race theory, and the like.

3 Consider, Ledesma and Calderón (2015); see the various articles in the 'Special Issue' of *Education Sciences* (2015) edited by Lindsay Pérez Huber & Susana Muñoz exploring how critical race theory and related approaches have become integrated into teacher education; and note the survey and discussion in Zach Goldberg and Eric Kaufmann (2023):

https://media4.manhattan-institute.org/sites/default/files/school-choice-not-enough-impact-of-critical-social-justice-ideology-in-american-education.pdf.

4 Appiah (2006: 15)

5 Alcoff (2006: 312)

6 Fraser (2000: 107). For Fraser, the rise of identity politics 'encourages both the reification of group identities and the displacement of redistribution' (110) – that is, cultural or identitarian concerns come to override class or economic ones. Relevant for our purposes is her suggestion that the identitarian model supposes that 'a group has the right to be understood solely in its own terms – that no one is ever justified in viewing another subject from an external perspective or in dissenting from another's self-interpretation' (112), the consequence of which is 'less to foster interaction across differences than to enforce separatism, conformism and intolerance' (119).

7 Alcoff and Mohanty (2006: 2)

8 LaCapra (2005)

9 For discussion of this debate, see Zammito (2000) Bilgrami (2006: 10–11) and Jung (2006: 33–34); Bernstein (2005: 47–74). The most common reason post-structuralists are concerned about contingency's role in identity formation is that 'the moment of subjectification – the moment we attain the status of subject – is simultaneously the moment of subjection,' and thus identity may be the product of oppression, which they claim should be dismantled, as Foucault and others following him have argued. This is not to say identity claims are altogether precluded, as some who believe identity to be illusory nevertheless suggest it should be adopted 'as a strategy, through a strategic essentialism' that effectively employs identity as a political weapon (Alcoff 2006: 319–325). It is just this sort of weaponisation that other identitarian thinkers are concerned about. As Appiah writes: 'here is a kind of identity politics that doesn't just permit but *demands* that I treat my skin color or my sexuality as central to my social life. Even though my "race" or my sexuality may be elements of my individuality, someone who insists that I organize my life around these things is not an ally of individuality.' (Appiah 2006: 20–21)

10 Suzanna Danuta Walters, 'In Defense of Identity Politics,' *Journal of Women in Culture and Society*, Vol. 43, No. 2 (2016): 480.

11 LaCapra (2005: 238–239); Hartsock (2006: 183); Haraway (1988). Commenting on this approach, Rufo writes, 'there is no neutral frame for interpreting society, but rather a plurality of racially contingent frames based on one's position as either "the oppressed or the oppressor" all of which depends on one's racial identity and related traits. There is, therefore, often a 'nebulous epistemological foundation' to identitarianism, insofar as 'personal offense becomes objective reality; evidence gives way to ideology; identity replaces rationality as the basis of intellectual authority' Rufo (2023: 236–237).

12 Hartsock (1998: 114–115, 122–123). Overcoming such 'boundaries' of experience between women and men is ultimately only possible through a revolutionary reordering of society and the present 'phallocratic world,' and thus not by any act of imaginatively entering into the lives of others.

13 What is more, it is not self-evident that the individual undergoing the experience is ever and always the best interpreter of the meaning of an event in which he or she is involved, and that others for reasons, say, of superior intellect, depth and extent of experience, education, self-consciousness of biases, and so on might be in a better position to understand and even judge such occasions, all of which requires leaving open the possibility that others may imaginatively participate in the lives of others.

14 Fukuyama (2018: 109–111) (emphasis in original).

15 Hekman (1997: 341). Rolin (2009: 218–226). For an additional account of limitations on understanding due to experience's non-transferability based on one's embodied position, see Harding (1992).

16 For critical discussions, including a review of some of the debates and literatures on standpoint epistemologists and their detractors, see Gregor McLennan (1995: 391–409); Ward, (1997).

17 Hekman (1997: 342). As Hekman adds: 'It is my contention that feminist standpoint theory represents the beginning of a paradigm shift in the concept of knowledge, a shift that is transforming not only feminist theory but also epistemology itself.'
18 Valdez (2001: 70)
19 Harnois (2010: 70)
20 Collins (1986: 29)
21 Criticism of cultural appropriation under the label 'cultural racism' can be found in Kendi (2019), esp. Ch. 7; cf. Coates (2015) who speaks of such appropriation in terms of 'plunder'; see also Johnson (2016).
22 For discussion of the many intellectual challenges and practical difficulties regarding cultural appropriation, not least of all in how best to define 'culture' and what exactly it means to 'appropriate,' see Young (2005). While significant, entering into these issues would distract from the more narrow focus here of how certain opponents of cultural appropriation rely on a specific epistemology that explicitly limits the powers and purview of human imagination. Compare with Lenard and Balint (2020), who make important distinctions between appropriation, offence, and misrepresentation, and discuss reasons for amplification of concerns on social media and in our culture today.
23 Ziff and Rao (1997: 17)
24 For details on these debates in the Canadian context, see Coombe (1997), Nourbese Philip (1997) Rowell (1995).
25 Quoted in Ziff and Rao (1997: 18).
26 See Berman (2004).
27 Coombe (1997: 76–78). For Coombe, 'if the imperialist claims of the Romantic author colored one side of this debate, the essentialising voice of Orientalism crept into the other' (78). 'Ultimately,' Coombe concludes, 'questions of culture and its appropriation are political, rather than ontological, ones that demand *empathetic identifications* rather than formal resolutions – a situational ethics to which we must always attend' (93; emphasis added). Compare with Brown (1998).
28 See Tsosie (2002), Prior (2019), and Lenard and Balint (2020: 341–344). For discussion of various American examples of cultural appropriation by whites of black culture and criticism suggesting an inability for whites to genuinely understand the black experience, see the essays in Tate (2003).
29 Greenberger (2017)
30 Beauchamp (2017). Beauchamp lists several other famous paintings that would not meet the standards for creation according to 'identity aesthetics.'
31 Shriver's full speech, 'I Hope the Concept of Cultural Appropriation is a Passing Fad,' can be found here: https://www.theguardian.com/commentisfree/2016/sep/13/lionel-shrivers-full-speech-i-hope-the-concept-of-cultural-appropriation-is-a-passing-fad. Further reflections by her on the reaction to her speech are recounted in Shriver (2016): https://www.nytimes.com/2016/09/23/opinion/will-the-left-survive-the-millennials.html. See also Albano (2022).
32 Smith does address the problem of faction; see Sandra J. Peart and David M. Levy (2009). The scholarship and debate over Smith's view on the political as well as on his political views is extensive, much of which has been ably summarized in Liu (2022), who suggests that Smith's politics 'resisted the temptation to fall into convenient categories' and the defining characteristic of Smith's politics is such that it cannot 'be found prepackaged with any clear labels' (272–73). For an important corrective of the dominant interpretation of Smith's comments on the 'crafty politician' as wholly negative, see Schliesser (2021).
33 Muller (1993: 5). Ryan Patrick Hanley (2009) makes the most convincing case for Smith's 'propensity to dialectic' and to 'the resolution of seeming opposites through a synthesis that in turn makes possible the realization of new horizons that require our renewed application' (209).
34 As Blosser (2016: 164) rightly claims, 'In addition to self-love, Smith saw that an economically and morally robust society needs people capable of using our imaginations,

sympathy, and virtues to respond properly to each other and our world.' Regarding the elusiveness of the imagination, see Brann (1991).

35 As Hanley writes, 'We today tend to assume that self and society are distinct. But Smith pushes back against this. In some deep sense, all of us, even in seeking to realize our individuality, are bound to the people around us in inescapable ways. This has important social and political implications, of course' (Hanley 2019: 17). Indeed, the implications are social and political, and what makes the bonds between us 'inescapable' is the result of imagination.

36 Remy Debes (2016: 193) uses the apt phrase of 'ground' in this way to indicate the fundamental role the imagination plays.

37 Adam Smith, *The Theory of Moral Sentiments* (Indianapolis: Liberty Fund, 1976), III. iv.4, 158. Adam Smith, *The Theory of Moral Sentiments* (Indianapolis: Liberty Fund, 1976). All references to this work will be noted parenthetically in the essay by Part, Section (where applicable), Chapter (where applicable), Paragraph, and Page Number.

38 TMS III.ii.4, 115

39 This is likewise noted by Charles L. Griswold, Jr. (2006). Griswold's essay is the best, and a rare, effort to reconstruct Smith's teaching on the imagination, which he rightly describes as 'a continuous and important theme throughout his work' that would no less have 'likely have been an important theme in the work he did not live to complete' (22).

40 Griswold (2006: 105).

41 Griswold (2006: 105).

42 Lewis (2000) provides compelling arguments about the underlying role of speech and persuasion in Smith's political economy.

43 See Winch (1998).

44 Smith is not bothered by what contemporary philosophers call the 'other minds' problem, for the imagination's powers provide an entrée into minds like our own. See Thomson (2021).

45 Smith underlines the detail to which the imagination can and must attend: 'the spectator must, first of all, endeavor, as much as he can, to put himself in the situation of the other, and to bring home to himself *every little circumstance* of distress which can possibly occur to the sufferer. He must adopt *the whole case of his companion with all its minutest incidents*; and strive to render *as perfect as possible*, that imaginary change of situation upon which his sympathy is founded' (I.i.4.6, 21; emphasis added).

46 Letter from David Hume, London, 28 July 1759, #36, in *Correspondence of Adam Smith* (Corr.: 43).

47 No mere changing of places or perspectives with the other, 'he also asks them to imagine to be like the other' Carrasco and Fricke (2016: 255).

48 Debes (2016: 193, 195).

49 Phillipson (1983: 183).

50 To the extent that the obvious emphasis is on sentiments or emotions, the mind is clearly involved in an important way; human sentiment and imagination – and therefore sympathy as the basis of morality – are here distinctive traits from animals, who are not capable of the same. Consequently, Smith's account here contrasts in an important way from Rousseau's view of *pitié*, which is a sentiment he suggests as pre-rational and pre-social and therefore shared by beasts. See Schwarze and Scott (2018).

51 Griswold (2006: 26).

52 Smith, 'History of Astronomy,' *Essays on Philosophical Subjects*, II.12, 45–46ff.

53 For discussion of *TMS* itself as a work of moral education, see Heydt (2008).

54 For an argument that it is 'absurd' or a form of 'conventional mythology' to hold that science is 'disinterested' and 'impartial,' and that it is 'futile to imagine that one can locate an impartial, dispassionate, disinterested' perspective of judgement, see Harding (1991:10, 11, 237–238 and Haraway (1988).

55 Muller (1993: 101); Heilbronner (1982) suggests that 'running concerns with the issue of social stability' are one of the three great themes of *TMS* (428–29ff).

56 The zero-sum nature of mercantilist politics, and the injustice of such a mutually exclusive logic more broadly in politics and law, is a crucial target of Smith's criticism. See, for example, Muller (1993: 79–82); Lieberman (2006).
57 On one reading of Smith the 'impartial spectator' is likened to conscience, the latter of which Smith says 'may be called the natural eye of the mind,' and so just like observing objects on the landscape requires that we 'change our position' to get a clearer and fuller view, we need look 'with the eyes of a third person, who has no particular connection with either, and who judges with impartiality between us' (TMS III.3.2–3, 135). Need for this perspectival approach is especially keen insofar as '[t]he great source of both the misery and disorders of human life, seems to arise from over-rating the difference between one permanent situation and another' (TMS III.3.31, 149).
58 Forman-Barzilai (2010: 11–25)
59 For an interpretation of Smith that takes up the question of modern categories of identity as well as post-modern critiques, see Weinstein (2013). Weinstein suggests that Smith's theory of pluralism (a term he acknowledges that well predates Smith) is bound up with his capacious understanding of rationality that is not reducible to economistic calculus but includes sensitivity to heterogeneous motivations and needs; hence the importance of imagination to appreciate this richness, as well as the role of education. As Weinstein argues, 'Sympathy is built on the imagination, which is itself dependent on and cultivated through education. However, for Smith, while socialization and education cultivate difference, they also help to bridge it because they enable spectators to enter into the experiences of others. Imagination is the bridge between people that creates community' (81).
60 Minowitz (1993: 47). On the theme of 'neutralization,' Heilbronner likewise suggests that sympathy enables us 'to perform the mysterious act of interpersonal identification, and thereby to achieve the insight and understanding that releases each person from the grip of his self-directed drives, delivering him or her over to the kingdom of choice and responsibility.' Heilbronner (1982: 431).
61 Phillipson (1983: 187)
62 McAleer (2025) has written most insightfully on this topic in various pieces of public commentary pieces. See also Lipovestky (1994).
63 Early in *TMS* Smith also speaks of 'the great leader in science and taste' as one who 'directs and conducts our own sentiments, the extent and superior justness of whose talents astonish us with wonder and surprise, who excites our admiration, and seems to deserve our applause,' for their intellectual virtues but also for their judgement, 'not as something useful, but as right, as accurate, as agreeable to truth and reality' (TMS I.i.3–4, 20). Further study might enumerate and elaborate the various models that Smith's pedagogical work offers, and rank them accordingly, in light of his own broader vision and defense of the commercial society.
64 Weinstein (2013: 83, 107)
65 Court (1985: 327)
66 (Court 1985: 331). Notably, Court writes, 'For the first time in British educational history, Smith had linked the study of social psychology directly with the teaching of English literature' (333). Compare with Wright (2006).
67 Weinstein (2013: 106)
68 Griswold (2006: 45), Weinstein (2013: 95)

References

Albano, M. (2002) 'Identity Politics Is Killing Fiction', *Spiked*, January 27, 2022. https://www.spiked-online.com/2022/01/27/identity-politics-is-killing-fiction/

Alcoff, L. M. (2006) 'Who's Afraid of Identity Politics?', in P. M. L. Moya and M. R. Hames-Garcia (eds.) *Reclaiming Identity: Reality Theory and the Predicament of Postmodernism*. Berkeley, CA: University of California Press, pp. 312–344.

Alcoff, L. M. and Mohanty, S. P. (2006) 'Reconsidering Identity Politics: An Introduction', in L. M. Alcoff et al. (eds.) *Identity Politics Reconsidered*. London: Palgrave Macmillan.
Appiah, A. (2006) 'The Politics of Identity', *Daedalus*, 135(4, Fall): 15–22.
Beauchamp, G. (2017) 'Open Casket and Cultural Appropriation', *The Antioch Review*, 75(5, Fall): 458–459.
Berman, T. (2004) 'Cultural Appropriation', in T. Biolsi (ed.) *A Companion to the Anthropology of American Indians*. Malden, MA: Blackwell Publishing, pp. 383–397.
Bernstein, M. (2005) 'Identity Politics', *Annual Review of Sociology*, 31: 47–74.
Bilgrami, A. (2006) 'Notes Toward the Definition of "Identity"', *Daedalus*, 135(4, Fall): 5–14.
Blosser, J. (2016) 'More Than Free Markets: Adam Smith and the Virtue of Responsibility', *Journal of the Society of Christian Ethics*, 36(1, Spring/Summer): 163–179.
Brann, E. (1991) *The World of the Imagination: Sum and Substance*. Savage, MD: Rowman & Littlefield Publishers.
Brown, M. F. (1998) 'Can Culture Be Copyrighted?', *Current Anthropology*, 39(2, April): 193–222.
Carrasco, M. A. and Fricke, C. (2016) 'Adam Smith's Impartial Spectator', *Econ Journal Watch*, 13(2, May): 312–318.
Coates, T.-N. (2015) *Between the World and Me*. New York: Penguin.
Collins, P. H. (1986) 'Learning from the Outsider Within: The Sociological Significance of Black Feminist Thought', *Social Problems*, 33(6, October–December): S14–S32.
Coombe, R. J. (1997) 'The Proprieties of Culture and the Possession of Identity: Postcolonial Struggle and the Legal Imagination', in B. Ziff and P. V. Rao (eds.) *Borrowed Power: Essays on Cultural Appropriation*. New Brunswick: Rutgers University Press, pp. 74–96.
Court, F. E. (1985) 'Adam Smith and the Teaching of English Literature', *History of Education Quarterly*, 25(3): 325–340.
Crenshaw, K. W. (1991) 'Mapping the Margins: Intersectionality, Identity Politics, and Violence against Women of Color', *Stanford Law Review*, 43(July): 1241–1299.
Davis, P. C. (1989) 'Law as Microagression', in K. Crenshaw (ed.) *Critical Race Theory: The Cutting Edge*. New York: The New Press, pp. 141–151.
Debes, R. (2016) 'Adam Smith and the Sympathetic Imagination', in R. P. Hanley (ed.) *Adam Smith: His Life, Thought, and Legacy*. Princeton: Princeton University Press, pp. 192–207.
Forman-Barzilai, F. (2010) *Adam Smith and the Circles of Sympathy: Cosmopolitanism and Moral Theory*. Cambridge: Cambridge University Press.
Fraser, N. (2000) 'Rethinking Recognition', *New Left Review*, 3(May/June): 107–120.
Freeman, A. D. (1995) 'Derrick Bell – Race and Class: The Dilemma of Liberal Reform', in K. Crenshaw (ed.) *Critical Race Theory: The Cutting Edge*. New York: The New Press, pp. 573–578.
Fukuyama, F. (2018) *Identity: The Demand for Dignity and the Politics of Resentment*. New York: Farrar, Strauss, and Giroux.
Goldberg, Z. and Kaufmann, E. (2023) 'School Choice Is Not Enough: The Impact of Critical Social Justice Ideology in American Education', *Manhattan Institute Report*, February 2023. https://media4.manhattan-institute.org/sites/default/files/school-choice-not-enough-impact-of-critical-social-justice-ideology-in-american-education.pdf
Greenberger, A. (2017) '"The Painting Must Go": Hannah Black Pens Open Letter to the Whitney About Controversial Biennial Work', *ARTnews*, March 21, 2017. https://www.artnews.com/artnews/news/the-painting-must-go-hannah-black-pens-open-letter-to-the-whitney-about-controversial-biennial-work-7992/
Griswold, Jr., C. L. (2006) 'Imagination: Morals, Science, and Arts', in K. Haakonssen (ed.) *The Cambridge Companion to Adam Smith*. Cambridge: Cambridge University Press.
Hanley, R. P. (2009) *Adam Smith and the Character of Virtue*. Cambridge: Cambridge University Press.
Hanley, R. P. (2019) *Our Great Purpose: Adam Smith on Living a Better Life*. Princeton: Princeton University Press.

Haraway, D. (1988) 'Situated Knowledges: The Science Question in Feminism and the Privilege of Partial Perspective', *Feminist Studies*, 14(3): 575–559.
Harding, S. (1991) *Whose Science? Whose Knowledge? Thinking from Women's Lives*. Ithaca, NY: Cornell University Press.
Harding, S. (1992) 'Rethinking Standpoint Epistemology: What Is "Strong Objectivity?"', *The Centennial Review*, 36(3, Fall): 437–470.
Harnois, C. (2010) 'Race, Gender, and the Black Women's Standpoint', *Sociological Forum*, 25(1, March): 68–85.
Hartsock, N. (1998) 'The Feminist Standpoint: Developing the Ground for a Specifically Feminist Historical Materialism', in *The Feminist Standpoint Revisited, and Other Essays*. London: Routledge, pp. 147–164.
Hartsock, N. C. M. (2006) 'Experience, Embodiment, and Epistemologies', *Hypatia*, 21(2, Spring): 178–183.
Heilbronner, R. (1982) 'The Socialization of the Individual in Adam Smith', *History of Political Economy*, 14(3): 427–439.
Hekman, S. (1997) 'Truth and Method: Feminist Standpoint Theory Revisited', *Signs: Journal of Women in Culture and Society*, 22(2): 341–365.
Heydt, C. (2008) '"A Delicate and an Accurate Pencil": Adam Smith, Description, and Philosophy as Moral Education', *History of Philosophy Quarterly*, 25(1, January): 57–73.
Johnson, M. Z. (2016) '5 Things You Don't Realize When You Defend Cultural Appropriation', *Everyday Feminism*, May 29, 2016. https://everydayfeminism.com/2016/05/defending-cultural-appropriation/
Jung, C. (2006) 'Why Liberals Should Value "Identity Politics"', *Daedalus*, 135(4, Fall): 32–39.
Kendi, I. X. (2019) *How to Be an Antiracist*. New York: Random House.
LaCapra, D. (2005) 'Experience and Identity', in L. M. Alcoff, M. Hames-Garcia, S. P. Moharty and P. M. L. Moya (eds.) *Identity Politics Reconsidered*. London: Palgrave Macmillan, pp. 228–245.
Ledesma, M. C. and Calderón, D. (2015) 'Critical Race Theory in Education: A Review of Past Literature and a Look to the Future', *Qualitative Inquiry*, 21(3): 206–222.
Lenard, P. T. and Balint, P. (2020) 'What Is (the Wrong of) Cultural Appropriation?', *Ethnicities*, 20(2): 331–352.
Lewis, T. J. (2000) 'Persuasion, Domination and Exchange: Adam Smith on the Political Consequences of Markets', *Canadian Journal of Political Science/Revue canadienne de science politique*, 33(2, June): 273–289.
Lieberman, D. (2006) 'Adam Smith on Justice, Rights, and Law', in K. Haakonnssen (ed.) *The Cambridge Companion to Adam Smith*. New York: Cambridge University Press, pp. 214–245.
Lilla, M. (2017) *The Once and Future Liberal: After Identity Politics*. New York: Harper.
Lipovestky, G. (1994) *The Empire of Fashion: Dressing Modern Democracy*, (trans. C. Porter). Princeton: Princeton University Press.
Liu, G. (2022) *Adam Smith's America: How a Scottish Philosopher Became an Icon of American Capitalism*. Princeton: Princeton University Press.
McAleer, G. J. (2025) *Veneration & Refinement: The Ethics of Fashion*. https://ethicsoffashion.com/
McLennan, G. (1995) 'Feminism, Epistemology and Postmodernism: Reflections on Current Ambivalence', *Sociology*, 29(2, May): 391–409.
McWhorter, J. (2021) *Woke Racism: How a New Religion Has Betrayed Black America*. New York: Penguin.
Minowitz, P. (1993) *Profits, Priests, and Princes: Adam Smith's Emancipation of Economics from Politics and Religion*. Stanford: Stanford University Press.
Mitchell, J. (2020) *American Awakening: Identity Politics and Other Afflictions of Our Time*. New York: Encounter Books.
Mounk, Y. (2023) *The Identity Trap: A Story of Ideas and Power in Our Time*. New York: Penguin.

Muller, J. Z. (1993) *Adam Smith in His Time and Ours: Designing the Decent Society.* New York: The Free Press.

Nourbese Philip, M. (1997) 'The Disappearing Debate; or, How the Discussion of Racism Has Been Taken Over by the Censorship Issue', in B. Ziff and P. Rao (eds.) *Borrowed Power: Essays on Cultural Appropriation.* New Brunswick, NJ: Rutgers University Press, pp. 97–108.

Peart, S. J. and Levy, D. M. (2009) 'Adam Smith and the Place of Faction', in J. T. Young (ed.) *The Elgar Companion to Adam Smith.* Cheltenham: Edward Elgar, pp. 335–345.

Phillipson, N. (1983) 'Adam Smith as Civic Moralist', in I. Hont and M. Ignatieff (eds.) *Wealth and Virtue: The Shaping of Political Economy in the Scottish Enlightenment.* Cambridge: Cambridge University Press.

Prior, A. (2019) 'What's Wrong with Cultural Appropriation? A Philosophical Investigation', *Masterarbeit Universität Hamburg* (June): 50–87.

Rolin, K. (2009) 'Standpoint Theory as a Methodology for the Study of Power Relations', *Hypatia*, 24(4, Fall): 218–226.

Rowell, J. (1995) 'The Politics of Cultural Appropriation', *The Journal of Value Inquiry*, 29: 137–142.

Rufo, C. F. (2023) *America's Cultural Revolution: How the Radical Left Conquered Everything.* New York: Broadside Books.

Schliesser, E. (2021) 'Adam Smith on Political Leadership', in R. J. W. Mills and C. Smith (eds.) *The Scottish Enlightenment: Human Nature, Social Theory, and Moral Philosophy: Essays in Honour of Christopher J. Berry*. Edinburgh: Edinburgh University Press, pp. 132–163.

Schwarze, M. A. and Scott, J. T. (2018) 'Mutual Sympathy and the Moral Economy: Adam Smith Reviews Rousseau', *The Journal of Politics*, 81(1): 65–80.

Shriver, L. (2016) 'Will the Left Survive the Millennials?', *The New York Times*, September 23, 2016.

Smith, A. (1976) [1759] *The Theory of Moral Sentiments*, (ed.) D. D. Raphael and A. L. Macfie. Indianapolis: Liberty Fund.

Smith, A. (1982) [1795] *Essays on Philosophical Subjects*, (ed.) W. P. D. Wightman. Indianapolis: Liberty Fund.

Smith, A. (1987) *The Correspondence of Adam Smith*, (ed.) I. S. Ross. Indianapolis: Liberty Fund.

Táíwò, O. O. (2022) *Elite Capture: How the Powerful Took Over Identity Politics (and Everything Else)*. London: Pluto Press.

Tate, G. (2003) *Everything but the Burden: What White People Are Taking from Black Culture*. New York: Random House.

Thomson, J. (2021) 'The Problem of Other Minds: A Disturbing World of Polite, Smiling Zombies', *Big Think*, August 19, 2021. https://bigthink.com/thinking/problem-other-minds-js-mill/

Tsosie, R. (2002) 'Reclaiming Native Stories: An Essay on Cultural Appropriation and Cultural Rights', *Arizona State Law Journal*, 34: 299–359.

Valdez, J. (2001) 'Standpoint Epistemology and Women of Color', in D. L. Hoeveler and J. Boles (eds.) *Women of Color: Defining the Issues, Hearing the Voices*. Santa Barbara, CA: Greenwood Press.

Walters, S. D. (2016) 'In Defense of Identity Politics', *Journal of Women in Culture and Society*, 43(2): 473–488.

Ward, S. (1997) 'Being Objective about Objectivity: The Ironies of Standpoint Epistemological Critiques of Science', *Sociology*, 31(4, November): 773–791.

Weinstein, J. R. (2013) *Adam Smith's Pluralism: Rationality, Education, and the Moral Sentiments*. New Haven: Yale University Press.

Wildman, S. M. and Davis, A. D. (1995) 'Language and Silence: Making Systems of Privilege Visible', *Santa Clara Law Review*, 35(3): 881–906.

Winch, D. (1998) 'Adam Smith and the Liberal Tradition', in K. Haakonssen (ed.) *Adam Smith*. London: Dartmouth Publishing, pp. 359–382.
Wright, J. B. (2006) 'Adam Smith's Ethics and the "Noble Arts"', *Review of Social Economy*, LXIV(2, June): 155–180.
Young, J. O. (2005) 'Profound Offense and Cultural Appropriation', *The Journal of Aesthetics and Art Criticism*, 63(2, Spring): 135–146.
Zammito, J. H. (2000) 'Reading "Experience": The Debate in Intellectual History among Scott, Toews, and LaCapra', in P. M. L. Moya and M. R. Hames-Garca (eds.) *Reclaiming Identity: Realist Theory and the Predicament of Postmodernism*. Berkeley, CA: University of California University Press, pp. 279–311.
Ziff, B. and Rao, P. V. (1997) 'Introduction to Cultural Appropriation: A Framework for Analysis', in B. Ziff and P. V. Rao (eds.) *Borrowed Power: Essays on Cultural Appropriation*. New Brunswick: Rutgers University Press.

11 Adam Smith on imagination and self-command

Eric Entrican Wilson

Introduction

This chapter is about the role of imagination in Smith's theory of self-command, which he defines as emotion regulation or the 'control of our passive feelings' (*Theory of Moral Sentiments* III.3.20).[1] Other commentators have acknowledged the importance of imagination to Smith's theory, but none has focused on it in detail or analysed the mechanics of imagination's contributions to the process of regulating emotion. My approach fills this gap in the scholarship.

The central argument advances two main claims. First, imagination plays a necessary and prominent role in Smithian self-command. Control over the imagination is what makes possible the mode of 'sensibility' on which self-command rests. The second main claim is that imagination makes two distinct contributions to self-command. It makes its first contribution by enabling A to switch perspectives with B and form an idea of B's situation and feelings. By means of this imaginative operation, A recruits the sympathetic process that alters her existing or anticipated passions.[2] Imagination makes its second contribution by providing a target or goal for self-command. The process is goal-directed, and Smith believes the goal is to align one's passions with a standard represented by the imagination.

In some ways, my approach is similar to Kopajtic (2020). However, we emphasise different aspects of Smith's theory. She argues against recent 'rationalist' interpretations of Smith by focusing on the role of emotion and sociability in self-command. I agree with much of what Kopajtic says about these factors and see no reason to repeat her arguments against Montes and Carrasco, which speak for themselves (2020, pp. 19–21). However, by focusing on imagination, my approach emphasises the role of *cognitive* control. Self-command, according to Smith, depends on the ability to control one's ideas by means of the imagination. Regulation of the passions is an *effect* of this control over one's ideas.

Therefore, I would not call Smith's view 'sentimentalist.' The label risks obscuring the centrality of cognitive control – or *idea* regulation – to Smith's theory. Furthermore, the label risks grouping his view with Hutcheson's, which would be a mistake.[3] Hutcheson may be a sentimentalist, but his account of emotion regulation belongs to the reason-based tradition, broadly construed. On his view, the 'violent' passions are regulated by the understanding, which affords belief correction and

DOI: 10.4324/9781003767824-14

rational reflection on general truths and 'superior goods.' Such operations arouse 'calm' emotions that counteract the violent ones we wish to control (Hutcheson 2006, p. 127; Hutcheson 2002, p. 32).[4] Smith, as will become clear, disagrees. However, the issue of labelling is not my focus. While we disagree on a few issues, my approach complements Kopajtic's interpretation more than challenges it. Indeed, it strengthens her case against recent 'rationalist' readings by downplaying reason and giving pride of place to the imagination.

Imagination and sensibility to the feelings of others

According to Smith, the imagination plays a necessary and prominent role in the process of self-command. This is because when a person tries to regulate their emotions, they must do so by using their imagination. Smith does not make this claim explicit, so my intention is to do that here. The point is easily gleaned from many of his examples, and it follows quite naturally from his more explicit remarks about the basis of self-command.

Smith claims that, 'our sensibility to the feelings of others . . . is the very principle upon which [self-command] is founded' (TMS III.3.34). Elaborating, he writes that, 'this very same principle' that 'prompts' us to 'compassionate' another's sorrow also 'prompts us to restrain our own,' and the same principle which 'prompts us to congratulate his joy . . . prompts us to restrain the levity and intemperance of our own joy' (TMS III.3.34). Similarly, he claims that self-command rests on 'a regard to the sentiments of the real or supposed spectator of our conduct' (TMS III.3.21). The fundamental point here is straightforward: *self-command is based on 'sensibility.'* The context of such remarks makes it clear that Smith wishes to break the usual associations between self-command and cold rationality or Stoic apathy. Correlatively, he wants the reader to associate self-command with imagination, emotion, and human sociability.

Smith does not define 'sensibility,' but following common usage, he thinks of it as receptivity to stimuli. Being 'receptive' to x is being susceptible to x or capable of being affected by it. The five corporeal senses are paradigmatic forms of sensibility. Your sense of sight, for instance, makes you receptive to the redness of strawberries. Smith's remarks in TMS and his early 'Of the External Senses' suggest that being sensible to the feelings of others is a matter of *feeling with* or *for* them.[5] This idea is found throughout Smith's discussion of self-command. For example:

> [T]he man who feels the most for the joys and sorrows of others, is best fitted for acquiring the most complete control of his own joys and sorrows. The man of the most exquisite humanity, is naturally the most capable of acquiring the highest degree of self-command.
>
> (TMS III.3.36)

The phenomenon is at the centre of TMS, of course, and his term for it is 'sympathy.' Given this, we can draw a conclusion that Smith does not actually formulate, namely, *sympathy is the basis of self-command.* Here 'sympathy' refers primarily to the sympathetic *process,* which consists of 'changing places in fancy' with another person, imagining how you would feel in her place or if you were her, and responding emotionally to that change of place or character (TMS I.i.1.3).[6] It is this process that makes us receptive to the feelings of others, just as it is the sense of smell that makes us receptive to the aromas in our environment.

This brings us to the central focus of the chapter: imagination's role in the process. As Smith's language indicates, the bulk of the work in sympathy is performed by 'fancy' or the imagination.[7] Its role is crucial because we cannot directly perceive the feelings of others.[8] Instead, we must represent or 'conceive' of them, which we do by imagining how we would feel in their situation (TMS I.i.1.2–4). As many scholars have discussed, Smith describes two forms of this process. In some cases, you imagine how you would feel *as you* in my situation. In other cases, you imagine how you would feel *as me* in my situation.[9] All sympathy involves an imaginative change of *place*, but the latter form of sympathy also involves the more strenuous and creative process of changing *characters* or *persons* (TMS VII.iii.1.4). This seems to parallel the way an actor might work out how to play a scene. Keanu Reeves imagines how John Wick (the character) would feel when such-and-such happens, not how *he* (the actor) would feel.[10]

The centrality of imagination to Smith's account of sympathy is widely recognised. Griswold, for example, writes that 'sympathy is an act of the imagination' (1999, p. 85).[11] Similarly, Raphael claims that in sympathy, 'imagination does most of the work' (2006, p. 163; cf. 2007, pp. 13–15). Even scholars who disagree about key aspects of Smith's view agree that imagination does most of the work. Unlike many interpreters, Nanay thinks of Smithian sympathy as 'quasi-automatic,' but he holds that imaginative processes are 'at the center of Smith's analysis' (2012, p. 101). Schliesser challenges Fleischacker's 'projectionist' view, but they both believe that most phases of the sympathetic process are carried out by the imagination Schliesser (2017, pp. 23–48). For Fleischacker, changing places in fancy with another person is 'the very essence of [Smithean] sympathy' (2012, p. 281 n.14). The prominent and active role of imagination is what chiefly distinguishes Smith's view from Hume's, according to Fleischacker (2019, p. 11). 'Smith,' he argues, says that 'the imagination [helps] us sympathize by enabling us to picture what it would be like to *inhabit the other person's situation*' (2012, p. 292).[12]

The first main claim of the chapter follows from the points just established. The core concept of self-command is deliberate, goal-directed emotion regulation. Self-command is based on our sensitivity to the feelings of others. Such sensitivity is made possible by the sympathetic process. Yet the bulk of the work in this process is performed by the imagination. Therefore, control over the imagination plays a necessary and prominent role in emotion regulation. When attempting to regulate our emotions, we use our imagination to awaken our 'sensibility' to the emotions of others and thereby open our own mental lives to the regulating influence of those emotions (as we imagine them to be).

Versions of this conclusion have been acknowledged or articulated by others (e.g. Kopajtic, 2020; Fleischacker, 2019, p. 21; Griswold, 2006, p. 41). However, this point has not received enough scholarly attention. My aim has been to state it explicitly and to show how it follows directly from Smith's theory of sympathy and his clearest statements about the underlying 'principle' of self-command. My next task is to examine imagination's role in detail. Smith's account is short on explicit theory and long on examples, so I attempt to glean the former from the latter.

Imagination's two main contributions to self-command

Smith's first description of emotion regulation occurs in Part I of TMS (TMS I.i.4.6–8).[13] The passage is worth quoting at length, and I shall return to it throughout this chapter. In the passage, Smith describes regulating your emotions for the sake of mutual sympathy with others. He focuses, in particular, on the difficulty of achieving mutual sympathy in situations where we don't see eye to eye or feel the same way about something. You don't resent the injuries I have suffered, and I feel no pity for your losses. As a result, it is hard to relate, and we may even 'become intolerable to one another' (TMS I.i.4.5). Absence of mutual sympathy is painful, so we both want to avoid being out of sync. Because it does not occur automatically, mutual sympathy in such circumstances requires self-command. Here is what we must do:

> In all such cases, that there may be some correspondence of sentiments between the spectator and the person principally concerned, the spectator must, first of all, endeavor, as much as he can, to put himself in the situation of the other, and to bring home to himself every little circumstance of distress which can possibly occur to the sufferer. He must adopt the whole case of his companion with all its minutest incidents; and strive to render as perfect as possible, that imaginary change of situation upon which his sympathy is founded.
> (TMS I.i.4.6)[14]

Smith mentions imagination only once, but it performs two main functions here. First, the spectator tries to imagine the feelings of the person principally concerned (the sufferer). We know from the beginning of TMS that the spectator must do this by imagining how she would feel in the sufferer's shoes (TMS I.i.1.2). This is the 'imaginary change of situation upon which his sympathy is founded.' As I have argued, this imaginative change of perspective is how the spectator recruits the sympathetic process, which opens their own passions to the influence of others.' In this passage, Smith also emphasises that in cases where two parties dislike each other or have opposed interests, the spectator must use their imagination to add detail, texture, and specificity to their representations of the sufferer's feelings and circumstances. This is how the spectator 'brings home' the sufferer's misfortune and their responses to it. Without the extra effort, the spectator's idea of the sufferer's feelings about her situation might be too dull to alter their own feelings

(TMS I.i.1.2). Her attempt to regulate her own passions by recruiting sympathy will be ineffective.

The passage also indicates that imagination plays a second key role in the process of emotion regulation. We know from the context that the spectator's endeavour is goal-directed. She is trying to align her feelings with the passions of the sufferer in the hopes of achieving mutual sympathy. The latter is represented by the spectator's own imagination. (Meanwhile, the sufferer tries to do the same.) Therefore, since those feelings are represented by the spectator's imagination, it is her imagination that supplies her endeavour with its target or standard. Because of her desire for mutual sympathy, the spectator's goal is to alter her passions to meet this standard.

First contribution

Let us now examine imagination's first contribution more closely. In the passage quoted earlier (TMS I.i.4.6) Smith claims that to regulate her passions, a person must put herself 'in the situation of the other.' As we know, this is accomplished by means of the imagination. The basic process consists of A imagining how things appear and feel from B's perspective, which A accomplishes by imagining how *she* would feel in B's circumstances. This is imagination's first main contribution to self-command.

The person's change of perspective has two important effects. First, it distances her from her own perspective and passions. The distance loosens the grip of those passions, making it easier to attend to considerations that lie outside the scope of her most immediate perspective – such as her future self's interests and the interests of others. (It also facilitates the moral self-assessment Smith explains in TMS III.) Second, it opens her up to the feelings of others, making her state of mind, including her own passions, susceptible to the influence of others. As noted earlier, this is what Smith calls being 'sensible to the feelings of others,' and it is the basis of self-command (TMS III.3.34). Therefore, this first contribution is central to the process of governing one's passions.

Not surprisingly, the imagination's first contribution to self-command appears in many of Smith's examples. Consider, again, his description of the mutual adjustment often necessary for mutual sympathy. When two parties are not on the same page, emotionally speaking, mutual sympathy requires self-command. The spectators make their effort by recruiting the sympathetic process, which they initiate by means of the imagination. Meanwhile, the sufferer does the same. Just as the former are

> continually placing themselves in his situation, and thence conceiving emotions similar to what he feels; so he [the sufferer] is as constantly placing himself in theirs, and thence conceiving some degree of that coolness with which he is sensible that they will view it. As they are constantly considering what they themselves would feel, if they actually were the sufferers, so he is as constantly led to imagine in what manner he would be affect if he was only one of their spectators of his own situation.
>
> (TMS I.i.4.8)

Here we see imagination playing the role described earlier.

The language is slightly different, but imagination makes the same contribution in many examples from Smith's discussion in TMS III. Consider the 'man of a little more firmness' (TMS 3.3.24). In Smith's scenario, this moderately self-governed person has suffered some significant misfortune, but he wishes to regulate his grief and sorrow in the presence of company. His effort to do so matches the process described in the above example. When visited by strangers or friends, 'he endeavours, as much as he can, to fix his attention upon the view which the company is likely to take of his situation' (TMS 3.3.24). The moderately self-governed man tries to perceive how his visitors view and feel about his responses to his misfortune. Do they shrink from his displays of grief, or do they approve of the way he handles himself? Imagination isn't mentioned here. But it is reasonable to think Smith equates fixing one's attention on the perspective of others with the process of 'changing places in fancy' with them. For Smith, there is no other way to form an idea of how others feel (TMS I.i.1.2). Hence, the process of fixing attention is performed by means of the imagination.

Similar efforts are made by the 'wise and just man,' whose 'constancy and firmness' reveal a much greater degree of self-command (TMS III.3.25). But he directs his imagination differently, focusing instead on the perspective and feelings of an *impartial* spectator. 'With the eyes of this great inmate he has always been accustomed to regard whatever relates to himself' (TMS III.3.25). Again, there is no explicit mention of imagination. But context and the arc of TMS make it clear that the wise and just man recruits the sympathetic process by imagining how an impartial spectator would respond to the passions he wishes to govern. Indeed, through a lifetime of practice, the former has become so adept at this that he 'almost identifies himself with' this product of his imagination (TMS III.3.25).

Examples of this type illustrate imagination's first contribution to self-command. Since we have no direct perception of others' feelings, we must imagine them, which we do 'by conceiving what we ourselves should feel in the like situation' (TMS I.i.1.2). This requires changing places in fancy with the other person, and it is this act of imagination that makes possible the sympathy, or 'sensibility to the feelings of others' (TMS III.3.34), which is the basis of self-command. As I have argued, the 'imaginary change of situation' is what recruits the process of sympathy for the purposes of emotion regulation. Smith's theory, then, tells us that self-command depends on, and is partially constituted by, this initial contribution from the imagination. He does not deny that other faculties, such as reason or understanding, often assist the imagination (cf. Kopajtic, 2020, pp. 9–10). But imagination plays the main role. Sensitivity to the feelings of others is the basis of self-command, and it is imagination that provides that sensitivity.

My discussion might seem incompatible with Smith's earthquake-in-China example, which Carrasco cites in favour of her more 'rationalist' reading (2012, p. 398). Smith describes *reason* as 'astonishing [and thereby overriding] the most presumptuous of our [selfish] passions' (TMS III.3.4). This emotional response occurs when we recognise that we are 'but one of the multitude,' no more important than anyone else (TMS III.3.4). The appearance of 'reason' here can make it tempting to read this as a case of emotion regulation by means of reason. However, we should resist this temptation.

First, in the passage Smith equates reason with 'conscience,' 'the inhabitant of the breast,' and 'the man within,' etc. Much of TMS I–III is devoted to explaining how the representation of this 'inhabitant' is generated by the imagination, sympathy, and social interaction. Again, reason and experience support the formation of our idea of 'the man within,' but it is hard to conclude from TMS I–III that this idea is produced directly by reasoning (cf. Kopajtic, 2020, p. 23 n.12).[15] Smith doesn't insist on the point because he has a different agenda here. He wants to focus on the function and phenomenology of conscience, something most readers will find familiar. The capacious list of seemingly equivalent terms serves the ecumenical function of directing the reader's attention away from the debate about which faculty grounds moral judgement – a debate which Smith enters in TMS VII, siding *against* 'the rationalists' (TMS VII.III).

Second, in this same passage, Smith says that it is from the inhabitant of the breast that 'we learn the real littleness of ourselves, and of whatever relates to ourselves, and the natural misrepresentations of self-love can be corrected only by *the eye* of this impartial spectator' (TMS III.3.4; my emphasis). Reference to the 'eye' invokes the beginning of III.3, where he explains how the imagination corrects our visual perception when we underestimate the size of remote objects. Sitting at my desk in my office, the mountain range seen outside the window appears no larger than the office in which I sit. But this impression is corrected when I 'transport' myself, 'at least in fancy, to a different station, from whence I can survey both at nearly equal distances' (TMS III.3.2). From this imaginative perspective, I can more accurately represent the comparative dimensions of objects in my visual field. If we take the analogy seriously, you must use your imagination to distance yourself from your own interests and recognise that you are *but one of the multitude* – just another person whose interests are morally equivalent to the interests of others.

Third, it is instructive to compare TMS III.3.4 with analogous passages from figures such as Samuel Clarke and John Balguy. They are quite emphatic about reason or understanding being the source of insight into moral equality. Unlike Smith, they explicitly compare it to the understanding's grasp of mathematical and logical truths. For instance, Clarke writes,

> [W]hatever I judge reasonable or unreasonable for another to do to me; that, by the same judgment, I declare reasonable or unreasonable, that I in the like case should do for him. And to deny this either in word or in action, is as if a man should contend, that, though two and three are equal to five, yet five are not equal to two and three.
>
> (Clarke, 1991, p. 242)

There is nothing like this in Smith.

Furthermore, Smith's description of being *moved* by the idea of moral equality differs from what is found in these thinkers. For instance, Smith says we are 'astonished' by 'the voice' of the impartial spectator and stirred to action by our *love* of 'the grandeur, the dignity and superiority' of virtue (TMS III.3.4).[16] Balguy, by contrast, claims that

> the same necessity which compels men to *assent* to what is *true*, forces them to approve what is *right* and fit. . . . In both cases the mind necessarily acquiesces, without regarding or considering the effects of tendencies of either.
> (Balguy, 1991, p. 453)

Again, there is nothing like this in TMS. Our feelings, thoughts, and actions are not altered by rational assent. Instead, they are altered by an emotional response to a representation of the imagination. In this case, passions are overridden by the view of ourselves gained by imagining how an impartial spectator would see things. The view 'astonishes' our self-interested passions. In terms Smith uses elsewhere, it 'flattens' their 'pitch.' There is nothing here about rational assent (or 'acquiescing' to truth).

Read in full, TMS III.3.4 calls to mind other experiences of seeing yourself as part of something immense. To my ears, his language evokes the sublime. To think of the 'real littleness' of yourself may be akin to imagining yourself at the base of the Alps, adrift on the open sea, or in an open field beneath the night sky. It is more like picturing yourself as a small part of a vast expanse than it is like rational assent to an abstract truth. Seeing yourself as 'but one of the multitude' also has something in common with seeing yourself as but one part of the cosmos. This is a matter of viewing yourself as part of an enormous system. I mention the similarity because Smith thinks such systems are represented by ideas of the imagination. The history of physics is, he believes, populated by ideas of natural systems, and these ideas are imaginative representations. The most successful of them stick partly because of their force and vivacity (Smith, 1980b, pp. 104–105).

TMS III.3.4 resists definitive interpretation. However, Smith's discussion does not closely resemble similar remarks from Clarke or Balguy. He does not *sound* like a rationalist here. On my reading, III.3.4 describes an act of imagination which produces an emotional experience capable of checking self-interest and inspiring virtuous conduct. Broadly speaking, it fits what I have said about the imagination and its first main contribution to self-command.

Second contribution

We can now turn to imagination's second major contribution to self-command. Recall that self-command is a goal-directed process. When we regulate our passions, we try to alter them in a particular direction, adjusting them to match some standard or target. This feature is central to Smith's understanding of the phenomenon. According to his theory, the goal of self-command is to meet a standard provided by the imagination.

TMS I.i.4.6, discussed earlier, belongs to Smith's extended discussion of the emotional adjustments frequently required for mutual sympathy. Here, he describes how a sufferer's grief or sorrow is compounded by an awareness that others probably don't share it. Even if they sympathise, their sympathy will be 'imperfect' because it is painful to 'enter into' grief, and most of us try to avoid pain (e.g. TMS I.ii.5.3). The sufferer's sorrows can be intensified by a painful lack of mutual sympathy. Smith describes how the sufferer manages his disagreeable and dissonant passions by regulating them:

> He [the sufferer] longs for that relief which nothing can afford him but the entire concord of the affections of the spectators with his own. . . . But he can only hope to obtain this *by lowering his passion to that pitch, in which the spectators are capable of going along with him. He must flatten, if I may be allowed to say so, the sharpness of his natural tone, in order to reduce it to harmony and concord with the emotions of those who are about him.*
>
> (TMS I.i.4.7; my emphasis)

This passage illustrates, again, imagination's first contribution to self-command. The sufferer puts himself in the shoes of the spectator and imagines how they feel about him, which makes him 'sensible' to their feelings and susceptible to their influence on his own. But Smith also describes a second contribution. The sufferer does not merely imagine the feelings of others. To obtain the relief of mutual sympathy, he tries to adjust his own sorrow so that it conforms to the 'pitch' of the spectators' sympathetic sorrow, which is typically less intense.[17] Harmony with their feelings is the goal of his effort. The closer he gets to this standard, the more the sufferer will be relieved by the process of self-command, which not only reduces his painful feelings but also affords him the compensatory pleasures of mutual sympathy.

Imagination represents the standard or goal that the self-commanding agent tries to meet.[18] This is imagination's second major contribution to the process of self-command. The process is goal-directed, and the goal is to conform one's passions to a standard supplied by the imagination. The point follows from what has already been said about Smith's theory. As TMS I.i.4. makes clear, when you regulate your passions, you attempt to align them with the emotions of those around you, or with an emotion they'd be 'capable of going along with' (cf. TMS I.i.5.1). For Smith, there is no way to form an idea of such passions except by representing them with your imagination, which you do by imagining how you would feel in the other's circumstances (TMS I.i.1.2). Hence, the standard or target of your efforts is provided by your imagination.

This feature of Smith's theory appears in many of his examples. For instance, in the same extended discussion, he describes the other party (the spectators) making the very same goal-directed efforts. Just as the sufferer adjusts his passions to harmonize with the spectators,' so they adjust theirs to harmonise with his. The latter serves as the target of the spectators' own attempt to govern their responses to the sufferer. They, too, try to alter their passions to conform with a target provided by their imaginations (namely, their representations of the sufferer's sorrow). Recall, also, the 'man of a little more firmness' from TMS III. He tries to govern his own passions by first directing his attention to the perspective and passions of his visitors. He does this by imagining how they feel about his feelings. If the latter are painful to him or he recognises that his passions are out of sync with theirs, he tries to alter them. Smith describes this as a goal-directed process. The man tries 'to feel [his misfortune] no further than they are capable of feeling it' (TMS III.3.24). Smith also describes the less mature self-command of 'the weakest man' aiming at the same target. The effort is too taxing, however, so he stops trying to regulate his own passions and starts trying to manipulate his visitors' feelings instead (TMS III.3.23).

Smith's discussion of self-command in different cultures also incorporates this aspect of his theory. Consider the 'savages in North America,' whose 'heroic' degree of self-command is 'almost beyond the conception of Europeans' (TMS V.2.9 and 10). Smith focuses on the former's ability to regulate passions such as romantic love, fear, and resentment (TMS V.2.9). Due to variations in cultural norms and expectations, the North American 'savage' is capable of 'going along with,' perhaps even feeling and expressing, only much flatter emotional notes. Less metaphorically, the typical 'savage' is prone to be less sensitive or receptive than the typical 'civilized' European is to intense feelings and expressions of fear, resentment, or romantic love. Smith's point is that how you imagine the feelings of others depends partly on the setting in which you were raised. This affects the standards or targets you imagine when developing and exercising self-command.

According to Smith, the 'heroic and unconquerable firmness, which the custom and education of his country demand of every savage, is not required of those who are brought up to live in civilized societies' (TMS V.2.10). Simply put, the 'savage' and the 'civilized' European spend their lives practicing self-command with a different target. Smith clearly thinks this gives the former an advantage when it comes to regulating passions such as fear and resentment. If self-command exists on a spectrum that spans from childlike weakness (TMS III.3.23) to 'constant firmness' (TMS III.3.25), the average 'savage' is much closer to the latter pole than the average 'civilized' person.

This part of Smith's theory contains several important nuances. His main claim is that the goal of self-command is to meet a standard or target that is provided by your imagination. But Smith characterises the target in several different ways. For instance, in TMS I.i.4.7, Smith describes regulating your passions so that they harmonise 'with the emotions of those who are about' you. Here, your goal is to match what you imagine to be the actual passions of a set of real spectators. But in TMS I.i.4.7, Smith also says that a person may try to lower 'his passion to that pitch, in which the spectators are capable of going along with him.' Instead of aligning your own passions with my actual passions, you try to alter them to a point where my passions are likely to follow (given the facts about human nature and prevailing cultural norms). I am not likely to abandon myself to agonising grief, but if you can reduce its intensity, I may very well 'go along with' calmer and more reserved feelings of loss. Here the target is a passion somewhere in the middle between us. Your imagination represents this target, and if you strive effectively for it, you may very well draw my passions towards it as well. This effect is made more likely by the fact that I, too, dislike want of mutual sympathy, so I will often be making parallel efforts to regulate my own passions. When this occurs, the result is greater mutual sympathy between us and an emotional harmony found somewhere between the initial extremes of my indifference or antipathy and your agonising, relatively 'violent' grief.

All these passages from TMS illustrate imagination's second major contribution to self-command. According to Smith our goal in self-command is to meet a standard represented by the imagination. In some cases, this is what you imagine to be the actual emotions of those around you, be they friends or strangers (TMS III.3.38–40), and in others, it is what you imagine to be the sentiments of a well-informed, impartial spectator. The truly virtuous person has an entrenched habit of focusing on the latter rather than the former. But, like the rest of us, the goal of her efforts at self-command is to meet a standard represented by the imagination.

'Rationalist' versus 'Sentimentalist' interpretations of Smith's theory

Kopajtic contrasts her 'sentimentalist' interpretation with 'rationalist' interpretations that assimilate his theory to the reason-based tradition that stretches from Socrates to Kant. My account is much closer to Kopajtic's, but neither label captures what I have tried to argue. This is easiest to see if we consider each of imagination's two major contributions to self-command. In my view, neither contribution should be assimilated to either sentiment or reason. The imagination's role is distinctive.

Let's start with the second contribution. I have argued that self-command is a goal-directed process in which one's goal is to align one's passions with a standard set by one's imagination. This claim closely resembles a key claim in Kopajtic's 'sentimentalist' interpretation of Smith's position (e.g. 2020, pp. 14–15). However, there are two important differences.

First, Kopajtic describes the standards of self-command as *sentiments*. This is true in one sense. When I regulate my self-pity for the sake of mutual sympathy with my visitors, for example, I am trying to align my feelings for myself with their feelings for me. But their feelings cannot be directly perceived or 'felt' on Smith's view. They must be represented by my imagination. Therefore, it is imagination that provides the standards involved in self-command, and – given Smith's conception of imagination – these standards take the form of *ideas*, not sentiments. They are cognitive states, broadly speaking. I'm trying to make my passions fit with what I *think* they feel about my situation. I produce and attend to this idea by imagining how I would feel if I were in their shoes. Hence, the standards or targets of self-command are cognitive representations of sentiments (ideas) rather than actual sentiments (feelings).

Second, Kopajtic seems to hold that the 'standard-setting sentiments' are necessarily those felt by an impartial spectator. But, as my discussion suggests, this over-moralises the phenomenon of self-command.[19] Smith describes a range of standards for self-command. In some cases, the self-commanding agent tries to attain the approval of the 'supposed' impartial spectator, but in others she tries to align her passions with those of 'real' spectators, who are often quite partial (TMS III.3.21). Smith also thinks the standard can be one's idea of what real spectators are 'likely to go along with,' given the circumstances and the spectators whose sympathy is being solicited. Finally, the person attempting to regulate her passions may aim for a standard set by her representation of unsavoury, even vicious, passions (TMS VI.iii.12). Such cases count as *moral* failures, but moral failures, such as 'dark and deep dissimulation,' sometimes require being quite effective at governing the passions (TMS VI.iii.12). Kopajtic acknowledges these remarks from Smith and notes that her account is not designed to explain them (2020, pp. 24 n.28). But I think they fit Smith's basic theory quite easily once one accepts that it describes a psychological process rather than a moral virtue.

The more 'rationalist' interpretations of Smith's view might object that reason can, and often does, provide the standards or goals of self-command. I do not think this is true, but considering the objection further clarifies what is distinctive about imagination's contribution and why his theory resists any kind of 'rationalist' reading.

Are there places in TMS where Smith claims that the goals of self-command are provided by reason (or the understanding or the intellect)? Yes, there are a few such passages. For example, Smith writes that we 'model the tenor of our conduct' on the 'vague and indeterminate ideas' provided by reason (TMS VII.iii.2.6), and, similarly, that 'our most solid judgments . . . with regard to right and wrong, are regulated by maxims and ideas derived from an induction of reason' (TMS VII.iii.2.6). Such remarks might suggest that the standards involved in self-command are often provided by reason. That is, based on the ideas and maxims of reason, you make inferences about how you ought to feel in such-and-such circumstances. Then you attempt to align your current (or anticipated) passions with those that reason represents as correct or proper. If this is Smith's claim, then reason, at least sometimes, provides the targets involved in self-command.

However, the context indicates that Smith's point is narrower than it might appear to be. In this portion of TMS, Smith is conceding ground to Cudworth's 'rationalist' account of moral judgement. The main topic is *moral judgment*, and Smith's concession to Cudworth is at least partly rhetorical and strategic. It serves the ecumenical aims of his larger discussion.[20] Smith's other remarks about rational standards seem similarly restricted. For instance, he writes,

> the regard to those general rules of conduct [formed by induction], is what is properly called a sense of duty, . . . and this is the only principle by which the bulk of mankind are capable of directing their actions.
>
> (TMS III.5.1)

Basically, Smith argues here that most of the time, plenty of decent people are behaving decently simply by following 'the established rules of behavior' (TMS III.5.1).[21]

In this discussion, Smith describes cases where a person regulates their behaviour *without* regulating their passions. A cold person may feel no gratitude towards their benefactor. But a decent person who has received 'great benefits' will 'strive to act' *as if* they do – endeavouring 'to pay all those regards and attentions to his patron which the liveliest gratitude could suggest' (TMS III.5.1). Similarly, a dutiful wife may not feel much 'tender regard' for her husband. But if she has been 'virtuously educated,' 'she will endeavor to act *as if* she felt it' (TMS III.5.1; my emphasis). In these two cases, one acts from a sense of duty and tries to obey the general rules of propriety. In this respect, those rules are the guiding standards of the person's regulatory efforts. But Smith explicitly excludes sentiment and passion from the scope of the regulatory process he describes. The focus is on outward behaviour, not emotion. If self-command is defined as 'control of our passive feelings' (TMS III.3.21), then these passages about reason and its rules do not directly concern the core phenomenon of self-command. Therefore, they do not speak against my claim that the targets or goals involved in self-command are provided by imagination.[22]

Now for imagination's first contribution. Here my approach has much in common with Kopajtic's 'sentimentalist' approach. She claims that 'self-command works by imaginatively taking up the perspective of an impartial spectator on oneself and sympathetically imagining the feelings of such a spectator' (2020, p. 11). We agree that self-command works by 'imaginatively taking up' the perspective of another person. But we differ in emphasis and focus. Kopajtic thinks the 'operation' of self-command involves three steps (2020, pp. 13–18). My approach concentrates on her first step, namely, imaginatively taking up the other's perspective. In my view, this is a cognitive process, broadly speaking. The self-regulator attempts to regulate her passions by using imagination to alter her *ideas* (about the other's perspective, how it feels to be in it, etc.). By contrast, Kopajtic tends to focus on steps two and three – the subsequent emotional responses produced by the work of imagination. My approach shifts our focus to the latter. In self-command, it is the imagination, not emotion, over which the person exercises primary and direct control. Using her imagination is how she activates her sensibility to the feelings of others, so any effect those feelings have on her own emotions must depend upon her imaginative efforts. For this reason, I hesitate to call Smith's view 'sentimentalist.' This label is perhaps fine for his theory of moral judgement, but here it risks obscuring Smith's emphasis on cognitive control by means of the imagination. 'Sensibility' and sympathetic emotion cannot do their regulatory work in his theory of self-command unless they are aroused and recruited by the process of controlling our imaginative representations.

My approach diverges much more sharply from any kind of 'rationalist' interpretation, including the ones that Kopajtic rejects. I would never deny that reason sometimes plays a role in activating sensibility and influencing the process of emotion regulation. But its role is always supportive. It assists one's attempts to *imagine* the perspective of another. Therefore, it's a mistake to describe the perspective-switching involved as a 'reflexive movement of reason' (Carrasco, 2012, p. 396). And I do not believe that self-command 'requires . . . rational assessment,' or 'implies a deliberative process' (Montes, 2020, pp. 122–123). Not much in TMS supports these claims. Moreover, they fail to recognise how much Smith seeks to distance himself from reason-based theories of self-command so that he can focus on the distinctive contributions of imagination.

Smith *never* claims that we recruit or activate the sympathetic process by means of reason. That is, he never claims that we use this faculty to put ourselves in the shoes of another. Instead, we do this 'in fancy' (TMS I.i.1.3). It is by means of imagination that I 'assume' your circumstances and 'conceive or . . . imagine' how it feels to be in such circumstances (TMS I.i.1.2). This point is not controversial. As noted earlier, Fleischacker describes this imaginative process as 'the very essence' of Smithian sympathy (2012, p. 281 n.14). If Smith saw himself as part of the reason-based tradition, he could have built on the work of Hutcheson, who argues that we regulate our 'violent' emotions by means of 'calmer' ones, which we arouse and recruit by using reason, or the understanding, to correct our beliefs (e.g. 2006, pp. 136–137; Wilson 2025b).[23] Smith could have said something similar by arguing that we regulate our passions by *using reason* to activate sensibility or recruit sympathy. But he does not do this. He never mentions Hutcheson's account of emotion regulation or even nods to it. Indeed, he seems to refer to the whole reason-based tradition only once, when he dismisses it by saying that the 'control of our passive feelings' cannot be acquired 'from the abstruse syllogisms of a quibbling dialectic' (TMS III.3.21).[24]

Furthermore, Smith uses standard modern terminology to characterise the output of the imaginative perspective-switching process as an *idea*. His descriptions of the ideas involved in sympathy and self-command strongly suggest they are not produced by reason. According to Smith, we can do four main things by means of reason.[25] We can predict the consequences of our actions and foresee their advantages and disadvantages (TMS IV.2.6). We can infer general rules of justice (TMS VII.iii.2.6). We can form 'those more vague and indeterminate ideas' of propriety that often guide our conduct (TMS VII.iii.2.6). And we can, by means of experience and induction, form 'general maxims of morality' (TMS VII.iii.2.6). None of Smith's descriptions of changing places in fancy suggest such outputs. Assuming the circumstances of another does not yield rules; it yields ideas. In fact, they are usually representations of particulars – specific people experiencing specific emotions in specific circumstances. When I change places in fancy with you, I imagine how *you* feel by imagining how *I* would feel in your circumstances, or how it would feel to *be you* in your circumstances.

Finally, such ideas are typically not 'vague and indeterminate.' Smith emphasises this point repeatedly. He says that when you attempt to regulate your passions, you switch perspectives by means of imagination and try to 'bring home' to yourself 'every little circumstance . . . that can possibly occur to the sufferer' (TMS I.i.4.6). Sympathy with the dead, for instance, involves forming ideas of what it would be like to be 'deprived of the light of the sun; to be shut out from life and conversation; to be laid in the cold grave, a prey to corruption and the reptiles of the earth' (TMS I.i.1.10). When the mother sympathises with her sick child and conceives of what it would be like to be in the child's situation, she thinks of feeling helpless and terrified by the 'unknown consequences of [the] disorder' (TMS I.i.1.12). These outputs of the perspective-switching process are not rules derived from an inferential process, and they are not usually 'vague and indeterminate.'

In these examples, Smith emphasises not just the specificity of the representations involved but also their *vivacity*. The mother's ideas are vivid and forceful, as are the thoughts of lying alone and forgotten in the cold grave. Smith emphasises their vivacity because it is essential to his theory of sympathy. He makes the point in the second paragraph of TMS, where he describes viewing 'our bother upon the wrack' (TMS I.i.1.2). It is 'by the imagination [that] we place ourselves into his situation' and form thoughts of his 'agonies' and 'torments' (TMS I.i.1.2). Such thoughts are ideas (cognitive representations) produced by the imagination, and these ideas alter our current emotional state only if they are sufficiently vivid and forceful. As Smith puts it, your idea of your tortured brother's agony 'excites some degree of the same emotion, *in proportion to the vivacity or dullness of the conception*' (TMS I.i.1.2; my emphasis).

The ideas of reason, according to Smith, are comparatively 'dull' and lack the detail and specificity of imaginative representations. They also lack the latter's direct connection to the comparatively forceful and vivid impressions of sense experience. Thus, ideas produced by reason are less likely to excite any emotional change. (Here, Smith agrees with Hume, as the language of 'vivacity' suggests.) Therefore, reason would be ineffective as a means of self-command.

To effectively regulate your passions, you must use your imagination to specify and vivify your conception of how it feels to be in your tortured brother's situation. Smith describes this as a matter of 'bringing home to ourselves' the details of the other person's situation and their emotional response to that situation (e.g. TMS I.i.1.4.6). You cause yourself to 'tremble and shudder at *the thought of what he feels*' (TMS I.i.1.2; my emphasis) by using imagination to produce detailed and forceful representations of those feelings, and to really look at *his situation* from *his* perspective (as you imagine it). This is not accomplished by using reason to form generalisations about how human beings are likely to feel in this type of situation. Imaginative ideas represent particulars, which are more likely to have the force and vivacity needed to excite emotional change (TMS I.i.1.2).[26]

Conclusion

Imagination plays a major role in Smith's theory of sympathy, and sympathy plays a major role in his theory of self-command. My chapter has tried to connect these two prominent features of Smith's work. On my reading, Smith believes that imagination is the primary means or basis of self-command. We use imagination to recruit the sympathetic process that alters the passions we wish to regulate, and imagination gives direction to this endeavour by supplying it with a target or goal. According to Smith, the faculty of imagination is therefore what enables us to alter or modify our passions in a deliberate, goal-directed manner. With this account of the primary means of emotion regulation, Smith's theory of self-command offers a rich alternative to the reason-based tradition that dominates the history of philosophy.[27]

Notes

1 *Theory of Moral Sentiments* hereafter cited as TMS. Throughout this paper I follow Hanley in thinking of self-command as the general capacity to regulate one's passions (2009, p. 158, n.36). Such regulation can occur for the sake of vice as well as virtue (e.g., TMS VI.iii.12). Defined this way, self-command is a psychological phenomenon rather than a moral virtue. For a brief survey of eighteenth-century views, see Harris (2013) and Wilson (2025a). Also pertinent is Radcliffe (2019).

2 I owe the language of 'recruiting' to Scarantino (2020).

3 To be clear, Kopajtic (2020) doesn't mention Hutcheson's view.

4 On Hutcheson's view, see Harris (2013) and Wilson (2025b).

5 See Smith's interesting remarks about the ambiguity of 'feeling' and how you feel it when another living organism feels itself being touched by you (Smith, 1980a, pp. 136–41).

6 For detailed discussion of the distinction between sympathy as *process* and sympathy as *result*, see Schliesser (2017, pp. 107–47). Kopajtic tends to emphasise sympathy as *result* (e.g., 2020, p. 12), which leads her to emphasize the role of 'sympathetic emotion' in self-command (e.g., 2020, p. 13). By contrast, my account emphasizes the degree to which any such result (feeling) depends upon work performed by the imagination. There is no major disagreement here – just a difference in focus and emphasis.

7 The literature on Smithian sympathy is extensive, and the following remarks make no claim to originality.

8 This aspect of Smith's view is criticised by Fleischacker (2012, pp. 303–309).

9 Most scholars of Smithian sympathy discuss the two forms distinguished. See, for example, Nanay (2012) and Ben-Moshe (2020).

10 Hacker dismisses this form of sympathy (or empathy) as 'unintelligible,' but I disagree and he offers no argument in support of his (rather snooty) remarks (2018, pp. 366 and 391). Griswold writes in depth about the acting parallel and, more broadly, Smith's use of theatre metaphors (1999).

11 Griswold (2006 and 1999: chapter 2) places imagination at the centre of TMS.

12 For detailed comparisons between Smith and Hume, see Fleischacker (2012 and 2019, pp. 16–17, 23–31; and Sayre-McCord, 2015).

13 For an extensive and illuminating discussion of I.i.4.6–8, see Kopajtic (2020).

14 Smith's description continues from here to include the efforts made by the other party. I regulate my passions to align them with yours. Meanwhile, you regulate your passions to align them with mine. Through a process of mutual adjustment, we meet in the middle, achieving an emotional harmony that feels good and promotes cooperation. More on this long passage below.

15 Not surprisingly, I agree with Kopajtic's anti-rationalist take on this passage. However, she thinks it is 'the *sentiments* of [the supposed] spectator' that alter our passions. But, strictly speaking, this is not correct. We are not directly affected by the sentiments of others. We are affected by our *ideas* of those sentiments, which are produced by our own imaginations. This is especially clear in the case of the sentiments ascribed to a 'supposed' spectator, who does not have any actual feelings because she is not an actual person.

16 Smith's remarks call to mind Butler's claim that when conscience speaks, it '*magisterially* asserts itself' (2017, p. 29; my emphasis). But Smith places greater emphasis on the aesthetic dimension of this experience.

17 On Smith's musical metaphors, see Kopajtic (2020).

18 The standard at which self-regulation aims is like the temperature setting – or 'reference value' – on a thermostat. See Carver and Sheier (1998), which has informed my account of imagination's goal-setting contribution.

19 We agree, of course, that the proper standard of moral judgement is determined by the impartial spectator's responses. But the issue here is self-command, not moral judgement, and the latter is not necessary for the former.

20 Despite the concession to Cudworth, of course, Smith goes on to deny that reason is the basis of moral judgement (TMS VII.iii.2–3).

21 Smith thinks that most perfectly decent people are like this most of the time. His description is not a criticism.

22 My interpretation is also supported by the role of examples in *Theory of Moral Sentiments*. Smith's many detailed and value-laden examples provide the reader – and the pupils in his lectures – with specific targets for emotion regulation. These are neither 'rules and maxims' nor 'vague and indeterminate' ideas of reason. They are detailed imaginative representations (stories, character types, and figures from history and literature), based on observations of history and common life. On the importance of character sketches, narratives, and examples to Smith's work, see Griswold (1999). On their moral-pedagogical function in TMS, see Heydt (2008).

23 Hutcheson's account of emotion regulation ascribes no significant role to the imagination. Typically, he discusses it only to describe how the imagination's 'fantastick' associations of ideas cause the violent passions we seek to regulate (2006, p. 136; 2002, p. 69). His grimmer view of imagination is closer to Locke's than to Hume's or Smith's. See Harris (2013).

24 Judging from a later passage, Smith has Chrysippus – a 'mere dialectical pedant' – in mind (TMS III.ii.1.41). One might conclude that Smith rejects only a very specific and apparently faulty reason-based model of self-command. However, Smith's remark is telling. Either he has chosen to caricature the whole tradition of reason-based models of self-command, or he has carefully selected the implausible theories of Chrysippus to represent it.

25 The history of philosophy offers countless conceptions of reason. To keep things manageable, I focus on Smith's own characterisation of reason, gleaning it from his discussion of Cudworth (TMS VII.iii.2).

26 As Griswold notes, Smith also thinks the issue here is particularity rather than *accuracy* (1999, pp. 100–101). This distinguishes him from many in the reason-based tradition – for example, the Stoics, who would argue that you must regulate your emotional response to your tortured brother by basing it on a *correct* judgement about the actual evil, if there is any, that he undergoes. Smith's ethical theory has something to say about this, of course, but his psychological theory of emotion regulation sharply diverges from the Stoics.'

27 I thank an anonymous reader for insightful criticisms and suggestions. For helpful discussion of the ideas that drive this paper, I'm grateful to Colin Heydt and Andrea Scarantino.

References

Balguy, J. (1991) 'The Foundation of Moral Goodness', in D. D. Raphael (ed.) *British Moralists*, Vol. 1. Indianapolis: Hackett Publishing Company.

Ben-Moshe, N. (2020) 'Making Sense of Smith on Sympathy as Approbation: Other-Oriented Sympathy as a Psychological and Normative Achievement', *British Journal for the History of Philosophy*, 28(4): 735–55.

Butler, J. (2017) *Fifteen Sermons and Other Writings on Ethics*, (ed.) D. McNaughton. New York: Oxford University Press.

Carrasco, M. (2012) 'Adam Smith: Self-Command, Practical Reason, and Deontological Insights', *British Journal for the History of Philosophy*, 20(2): 391–414.

Carver, C. and Sheier, M. (1998) *On the Self-Regulation of Behavior*. New York: Cambridge University Press.

Clarke, S. (1991) 'A Discourse Concerning the Unchangeable Obligations of Natural Religion', in D. D. Raphael (ed.) *British Moralists*, Vol. 1. Indianapolis: Hackett Publishing Company.

Fleischacker, S. (2012) 'Sympathy in Hume and Smith: A Contrast, Critique, and Reconstruction', in C. Fricke and D. Føllesdal (eds.) *Intersubjectivity and Objectivity in Adam Smith and Edmund Husserl*. Ontos, pp. 273–311.

Fleischacker, S. (2019) *Being Me Being You: Adam Smith and Empathy*. Chicago: University of Chicago Press.

Griswold, C. (1999) *Adam Smith and the Virtues of Enlightenment*. Cambridge: Cambridge University Press.

Griswold, C. (2006) 'Imagination: Morals, Science, and Arts', in K. Haakonseen (ed.) *The Cambridge Companion to Adam Smith*. Cambridge: Cambridge University Press, pp. 22–56.

Hacker, P. M. S. (2018) *The Passions: A Study of Human Nature*. Oxford: Wiley-Blackwell.

Hanley, R. (2009) *Adam Smith and the Character of Virtue*. Cambridge: Cambridge University Press.

Harris, J. (2013) 'The Government of the Passions', in J. Harris (ed.) *The Oxford Handbook of British Philosophy in the Eighteenth Century*. New York: Oxford University Press, pp. 270–288.

Heydt, C. (2008) '"A Delicate and an Accurate Pencil": Adam Smith, Description, and Philosophy as Moral Education', *History of Philosophy Quarterly*, 25(1): 57–74.

Hutcheson, F. (2002) *An Essay on the Nature and Conduct of the Passions, with Illustrations on the Moral Sense*, (ed.) A. Garrett. Indianapolis: Liberty Fund.

Hutcheson, F. (2006) 'A Synopsis of Metaphysics Comprehending Ontology and Pneumatology', in J. Moore and M. Silverthorne (eds.) *Logic, Metaphysics, and the Natural Sociability of Mankind*. Indianapolis: Liberty Fund.

Kopajtic, L. (2020) 'Adam Smith's Sentimentalist Conception of Self-Command', *The Adam Smith Review*, 12: 7–27.

Montes, L. (2020) 'The Relevance of Propriety and Self-Command in Adam Smith's *Theory of Moral Sentiments*', *Social Philosophy & Policy*, 37(1): 118–137.

Nanay, B. (2012) 'Adam Smith's Concept of Sympathy and Its Contemporary Interpretations', *The Adam Smith Review*, 5: 85–105.

Radcliffe, E. (2019) 'Ruly and Unruly Passions: Early Modern Perspectives', *Royal Institute of Philosophy Supplement*, 85: 21–38.

Raphael, D. D. (2006) 'Sympathy and the Impartial Spectator', in K. Haakonseen (ed.) *The Cambridge Companion to Adam Smith*. Cambridge: Cambridge University Press, pp. 158–188.

Raphael, D. D. (2007) *The Impartial Spectator: Adam Smith's Moral Philosophy*. New York: Oxford University Press.

Sayre-McCord, G. (2015) 'Hume and Smith on Sympathy, Approbation, and Moral Judgment', in E. Schliesser (ed.) *Sympathy: A History*. New York: Oxford University Press, pp. 208–246.

Scarantino, A. (2020) 'Exploring the Roles of Emotions in Self-Control', in A. Mele (ed.) *Surrounding Self-Control*. New York: Oxford University Press, pp. 117–141.

Schliesser, E. (2017) *Adam Smith: Systematic Philosopher and Public Thinker*. New Oxford University Press.

Smith, A. (1976) *The Theory of Moral Sentiments*, (eds.) D. D. Raphael and A. L. Macfie, Indianapolis: Liberty Fund.

Smith, A. (1980a) 'Of the External Senses', in W. P. D. Wightman and J. C. Bryce (eds.) *Essays on Philosophical Subjects*. Indianapolis: Liberty Fund, pp. 135–168.

Smith, A. (1980b) 'The History of Astronomy', in W. P. D. Wightman and J. C. Bryce (eds.) *Essays on Philosophical Subjects*. Indianapolis: Liberty Fund, pp. 33–105.

Wilson, E. E. (2025a) 'Emotion in the Eighteenth Century', in A. Scarantino (ed.) *Emotion Theory: The Routledge Comprehensive Guide Volume I – History, Contemporary Theories, and Key Elements*. New York: Routledge, pp. 129–147.

Wilson, E. E. (2025b) 'Hutcheson and the Stoics on Emotion Regulation', *Journal of Scottish Philosophy*, 23(2): 75–93.

12 Adam Smith on colour and solidity

Hannes Ole Matthiessen

Introduction

Adam Smith holds that solidity and colour play a fundamental role in perception: they are the properties that make us aware of objects. Solidity (the property by which we distinguish things from our own body) presents us with tangible objects. Colour (the property by which we distinguish parts of the visual field from each other) presents us with visible objects. The fundamental feature that enables solidity and colour to play this role is their spatiality – their perception is always accompanied by our conceiving of them (or their bearers) as extended, figured, divisible and mobile. Thereby, we experience tangible and visible objects as occupiers of real three-dimensional and visual two-dimensional space.

Solidity and colour stand in strong contrast to secondary qualities such as heat and cold, sound, taste and smell which are a-spatial in nature, according to Smith. Nevertheless, in other respects, colours are similar to secondary qualities in that they do not present objects as external to us and only allow us to perceive material objects in an indirect and (largely) acquired fashion.

After briefly introducing Smith's account of colour as the object of sight (the first section), I discuss Smith's account of touch and of secondary qualities to locate colour in Smith's framework. To that end, the second and third sections explain Smith's distinction between feeling solid bodies immediately via resistance and perceiving them *in virtue of* sensations. Then I lay out the Berkeleyan background of Smith's theory of vision (the fourth section) and discuss the relation between colours and secondary qualities (the fifth section). The sixth section and the conclusion recapitulate Smith's realist reading of Berkeley's theory of vision. Colours, for Smith, are not properties of material bodies, but they are also not merely internal sensations, properly speaking. They are objects in an internal world of vision that serves as a sign for the material world around us.

Smith on colour – a preview

The central idea behind Smith's theory of colour is that it should be understood in analogy to solidity, the property we attribute to *bodies* or *things* based on an experience of resistance. In ES § 46–47, he writes:

DOI: 10.4324/9781003767824-15

> The objects of Touch are solidity, and those modifications of solidity which we consider as essential to it, and inseparable from it; solid extension, figure, divisibility, and mobility.
>
> The objects of Sight are colour, and those modifications of colour which, in the same manner, we consider as essential to it, and inseparable from it; coloured extension, figure, divisibility, and mobility.

Reading this for the first time, one wonders: what does it even mean to treat solidity analogously with colour – does this make any sense? Following Locke, Adam Smith holds that the sense of touch furnishes us with the idea of solidity whenever we feel an external body *resisting* our body. Solidity, also, is what distinguishes a mere extent of space from a body that fills that space. Solidity is the property that 'exclude[s] all other substances' (Locke 1910: 2.4.2). Our idea of a certain region of space is different from the idea of that region of space filled with solid matter. Very broadly, the same holds for colours in the visual world: we can conceive a portion of the visual field of a certain size and shape, and that conception is different from one where a certain colour fills it. So just as solid bodies fill portions of the material world, coloured figures fill the visual world. The other similarity has already been mentioned: whenever solidity and colour are perceived, the bearer of these properties is conceived by us as spatial – as extended, figured, divisible, and mobile. Feeling something resist our hand, or seeing a colour stand out from a background, we cannot help but attribute all these spatial characteristics to the object we are aware of. This is the overall picture. To make it more solid, I will look at Smith's account of solidity next.

Smith on solidity and secondary qualities

Adam Smith's Essay *Of the External Senses* gives an account of the five senses – touch, smell, taste, hearing, and sight – in a phenomenologically and empirically informed manner. It begins with the sense of touch, which plays a fundamental role in acquainting us with mind-independent reality. In touching an object, I feel, on the one hand, a sensation of pressure 'as [an] affection of my hand' (§ 3). On the other hand, however, 'the thing which presses and resists I feel as something altogether different from those affections, as external to my hand, and as altogether independent of it' (2006: 136–137). So, besides the sensation that resides in my hand, I also feel an external object, a 'Solid Body or Thing' (§ 8). According to Smith, the perception of solidity, in turn, goes along with an 'idea or conception of a solid substance' that necessarily involves the 'qualities of extension, divisibility, figure, and mobility' (§§ 9–13).[1]

Both the affection of the touching organ (the sensation of resistance) and the object of touch are said to be *felt* (§ 3). They are, so to speak, two aspects of the overall experience of touching an object. The other qualities (extension, divisibility, figure, mobility) are assumed to belong to the perceived body, but not necessarily on a perceptual level (although, one may argue, we sometimes *feel* an object's extension, figure or divisibility as well). Rather, they are 'necessarily involved in the idea or conception of a solid substance' (§ 13). The notion of solidity Smith employs is, as Glenney (2014) rightly remarks, largely taken over from Locke (1910: 2.4). While Locke regards *solidity* as largely synonymous with *impenetrability* (2.4.1) and thereby opens up a whole lot of metaphysical issues (What does impenetrability amount to? How do we deal with holes and voids in an object? Cf. Stuart 2013: 58–62), Smith takes for granted that our impression of resistance brings about a notion of solidity and is more interested in the epistemic and conceptual consequences of this notion (cf. Glenney 2014: 122 ff.). Where Locke sees solidity as nearly synonymous with *impenetrability*, Smith considers the notions of solid and *substantial* as 'altogether, or as nearly synonymous' (§ 8). What is essential for our ordinary understanding of a solid body is the idea of 'a thing that subsists by itself, and independently of any other thing' (Glenney 2014: 122 ff.).

Note that, according to Smith, we feel objects not only as solid or as having a particular shape or size, but also as, for example, warm. Here, Smith argues, the sensation is felt as internal to the sense organ and attributed to the external object only indirectly:

> When we lay our hand upon a table, which is either heated or cooled a good deal beyond the actual temperature of our hand, we have two distinct perceptions: first, that of the solid or resisting table, which is necessarily felt as something external to, and independent of, the hand which feels it: and secondly, that of heat and cold, which by the contact of the table is excited in our hand, and which is naturally felt as nowhere but in our hand.
>
> (§ 20)

So, some perceptions that belong to the sense of touch are different from feeling bodies as solid and external.

In contrast to the sensation of resistance and the associated perception of solidity, Smith groups together the sensations of *temperature, taste, smell and sound,* classical secondary qualities. The distinction between primary and secondary qualities gained popularity in the seventeenth century and was well established in the eighteenth century. The basic idea is that primary qualities (extension, figure, motion, etc.) 'really' belong to the objects and are perceived basically as they are. The idea I get when I look at a triangle somehow *mirrors* the real shape of the triangle. Secondary qualities (smells, temperature, sounds, etc.) are in one way or another inadequately represented in perception: what we experience as a colour might, in fact, just be a microscopic surface structure built out of material that is in itself not coloured. What is experienced as a certain smell is really just a concentration of molecules in the air, consisting of parts that do not smell at all in themselves. Smith does mention secondary qualities but he seems to be somewhat sceptical about the terminology when he talks of 'These four classes of secondary qualities, as philosophers have called them, or to speak more properly, these four classes of Sensations; Heat and Cold, Taste, Smell, and Sound' (§ 25). One way to interpret his hesitation to adopt the jargon is that he has reservations about the term *secondary*. However, one may also understand the criticism as directed against the idea that we are dealing with *qualities,* since in reality, they are only sensations. Under this interpretation, it still seems legitimate to use the term 'secondary qualities' while being aware that Smith regards them as a sort of sensations (i.e. the sensations of temperature, taste, smell, and sound) and denies that they are also properties of objects.

Traditionally, in any treatments of secondary qualities, colours would naturally play one major role. Things are different in Adam Smith's account, as we will see in the fourth section. So, *secondary qualities,* for the time being, refer to temperature, taste, smell, and sound only.

The main characteristic of secondary qualities is that they are 'felt, not as resisting or pressing upon the organ; but as in the organ' (§ 25). They are 'naturally perceived . . . as mere affections of the organ, and what can exist nowhere but in the organ' (§ 25). So while a tactile sensation of pressure is accompanied by the perception of that which resists me, sensations of feeling temperature, taste, smell, and hearing are mere sensations that have no object external to the organ of sense. These sensations not only fail to adequately represent some properties of objects; they do not even *purport* to do so (§ 25). Smith however acknowledges that, at least for the sense of hearing, this view appears counter-intuitive since we often say 'that we hear a sound at a great or a small distance, on our right hand or on our left.' (§ 24) But this is just a façon de parler. In fact,

> the real sound, . . . the sensation in our ear, can never be heard or felt any where but in our ear, it can never change its place, . . . and can come therefore, neither from the right nor from the left, neither from before nor from behind us.
>
> (Glenney 2014: 122 ff.)

According to Smith, secondary qualities lack spatial properties altogether and can in no way be extended, figured, mobile, or divisible: 'They do not possess, nor can we even conceive them as capable of possessing, any one of the qualities, which we consider essential to, and inseparable from, the external solid and independent substances' (§ 26, cf. Also §§ 27–30).

At this point, it is important to remember that Smith does not restrict *sensation* to heat, smell, taste, and sound. We have already learned that there are tactile sensations of resistance and pressure (§3) as well. And there is little reason to suspect that these sensations differ in their spatial character from those of the secondary qualities.[2] A sensation of pressure, likewise, is neither square nor round. It is a pure feel. The *substances* or *things* only enter the scene when we attend to the objects that *exert* resistance or pressure. Those, not the sensations, are extended, figured, divisible, and so on. Sensations of temperature, taste, smell, and sound are just sensations that are not connected with resistance and, hence, do not make us aware of external objects in the same way sensations of resistance do.

They can make us aware of distant bodies in a different way, though. Although, according to Smith, a sound is only experienced in the ear, we can also reliably form beliefs about the whereabouts of the sounding body (§ 24). Which is to say, we may become aware of the locations of bodies through sensations of sound. Moreover, we may also be alarmed or scared by a loud sound. Since sound qua 'affection of the organ of Hearing, can in most cases neither benefit nor hurt us' (§ 87) this finds explanation in 'some vague notion of some external substance or thing which excites [the sound]' (Glenney 2014: 122 ff.). Similar things can be said about sensations of smell and heat. Since these distant bodies, when in contact with our body, could harm or benefit us, various sensations take on the role of informing us about such bodies. The idea is not original to Smith; we can also find it in authors such as Nicolas Malebranche and George Berkeley. The latter, in his *New Theory of Vision*, describes the function of visible ideas 'which in themselves are not capable of affecting, or any wise altering the frame of [our] bodies' as allowing 'to foresee . . . the damage or benefit which is like to ensue, upon the application of [our] own bodies to this or that body which is at a distance' (Berkeley 1993: §59). Brian Glenney, whose papers (2011, 2014, 2015) form the main body of scholarly literature on Smith's theory of perception, suggests two different ways to interpret the mechanism that makes us aware of distant bodies through sensations. On the one hand, he proposes to interpret indirect awareness of the sources of heat, smell and sound in terms of the 'simulati[on] of tactile environments' (Glenney 2011: 205). Upon hearing a loud noise or smelling pleasant food, we imagine the immediate presence of the source and have an adequate reaction. Another approach that seeks to highlight the continuities between ES and TMS (Glenney 2014) explains the apprehension of distal bodies through a mechanism of sympathy: upon perceiving a smell or sound, a perceiver attributes it to 'a particular object, projects him or herself into proximity with that object, and approximates the associated feelings that would be felt were the object made present' (Glenney 2015: 242) – a mechanism that is largely parallel to that we use moral evaluation of others (cf. Glenney 2014: 119).

Obviously, these two explanations are similar in spirit and probably not mutually exclusive. In the following sections, we can remain neutral regarding the question of whether one of the two is preferable to the other, or whether another interpretation should be adopted. The only thing that matters for our project is that Smith distinguishes between a direct acquaintance with bodies through the sense of touch and an indirect one that is – in one way or another – mediated by sensations that are, strictly speaking, limited to the organ of sense in which they are felt.

Solidity versus secondary qualities – two criteria

So far, Adam Smith provides two different means of perceiving bodies: on the one hand, we can become aware of a solid body immediately by feeling resistance. On the other hand, our perceptions of secondary qualities such as temperature, smell, taste and sound inform us in a less detailed way about the whereabouts and potentially useful or harmful features of bodies. The salient features of tactile perceptions of bodies as solid are the following:

Externality: Sensations of resistance make us aware of solid bodies with an independent and external existence.

Spatiality: These external objects are represented as space occupying, that is, as things that have the properties of extension, figure, motion, and divisibility.

Our perceptions of secondary qualities lack externality and spatiality, as they are described as inherently phenomenal in the perceiver and as a-spatial (neither extended, figured, divisible, nor mobile)[3]:

Non-externality: Secondary qualities are experienced as something that exists in the organ and couldn't exist anywhere else.

Non-spatiality: These sensations are a-spatial (i.e. neither extended, figured, movable, nor divisible).

The reason why Smith would conjoin non-externality and non-spatiality may have been quite obvious around the middle of the eighteenth century when Smith's Essay was, with all likelihood, composed (cf. Brown 1992). It was a widespread idea at that time that mental items – thoughts, ideas, sensations – could not be divisible because the mind itself was regarded as unitary and indivisible. As Hume puts it, it 'is impossible any thing divisible can be *conjoine'd* to a thought or perception, which is a being altogether inseparable and indivisible' (Hume 1969, 1.4.5.7). And he goes on:

> For can any one conceive a passion of a yard in length, a foot in breadth, and an inch in thickness? Thought, therefore, and extension are qualities altogether incompatible, and never can incorporate together into one subject.
> (Hume 1969, 1.4.5.7)

Independently of these considerations, it is also possible that Smith was led to the distinction between sensations of resistance (indicating external existence) and secondary qualities by phenomenological investigations. After all, it is possible to experience sensations of smell and sound devoid of all spatial meaning, even if this is not the typical attitude we normally have.

As we saw in the last section, the sensations of heat, smell, taste, and sound can, although not always, excite imaginations or apprehension of bodies, just as sensations of resistance do. The difference is that sensations of resistance give us immediate perceptual access to the body that we feel to resist, while the other sensations invoke some additional mechanism – suggestion, imagination, sympathy – to make us apprehend external bodies (cf. Glenney 2011: 211 for a similar outlook).

Smith never mentions colour in connection with his discussion of secondary qualities, which is surprising given that – from Descartes to Locke – colour is one of the prime examples of a secondary quality. As we shall now see, sensations of colour – and visual perception in general – have commonalities with secondary qualities for Smith: the objects of sight do not present themselves as external in the way solidity does. So whenever vision discovers to us the location and properties of distant objects, it does so in the same indirect (and often acquired) fashion in which heat, smell, and sound do so. In another aspect, however, the objects of vision are altogether unlike secondary qualities: they are necessarily spatial, that is, extended, shaped, divisible and mobile. So what are colours?

Smith on the objects of vision

Smith advertises his section on vision as a recapitulation of George Berkeley's theory of vision to which he has 'scarcely anything to add' (§ 43). The basic idea is that vision is a language of God: the immediate objects of vision function as word-like *signs* to signify the objects of touch, which become, so to speak, the mediate objects of vision. The immediate objects of vision, coloured patches arranged in two dimensions, are sometimes called *visible figures* by Berkeley. Smith does not use the term himself, although he alludes to *visible squares* and *visible circles* (§ 61). Something that, as an object of vision, is a brown (two-dimensional) trapezoid in the middle of the visual field signifies, to the experienced subject, a (three-dimensional) tabletop at a few yards' distance, oriented in a certain way. Just as Berkeley, Smith emphasises that the signification relation, as a linguistic one, is arbitrary and not grounded in resemblance or any necessary connection (§ 60).[4]

The immediate objects of vision possess two sets of properties: shapes and colours. Smith, however, does not treat visible shape and colour separately but observes two remarkable features of 'the objects of sight' (which are, remember, figured and coloured):

Smith *denies externality* for them for the reason that 'the objects of Sight are not perceived as resisting or pressing upon the organ which perceives them' (§ 44), and also because 'the principle of perception, it is probable, originally perceives [the objects of Sight] as existing in that part of the organ, and nowhere but in that part of the organ' (§ 45).

On the other hand, Smith *accepts spatiality* for them: the immediate objects of sight have 'coloured extension, figure, divisibility, and mobility.' (§ 47) It seems, then, as if the objects of sight *combine* properties of solid objects (spatiality) and of secondary qualities (non-externality).

Colour as a spatial object

By Smith's own lights, the objects of vision are neither the ordinary material objects we touch, nor are they mere sensations like those of sound or smell. What are they, then? Smith, in fact, proposes a very interesting intermediate status for them: he suggests that they form a special class of spatial objects with colour being the visual analogue to felt solidity: the bearer of spatial properties such as extension, figure, divisibility, and mobility:

> The objects of Touch are solidity, and those modifications of solidity which we consider as essential to it, and inseparable from it; solid extension, figure, divisibility, and mobility.

> The objects of Sight are colour, and those modifications of colour which, in the same manner, we consider as essential to it, and inseparable from it; coloured extension, figure, divisibility, and mobility.
>
> (§§ 46–47)

This central passage certainly leaves us with a few questions. Earlier, we learned that the resistance we experience in touching an object makes us aware of its solidity. It sounds quite artificial to say, as in the quote above, that solidity *is* the paradigmatic object of touch. Solidity is still a quality: this power or quality of resistance we call Solidity; and the thing which possesses it is the Solid Body or Thing (§ 8). The analogy to the visual case seems to be less than perfect: even if we may say that colours fill the visual field, we may not say that *solidity* fills the tangible space. The inhabitants of the external world are *solid bodies* or things that possess the quality of solidity (alongside the four essential spatial features associated with it).

The parallel between the tangible and the visible world can be salvaged. Instead of assimilating touch to sight, one can do it the other way around: just as solid *things* or bodies are the inhabitants of the material world, what fills the visual world are not *colours*, but coloured expanses, coloured patches, or coloured sections of the visual field. These possess colours just as things possess solidity. And the coloured expanses are what fill the visual world, as bodies fill the external world.

Solidity is the property that is immediately suggested by the tangible sensations of resistance, while other substantial properties (such as a *particular* size and shape etc.) depend on perceiving solidity. Something analogous holds for vision: we must be aware of colour (or better: of a contrast between two colours) to distinguish one object of vision from the background or from another object of vision in order to perceive distinct shapes and sizes. The analogy between solidity and colour thus gets us pretty far.[5]

Colours, for Smith, are markedly different from the secondary qualities of smell, temperature, and taste, which he regards as mere sensations phenomenally located in the organ of perception, without internal spatiality.

Smith does talk about *sensations* of colour several times, for example, in the context of describing what a person born blind would come to know upon first being endowed with sight (§ 48, cf. also $ 45). This, however, does not indicate that he takes colour to be a secondary quality akin to those of smell and sound. A sensation (*of resistance*) is also present in our perceptions of solidity, after all. So the analogy stands: there is a sensation of resistance here, and of colour there; as a result of which solidity and, respectively, colour are perceived.

The main difference between perceptions of secondary qualities, on the one hand, and perceptions of solidity and colour, on the other hand, lies in the aspect of spatiality. Secondary qualities are presented as modifications of the sense organ, and as such they are in principle incapable of any of the four spatial denominations of extension, figure, divisibility and motion – 'they do not possess, nor can we even conceive them as capable of possessing, any one of the qualities, which we consider as essential to, and inseparable from, the external solid and independent substances' (§ 26). Sensations of resistance and colour, on the other hand, draw our attention to objects distinct from the mere feeling in the organ. When we encounter an object with the sense of touch, we are immediately aware of a modification of our sensibility (a sensation) and also of that solid body that resists us and brings about this sensation. This object may be perceived as having a certain figure or size. We may also know a priori that it will necessarily have some figure and extension, and that it is in principle divisible and mobile. When we see something, what we are immediately aware of is perhaps a sensation of colour, but *also* a coloured patch in our visual field. Although visual experience confronts us with spatial coloured objects, and not only with modifications of our sense organs, it does not present us with externality, mind-independence, in the same way tactile experience does. Coloured patches do not resist the eye, and thus do not inform us of anything outside the eye. They are extended objects, but nevertheless internal.

Smith's theory of perception

Whereas the material world around us is inhabited by numerous solid bodies, the world of sight is filled with coloured shapes. These shapes resemble solid bodies in that they are also extended and figured, mobile and divisible. In a way, they are what make up the visible world, the objects of vision.[6]

At least this is what goes on in the visual world alone. As inhabitants of the world of solid bodies *we* are able to associate our visual experiences with the experiences of touch in such a way that we learn to interpret the visual objects as signs for real bodies. The perception of bodies through the sense of sight – though rich in detail and very reliable – is indirect, just as the perception of distance and size via sound, radiant heat, or smell.

What is really original in this story is that Smith is one of the few, perhaps the first, philosophers who argue consistently that the objects of vision – colours – possess spatiality while not exhibiting externality. But how can he be the first if his theory of vision is merely a recapitulation of Berkeley's theory of vision? Well, in fact, Smith digresses from Berkeley in an important respect: Berkeley would not accept the idea that the sense of touch presents us with externality. For him, ideas of touch are just as internal as all other sensory ideas and do not inform us about an object existing outside the mind.

Although Berkeley, in publishing the *New Theory of Vision*, was convinced of the doctrine of immaterialism (the *Principles of Human Knowledge,* which lay down his philosophical project, were to appear the next year) he chose not to be explicit about his views in the earlier work, probably in order not to offend his readers. Quite the contrary, there are a number of places where he contrasts 'internal' ideas of vision with 'external' ideas of touch (e.g. New Theory of Vision: §§45, 78, 99), without wholeheartedly supporting the distinction. It is not implausible to assume that Smith either did not know Berkeley's full philosophical outlook or chose to ignore it because he found it unpalatable. If that was the case, one might simply see Smith's Essay as a largely successful attempt to make sense of Berkeley's theory of vision in a realist framework. Its leading question is: what can we say about the senses and the way they inform us about the world? For secondary qualities, the answer is: we feel them as modifications of ourselves, mere feelings that have no spatial properties. However, in many circumstances, they make us (though rather vaguely) aware of bodies, particularly those that could possibly harm or benefit us. In vision, we are also acquainted with an inner realm, that of the objects of vision. However, these are capable of informing us about external bodies in a much more detailed and reliable way. To achieve that, they are themselves spatially organised, they are proper *objects*. Their spatial properties – their shapes, sizes, divisions, and movements – represent the spatial properties of the bodies they stand for.

The tactile perception of a body, for Smith, includes the awareness of resistance and, hence, of independent existence. This feature is absent in visual perception. Therefore, colours are not external bodies or things – which is a feature that colours share with secondary qualities: by Smith's lights, material objects are not warm because warmth, properly speaking, is just a sensation. Similarly, objects are not red or yellow. But this is not because colours are sensations. They are not. In contrast to sensations, colours are extended, shaped, mobile and divisible. In the light of what have seen so far, we can now distinguish *three* ways in which our senses enable us to perceive the material world:

- When we touch a body, we immediately perceive it as external and substantial (i.e. extended, figured, divisible, and mobile).
- Secondary qualities such as heat, smell, taste, and sound are experienced as internal to the organ of sense and as non-spatial (i.e. as neither extended nor figured, divisible or mobile). These sensations, however, can – in an instinctive or acquired manner – suggest the locations and dimensions of bodies to us.
- The immediate objects of vision are perceived as non-external (since they do not resist the eye) but also as spatial (i.e. extended, figured, divisible, and mobile) objects. They suggest bodies to us in a much more systematic, detailed, and reliable manner than the sensations mentioned earlier.

Secondary qualities and colours play similar roles in our interactions with the environment. Although neither of them belongs to external objects, both of them make us aware of them. The manifold of coloured patches in the visual field makes us, as competent perceivers, aware of the layout of bodies in our environment. Although with less detail and perfection, the same is generally true for perceptions of sound and smell. They also make us aware of certain bodies (typically by making us aware of events), and of their position in space.

Conclusion

Although he may not be aware of this himself, Smith achieves more than he claims. Instead of merely recapitulating Berkeley's views on vision, he gives them an interesting turn: being not fully aware of Berkeley's complete metaphysical outlook (or at least ignoring it), he takes the remarks about the 'internality' of vision and the 'externality' of touch at face value and figures out how such a theory might be in some detail. A world of spatial, yet non-external, visual objects is opposed to the mind-independent, solid bodies which are signified by them. Even if, according to this view, colours are no secondary qualities, they are in a way less real than material objects. After all, they are merely signs for what is 'really out there.' Concerning their metaphysical status, Smith gives us just hints: in discussions of the secondary qualities of temperature, smell, and taste he mentions the Lockean idea that objects possess powers to produce sensations (§§ 21, 22, 23) in us.[7] About the power to produce sensations of colour, Smith writes: 'The powers by which different bodies excite in the organs of Sight the Sensations of different colours, probably depend upon some difference in the nature, configuration, and arrangement of the parts which compose their respective surfaces.' (§ 48) This surface property, though responsible for our sensations, is not *identical* to colour. The main reason for this is the incommensurability of visible and tangible objects. 'We cannot, even in imagination, conceive an object of Touch to be prolonged into an object of Sight, or an object of Sight into an object of Touch' (§ 50) For Smith, as for Berkeley, the objects of touch and vision are so different that even our ideas of tangible and visible triangles are utterly dissimilar and only connected by habituation (§ 61f.). As a result,

> the objects of Sight and those of Touch constitute two worlds. . . . The tangible world, as well as all the different parts which compose it, has three dimensions, Length, Breadth, and Depth. The visible world, as well as all the parts which compose it, has only two, Length and Breadth. It presents us only a plain surface, which, by certain shades and combinations of Colour, suggests and represents to us . . . certain tangible objects which have no Colour. (§ 50)

The visible world, the product of sensations of colour, is a two-dimensional manifold of coloured shapes. Its inhabitants are experienced as internal to the eye and yet have, unlike secondary qualities, all the marks of objects, namely figure, extension, divisibility, and mobility. Their colours are to the eye what solidity is to the touch.

Acknowledgements

A precursor of this paper has been presented at the conference *Smith, Ferguson, and Witherspoon at 300* that took place at the University of St. Andrews in July 2023. I am grateful for helpful comments from the audience, particularly to Michele Bee, James Foster and David M. Levy. Also many thanks to anonymous referees for the Adam Smith Review and to Bernhard Thöle, whose criticisms helped to improve this paper.

Notes

1 One *might* think that Smith has a sign-signified relation in mind, here, such that the sensation of pressure leads us to an automatic *judgement* about externality. But his formulations strongly suggest that no element of judgements is present: he says that a table is

not *judged* external but 'felt accordingly' (§ 3) and 'felt as something altogether different from those affections' (Griswold 1999: 100–101). Glenney (2014), in the same vein, suggests that tactile resistance represents external objects 'directly' (p. 222). I will assume this reading throughout.

2 At least there is no reason to suspect that Smith makes a difference here. Systematically, it has recently been argued that although we can, in experiences of touch, distinguish between a body-directed sensation and the awareness of the object that resists, both of them are spatial in that the sensation is still experienced as being located at a certain part of the body (cf. e.g. Martin 1992: 204ff.).

3 This is the case as long as we consider the secondary qualities in themselves, without their ability to inform us about bodies at a distance.

4 Though he acknowledges in §§ 61 and 62 that certain visible ideas – even if not similar to tangible ideas – are 'better fitted' to represent certain tangible ideas than others – a thought that is also discussed in Berkeley's New Theory of Vision (§ 142, § 152). This may weaken the language analogy, but it does so in Smith to the same degree as it does in Berkeley.

5 A disanalogy which Smith fails to detect is the following: While solid bodies exclude each other, such that one body resists the movement of another body and either moves out of place or stops the other's movement, colours in the visual field behave differently: while they sometimes expel each other (as when we observe two balls bumping into each other), it is more often the case that one visual object occludes the other (as the moon occludes the sun in a solar eclipse). Thomas Reid mentions that imaginary purely visual observers, the Idomenians, speak about the 'overcoming quality of bodies' (Reid 1997: 111), here. In this respect, colours are not as solidity, although they fill the visual world.

6 The picture that emerges has a remarkable similarity to what Hutcheson, Smith's teacher in Glasgow, writes about the ideas belonging to specific senses: 'Some *Ideas* are found accompanying the most different sensations, which yet are not to be perceived separately from some *sensible Quality;* such are *Extension, Figure, Motion,* and *Rest,* which accompany the *Ideas* of Sight, or Colours, and yet may be perceived without them, as in the *Ideas of Touch,* at least if we move our Organs along the Parts of the Body touched. *Extension, Figure, Motion,* or *Rest* seem therefore to be more properly called *Ideas accompanying* the Sensations of *Sight* and *Touch,* than the sensations of either of these senses' (Hutcheson 2002: 16).

7 Note that Smith warns against using the same word for the power and the resultant sensation. For secondary qualities at least, he wants the name to be reserved for the sensation. The power is just some physical constellation that helps the senses to do their job of informing us about bodies.

References

Berkeley, G. (1993) 'An Essay towards a New Theory of Vision', in M. R. Ayers (ed.) *Philosophical Works: Including the Works on Vision*, London: Everyman, pp. 1–70.

Brown, K. L. (1992) 'Dating Adam Smith's Essay Of the External Senses', *Journal of the History of Ideas*, 53: 333–337.

Glenney, B. (2011) 'Adam Smith and the Problem of the External World', *Journal of Scottish Philosophy*, 9(2): 205–223.

Glenney, B. (2014) 'Adam Smith on Sensory Perception: A Sympathetic Account', in David Hardwick and Leslie Marsh (eds.) *Propriety and Prosperity: New Studies on the Philosophy of Adam Smith*. Basingstoke: Palgrave Macmillan, pp. 118–135.

Glenney, B. (2015) 'Perception by Sympathy: Connecting Smith's "External Senses" to his "Sentiments"', *The Adam Smith Review*, 8: 241–255.

Hume, D. (1969) *A Treatise of Human Nature*. London: Penguin Books. (Cited by book.part.section.paragraph).

Hutcheson, F. (2002) *An Essay on the Nature and Conduct of the Passions and Affections, with Illustrations on the Moral Sense*. Indianapolis: Liberty Fund.
Locke, J. (1910) *An Essay Concerning Human Understanding*. London: Routledge.
Martin, M. G. F. (1992) 'Sight and Touch', in T. Crane (ed.) *The Contents of Experience: Essays on Perception*. Cambridge: Cambridge University Press, pp. 196–215.
Reid, Thomas. (1997) *An Inquiry into the Human Mind on the Principles of Common Sense*, (ed.) Brookes. Edinburgh: Edinburgh University Press.
Smith, A. (1978) 'Of the External Senses', in W. P. D. Wightman and J. C. Bryce (eds.) *Essays on Philosophical Subjects*. Oxford: Oxford University Press, pp. 131–168. (ES).
Stuart, M. (2013) *Locke's Metaphysics*. Oxford: Oxford University Press.

Part III

Roundtables

13 Introduction to the authors-Meet-Critics symposium

Andreas Ortmann and Benoît Walraevens

As the title of our book suggests, ours is an exercise in finding coherence in Adam Smith's work. As the subtitle of our book indicates, we take seriously Smith's work on languages, rhetoric, and conjectural history. Our point of departure is Smith's *Lectures on Rhetoric and Belles Lettres,* which preceded his *Theory of Moral Sentiments* and *The Wealth of Nations* by almost two and four decades respectively, but which he continued teaching for many years.

> Had Smith had more confidence in his own thoughts on rhetoric, and his lectures published earlier, then perhaps his own use of rhetoric, and its connection with his moral philosophy, would have led to a different interpretation of his economics.
>
> (Dow 2009: 18)

The use of persuasive language and argumentation can shape perceptions of economic actors and outcomes, thus influencing individual decision-making and public policies. As we documented in Chapter 2, titled *The Rhetorical Structure of Adam Smith's The Wealth of Nations (and what caused it),* Smith was very much aware of this. Specifically, he understood that speakers' (writers') and listeners' (readers') interests might be conflicted, and anticipated correctly (Fleischacker 2004: 16) that his targets (merchants, manufacturers, and their political supporters) would not take kindly to his 'very violent attack' (*Corr. Letter* 208: 251; Smith 1987) on the mercantile system they represented. Hence, his argumentation had to be strategic, using what he called the 'Socratic' method:

- He initially kept away from the main point to be proved – that the system of commerce of Great Britain of his time was dysfunctional, and in any case, far inferior to a system that would not be riddled by mercantile regulations.
- Instead, Smith outlined in Books I through III the optimality of a rigorously developed system of political economy (whose descendants still reign supreme

Adam Smith's System: A Re-Interpretation Inspired by Smith's Lectures on Rhetoric, Game Theory, and Conjectural History, Palgrave Macmillan, 2022.

DOI: 10.4324/9781003767824-17

in today's economic textbooks), assuming away problems of public good provisions or externalities and, for the most part, asymmetric information.
- In these first three books, Smith sometimes implicitly showed the damage done by an economic system catering to vested interests (see *WN,* I.viii.13, 84; I.x.c.25, 144; I.xi.p.10, 267; Smith 1976b), but he refrained from identifying the opponent, that is, the mercantilist system or the collusion between the merchant class and legislators.
- He did so only in Book IV, *Of Systems of Political Economy*, where he attacks the mercantile system in his own country and time frontally and relentlessly. The reader, if he or she bought into the arguments mustered in Books I-III, could only grant the validity of the conclusion that the system of commerce in Great Britain during Smith's time was dysfunctional.

In our view, Smith meant Book V to be a central book of *WN* and much more than an afterthought to his summary of the 'didactic' and impartial 'system of natural liberty' at the end of Book IV.

- In Book V Smith introduced public good provision problems, (what is nowadays called) externalities, and other incentive alignment problems. He argued persuasively for incentive-compatible solutions, anticipating modern theories of the firm, reputational enforcement, and public finance (Ortmann and Meardon 1995; Ortmann 1999; see also West 1990: Ch. 5, 7–9).
- He also finished the book, quite rhetorically, on the most pressing political issue of his time: the fate of the British Empire. To argue that Smith's treatment in Book V of public expenditure, revenue, and debts was *primarily* historical seems like a misreading of it.

> Many of the difficulties in Smith's views and arguments arise from the fact that he was dealing with questions that remain difficult for us today. . . . We can learn from Adam Smith today, but to do so we need to distinguish carefully between his local and universal teachings.
>
> (Fleischacker 2004: xvi–xvii)

Game theory is a branch of mathematics for the social sciences that studies decision-making in situations where two or more individuals or groups interact, often (but not always) having conflicting interests. The central idea of game theory is that the best outcome for each player depends not only on their own actions but also on the actions of their opponents.

Game theory comes in two flavours, in Binmore's terminology: 'eductive' and 'evolutive' (Binmore 1990, 2008). A Nash equilibrium is the most prominent solution concept of eductive game theory; it is a 'state of play' in which none of the players, conditional on the other players' choices of actions, has an incentive to change their choice of action. Importantly, under weak conditions on the dynamics,

Friedman (1991) has shown that the Nash equilibrium of the so-called normal form of, say, principal-agent games (about which more below) is the fixed point of the evolutive process that it defines. This connects eductive and evolutionary game theory with each other.

The advantages of bringing game theory to Smith are:

> Firstly, it allows us to bring a well-established, precise language (eg., players' actions, payoffs, information conditions) and an impressive conceptual apparatus (eg., the distinction of the equilibrium outcomes of finitely and indefinitely repeated stage games, something that routinely confounds (Smith) scholars because they do not understand the observational equivalence of behaviour resulting from indefinitely repeated actions such as the game of life, and pro-social preferences) to the subject matter. This turns out to be important when, to give just one of many possible examples, one wants to properly conceptualize the acquisition of self-command which is now recognized as a necessary step to recover the connection between Smith's political economy and moral philosophy.
> (Montes 2016: 152; 2019)

- Second, it allows us to identify Smith's universal take-home messages and arguments, many of which remain controversial. Using the language of game theory gives us the opportunity to strip away context ('the local teachings' in Fleischacker's words) and focus on the incentive structure that the interacting players face, to identify what one might want to call problem isomorphs, that is, structurally identical incentive problems which otherwise may be read as different problems because of the context in which they are shrouded. This allows us to infer what Smith would have argued in contexts that did not exist in his time and place.

We have demonstrated (e.g. Chapters 2 and 3 of our book) that the speaker-listener stage game is isomorphic to the game that Man Today and Man Tomorrow play in the *TMS* and that the buyers and sellers of goods of adjustable quality play in the *WN*. In Matrix 1 (taken from Meardon and Ortmann 1996), the socially optimal outcome would be the cell in the upper left corner. In a one-off game, Man Yesterday faces the temptation of choosing the improper action over the proper action. For example, instead of having a glass or two the night before a presentation, and assuming that Man Today will just go about business as usual ('routine'), he empties the whole bottle of fine Scottish strawberry wine. As the cell in the lower left demonstrates, this leads to a negative payoff (aka hangover) for Man Today on the day of the presentation. This, however, is only the likely result of a one-off game between the two. (Note that it is not an equilibrium.) In a repeated game, and under certain reasonable conditions, Man Yesterday will learn to adjust his consumption in a way that would make him the prudent man Adam Smith would approve of. The outcome in the game of life thus played would be the cell in the upper left corner, which is the outcome where the total payoff is the highest.

Matrix 1 The game of self-command

Man Yesterday \ Man Today	Routine	Real
Proper	(1, 1)	(0, 0)
Improper	(2,−1)	(0, 0)

We have likewise analysed, game-theoretically (eg., Ch. 4), the proper role of government in Smith by sketching out in the language of game theory the incentive problems that joint-stock companies, teachers, and preachers face. Incentive problems we add that Adam Smith understood, famously, very well: 'In every profession, the exertion of the greater part of those who exercise it, is always in proportion to the necessity they are under of making that exertion' (*WN*, V.i.f.4: 759).

We also sketched out (with the help of Steve Meardon, see Ch. 5) a rich class of models that represent phenomena as varied as (asymmetrically structured) seller-buyer transactions of goods of adjustable quality or employee-employer relations ('principal-agent'), or (symmetrically structured) attempts at collusion, public goods provision, and externalities ('social-dilemma'), and again the proper role of government in these situations.

Throughout our book, we underline that for Smith, people are naturally sociable creatures, 'commercial animals' (see Walraevens 2010: Ch. 6) that take pleasure in exchanging ideas, sentiments, and goods. They look after the approbation of their opinions, conduct, and valuation of goods by their fellow animals (and by themselves).

The unity of Smith's conception of humans is not based on self-interest (although Smith overall left little doubt that self-interest is a major driver of people's motivations) but rather on sociability. The *game of life* is a repeated interactive game. Our languages and ideas, moral sentiments, and modes of commercial exchange evolve and are not God-given, a provocative idea when and where Smith lived and worked.

In Chapter 7, a capstone chapter of sorts, we identify the Wonder-Surprise-Admiration mechanism as the precursor of the prediction error minimisation mechanism now widely accepted in neuroeconomics as the driver of evolutionary processes.

Schematically . . .

We call the W-S-A mechanism a meta-routine and, in that chapter, identify, based on the stepping-stone analysis in the preceding chapters, three reasoning routines (RRs) that Smith used consistently from the get-go. It turns out that these reasoning routines map nicely in the eductive and evolutive game theory versions. We call RR1 Smith's Newtonian-deductive view of the world, as prominently on display first in Smith's *History of Astronomy* (*EPS,* IV.68–76: 99–105). RR2 captures the fact that Smith understood well the strategic nature of all things rhetorical,

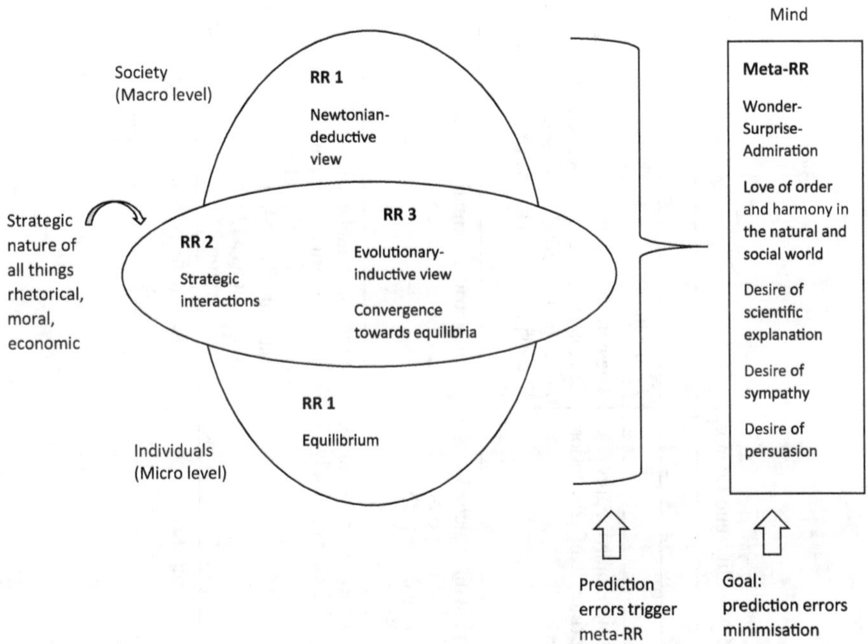

Figure 13.1 [Figure 1 in Chapter 7 of *Adam Smith's System: A Re-Interpretation Inspired by Smith's Lectures on Rhetoric, Game Theory, and Conjectural History* by Andreas Ortmann and Benoît Walraevens]

moral, and economic. Game theory, as we have argued, is well-suited to frame our understanding, and it represents, in its eductive version, very much a Newtonian view of the world. We call RR3 Smith's Evolutionary-inductive view of the world. Smith believed that human capacities such as languages or moral sentiments, as well as institutions like property rights, cultures, governments, and philosophical systems, evolve over time. He demonstrated this evolutionary mode of thinking in most, if not all, of his major published and unpublished works (Ortmann and Walraevens 2022: 182). Importantly, over time Smith, who initially seemed to have believed that the social sphere, like nature, was God-given, became increasingly doubtful about this somewhat Panglossian view. This made him understand that, rather than evolutionary processes always moving towards a unique equilibrium, there may be many, generating interesting equilibrium selection problems.

Table 1 summarises how Smith's RRs (and meta-RR) show up in his analysis of languages, rhetoric, morality, and economics. Following Newton's method, RR1 aims to identify very few principles to explain a variety of phenomena. In Smith's project of establishing a science of society, it means identifying principles of human nature implemented by the Deity to realise her ends (the perpetuation, propagation, and happiness of the species). Smith insists on the faculty of language and the (natural) desire to persuade in his analysis of languages and rhetoric, on

Table 13.1 The Reasoning Routines in Smith's analysis of Language and Rhetoric, Morality, and Economics

	Domains of application		
Reasoning Routines	*Language and Rhetoric*	*Morality*	*Economics*
1. Newtonian, deductive view of the world: equilibrium	The faculty of language and the desire (and need) to persuade	The faculty/principle of sympathy (empathy), the principle of gravitation of the social world	The natural propensity to truck, barter, and exchange, and the desire to better our condition are the two principles that explain how nations can increase their wealth.
2. Strategic interactions	Persuasion as strategic interaction, possibly in the form of conflicting interests/informational asymmetries, and hence as principal-agent games	Social interaction, with principal-agent game as the building block of self-command, mutual sympathy	Asymmetric information, strategic interactions, and reputation
3. Evolutionary, inductive view of the world: convergence towards equilibrium	Social interactions and language rules as conventions, driven by propriety of style	The emergence and evolution of moral norms, driven by (lack of) propriety of conduct	The formation and evolution of economic 'norms': the principle of *gravitation* of market prices around the natural price. Market prices as conventions and markets as evolutionary processes
Meta-Routine:	Pleasure of persuading	Pleasure of mutual sympathy	The pleasure to exchange is a pleasure to persuade

the faculty of sympathy and the (natural) desire for approbation in his moral analysis, and on the natural propensity to truck, barter, and exchange and the desire to better our condition in his economic analysis. RR2 highlights the strategic nature of social interactions in Smith, whether it be in the exchange of words and ideas, moral sentiments, or goods and services. These interactions between a writer and their reader(s), a speaker and their audience, an agent and their spectators (real or imaginary), or a seller and their buyers, are usually characterised by asymmetric information and conflicting interests and can be framed game-theoretically, as we show in the book. RR3 underlines the evolutionary nature of social norms, seen as human conventions founded on the natural desire (and pleasure) of propriety and approbation of our language and ideas, moral sentiments, or valuation of goods and services. Lastly, the Meta-RR underlines Smith's peculiar insistence on Man's desire for agreement, order, and harmony with others (including themselves), which restores the equilibrium and tranquillity of his mind. This aesthetic love of systems and harmony of minds plays a huge role in Smith's analysis of language, rhetoric, morality, and economics.

Identifying these different reasoning routines, relating them to important events in Smith's personal and intellectual life (see Ch. 7, the third section), and showing how he applied them in his various domains of analysis, helps us to provide a new systematic interpretation of his project of a science of society, unveiling the deep structure of his oeuvre.

References

Binmore, K. (1990) *Essays on the Foundations of Game Theory*. Cambridge, MA: Basil Blackwell.

Binmore, K. (2008) *Game Theory: A Very Short Introduction*. Oxford: Oxford University Press.

Dow, S. (2009) 'Knowledge, Communication and the Scottish Enlightenment', *Revue de philosophie économique*, 10(2): 1–23.

Fleischacker, S. (2004) *On Adam Smith's Wealth of Nations*. Princeton: Princeton University Press.

Friedman, D. (1991) 'Evolutionary Games in Economics', *Econometrica*, 59(3): 637–666.

Meardon, S. J. and Ortmann A. (1996) 'Self-Command in Adam Smith's Theory of Moral Sentiments: A Game-Theoretic Reinterpretation', *Rationality and Society*, 8(1): 57–80.

Montes, L. (2016) 'Adam Smith: Self-interest and the virtues', in R. Hanley (ed.) *Adam Smith: His Life, Thought, and Legacy*. Princeton: Princeton University Press, pp. 138–156.

Montes, L. (2019) 'Adam Smith's Foundational Idea of Sympathetic Persuasion', *Cambridge Journal of Economics*, 43(1): 1–15.

Ortmann, A. (1999) 'The Nature and Causes of Corporate Negligence, Sham Lectures, and Ecclesiastical Indolence: Adam Smith on Joint-Stock Companies, Teachers, and Preachers', *History of Political Economy*, 31(2): 297–315.

Ortmann, A. and Meardon, S. J. (1995) 'A Game-Theoretic Re-evaluation of Adam Smith's Theory of Moral Sentiments and Wealth of Nations', in I. H. Rima (ed.) *The Classical Tradition in Economic Thought. Perspectives on the History of Economic Thought Vol XI*. Brookfield: Edward Elgar, pp. 43–61.

Ortmann, A. and Walraevens, B. (2022) *Adam Smith's System: A Re-Interpretation Inspired by Smith's Lectures on Rhetoric, Game Theory, and Conjectural History*. Palgrave Macmillan.

Schumpeter, J. A. (1954) *History of Economics Analysis*. Oxford: Oxford University Press.

Smith, A. (1976b) *An Inquiry into the Nature and Causes of the Wealth of Nations*, (ed.) R. H. Campbell and A. S. Skinner, Glasgow edition. Oxford: Oxford University Press. Reprinted, Liberty Press (1981).

Smith, A. (1976b) *Essays on Philosophical Subjects*, (ed.) W. P. D. Wightman, Glasgow edition. Oxford: Oxford University Press. Reprinted, Liberty Press (1982).

Smith, A. (1982) 'The Principles which lead and direct Philosophical Enquiries illustrated by the History of Astronomy', in *Essays on Philosophical subjects* (Smith 1982 [1980]). pp. 33–105.

Smith, A. (1983) *Lectures on Rhetoric and Belles Lettres*, (ed.) J. C. Bryce, Glasgow edition. Oxford: Oxford University Press. Reprinted, Liberty Press (1985).

Smith, A. (1987) *Correspondence of Adam Smith*, (ed.) E. C. Mossner and I. S. Ross, 2nd edn., Glasgow edition. Oxford: Oxford University Press. Reprinted, Liberty Press (1987).

Walraevens, B. (2010) *Croissance et progrès chez Adam Smith*. PhD Thesis in Economics, Université Paris 1 Panthéon Sorbonne.

West, E. G. (1990) *Adam Smith and Modern Economics: From Market Behavior to Public Choice*. Aldershot: Edward Elgar.

14 Comments on Ortmann and Walraevans

Ryan Patrick Hanley

Andreas Ortmann and Benoît Walraevens' stimulating new book is titled *Adam Smith's System: A Re-Interpretation Inspired by Smith's Lectures on Rhetoric, Game Theory, and Conjectural History*. In what follows I want to say a bit about the book's claims on three of the four distinct categories invoked in its title: rhetoric, game theory, and systematicity. (I will leave it to my fellow contributors to this symposium to say something about conjectural history!) For on my reading, Ortmann and Walraevens' book has new and important things to say on all three of these fronts, and, in the space available to me, I'd like to try to do what I can to highlight what I take to be their most important contributions and also to raise a few questions.

First, rhetoric. One of the most useful elements of this book, to my mind, is the way in which Ortmann and Walraevens use various concepts that Smith developed in his early rhetoric lectures of the 1740s and 1750s to shed light on the structure and substance of his later published corpus, especially the structure and substance of *The Wealth of Nations*. Ortmann and Walraevens of course are hardly the first to document connections between Smith's rhetorical theory and the other elements of his corpus; to name just two important scholarly contributions on this front, Vivienne Brown's (1994) pioneering study did much to document a number of important connections between Smith's rhetoric and his moral theory, and James Otteson's subsequent study, in a somewhat different vein, did much to help Smith scholars see the ways in which Smith's understanding of language and its evolution shaped Smith's understanding of what Otteson (2002) calls his 'marketplace of life.' But at least part of the value added by Ortmann and Walraevens on this front is to show the degree to which Smith's presentation of his normative arguments in *The Wealth of Nations* draws on concepts elucidated in the rhetoric lectures. In particular, they persuasively showed how sensitivity to Smith's use of the 'Socratic' rhetorical style that he himself described in *LRBL* can help us see how and why he structured his presentation of his public goods policy provisions in Book V of *WN* in the way that he did. For as Ortmann and Walraevens rightly noted, Smith was deeply aware of how radical his policy proposals were likely to seem to the political and economic elites he sought to persuade. Smith's use of rhetoric thus allowed him to make radical proposals in a subtle and gentle way, and indeed in a way that

DOI: 10.4324/9781003767824-18

was more likely to gain for them a receptive hearing from those who might otherwise have dismissed them out of hand.

Now, all of these claims regarding the connections between Smith's rhetoric lectures and *The Wealth of Nations* seem to me insightful and fruitful. Let me raise just two points in response. First, the more I study Smith the more I think we'd all do well not only to attend to the rhetorical elements of *WN* but also to read *WN*'s rhetorical elements in light of the lectures on rhetoric. Additionally, we should read *WN*'s rhetoric and substance in light of the lectures on jurisprudence. For when we read *LJ* and *WN* next to each other, it becomes very evident that Smith very often made the very same point in very different ways in his published and unpublished works. But as far as I know, no one has yet tried, in any systematic way, to account for exactly why this is – though this would, I think, be an extremely interesting and welcoming project. Also, on the rhetoric front, a question for the authors might be raised: namely, how reliable can *LRBL* be as a guide to Smith's own rhetoric? After all, *LRBL* is essentially a history or catalogue of rhetorical concepts; in this sense *LRBL* does for the history of rhetoric what *TMS VII* does for the history of moral philosophy, or *HA* does for the history of astronomy. But no one would say, at least without heavy qualification and extensive justification, that some discrete point Smith makes about Aristotle or Hobbes or Mandeville in *TMS VII* explains what he is up to in his own name in the first six parts of *TMS*. So what then, we might wonder, justifies the hermeneutic move of applying to Smith's own thought rhetorical devices that he describes in *LRBL*?

Let me turn now to the second of the three title categories, game theory. Here, I think it's fair to say that this is where the book's heart lies, and Ortmann and Walraevens make a number of important claims. Space limitations require me to limit myself to highlighting the two claims about game theory that they themselves have highlighted as central to their project. First, Ortmann and Walraevens argue that game theory is a useful lens to apply to Smith's social analysis insofar as it reveals a consistency in Smith's social analysis that other Smith scholars have often failed to see. Specifically, their claim is that seeing Smith through the lens of game theoretical equilibrium outcomes helps us see the degree to which Smith consistently viewed what they call 'the game of life' as an infinite number of discrete stage games.

This is a helpful claim of course. But I wonder about the degree to which other scholars have missed this, and, in turn, whether Ortmann and Walraevens are perhaps using a different conceptual language to define an idea that may already be familiar to certain types of Smith scholars. I think particularly of certain moral philosophers who have written on Smith, and especially Otteson, mentioned earlier. One thing Otteson's idea of Smith's 'marketplace of life' helped many of us see is the degree to which Smith in fact sees life as an iterated series of intersubjective exchanges – in economic life, exchanges of goods and services, and in moral life, exchanges of sympathy. Otteson, to be sure, doesn't speak the game theoretic language of plays and payoffs, but it's not clear to me that his basic framework is all that different from that of the authors. The authors themselves at several points engage Otteson's work and suggest broad sympathy with it (e.g. pp. 210–211).

However, on their view, the interpretation advanced by Otteson is flawed insofar as Otteson 'misses the principal-agent aspect which differentiates the processes of the formation of languages and moral sentiments, for example, from the price discovery process' (p. 19). This may be right, but it would be helpful to hear more from the authors about whether they see themselves as supplementing Otteson's view by remedying or filling out lacunae, or if they see themselves as offering something fundamentally and radically different with their focus on the significance of the principal-agent aspect.

A second point on the game theory front: Ortmann and Walraevens also suggested that another reason why the game theory approach is so useful is that it helps us to distinguish the idiosyncratic from the universal in human exchange. The authors themselves capture this distinction by using the language of 'local teachings' or context on the one hand and 'problem isomorphs' on the other. Here again this seems to me fruitful, especially insofar as it reminds us of the degree to which Smith saw social interaction in terms of universal natural principles. But I suspect that Smith would also be the first to say that when it comes to moral choices, context matters. The texts here are familiar: for example, how do we know whether to sympathise with the man crying in the street until we know why he's crying? Here, as elsewhere, knowing the context matters. And thus I wonder how far the authors want to push their claim about 'problem isomorphs,' and whether too much focus on these isomorphs can lead us to minimise Smith's rich appreciation of the importance of context (to say nothing of his rich appreciation of human diversity and social pluralism). The importance of such context-specific action has been emphasised by Vernon Smith and Bart Wilson in their own important recent study. For their part Ortmann and Walraevens tend to emphasise the degree to which they are broadly following the same path as Smith and Wilson (2019) (e.g. pp. 4, 21), but here it seems to me there might be one place they diverge.

Since time and space are short, let me end by briefly turning to the third category, systematicity. I couldn't agree more with the authors that any interpretation of Smith that is worth its salt has to account for how Smith understood the concept of a system, as well as how he himself understood his work to hold together as a system. This itself has been the focus of recent books on Smith, including especially Eric Schliesser's (2019) *Adam Smith: Systematic Philosopher and Public Thinker*. I thus welcome the authors' efforts to uncover the 'deep structure' of Smith's thought (see especially 169f.). At the same time, I wonder whether we can fully uncover this deep structure without attending to the way in which Smith drew on concepts of natural religion and providentialism, both of which are fundamental elements of Smith's thought, albeit somewhat underemphasised in Ortmann and Walraevens' otherwise very illuminating and welcoming study.

References

Brown, V. (1994) *Adam Smith's Discourse: Canonicity, Commerce, and Conscience*. London: Routledge.

Otteson, J. R. (2002) *Adam Smith's Marketplace of Life*. Cambridge: Cambridge University Press.

Schliesser, E. (2019) *Adam Smith: Systematic Philosopher and Public Thinker*. Oxford: Oxford University Press.

Smith, V. L. and Wilson, B. J. (2019) *Humanomics: Moral Sentiments and the Wealth of Nations for the Twenty-First Century*. Cambridge: Cambridge University Press.

15 Adam Smith as persuader

Wonder-Surprise-Admiration

Lisa Hill

Andreas Ortmann and Benoît Walraevens bring us a new and fresh reading of Smith that focuses on its game-theoretical aspects, emphasising 'the importance of persuasion' in dealing with 'information asymmetries' in 'strategic interactions' where there are 'conflicting interests.' Smith's thought, they argue is 'prominently about persuasion.' I tend to agree and focus here on a case where this is exemplified in Smith but which they do not include in their book, no doubt because it is found in the *Theory of Moral Sentiments* and not the too often neglected sources upon which they uniquely rely for their new reading.

I discuss here how conflicting interests and asymmetric information can be affected by, or be an artefact of, a lack of motivation to genuinely care about how to manage a commercial state properly and thereby secure the welfare of the public. How to move politicians from a selfish to a more sociable attitude towards the public by a method that did not lower itself to berating their lack of public virtue. It is not that Smith was above moralising; only that he does not wish to waste his time on an argumentative strategy that would have no effect in this case. So, I explore how Smith seeks to overcome the problems caused by a lack of interest and an absence of public virtue on the part of the nation's political leaders. In this case the information asymmetry is not an inevitable or unintentional part of the strategic interaction (as seems to be Ortmann and Walraeven's assumption) but wilful due to apathy and lack of virtue. In any case, the following discussion is not so much critical of Ortmann and Walraeven's book as an effort to fill out or expand on some of their key points.

Ortmann and Walraevens propose that Smith used the meta-reasoning routine 'Wonder-Surprise-Admiration' to generate satisfactory explanations for puzzling social phenomena. We begin in a state of psychological 'equilibrium' when 'everything we observe happens as expected, when our world is in order.' But when 'unexpected events' occur we experience 'wonder' and 'surprise.' This creates an 'unpleasant gap in sense-making 'which we are motivated to fill in order to return to a state of imaginative '"tranquility and composure"' (pp. 184–185). Smith, they point out, not only used this routine to understand 'the ways our thoughts on the natural and social world come about' but also to talk about how 'we communicate them, for entertainment and/or persuasion' (p. 173). As I show here, Smith used this reasoning routine as a persuasive tool to provoke curiosity first, and then a

DOI: 10.4324/9781003767824-19

spirit of public virtue in legislators. He wanted to disrupt the mental tranquillity of the statesmen of his time and encourage them to allay their psychological disequilibrium through the policies he recommended.

Although we like to imagine Smith as a reserved and serious scholar (which he undoubtedly was), he was also a skilled 'ideas entrepreneur,' a marketer of ideas who knew how to make his ideas politically relevant and attractive. As we see in the example below, one of his techniques was to frame contemporary events as a series of crises in order to provide converts with the ammunition they needed to further his attempts to reform the British state (Morrison 2012: 405). These depictions of crises (surprise and wonder) were also designed to inspire legislators themselves to want to change things according to the solutions he provided.

Smith not only showed us that humans are 'fundamentally moral (self-reflective) and speaking (persuasive) animal moved by . . . imagination and passions/emotions' (p. viii); he also showed himself to be a successful and strategic persuader able to engage the imaginations and passions of his readers in order to get what he himself wanted, namely, 'the approbation and sympathy for [his] opinions and ideas' (p. 210), in this case, his ideas about how the economy should be managed. But as Ortmann and Walraevens note 'Smith, faced . . . a hostile crowd in the merchants and political elite of the day' and expended much energy in 'laying out the logic of a competitive market economy not afflicted by counterproductive trade restraints, public-good provision problems, and externalities.' Smith wanted to communicate that his 'Newtonian view' of how things should work was often frustrated by ill-aligned incentives in the marketplace and the influence of 'vested interests' in the legislature. Since in this case the information asymmetry on the opposing side was wilful moral laziness – or at least a passive form of self-interest – he had to manage 'this strategic interaction' carefully and gamefully.

Smith's mission

Smith pioneered a tradition whereby the scholar takes it upon themselves 'the duty to shape and judge public policies, to lead public opinion, to define the desirable ends.' This entailed a belief that economics should be taught to both leaders and the public alike (Schumpeter 1952: 207). Smith took this self-appointed task very seriously, opining that a 'just, reasonable and practicable . . . political disquisition' was just about the 'most useful' kind of scholarly project he could think of; at the very 'least,' it might 'animate the public passions of men, and rouse them to seek out the means of promoting the happiness of the society' (TMS IV.i.11, 186).

This mission was by no means straightforward. Smith understood that 'prejudice and ignorance' played a much larger role in 'political life' than 'in ordinary economic affairs' (Stigler 1975: 241). Most of what was wrong with the way the state operated in his time was due to either ignorance, knavishness, or a lack of sincere regard for the public good. Smith's first and most pressing task, therefore, was to persuade the legislator to *care*; once he had achieved that and secured the attention of the only actors who could fix it, the problem – and its solution – could be laid out and, importantly, *heeded*.

But how could he animate them when it seemed to Smith that, given the state of British public affairs, none of them cared a bit about the national welfare? I show below that Smith seems to have used the 'Wonder-Surprise-Admiration' meta-heuristic to get the statesmen of his day to take an interest in public affairs. He would show them that the state of the English economy was once magnificent but now badly broken machine that could be remediated by an integrated, Newtonian approach that would evoke the form of pleasure associated with our innate 'aesthetic love of order and systems' (p. 183) and thereby inadvertently evoke a more sociable approach to public policy.

Wonder-Surprise-Admiration

As Ortmann and Walraevens see it, the process of philosophising always begins with wonder and surprise; a disruption of a state of psychological equilibrium when things are not as we would expect or wish them to be (wonder-surprise). It concludes or is reconciled by a pleasing and satisfactory explanation, 'a new understanding' (admiration) (p. 184). In prosecuting his political economy, Smith believed that he was engaged in an enterprise so noble and absorbing that its successful execution embodied an aesthetic dimension insofar as confusion about why the economy struggled was to be met by the production of an explanation both elegant and calming. It was elegant and calming because the solution was already embedded in the diagnosis, an argumentative technique Smith often used to great effect, as Ortmann and Walraevens note. If Britain's economic woes were caused by corruptions of the system of natural liberty then the solution was obviously to remove the corruptions and restore the system to its natural and correct state.

For Smith, the system of 'natural liberty' was both an explanatory device and a real system governed by natural laws and it was the foundation of his entire political economy. It was a beautiful 'machine' 'contrived' from 'all eternity' by the 'Author of Nature' (TMS II.ii.3.5; see also Hill 2001). That this system embodied divine intention allowed Smith to generate an especially urgent sense of crisis around it; it also authorised him to (sometimes mercilessly) moralise against those who abused it. In a sense, in order to please 'God,' this beautiful and natural system needed to be untangled from its myriad 'obstructions' and corruptions.

So, how did Smith use the reasoning routine of Wonder-Surprise-Admiration to animate the legislators of his day to first care about the state of the British economy; then to see things his way; and thereafter to reform the economic system according to his prescribed methods?

Smith's argumentative strategy

Evidently assuming that most of the politicians of his days were 'heedless of the interest of [their] country,' Smith reflected on how he might stir that interest and 'implant public virtue in the breast[s]' of the nation's leaders. He cynically – or perhaps sensibly – surmised that it would be a waste of time to point out the public benefits: 'the superior advantages the subjects of a well-governed state enjoy,' how they 'are better lodged . . . better clothed [and] . . . better fed.' Therefore, Smith decides that his best strategy is to appeal to the amateur engineer inside every political actor, who, it should be noted at this point, he automatically assumed to be male. In any case, rather than advert to the public benefits, it is better to write of a social and economic system as though it were an exquisitely complicated machine that needed explaining. As Smith put it:

> [y]ou will be more likely to persuade, if you describe the great system of public police which procures these advantages, if you explain the connexions and dependencies of its several parts, their mutual subordination to one another, and their general subserviency to the happiness of the society.
> (TMS IV.i.11, 186) (Stage 1: psychological equilibrium)

On this reasoning, all eyes would now be trained on him as he lifted the hood of the engine that needed fixing, and all heads would now be inside the metaphorical hood, transfixed by curiosity.

The next step was to show in what ways and by which mechanisms this beautiful machine was being improperly driven and therefore damaged by its irresponsible operators (Stage 2: wonder and surprise). Smith wrote that 'if you show how this system might be introduced into his own country, what it is that hinders it from taking place there at present, how those obstructions might be removed, and all the several wheels of the machine of government be made to move with more harmony and smoothness, without grating upon one another, or mutually retarding one another's motions,' much like the gears of an automobile engine, it is almost impossible for 'a man' to 'listen to a discourse of this kind, and not feel himself animated to some degree of public spirit.' The same dynamic is at play when I explain to my son, as I am teaching him to drive, the destructive effect that his careless grinding of the gears has on the car's gear box. Once I explain this, he is motivated to change gears with more attention because he prefers, not so much to be virtuous, but to be a skilful driver who avoids damaging the machine. It also gives him a better sense of how to do so properly because the action of the mechanism has now been explained to him. Afterwards, Smith suggests that one must offer a neat and elegant solution to fix the problem, that is, to 'guard against' the 'dangers to which' the legislator's nation 'may be exposed' (TMS IV.i.11: 186). Smith understands that one must first paint a picture of order and tranquillity to imaginatively evoke a sense of psychological equilibrium (in this case, an idealised and properly functioning system of natural liberty designed by God), then create a sense of crisis around that picture (wonder and surprise), and finally inspire the legislator's curiosity about the solution and a strong 'desire' to apply that solution ('admiration'). By proceeding in this fashion, Smith believes he will produce the desired effect on the legislator who 'will, at least for the moment, feel some desire to remove those obstructions, and to put into motion so beautiful and so orderly a machine' (TMS IV.i.11: 186).

I will now discuss how Smith took his reader through the various stages of 'wonder-surprise-admiration' with respect to the system of natural liberty and its afflictions. This began by describing the beautiful machine in its natural state.

The discombobulating problem

The system – or 'machine,' – of which intricate workings Smith sought to describe and celebrate was the management of the economy under conditions of 'natural liberty.' The latter, he explained was a natural, invisible but very real system of non-state, voluntaristic, private, non-monolithic and decentralised means for the self-government of people that was capable of delivering prosperity and exponential improvement. It existed as a perfectly self-equilibrating ecology that the leaders of his time seemed oblivious to, as evidenced by their routine mistreatment, distortion and pollution of it. Smith described at length how it was burdened by the 'folly of human laws' and the weight of artificial, mercantilist, and 'impertinent obstructions' imposed on it. Such obstructions destructively 'encumber [the] operations' of the market (WN IV.v.b.43, 540) and infringe upon our natural economic rights (WN I.x.c.12, 138; WN IV.vii.b.44, 582).

Among the various distortions and afflictions entangling and distorting the free play of the market were such institutional impediments as monopolies, laws restricting free trade, burdensome taxes, laws of settlement, corporation laws, patronage and nepotism, and archaic laws controlling inheritance and workers' rights. All of these obstacles productivity and individual effort and threatened the prosperity and security of entire nations; they should, therefore, be eliminated wherever possible so that the 'machine' could work properly and the people could enjoy their economic citizenship rights. For example, whereas the system of natural liberty would 'naturally dispose' the 'private interests and passions of individuals . . . to turn their stock towards the employments which . . . are most advantageous' and 'agreeable to the interest of the whole society,' mercantilism, whose 'sole engine' is monopoly, 'necessarily derange[s] more or less this natural and most advantageous distribution of stock' (WN vii.c.88–89, 630).

Smith's economic thought is effectively a protracted diatribe against elite manipulation of the state and the market; against corruption, mercantilism and crony capitalism (WN IV.viii.54, 661–662). Having created a sense of crisis around the abuse and corruption of the Creator's beautiful system, Smith then went about proposing a solution that would restore it to its natural state and bring forth 'admiration.'

The Mechanic's cure

A society managed according to the laws and principles of natural liberty and freed from the cumbersome constraints of bad public administration had the potential to be a thing of beauty. Smith likened it to a perfectly calibrated machine whose smooth operation was capable of evoking aesthetic pleasure.

> The perfection of police, the extension of trade and manufactures, are noble and magnificent objects. The contemplation of them pleases us, and we are interested in whatever can tend to advance them. They make part of the great system of government, and the wheels of the political machine seem to move

> with more harmony and ease by means of them. We take pleasure in beholding the perfection of so beautiful and grand a system, and we are uneasy till we remove any obstruction that can in the least disturb or encumber the regularity of its motions.
>
> (TMS V.i.11, 185)

We must free the system of natural liberty from the clogs that were interfering with 'the regularity of its motions' and causing its various parts to 'grat[e] upon one another.' This meant government restraint, the eradication of superfluous jams on its natural workings and the liberal oiling of its components with economic freedom. As he famously wrote, when maladaptive 'systems either of preference or of restraint' have been eradicated, 'the obvious and simple system of natural liberty establishes itself of its own accord' (WN IV.ix.51, 687).

Smith's persuasive strategy seems to have worked. According to Jeremy Bentham, his ideas produced 'an evident change in public opinion . . . on all points of political economy' (Bentham in *Corr. Letter*, App. C: 386). While the full extent of the impact of Smith's ideas in his own time has been debated (Teichgraeber 1987: 339), it is fair to say that, regardless of how much influence they exerted in the eighteenth century, that influence has proved to be steady and enduring, intensifying progressively in the subsequent centuries.

References

Hill, L. (2001) 'The Hidden Theology of Adam Smith', *European Journal of the History of Economic Thought*, 8(1): 1–29.

Morrison, J. A. (2012) 'Before Hegemony: Adam Smith, American Independence and the Origins of the First Era of Globalization', *International Organisation*, 66(3): 395–428.

Schumpeter, J. A. (1952) *Ten Great Economists: From Marx to Keynes*. London: George Allen and Unwin.

Smith, A. (1976) [1759] *The Theory of Moral Sentiments*, (eds.) D. D. Raphael and A. L. MacFie. Oxford: Clarendon Press.

Smith, A. (1978) *Lectures on Jurisprudence (A and B)*, (eds.) R. L. Meek, D. D. Raphael and L. G. Stein. Oxford: Oxford University Press.

Smith, A. (1979) [1776] *An Inquiry into the Nature and Causes of the Wealth of Nations*, (eds.) R. H. Campbell and A. S. Skinner. Oxford: Clarendon Press.

Smith, A. (1980) *Essays on Philosophical Subjects*, (ed.) I. S. Ross. Oxford: Clarendon Press.

Smith, A. (1987) *The Correspondence of Adam Smith*, (eds.) E. C. Mossner and I. S. Ross. Oxford: Oxford University Press.

Stigler, G. (1975) 'Smith's Travels on the Ship of State', in A. S. Skinner and T. Wilson (eds.) *Essays on Adam Smith*. Oxford: Clarendon Press, pp. 237–246.

Teichgraeber, R. F. (1987) *"Free Trade" and Moral Philosophy: Rethinking the Sources of Adam Smith's Wealth of Nations*. Durham, NC: Duke University Press.

16 The dualities of Smith's system

Ecem Okan

As true Smithians who embrace his *Principles Which Lead and Direct Philosophical Enquires; Illustrated by the History of Astronomy,* among others, Andreas Ortmann and Benoît Walraevens provide us with a new system of Smith's thought by binding together its parts – language and rhetoric, morality, economics – with invisible chains or what they call reasoning routines (RRs). These core observations about the way in which Smith conceptualised his Humean 'science of man' (Ortmann and Walraevens 2022: 173, 274; cf. Phillipson 2010: 2) are analysed throughout the book with various illustrations drawn from textual evidence. Such an exercise in finding 'coherence' (p. vii) in Smith's work implies reducing its complexity to soothe our imagination and gain our admiration. Overall, their book fulfils these conditions. It is hard not to agree with their insistence on how rhetoric is crucial for understanding Smith in general; or to admire how smoothly they manage to lead our imagination across the five books of *The Wealth of Nations.* They argue that rather than its content (as commonly found in Smith scholarship), it is the form of the book which is rhetorical.

The present opportunity to assess their book then calls for, in Smithian terms, attentive observation in order to discover difficulties that tend to embarrass and confound the imagination in its effortless flow from one idea to another. It is an impossible task to avoid gaps or intervals in the study of such a rich and widely discussed thinker. The book avowedly does not explain Smith's complete oeuvre (p. vii, 223). I assume that the authors leave out material for the sake of argumentation and clarity. Rather than pointing out what's missing from the whole picture, I'll stick to the difficulties arising from the gaps in their narrative of Smith's system that I classify under three kinds of duality: the philosopher and common people, the impartial and partial, the general and particular. The fact that Smith himself is equivocal about which point of view he approaches a specific issue from leaves the reader desiring a little more discussion than the authors so fruitfully begin.

The philosopher and common people

The first difficulty is the lack of a clear distinction between how (and what) Smith, as a philosopher, thinks, and how (and what) Smith, as a philosopher, thinks about how (and what) people think. There are two areas in which this absence is striking.

DOI: 10.4324/9781003767824-20

First, in the definition of reasoning routines, the authors argue that Smith's deductive (RR1) and inductive view of the world (RR3), and his understanding of problems arising from strategic interactions (RR2) are all triggered by a meta-routine which is equated to, among others, Smith's method of scientific inquiry (meta-RR) – and which, as I suggest in the opening passages, is also the method adopted by the authors for their study of Smith. In a similar vein, they draw analogies 'between this process of scientific discovery and his concept of gravitation of the market price around the natural price' (p. 184), between the desire for scientific explanation and the 'desires of persuasion and sympathy' (p. 209), or between 'moral and intellectual judgments' (p. 206) on the grounds that 'similar cognitive processes and motivations are at work' (p. 226). Even though the authors qualify these observations regarding to *people* with lesser cognitive abilities (p. 226, my emphasis) and note that Smith's overriding interest is to understand how *people* reasoned and thought about the natural and social world, the qualification itself, along with the above observations, makes the mistake of conflating two distinct points of view: that of the philosopher and the commoner.

The distinction is implicit in most of Smith's works (although there are exceptions, as in *Astronomy* (II.12.11, 45) where Smith distinguishes between philosophers who perceive an interval between two objects and the bulk of mankind who consider them as connected); and it corresponds to the two kinds of relation, natural and philosophical (*T* 1.1.5.1), identified by Hume (2000) in the *Treatise* (whose influence is stressed by the authors as well as the editor of *ESP*, Bryce: 42). The natural relations of resemblance, contiguity and causation connect two ideas in such a way that the experience of one idea naturally introduces another. While they have a 'connecting [or associating] principle' (*T* 1.1.5.1; Astronomy IV.19, 66), philosophical relations don't: it is when two ideas are voluntarily and arbitrarily compared together that 'the ideas of philosophical relation' are produced (*T* 1.1.5.2). The way in which the understanding or cognitive processes operate differs greatly, for example, when 'we are uneasy when people differ from us in sentiments and opinions' (Ortmann and Walraevens 2022: 209) or when Copernicus is unsatisfied with the system of Ptolemy (Astronomy IV.27,71). It would have been useful to express this core distinction and put it to the fore in an analysis of reasoning routines, even if emotions (such as wonder, surprise, and admiration) are universal.

Second, the account of morality as emerging conventionally through experience of common life does not explain how the philosopher comes to form a critical and objective point of view. However, this is essential for the analysis of Smith's RR and also for buttressing the suggestion that 'the system of natural liberty is a 'didactic discourse' of a philosopher or impartial spectator who takes a distanced, well-informed, unbiased view on political economy' (pp. 57–58). Of course, the former is a famous critique addressed to Smith himself that usually goes hand in hand with the endless debate about the normative or descriptive dimension of his moral theory. Smith's appeal to the distinction between the desire to be praised and to be praiseworthy or to an idea of perfection is much discussed on this matter. The book doesn't overtly address this problem, and it seems as though both the social and ethical standards (in its strict sense), that is, both 'moral' standards, are explained by the same principles.

On the one hand, the authors note that the impartial spectator, as the ethical standard or conscience, corrects the imperfections of the judgements of the actual spectators (pp. 74, 150). On the other hand, it is implicitly accepted that the standard of the impartial spectator is not sufficient to prevent the corruption of morals. A proof is the mercantile system, the social standard considered as human interference with the divine plan (pp. 187–188). Smith is subject to a similar ambiguity, for instance, when he condemns Aristotle's and Plato's views on infanticide (TMS V.ii.15), as they apparently cannot provide moral judgements that transcend the social norms. But how can the 'partial' mercantile system and Smith's 'impartial' system of natural liberty both be explained by the same principles? The observation that Smith's emphasis shifted from the deductive to the evolutionary view (p. 187), if intended as an oblique response to this problem, is unsatisfactory. This is because while the late additions to the *TMS* pertain to the partial, the delay of and revisions to the *WN* also relate to the impartial according to the author's analysis.

The impartial and partial

The second difficulty has to do with the characterisation of the system of natural liberty as impartial in contrast to the partial mercantile system. In their presentation of the system of natural liberty, the authors follow many scholars by stressing 'the natural right every man has to choose how to use his capital or faculties as he sees proper' (p. 53), which would be established once an exact administration of justice is secured. The implications of the direct link Smith forges between this system and the natural progress of opulence are, again, as conventional, glossed over. Even though the authors remark on the link (p. 54), their comments – for example, 'Once they are free to . . . employ their capital as they see fit, the economy will follow the natural, optimal order of progress toward opulence' – de-emphasise it. Rather, Smith suggests that if people are free to choose how to use their capital, they would choose to invest in the order dictated by the natural progress of opulence: first agriculture, then manufactures, and lastly foreign commerce (WN III.i.9, 380 Cf. WN II.v). It is surprising to see how often the condition Smith sets for the natural system of liberty to be beneficial is forgotten, especially when we consider that Smith's argument is as conspicuous as it gets in the famous invisible hand passage (WN IV.ii.9, 456).

Why would this matter for the present book? Arguably because it could further develop the line of interpretation the authors competently adopt regarding the important role of rhetoric in Smith's system. On the one hand, it sheds light on Smith's conception of the natural progress of opulence as the direct opposite of the mercantile system by magnifying the importance of agriculture while diminishing the role of foreign commerce. On the other hand, it demonstrates Smith's capacity to persuade the reader, as well as the present authors (p. 35), into believing that North American colonies follow the natural order of progress contrary to the inverted one followed by Europe. The reasons why North American colonies' progress is not natural have been discussed (e.g. Paganelli 2022); suffice it to mention two of them: colonies were not free to choose how to use their capital (as Smith and the authors are well aware) because of the Acts of Navigation, among others. Smith is also explicit that the North American colonies could invest most of their capital in agriculture because it was British capital that carried on the other sectors (WN II.v.21, 366). Consequently, it is possible to advance that the natural system of liberty partakes in a rhetorical rather than a didactic discourse, because while the system itself promotes an impartial regard for different sectors (and social classes), Smith's conceptualisation of the system is partial to the extent that, without 'carefully weighing the pros and cons of his argument' (LRBL i.150: 62; Ortmann and Walraevens 2022: 52), Smith seems to be aiming for persuasion rather than instruction. It is also notable that Smith simply does not elaborate on it. Maybe he even tries to appeal to our tendency to admire simple and beautiful systems (TMS IV.i.11; Astronomy *II.12*) to motivate us towards liberty and progress by making them appear so natural and spontaneous. All these points further justify the authors' sharp observation that North American colonies illustrate 'the possible benefits of his ideal system of natural liberty and the dangers of the mercantile system' (p. 35).

The general and particular

The last difficulty has to do, in very broad terms, with the interplay between what is general and particular in Smith's thought. I thereby allude to Fleischacker's (2004) distinction, endorsed by the authors, between the function of the *WN* as a tract and treatise and between Smith's 'universal and local teachings' (p. 23). The authors take on the task of separating Smith's universal and local teachings with their analysis of RRs, especially with their use of game theory (RR2), to extract what is universal in Smith's thought (pp. 5, 23), which leads them to qualify Smith ultimately as an experimental philosopher and a cognitive and social psychologist in the introduction and conclusion of the book (pp. 11, 234). I think there is a missed opportunity here in qualifying Smith as a political thinker as well. In other words, in assessing Smith's contribution to politics not only in its particular context (as the writer of a political tract) but also in its universal scope (as a writer of a political treatise).

In emphasising North American colonies as illustrating the dangers of the mercantile system, the authors point to the *political* danger that Great Britain faced regarding the fate of the empire. They correspondingly 'conclude that *WN* should be read as a very political book' (p. 34), that is, as a tract, in addition to its function as a treatise (Fleischacker's 2004). Considering that Smith deemed *WN* to be 'a very violent attack against the commercial system of Great-Britain' (*Corr. Letter* 208: 251), the authors successfully show how his attack is built gradually across the five books of the *WN* culminating in the final blow in the last book – which demonstrates the central importance of Book V (pp. 6, 32). It is concomitantly argued that 'what started out as a treatise increasingly took on the nature of a tract' (p. 33), while they also admit that Book V contains elements of a treatise on optimal and just taxation and spending.

Arguably, at least one of Smith's universal political teachings in Book V is the coupling and decoupling of the not-yet-conceptualised concepts of mercantilism and colonialism. While Smith's coupling of these two is commonplace, his decoupling of the two – with his project of a free trade empire – is underemphasised. The direct links Smith forges between colonies and the mercantile system are stressed by more and more studies like the present one, which shows that for Smith, the most dangerous political consequence of the mercantile system was, in Humean terms, the 'death' of the British empire. On this point, even though the authors seem to agree with Hill's (2020) pragmatist approach to politics – who 'argues that the project of union with the American colonies . . . [was] rather a second-best solution knowing the interests, pride, and prejudices of people and politicians on both sides of the Atlantic' (48 n.45) – their insistence on Smith's concerns about the survival of the empire indicates the contrary. Moreover, although the authors pay close attention to Smith's intellectual evolution and historical developments in the North American colonies before the publication of the *WN*, the question of why Smith did not revise his projections about the outcome of the British empire throughout numerous editions of the *WN* (even after the independence of the colonies) is curiously not raised. The fact that Smith maintained his project for empire (and the fact that he advanced it because even by 1776 it was a lost cause) indicate that rather than a pragmatic solution, it might be a thought experiment attesting to the possibility of conceiving colonialism without mercantilism. Smith might have been right after all; even if colonialism can be considered a mercantile enterprise (e.g. Richard Hakluyt 1877 [1584]), the demise of mercantilism wasn't followed by that of the British Empire.

To conclude: besides considering Smith as a system builder in light of Phillipson's work (2010), the authors themselves endorse the spirit of system in arranging and methodising Smith's system-building into a new interpretative system. Smith was apprehensive about philosophers becoming too attached to their own system rather than to the truth. With its caution and modesty, this new system sides with the evidence and the truth. With its simplicity and economy, it sides with the agreeable. And as with any system of philosophy, it is subject to constant revision.

References

Fleischacker, S. (2004) *On Adam Smith's Wealth of Nations: A Philosophical Companion*. Princeton: Princeton University Press.

Hakluyt, R. (1877) [1584] *A Discourse Concerning Western Planting*. Cambridge, MA: Press of J. Wilson.

Hill, L. (2020) *Adam Smith's Pragmatic Liberalism: The Science of Welfare*. London: Palgrave Macmillan.

Hume, D. (2000) [1739–1740]. *A Treatise of Human*, (eds.) David F. Norton and Mary J. Norton. Oxford: Oxford University Press.

Ortmann, A. and Walraevens, B. (2022) *Adam Smith's System: A Re-Interpretation Inspired by Smith's Lectures on Rhetoric, Game Theory, and Conjectural History*. Palgrave Macmillan.

Paganelli, M. P. (2022) 'Adam Smith and Economic Development in Theory and Practice: A Rejection of the Stadial Model?', *Journal of the History of Economic Thought*, 44(1): 95–104.

Phillipson, N. (2010) *Adam Smith: An Enlightened Life.* New Haven: Yale University Press.

Smith, A. (1976a) 'An Inquiry into the Nature and Causes of the Wealth of Nations', in R. H. Campbell and A. S. Skinner (eds.) *The Glasgow Edition of the Works and Correspondence of Adam Smith*, Vol. 2a+2b. Oxford: Oxford University Press.

Smith, A. (1976b) 'The Theory of Moral Sentiments', in A. L. Mackie and D. D. Raphael (eds.) *The Glasgow Edition of the Works and Correspondence of Adam Smith*, Vol. 1. Oxford: Oxford University Press.

Smith, A. (1977) 'The Correspondence of Adam Smith', in E. C. Mossner and I. S. Ross (eds.) *The Glasgow Edition of the Works and Correspondence of Adam Smith*, Vol. 6. Oxford: Oxford University Press.

Smith, A. (1980) 'Essays on Philosophical Subjects', in E. C. Mossner and I. S. Ross (eds.) *The Glasgow Edition of the Works and Correspondence of Adam Smith*, Vol. 3. Oxford: Oxford University Press.

17 The obsessive lovers of systems in Adam Smith

Spyridon Tegos

Framing Adam Smith's project in game-theoretical terms seems a bold enterprise, notwithstanding scientific jargon issues arising from such a venture between the social sciences and philosophy. Nonetheless, this book project stands out for originally blending the game theoretical and rhetorical belletristic traditions. The avant-garde and archaic elements are both mobilised. Interestingly, the authors seem to argue that a replica of the Adam Smith Problem, an epistemological obstacle of a kind, was lurking behind Adam Smith scholarship well beyond the discovery and publication of the *Lectures on Rhetoric & Belles Lettres* in 1963. Neglecting the pivotal role of persuasion and communication throughout all branches of Adam Smith's oeuvre has erected a mental barrier. Ignoring the rhetorical structure that pervades Adam Smith's books simply overshadows attempts to make sense of Adam Smith's system. Ortmann and Walraevens remove this veil of misprision regarding the belletristic lens as a road to what they call the 'deep structure' of Adam Smith's oeuvre as a whole.

Be that as it may, applying Smith's rhetoric to his own oeuvre is a necessary but not sufficient condition to make sense of the 'very systematic' philosophy of Adam Smith. (For a different perspective on Adam Smith as a systematic thinker, see Schliesser 2017.) In this distinctively avant-garde book, the complementary key component to unfold Smithian structural analogies lies in the game theory tradition. Ortmann and Walraevens argue that Smith's philosophy rests on a modern conception of the self as a sympathetically construed entity, emerging through the real and internalised gaze of his fellows. The strategic interactions between self-interested yet empathetic individuals involve the still much-debated issue of asymmetric information between the agent and the principal.

To be sure, one can legitimately wonder whether transcribing Adam Smith's philosophy in those terms is necessary. Game theory brings an impressive conceptual apparatus leading to the 'distinction of the equilibrium outcomes of finitely and indefinitely repeated stage games' (Ortmann and Walraevens 2022: 239) and enables us to

> focus on the incentive structure that the interacting players face, to identify what one might want call problems isomorphs, ie. structurally identical

DOI: 10.4324/9781003767824-21

> incentive problems which otherwise may be read as different problems because of the context in which they are shrouded.
>
> (p. 240)

Along these lines, the authors also focus on the *WN* V, a book neglected according to their reading, especially regarding the incentive-compatible organisation of institutions, governmental, corporative, educational, and ecclesiastical. Therefore, game theory provides a rich conceptual toolbox that can refresh both Adam Smith scholarship and contemporary debates in economy and social sciences.

In this view, Adam Smith's system consists of homologous structures, structural analogies between subfields, science, rhetoric, morality, and political economy. In other terms, it involves reasoning routines as the authors dub them.

The first reasoning routine sheds light on the connecting principle that explains the diverse phenomena in each field, following a Newtonian-deductive model. Ortmann and Walraevens set out to formulate RR1 as follows: the faculty of language and the desire (need) to persuade; rhetoric; the faculty/principle of sympathy (morality); the natural propensity to truck, barter, and exchange; and the desire to better our conditions (social science and economy) are the principles that respectively explain the diverse scientific, linguistic, moral, and socio-economic phenomena.

The second reasoning routine introduces the game-theoretical context and rests on the strategic interaction between speaker (writer) and listener (reader). As a result, 'asymmetric information, strategic interaction, and reputation in economics and morality/between writers and readers, buyers and sellers' provide a game theoretical framework that explains thoroughly the 'subtleties of reputational enforcement' in morality and economics (pp. 197–201, 214–216).

The third reasoning routine emphasises the evolution of norms, the conjectural history of systems based on inductive/evolutionary principles. The evolution of rhetoric, linguistic, moral, and economic norms fits into the same pattern provided the necessary adjustments: market prices, for instance, gravitate around the natural price, while the latter puts order into the apparent chaos of prices. As a convention, it follows the same evolutionary path.

Ultimately, the meta-reasoning routine is triggered by wondrous and surprising objects or events that disturb the imagination's ordinary course. This course is restored by 'the pleasure of persuasion, the pleasure of mutual sympathy . . . the pleasure to exchange is the pleasure to persuade someone, ie., a pleasure to find an agreement on the valuation of goods and services we value' (209, 212). The respective kind of pleasure restores the imagination's tranquillity and triggers admiration for the respective systems.

I think that the book subtly pinpoints the gaps in scholarship, especially regarding the links between the interrelated fields of aesthetics, rhetoric, morality, and economics. Yet I'm inclined to think that politics somehow lags behind. In the remaining part of this essay, I focus on the category of conjectural history firmly embedded in Ortmann and Walraevens' project paying special attention to Adam Smith's politics. Within this framework, there are four interconnected points to bring up for consideration.

First, the issue of (moral) corruption and its place in the 'conjectural history of systems based on inductive/evolutionary principles.' The Smithian connection between polite sociability and rhetorical propriety reflects the double life (McKenna 2016: 290) of propriety in the discipline of rhetoric and ethics. Hence the recurring concern throughout the book is to remind us that the game theoretical background reflects Smith's emphasis on persuasion as opposed to domination in strategic interactions between empathetic individuals. The human tendency to dominate is corrupting for both the master and the servant and undermines the proper functioning of all systems. The authors claim that there is no incompatibility between morality and prosperity within commercial societies while taking into consideration Smith's emphasis on the 'malevolent side of exchange' ingrained in market power relations (pp. 142, 148). The rise of standards of living and the development of commercial virtues such as prudence, frugality, industry, and middle-class moderation can potentially counterweight commercial flaws and lead to a flourishing society. Yet Smith's critique in *WN* V regarding the alienation of the provincial worker moving into an urban setting or the detrimental impact on the labouring poor's psyche of the advanced division of labour deserves more attention. Overall, I think that Ortmann and Walraevens should focus more on Smith's pessimistic credo, shared with Hume, expressed throughout *WN* III and V, *TMS* I, VI, and *LJ* of an extremely frail and reversible progress of commercial society. Alongside the public credit debate, these worries may not transform Smith into a critic of commercial society but possibly a sceptic concerning its endemic threats.

The second point I wish to raise pertains to the evolution of norms in the field of politics and ethics: Smith's concern about moral corruption due to wealth worshipping (TMS I.iii.ii-iii) alongside the conjectural account of socio-economic transformations from the Middle Ages to modernity invite some clarifications. Again, the issue of persuasion vs. domination looms large. *WN* and *LJ* provide reasons why wealth is perceived as a source of authority and, concomitantly, why we naturally admire (and Smith translates this admiration in terms of sympathy with wealth and greatness) our superiors. However, one may wonder to what extent both claims (perception of wealth as a source of authority/natural admiration of superiors as a universal trait) address the same problem. I think there are grounds to challenge this view. The authority of wealth does not trigger sympathy throughout history, at least not the same kind of sympathy. By the same token, deference to authority undermines any kind of persuasion in morality and politics.

In the pastoral stage, Smith draws attention to the direct dependence on the chieftain both of the poor and of the less important proprietors of flocks and herds. The lesser shepherds realise that the security of their flocks depends on the security of the chieftain and the authority of their restricted nobility on the great authority of the rich chieftain (LJA, 7–9: 202–203). To be sure, no recourse to naked violence was needed to account for shepherd inequality; the military chief has served as a judge during peace and has amassed great wealth through gifts from the clients who require his service as an arbiter of private conflicts (Hont 2009: 154; Tegos 2020: 121–122). As a result every leader creates a mass of servitors who depend on his jurisdiction and survival during peace while they obey his orders and follow him blindly into war (LJA 130–2: 322).

In *TMS* I.iii.2–3, Smith clearly states that sympathy with the wealthy and great is disinterested ('disinterested admirers and worshippers of wealth and greatness'). Therefore, there is no sympathy strictly speaking with the chieftain. The issue that lurks behind is whether sympathy with authority, based on human nature, is a transhistorical or modern phenomenon proper to commercial modernity. In *WN* III, ii-iii and *LJA-B*, the transition from feudal/tribal societies to commercial modernity is depicted as a transition from admiration for the leader as protector to the sympathy with the leader based on mere prestige: 'for in general the poor are independent and support themselves by their labour, yet though' they expect no benefit from them they have a strong propensity to pay them respect' (LJB 401). Therefore deference to authority undermines a conjectural history of politics based on inductive/evolutionary principles as domination gives way to servility towards prestige.

Third, the evolution and refinement of Smith's concept of system stretch across aesthetics, morality, economics and politics and prompt further reflection on the 'love of system.' It is more the *History of Astronomy* and *TMS* IV than the belletrist tradition that moves centre stage. At this juncture, one should understand the disinterested 'sympathy with the rich and great,' mainly developed in *TMS* I.iii.ii-iii, through the lenses of *TMS* IV.i. In *TMS* IV.i, the disposition of individuals to admire the wealthy is understood as a love of the system of means at the wealthy's disposal neatly adjusted to the end (pleasure-happiness). Smith moves beyond Hume's account of the 'sympathy with the wealthy' based on ambition, emulation and vanity. The latter explains for Smith the distinction of ranks, but it does not fully account for the phenomenon of admiration of superiors. Taking a step further, the idea of admiration for systems found in *TMS* IV.i should be traced back to Smith's juvenile works on aesthetics and epistemology (Tegos 2024). Indeed, the 'beauty of a systematic arrangement,' the adjustment of means, the fitness of an object to fulfil an end trigger for Smith a 'sensual and intellectual sentiment' of admiration that accounts for the disposition to submit to our superiors, provided that we understand superiority as a superior system-building capacity (Diatkine 2020). I think that Smith's thought cuts even deeper. In *TMS* I.iii.3, Smith accounts for the deference to royal authority in terms of admiration for the supposedly countless 'means to be happy' at the king's disposal. The king is also the supreme political speculator colonising the political imaginary, endowed with the maximum of means to reach any desirable political end; thus, he colonises the political imaginary. Simultaneously, Smith embraces a pre-sociological theory of prestige and detects a distinct disposition to submit to royal prestige, a fetishism of royal greatness (TMS I.iii.2.3: 'Even when the people have been brought this length, they are apt to relent every moment, and easily relapse into their habitual state of deference to those whom they have been accustomed to look upon as their natural superiors.'). In this vein, Smith turns slightly ironic: the kings make no effort to gain sympathy; they are self-absorbed free riders in the social sympathetic exchange, undermining the mechanism of mutual sympathy; yet they catch everyone's eye and dominate spectatorial sympathy (TMS I.iii.2.30), 'We could even wish them immortal . . . Great King, live forever! is the compliment which, after the manner of eastern adulation, we should readily make them, if the experience did not teach us its absurdity' (TMS I.iii.2.3). Therefore, deference to the authority of the wealthy cannot fully account for the kind of love of system associated with royal greatness. Deference to royalty, a 'peculiar sympathy' as Smith calls it, constitutes a mode of sympathy per se. It undermines persuasion and entails submission through the love of the royal system. Yet Smith thinks it is necessary for the social order although his recurring irony towards the human propensity to submit to royal prestige leaves no doubt about his assessment of it.

In his idiosyncratic doctrine of romantic love, Adam Smith condemns love for being exclusive and rejecting any alternative sociability. There are striking parallels between lovers and kings. To be sure, the main flaw in a lover's character is the indifference to spectators, let alone the impartial spectator. In this vein, Smith points to the impermeability, the quasi 'autism' of lovers who live in their own exclusive world, indifferent to the sympathy of others, self-absorbed free-riders in the social sympathetic exchange (TMS I.ii.2). I think this aspect of Adam Smith's doctrine of love cannot be lightheartedly dismissed, especially its potential linkage with the love of system.

Ultimately, a fourth issue to raise regarding political systems is the love of political systems and its dark side when it becomes excessive. Ortmann and Walraevens claimed that coherent systems based on a few simple principles capable of explaining a wide range of phenomena give aesthetic and intellectual pleasure to those who observe them. This kind of aesthetic appreciation can also be applied to all fields including economics and politics: 'Human society, when we contemplate it in a certain abstract and philosophical light appears like a great, an immense machine, whose regular and harmonious movements produce a thousand agreeable effects' (TMS VII.iii.1). Smith criticises speculative political philosophies that seek to prescribe in normative terms how society should be structured, even when their theories conflict with observable human experience. Yet Smith goes beyond utopianism. Specifically, he calls the speculative philosopher a 'man of the system,' blinded by his or her own sublime vision of economics and politics. The 'man of the system' looms large when fascination with beautiful systems gives way to delusions of grandeur: 'The man of system . . . is often enamoured with the supposed beauty of his own ideal plan of government, that he cannot suffer the smallest deviation from any part of it' (TMS VI.2).

It is probably worth analysing the extent to which Smith thinks that a form of moderate charismatic leadership is possible although rare. Provided certain checks that generate a moderate spirit of system, the ideal of modern statesmanship is not chimerical: 'Some general, and even systematical, idea of the perfection of policy and law, may no doubt be necessary for directing the views of the statesman' (TMS VI.ii.18).

Overall, this stimulating book prompts the reader to extend its multilayered, game-theoretically updated conception of Smithian interrelated systems to surprising fields within or beyond Adam Smith studies. This wondrous and surprising experiment contributes to the tranquillity of the imagination through admiration.

References

Diatkine, D. (2020) 'Vanity and the Love of System in Theory of Moral Sentiments', *The European Journal of the History of Economic Thought*, 17(3): 383–404.

Hont, I. (2009) 'Adam Smith's History of Law and Government as Political Theory', in R. Bourke and R. Geuss (eds.) *Political Judgment: Essays for John Dunn*. Cambridge University Press.

McKenna, S. (2016) 'Adam Smith and Rhetoric', in R. P. Hanley (ed.) *Adam Smith: His Life, Thought and Legacy*. Princeton: Princeton University Press.

Ortmann, A. and Walraevens, B. (2022) *Adam Smith's System: A Re-Interpretation Inspired by Smith's Lectures on Rhetoric, Game Theory, and Conjectural History*. Cham: Palgrave Macmillan.

Schliesser, E. (2017) *Adam Smith: Systematic Thinker and public Philosopher*. Oxford: Oxford University Press.

Tegos, S. (2020) 'Deference to Authority in Adam Smith', *Adam Smith Review*, 12: 117–133.

Tegos, S. (2024) 'Pre-Weberian Theories of Charismatic Leadership and the Aesthetics of Deference in the Scottish Enlightenment', in T. Demeter (ed.) *The Sociological Heritage of the Scottish Enlightenment*. Edinburgh: Edinburgh University Press.

18 Replies to authors-Meet-Critics-Symposium comments

Andreas Ortmann and Benoît Walraevens

We are delighted to have been able to attract such a stellar group of critics for our book, and we are humbled by, but also very pleased with, their generous characterisations of it [Hanley: 'stimulating new book,' (411) 'very illuminating and very welcome study' (415); Hill: 'A new and fresh reading of Smith' (417); Tegos: 'this book project stands out for originally blending the game theoretical and the rhetorical belletristic traditions,' 'this distinctively avant-garde book' (435)], as well as by the unexplored avenues that they have identified for further research.

Our critics' diverse contributions overlap only on occasion (e.g. in Hanley's and Tegos' wondering about the value added of our game-theoretical framing, and our relative neglect of Smith's political theory; see the comments by Hill, Okan, and Tegos).

Since there is little overlap in the comments, we will address them one by one.

Hanley: Ryan asserts that we have 'new and important things to say' (411) about three of the four categories invoked in the title and subtitle of our book: *rhetoric, game theory, and systematicity*. (He defers on our use of conjectural history to the other contributors. See below our reply to Spiros Tegos' comments.)

Regarding rhetoric, he notes that we are 'hardly the first to document the connections between Smith's rhetorical theory and the other elements of his corpus' (411); we are happy to concede that much and have made it quite clear in our book. Ryan raises two points. We agree that the first one ['To read WN's rhetoric and substance in light of the lectures on jurisprudence. For when we read *LJ* and *WN* next to each other it becomes very evident that Smith very often made the same point in very different ways in his published and unpublished works.' (412)] would be an extremely interesting project that might address a point that is also raised by Ecem and by himself, on our relative neglect of Smith's politics, which has recently attracted more attention (see in particular Sagar 2018, 2022). Along these lines, one of us has recently tried to unveil Smith's reinterpretation of the idea of good government in his different works, or his political economy of good government, and highlighted in this context an important change (from 'in all civilized societies' to 'in a well-governed society') that Smith made between the *Early Draft* to the *WN* and the published book in the famous passage on the division of labour creating 'universal opulence,' which extends to the lowest ranks of society (see *ED*, p. 566 and *WN*, I.i.10: 22, on which see Silvestri and Walraevens 2023: 427). For sure

DOI: 10.4324/9781003767824-22

the *LJ* and the *WN* have quite different statuses, purposes, audiences, and formats, requiring different rhetorical methods, as Smith taught in his lectures on rhetoric. This would be worth careful investigation.

His second point questions '[H]ow reliable in fact can *LRBL* be as a guide to Smith's own rhetoric? . . . what, we might wonder justifies the hermeneutic move of applying to Smith's own thought rhetorical devices that he describes in *LRBL*'? (412–413) We have made this case by way of (Smith's) revealed preference (e.g. regarding the structure of the *WN* – and the importance of the Book V in particular – as primarily a tract aimed at persuading the powers that be of the day). That required us to do considerable legwork, but we did it in our book and ultimately have to let the reader decide whether we succeeded (or not). Moreover, relying on Smith's own teachings on rhetoric is helpful for addressing the issue of the coherence of Smith's work, which cannot be ignored when one tries to provide a systemic reading of it. But of course, we don't deny that important insights into Smith's works can be reached through other conceptions of rhetoric than those taken from Smith's lectures.

Regarding game theory, 'where the book's heart lies' (413) according to his reading, Ryan wonders whether we are using a different conceptual language to define an idea that may already be familiar to certain types of Smith scholars, such as Otteson. Specifically, Ryan wants us to elaborate on whether we see ourselves 'supplementing Otteson's view by remedying or filling out lacunae,' or whether we are 'offering something fundamentally and radically different' with our focus on the significance of the principal-agent aspect. We like to think of our treatment of Smith as sharpening and enriching Otteson's agenda on Smith's 'marketplace of life.' The principal-agent aspect is an important element but not *the* focus of our work. The fact of the matter is that it captures rather precisely the theory of self-command, which benefits from being harnessed game-theoretically. Ryan also wonders in this context whether we overplay the attempt of identifying the problem isomorphs (i.e. the universal teachings) and the general rules at the cost of neglecting context-specific details of which Smith was obviously a master, especially in his moral analysis of people's evaluation of the propriety and merit or demerit of conduct, as Ryan underlines. We see the danger and maybe to some extent, have bent the rod too far to stress the usefulness of a game-theoretic reframing of problem isomorphs that show up in Smith's works on rhetoric, languages, moral sentiments, and economic concepts such as efficiency wages.

Regarding systematicity, Ryan wonders whether we have paid enough attention to 'the way in which Smith drew on concepts of natural religion and providentialism.' (414) In our book, we have made it clear at various places that we are persuaded – cue Kennedy's work on this issue – that Smith was not a believer in a supreme Creator or Deity, or more precisely, not late in his life. For sure, Smith drew on natural religion and providentialism all the way through *TMS,* but he seems to have fallen off the belief in a supreme Creator or Deity sometime, possibly around the time of his European travels. We have elaborated on this issue extensively in our book on page 177–188; see also footnote 11 on page 178.

Hill: Lisa expands on some of our key points, especially on our view of Smith as a persuader and his use of the meta-reasoning routine (the Wonder-Surprise-Admiration routine from the *Astronomy*), by using an example from Smith's *TMS*: his famous appeal to the love of systems to inspire 'the spirit of public virtues in legislators.' (418) She mentions (a point we have made in our book and elsewhere, for example, in our review of Phillipson's book, Ortmann and Walraevens 2012) that Smith, as much as he was a reserved and serious scholar, was 'a skilled "ideas entrepreneur," a marketer of ideas who knew how to make his ideas politically relevant and attractive,' and who wanted to change public policies for the common good. For her,

> one of his techniques was to frame contemporary events as a series of crises, in order to provide converts with the ammunition they needed to further his attempts to reform the British state. These depictions of crises (surprise and wonder) were also designed to inspire legislators themselves to want to change things according to the solutions he provided. (418)

That strikes us as a very astute application of the meta-routine that we identified as the main driver behind Smith's, and others,' thinking. Her case that, '[i]f Britain's economic woes were caused by corruptions of the system of natural liberty then the solution was obviously to remove the corruptions and restore the system to its natural and correct state,' (420) seems to us as very persuasive and indeed a very nice extension of our key points about rhetorical figures.

We also agree with her important point – also made excellently in her 2020 book (see Hill 2020) – that 'Smith's economic thought is effectively a protracted diatribe against elite manipulation of the state and market, against corruption, mercantilism, and crony capitalism. Having created a sense of crisis around the abuse and corruption of the Creator's beautiful system Smith then went about proposing a solution that would restore it to its natural state and bring forth "admiration"' (423) and tranquillity of mind, the beautiful system of natural liberty. Just a remark on this point, though. While Smith relied on the love of systems of politicians to motivate them to work for the public good, he also famously highlighted the dangers of an excessive spirit of system in politics, leading to radical reforms without taking into account the established interests and prejudices of the different ranks and orders of society. That's why he advocated cautious, moderate and gradual reforms towards the liberalisation of trade (especially the colony trade) and the implementation of the system of natural liberty, and appealed to wise legislators in the last edition of *TMS* to deal with the art of good government (see p. 47 in our book).

Where we part ways with Lisa is on her stance concerning the issue of Providence (e.g. Hill 2001) and the importance of a Creator or Deity for Smith's thinking. See our related comment above on Ryan's reservation. We have belaboured in our book that Smith's belief in the inevitable reality of a beautiful and grand system, at least in the social sphere, faded relatively early in his life, and that a necessary or natural convergence to an efficient equilibrium could not reasonably be expected (see Ch. 7).

Okan: Ecem agrees with our 'insistence on how rhetoric is crucial for understanding Smith in general' and our claim that the form of the book itself is rhetorical. She takes us to task for what she perceives to be gaps in our narratives.

For sure, we haven't tried nor pretended to offer an exhaustive, comprehensive or definitive interpretation of Smith's complete oeuvre, and it is impossible to capture all the richness of Smith's thought with only a few defining principles or reasoning routines, though it pleases our imagination. Ecem organises her reflection on the inevitable gaps in our narrative around what she sees rightly as three important kinds of duality in Smith's thinking: (i) the philosopher and the common people, (ii) the impartial and the partial, and (iii) the general and the particular.

Ecem argues that we have been conflating two separate points of view: that of the philosopher and the commoner. Distinct, not similar cognitive processes operate when we are uneasy when people differ from us in sentiments and/or opinions, and when a philosopher is unsatisfied with the system or explanation of another philosopher. Maybe we have pushed the analogy too far here and should have been more careful in underlining the differences between intellectual judgements, based on understanding, and social/moral judgements, based on sympathy.

Regarding the system of natural liberty as a rhetorical discourse: yes, it is rhetorical in part as well, a philosophical discourse aiming to arouse our love of systems and thus soothe our imagination by presenting society as an ideal, beautiful machine functioning harmoniously, against the disorders of the prevailing mercantile system. We also agree that American colonies are not a perfect example or ideal type of the natural order of progress (they benefited from some advanced British institutions and suffered from the monopoly of the colony trade), but rather what comes closest to it.

Another interesting suggestion Ecem makes is to delve further into the political aspect of Smith's *WN* and to consider the book as a true political treatise. In it, an original model of a free trade Empire is presented, decoupling mercantilism and colonialism. As mentioned earlier, we agree that Smith's political theory still needs further inquiry from Smith scholars. See also our comments on the other reviewers regarding the issue of universal insights vs. context-dependent ('local') learnings.

Tegos: Spiros, like Ryan, wonders about the value added of our game-theoretic framing but seems ultimately persuaded by our arguments. He says,

> [T]he book quite subtly pinpoints the gaps in the scholarship, especially regarding the links between the interrelated fields of aesthetics, rhetoric, morality and economics. Yet, I am inclined to think that politics somehow lags behind. . . . I focus on the category of conjectural history firmly embedded into Ortmann & Walraevens's project paying special attention to Adam Smith's politics. (437)

We are grateful for the discussion that follows. We restricted ourselves to rhetoric, morality, and economics and the related major (un)published works that we have from Smith. We made no attempt in our book project to also reflect deeply on Smith's unpublished work on jurisprudence and the science of the legislator, and acknowledge – in line with our acknowledgement of the intriguing research project Hanley has proposed on comparing *WN* and *LJ* along the categories enumerated in our subtitle and also in line with our agreement on Hill's application of the meta-routine that we identified to egg politicians towards decision-making for the greater good – our discussion in this respect is insufficient and the elaboration of how our system and approach apply to Smith's unfinished project of a science of the legislator would be a good thing that we might consider working on in the future.

Focusing on Smith's politics and conjectural history, Spiros discusses first the important issue of moral corruption in Smith (on which he made important contributions) and advises us to focus more on 'Smith's pessimistic credo,' (438) and especially on his fears concerning the alienation of urban factory workers as well as on the 'reversible progress of commercial society.' It is true that we could have done more on this point (see though p. 124 of our book, and Walraevens 2011 for a more extensive treatment of corruption in Smith). Then he addresses the evolution of norms in politics and ethics in Smith's conjectural history from the Middle Ages to modernity, thus filling a gap in our narrative by focusing on the authority of (and sympathy for) wealth owners and the admiration for our superiors throughout the ages. He rightly underlines that 'deference to authority undercuts a conjectural history of politics based on inductive/evolutionary principles as domination gives way to servility towards prestige.' (439) We could add that the advent of commercial society also raises new questions about deference to authority inside firms with the subordination relationship between 'masters' and their employees, or capitalists and workers (on which see Dellemotte and Walraevens 2015).

Afterwards, he reflects on the fact that Smith moves beyond Hume's account of the 'sympathy with the wealthy' (439) based on ambition, emulation and vanity, to emphasise the importance of the love of systems, and he discusses specifically Smith's views on the admiration of kings. Smith, Spiros notes, 'detects a distinct disposition to submit to royal prestige, a fetishism of royal greatness,' a 'peculiar sympathy,' (440) which does not need persuasion and entails submission. The admiration for kings is not surprising, though, because not only do they colonise 'the political imaginary' (and can generally exert absolute power over the property and life of their 'subjects'), they also concentrate different natural sources of authority (the superiority of wealth and birth). Spiros rightly underlines how Smith makes use of irony in his description of the authority of kings, an ironic tone that we can find in several parts of his work (e.g. in his description of the poor man's son or of global history). But Smith believes that the natural authority of rulers has some limits and will be contested when it becomes excessive and oppressive, thus legitimising the right of resistance (see *LJ*). Spiros then draws an interesting parallel that would deserve more development between lovers and kings in Smith, both being 'indifferent to the sympathy of others and self-absorbed free-riders in the social sympathetic exchange.' (441) Ultimately, we agree with him when he points out the dangers for Smith of an excessive love of systems in politics and the necessity to find a wise, charismatic, but unabusive legislator exhibiting a moderate spirit of system, as we underlined previously (see above our comment on Lisa Hill). All in all, Spiros reminds us that we might have paid insufficient attention in our book to the excesses and dangers of Smith's love of systems.

Summary: We are grateful to our critics for their sincere engagement with our project and their kind and constructive words about it.

References

Dellemotte, J. and Walraevens, B. (2015) 'Adam Smith on the Subordination of Wage-Earners in Commercial Societies', *European Journal of the History of Economic Thought*, 22(4): 692–727.

Hill, L. (2001) 'The Hidden Theology of Adam Smith', *European Journal of the History of Economic Thought*, 8(1): 1–29.

Hill, L. (2020) *Adam Smith's Pragmatic Liberalism: The Science of Welfare*. London: Palgrave Macmillan.

Ortmann, A. and Walraevens, B. (2012) 'Adam Smith, Philosopher and Man of the World: A Review Essay on Nicholas Phillipson's "Adam Smith: An Enlightened Life."', *History of Economic Ideas*, 20(1): 185–191.

Sagar, P. (2018) *The Opinion of Mankind: Sociability and the Theory of the State from Hobbes to Smith*. Princeton: Princeton University Press.

Sagar, P. (2022) *Adam Smith Reconsidered: Liberty, History, and the Foundations of Modern Politics*. Princeton: Princeton University Press.

Silvestri, P. and Walraevens, B. (2023) 'Liberty, Political Economy and Good Government in Adam Smith', *European Journal of the History of Economic Thought*, 30(3): 410–442.

Walraevens, B. (2011) 'Corruption des travailleurs et éducation dans les sociétés commerciales selon Adam Smith', *Cahiers d'Economie Politique*, 60: 11–44.

19 Author-Meet-Critics Symposium 2

Nir Ben-Moshe

On Smith, Hume (and Reid)
John Skorupski

Nir clearly knows his Smith very well. I have learned a lot from him and there are many aspects of Smith about which we agree. However, Nir's book has a very clear central thrust with which I am not so convinced. He interprets Smith's theory of moral sentiments within the framework of a Humean, or 'desire-belief,' account of practical reasons.

Nir endorses this framework, although he is well aware of the by the standard objections to it by now. Indeed a large part of the book is devoted to a response to these objections, which draws on Bernard Williams' paper, 'Internal and External Reasons, as well as Hume. (Incidentally, he takes Williams to be a Humean (p. 31), which I think is a mistake.[1] But this doesn't matter for what I want to say here.)

I don't myself find Humeanism in any way plausible. But I'm going to steer away from the familiar debate about the pros and cons of Humeanism and Williamsism. What I want to argue is that the Humean framework is unhelpful for understanding Smith. Smith's theory is a completely general naturalistic epistemology of the sentiments, or more precisely, of judgements about the *propriety* of the sentiments. By virtue of the link that Smith takes for granted between the propriety of sentiments and the propriety of actions, this becomes a sentimentalist epistemology of practical reasons. This account gives Smith no reason to accept Humeanism. Nor, as far as I am aware, does Smith anywhere discuss or endorse Humeanism (though I'd welcome any suggestions about that).

I should say that although Nir clearly endorses Humeanism I am not sure whether he thinks that Smith does. I guess he would say that Smithian insights, in particular those that centre on the 'impartial spectator,' can be used to rebut or at least weaken the force of the standard objections. And he might add that the Humean framework illuminates Smith's positions. Yet it seemed to me that the

Book Symposium on *Idealization and the Moral Point of View: An Adam Smithian Account of Moral Reasons by Nir Ben-Moshe*

DOI: 10.4324/9781003767824-23

discussion in the book, good as it is on both Smith and Humeanism, does not show that either illuminates the other.

So did Smith endorse Hume's account of practical reasons? There is, as far as I can see, no direct evidence that he did. And the usual historical warning applies: however influential Hume is in contemporary moral philosophy, we must guard against imputing his views to his contemporaries simply for that reason.

Humeanism did not have the influence in Smith's time that it has nowadays. Smith's contemporary, Thomas Reid (Smith, 1723–1790; Reid, 1710–1796) gave Hume's view of reason and the passions short shrift. At first sight, he says, it appears 'a shocking paradox,' . . . but when its meaning is elicited, it turns out, 'like other paradoxes,' to be 'nothing but an abuse of words.'

> For if we give the name of *passion* to every principle of action, in every degree, and give the name of *reason* solely to the power of discerning the fitness of means to ends, it will be true that the use of reason is to be subservient to the passions.
>
> (*Active Powers*, Essay III, Pt II, ch vi)

In another telling observation, Reid distinguishes between desire and volition:

> With regard to our own actions, we may desire what we do not will, and will what we do not desire; nay, what we have a great aversion to. . . . Desire, therefore, even when its object is some action of our own, is only an incitement to will, but it is not volition. The determination of the mind may be not to do what we desire to do.
>
> *Works*, 2 vols. Ed. W. Hamilton, 6th edn 1863 532a.

The point is not just that a contemporary of Smith, as influential in his time as Hume, and whom Smith would undoubtedly have read, dismissed the desire/belief view so crisply and took its dismissal to be simply a reassertion of common sense. More strongly, I think that Smith could have accepted both of Reid's remarks consistently with his own theory and his rejection of rationalism.

How can this be so? What Smith gives us is an *epistemological* account of the circumstances in which a judgement of the propriety of a feeling is *warranted.* Note that this account is a general theory of the propriety of all sentiments and how their propriety is judged; it does not apply just to the sentiments specifically involved in *moral* judgement (i.e. 'gratitude' and 'resentment'). In his theory, desire becomes just one of the sentiments.

Propriety is a normative concept. A sentiment is considered proper when there is sufficient reason for it. Sufficient reason for that degree of gratitude, say: the degree which is felt neither to be cold-hearted, insufficient, nor exaggerated, over the top. Thus, the epistemology of propriety is the epistemology of reasons for feelings – evaluative reasons, as I call them. Smith's aim is to accurately describe the psychological factors that constitute the epistemic ground of evaluative reasons and how these factors work through the capacity for sympathy and the ability to see ourselves as others see us (to quote another Scotsman). This latter capacity, as Smith fully appreciates, is not simply the capacity to see how the everyday crowd, whose view is easily distorted by their own sentiments, would see us. It is the capacity to see how a *disinterested spectator* would see us. More exactly, it is the capacity to see how and to what extent a spectator freed from distorting sentiments that arise from irrelevant personal interests would sympathise with the feelings and actions of an agent placed in some specified circumstances. (By the way, '*disinterested* spectator' is one of the phrases Smith uses. I've used it in preference to 'impartial spectator' because there's a tendency to see the latter as specifically concerned with theories of ethical impartiality. Smith's theory is fully general: it applies to all evaluative judgements and not just to specifically ethical ones, though it applies to those too.)

Now a rationalist might view all of this as unacceptable psychologism. In contrast, a naturalistic epistemologist could see it as simply a brilliantly observed account of the immanent rationality of the sentiments. Furthermore, Smith applies it to actions via a principle that he clearly assumes but never articulates sufficiently, and which I would put like this (though it could be put in terms of 'propriety'):

> Whatever facts give a person reason to feel a sentiment give that person reason to do the action 'most immediately and directly' prompted by the sentiment.

'Most immediately and directly' is Smith's phrase in this passage:

> Gratitude and resentment . . . are the sentiments which most immediately and directly prompt to reward and to punish.

In this sentence, the move from sentiment to action is psychological. But in context, its importance is also normative. The general idea is that many sentiments prompt a characteristic action, the action that is both 'natural and proper' to the sentiment. Thus, for example, the sentiment of gratitude prompts thanks, that of fear prompts flight, and that of anger prompts aggression. That being said, reasonable fear (justified fear) is a reason for flight, reasonable anger (justified anger) is a reason for a hard retort, and so on. The principle is fully general, providing a bridge from evaluative to practical reasons. It provides practical reasons with a sentimentalist source. The sentimentalist source may be combined with other sources, such as belief and will, as in Reid, or it may be presented as the sole source of practical reasons. This latter view gives us *comprehensive sentimentalism* about practical reason. It is plausible to assume that it is what Smith intended.

Comprehensive sentimentalism actually seems incompatible with Humeanism. True, the Humean might argue that every sentiment produces a desire to perform its characteristic action. I think Smith did not use the word 'desire' in this broad way. In any case, it does not help at the normative level. Suppose you go to a piano recital given by an acquaintance whom you thoroughly dislike. Your main emotional responses are envy, irritation, and the like. You feel no admiration, yet you see that there is a strong reason to admire because the disinterested man within your breast tells you so, and you are not so captured by envy as to hide from his verdict. So you clap and praise even though you have *no* desire to do so. In other words, it's the sincere, fair-minded belief that the performance is indeed worthy of admiration, not the sentiment itself, which you quite fail to feel, that causes your praise. You clap because you believe that the sentiment of admiration is the proper response to this performance, and hence by the bridge principle, that praise is the proper action. This action, therefore, is caused by a normative belief, not a desire.

There is, as far as I can see, no reason why Smith should deny the causality of normative beliefs any more than Reid does, though their story about what *warrants* the normative belief is very different. Or rather, in this example, Reid does not *have* a story because he does not accept that there are such things as evaluative reasons, as opposed to epistemic and practical reasons. But Smith can accept both that beliefs about evaluative and practical reasons are grounded in the sentiments and that those normative beliefs can cause actions. Thus he seems to come out ahead of both Hume and Reid!

Note

1 See my (2007) 'Internal Reasons and the Scope of Blame.'

Reference

Skorupski, J. M. (2007) 'Internal Reasons and the Scope of Blame', in A Thomas (ed.) *Bernard Williams.* Cambridge: Cambridge University Press, pp. 73–103.

20 Comments on Nir Ben-Moshe, *idealization and the moral point of view*

Remy Debes

Nir Ben-Moshe's *Idealization and the Moral Point of View* is a lively new attempt to situate the philosophies of David Hume and Adam Smith in contemporary metaethical and normative ethical debates. The result is a high-level analysis of interpretive trends on both thinkers, against the backdrop of what has come to be known as the 'informed desire theory' of moral reasons. Although the balance of the argument leans towards the advantages of Adam Smith's view, Ben-Moshe works out positive positions on both thinkers. Correspondingly, I recommend the book to scholars of Hume and Smith as well as contemporary theorists working on moral reasoning.

Originally, given some of my own work on Smith, I expected to focus my review on Ben-Moshe's final chapter, which explores a Smithian account of 'humanity,' especially its connection to the standpoint of the impartial spectator and the reasons this standpoint generates. Ben-Moshe does not spend much time discussing Smith's own use of the term 'humanity' or its cognates.[1] Moreover, outside of some remarks in the footnotes, he does not discuss how his conclusions in this respect align with other interpretations of Smith on the subject of human worth and moral respect. So, I anticipated pressing Ben-Moshe, first, to say more about Smith's terminology; and second, to elaborate on how his argument fits together with other scholarly attempts to position Smith as a kind of 'avant-garde' theorist of human dignity. Instead, I found myself drawn in by the groundwork of Ben-Moshe's inquiry. So, this is where I shall focus my review.

The big picture

I begin with two big-picture questions for clarification. First, the informed desire theory of Humean reasons that Ben-Moshe wants to defend, à la critical injections of Smith's philosophy, turns on a person's recognising the 'authority' of the desires of their 'ideal self,' the latter of which is defined in terms of 'suitable conditions' – that is, the conditions that define the 'viewpoint' or 'deliberative stance' one ought to judge from, and which thus (partly) determine their desires. In this regard, Ben-Moshe poses a hypothetical challenge to his own strategy. He writes, 'Why should an agent be any less opposed to being subjected to the values of their ideal selves than being subjected to the values of someone else

DOI: 10.4324/9781003767824-24

altogether?' In reply, he argues that there is a crucial distinction between 'a scenario in which the agent *could* recognise the authority of her alleged ideal self and one in which she could *not* recognize this authority.' In the former but not the latter, he continues, 'she has a certain type of epistemic authority over the desires that constitute her ideal self.' 'In other words,' Ben-Moshe writes, 'if the agent could *herself* recognize the authority of the standard in question, then, not only is it the case that the verdicts of the true or ideal self are authoritative because this self is under the relevant suitable conditions – although they *are* also authoritative for this reason – but, in addition, they are authoritative because the actual self could endorse the deferral to itself as the authoritative standard.' (manuscript, 26–27).

The phrasing of this final claim confuses me. Is the claim meant to be disjunctive or conjunctive? Must the judgements of the ideal self be made under suitable conditions *and* recognised as such? Or could either suffice? And what exactly *makes for* the 'authority' of these judgements? Obviously, the relevant conditions are supposed to be normative for the *correctness* of the judgements. But without an argument, it is not clear why these conditions render the judgement *authoritative*. Furthermore, what exactly is the relevant 'recognition'? That is, what kind of cognition is it? Is it a belief? Some kind of assent?

Second, Ben-Moshe wants to preserve in his theory of reasons a form of what is known as proportionalism. He thus writes of a hypothetical agent,

> [G]iven her skepticism about the motivational efficacy of reason, it is natural for the Humean theorist, especially if she is committed to the Humean theory of motivation, to assume that the relative strengths of an agent's desires (under suitable conditions) are the most plausible candidates for serving as the psychological component that determine the weights of our reasons.

I think this is correct *for the Humean*. But what of Hume himself? Here and elsewhere, Ben-Moshe glosses the work that the phenomenological peculiarity of moral feeling does for Hume, that is, in moral reasoning. Hume memorably writes:

> tis evident, that under the term pleasure, we comprehend sensations, which are very different from each other, and which have only such a distant resemblance, as is requisite to make them be expressed by the same abstract term. A good composition of music and a bottle of good wine equally produce pleasure; and what is more, their goodness is determined merely by the pleasure. But shall we say upon that account, that the wine is harmonious, or the music of a good flavour? In like manner an inanimate object, and the character or sentiments of any person may, both of them, give satisfaction; but as the satisfaction is different, this keeps our sentiments concerning them from being confounded, and makes us ascribe virtue to the one, and not to the other. Nor is every sentiment of pleasure or pain, which arises from characters and actions, of that peculiar kind, which makes us praise or condemn.
> (*Treatise*, 3.1.2.4)[2]

As far as I can tell, Ben-Moshe largely ignores this phenomenological element in Hume. Perhaps this is because he has no truck with claims about the peculiarity of approbation. And why should he? After all, it smacks of moral sense theory, and Ben-Moshe is adamantly out to defend a Humean theory of reasons for its naturalist, anti-realist bent. So, it would be risky to endorse the addition of a moral faculty to the human mind. At least, it would be risky to do so only on the basis of Hume's introspective claims.

And yet, I think there are complications in denying Hume this move, given the rest of Ben-Moshe's argument. I will mention one complication now and one in the next section. Consider that it is crucial to Ben-Moshe's overall argument to postulate *an* original faculty. Thus, in partial answer to my foregoing confusion about what makes the dictates of the ideal self authoritative, Ben-Moshe argues – consistent with the Humean theory – that the reasons of our ideal self are overriding when our *strongest desire* is to follow the dictates of that ideal self. He writes:

> One could potentially think of this idea as analogous to entering a practice: we are familiar with practices in which, while it may be up to us whether or not to enter the practice, once we are in the practice, someone else gets to dictate what we ought to do. For example, while one might choose whether or not to take Professor X's class, once one is enrolled in Professor X's class, one must adhere to the requirements that Professor X has specified in the syllabus. What I am suggesting is that committing to the authority of the ideal self ought to be conceived of along similar lines.

Ben-Moshe continues:

> [G]iven a certain desire that agents initially have, and regardless of the strength of this desire, they enter into the practice of allowing their reasons (and their weights) to be determined by the desires (and their strengths) of their ideal self, rather than those of their actual self.
>
> (manuscript, 29–30)

I find all of this very interesting. However, to talk about a 'certain desire that agents initially have' sounds very similar to what would follow from the Humean theory of mind after one posits an original faculty. Hence, the force of my initial request for clarification about why Ben-Moshe doesn't lean into Hume's talk of the peculiarity of moral approbation. If Ben-Moshe is willing to go in for one original faculty – namely, to explain why we recognise the authority of a certain practice of practical reasoning – then why not also accept a second faculty – namely, one that gives rise to the peculiar sentiment of approbation, and, in turn, all the benefits this peculiarity offers for moral reasoning?

Interpretive quibbles

As I noted at the start, Ben-Moshe's analysis involves several interpretive positions on Hume and Smith. In the spirit of constructive debate, I want to push back on a few elements of these innovations, starting with Ben-Moshe's proposed 'two-stage approach' for understanding Hume's argument on the general point of view.

First, I believe that if we are going to discuss 'stages' at all, then we need three, not two. According to Hume, to attribute any action to a person, we must make a judgement from the relevant effects (in this case, some action) to the likely cause (some quality of character). Ben-Moshe himself notes that 'individual actions are virtuous or vicious only insofar as they are *indicative* of an agent's character' (p. 36). However, Ben-Moshe doesn't pause to say that this itself is a judgement, let alone a judgement that already requires one kind of general point of view, namely, the one that allows generalising causal judgements (i.e. inferring effects from causes and vice versa). Making such generalisations is kind of abstraction, according to Hume. And, strictly speaking, this is the first *stage* of any moral judgement.

Ben-Moshe does note later that Hume appeals to the general point of view to develop general rules about probability, in part to respond to the well-known 'virtue-in-rags' objection. However, by this point in Hume's argument, this 'probability' use of the general point of view is normative: it *corrects* first order value judgements. For example, this kind (or stage) of abstraction is what allows us to say that 'helpful' actions, even if they fail, are still good. By contrast, and what my previous point aimed to underline, any first order judgement about the goodness or badness of an action already required a causal generalisation going the other way – something like, 'helping actions reflect a helpful character.' In this more basic generalisation, the 'effect' is the helping action, not the pleasure that this helpful action (probably) produces in another person who receives the help, and which pleasure, on Hume's theory, is the basis of our judgement about the goodness of that action. In short, what Ben-Moshe calls the 'first stage' of moral judgement is, according to Hume, usually the result of *two* different steps of abstraction or generalisation. Perhaps this sounds nitpicky. But the point is so often obscured in the scholarship, I felt a duty to correct it here.

Second, just after this, Ben-Moshe writes: 'Hume of the *Treatise* believed that sympathy – which denotes a widespread form of fellow-feeling with others' inclinations and sentiments (THN 2.1.11.2; SBN 316) – is 'the chief source of moral distinctions' (THN 3.3.6.1; SBN 618). Sympathy gives rise to sentiments of approval and disapproval in the following way: a sentiment of approval arises from a feeling of pleasure that is felt when we sympathise with the pleasure felt by the actor and/or those with whom she interacts insofar as a certain character trait of the actor is useful and/or agreeable to the actor herself and/or those with whom she interacts (and vice versa for a sentiment of disapproval).' (manuscript, 36). I believe this summary is misleading in a few ways.

(1) Sympathy is not required for all sentiments of approval and disapproval. Hume thinks that some actions and qualities of character, like wit, elicit a sentiment of approval immediately. (2) Bracketing the first point, it is contentious to claim that the *source* of this sentiment is sympathy, per se. Sympathy is the process or mechanism by which we come to feel the pleasures or pains of others, which the 'transmission' of feeling is a crucial catalyst to the actual sentiment of

approval. But, for Hume, there must be some further spring, faculty, or source – some disposition of our mind or nature – whence the sentiment of approval arises.[3]

After all, not only is approbation felt towards a new object (some person), but it is also a sentiment entirely distinct from the one felt *by* sympathy. For example, if Nir were to compliment Don for his generosity, then what I feel as the observer by sympathy is *Don's* pleasure (albeit in some more concrete passionate form, like gratitude). But my *approval* of Nir's complimentary remark is not the gratitude I share by sympathy with Don. It is a *new* passion. Indeed, it is a passion with a distinctive phenomenology. Or as Hume puts it in the *Treatise*, recalling my point above, it is a 'peculiar' sentiment. So, whence this sentiment? Something more must be added to sympathy – *some further source* – that can account for this new feeling.

But there is also this: Ben-Moshe spends considerable time criticising supposed weaknesses of Hume's general point of view, especially as it is presented in the *Treatise.* All in all, it is a rich and informed discussion, with interesting suggestions for how to read the development of Hume's thought. However, a fair bit of the supposed weaknesses Ben-Moshe identifies turn on complications of bias. And one of the explicit uses Hume makes of the phenomenological peculiarity of moral approbation, is our ability to use this peculiarity to distinguish moral approbation from the complications of self-love. Hume writes:

> It is only when a character is considered in general, without reference to our particular interest, that it causes such a feeling or sentiment, as denominates it morally good or evil. It is true, those sentiments, from interest and morals, are apt to be confounded, and naturally run into one another. It seldom happens, that we do not think an enemy vicious, and can distinguish betwixt his opposition to our interest and real villainy or baseness. But this hinders not, but that *the sentiments are, in themselves, distinct*; and a man of temper and judgment may preserve himself from these illusions.
>
> (*Treatise* 3.1.2.4, emphasis added)

To be clear, the present point does not constitute a rejection of Ben-Moshe's central claims. Specifically, it does not entail a rejection of his claim that conditions like full information and inter-personal consensus *also* help weed out bias and settle problems of variability in moral judgement. My point is only to underline the silence in Ben-Moshe's account about a critical claim in Hume and to suggest that its inclusion might greatly mitigate the supposed weaknesses of Hume's use of the general point of view, and in turn, Ben-Moshe's anxiety about them.

Notes

1 For Smith's use of 'neighbour' and other cognates of 'dignity, see Debes (2012).
2 All citations to Hume's *Treatise* are to *A Treatise of Human Nature*, eds. David and Mary Norton (New York: Oxford University Press, 2000), followed by book, part, section, and paragraph numbers.
3 For some elaborations on both these points, see Debes (2020).

References

Ben-Moshe, Nir. *Idealization and the Moral Point of View Manuscript*.
Debes, R. (2012) 'Adam Smith on Dignity and Equality', *British Journal for the History of Philosophy*, 20(1): 109–140.
Debes, R. (2020) 'Hume on Personal Merit: Virtue, Talent, and the Import of Appendix 4', in J. Taylor (ed.) *Reading Hume on the Principles of Morals*. New York: Oxford University Press.
Hume, D. (2000) *A Treatise of Human Nature*, (eds.) D. Norton and M. Norton. New York: Oxford University Press.

21 The demigod within the breast

Reflections on Ben-Moshe's (over)-*Idealization of the moral point of view*

Keith Hankins

The last 30 years have witnessed a renaissance of Smith scholarship. Once treated by philosophers largely as a footnote to Hume, Smith is now treated as an important moral philosopher in his own right. His accounts of virtue, sympathy, and moral judgement have received extensive attention, and the ways in which these accounts differ from (and arguably have meaningful advantages over) Hume's accounts of the same are widely recognised. Similarly, the 'Das Adam Smith Problem' that supposedly vexed Smith's account of the relationship between markets and morality has been thoroughly resolved. But while Smith's moral theorising has rightfully received attention from those favourably inclined to sentimentalism as well as those involved in the burgeoning PPE movement, his work has not received the attention it deserves among those engaged in the kinds of ethical debates shaped by whether one is inclined to be a Humean or Kantian about reasons (and the various metaethical implications of being one or the other).[1]

Nir Ben-Moshe's new book *Idealization and the Moral Point of View: An Adam Smithian Account of Moral Reasons* promises to rectify this. His book begins by boldly pronouncing his aim to do for Smith what Korsgaard did for Kant – that is, to present a comprehensive and distinctively Smithian account of the nature of our normative reasons for action – and in that he thoroughly succeeds. Indeed, my biggest complaint about the book may be that there was room for Ben-Moshe to have been more ambitious than he, in fact, was (more on that in a moment). It also warrants mentioning that the book Ben-Moshe has produced is admirably concise despite engaging with several interesting and distinct debates. Additionally, the explication of his view is very precise (almost to a fault).[2] That said, the point of an essay like this is not so much to flag what one admires and agrees with, but to explore the points where one has substantive disagreements. In my case, there are at least a couple of these. I will turn to those disagreements shortly, but before doing so, it will be useful to also say something about the framing of the book, because I think that framing provides useful context for the points of disagreement I want to hash out here.

Ben-Moshe suggests that the target audience of the book is contemporary ethicists sympathetic to an anti-realist, naturalistic metaethical framework, and in particular to moral sentimentalism. That framing allows him to more fully explore the contours of his own view instead of having to survey the wide terrain of alternative

DOI: 10.4324/9781003767824-25

views. More importantly, it allows him to do so without having to worry whether he has provided the best characterisations of views held by opponents he's unlikely to convert. However, as someone who falls squarely within Ben-Moshe's target audience, I think there was room for the book to have been a bit more ambitious in its framing. At the very least, the book could have done a bit more in the introduction to say something about why the way of thinking about morality it adopts is attractive. And since Ben-Moshe doesn't do this, I'll say here that I think a fruitful way of approaching the book is as an attempt to show why the Smithian account of reasons it develops makes an anti-realist, naturalistic metaethical framework more attractive and plausible than the realists tend to think. I should say, too, that I think it would have been worth framing things this way not just because it would make the project relevant to a broader audience but also because I suspect that Ben-Moshe himself is sympathetic to some of the claims made by realists. At the very least, Ben-Moshe seems to have implicitly endorsed some of the ways in which realists have framed debates about what it means for a reason to be a *moral* reason or for an account of morality to be persuasive. As we will see in what follows most of the disagreements I have with his account stem from the fact that I'm more sceptical of these framings, and I think Smith arguably was as well. My hope, then, is that this exchange can provide an opportunity for Ben-Moshe to clarify where his sympathies lie in this regard.

On to the disagreements. My first point of contention is with Ben-Moshe's suggestion that the moral point of view is (or should be) universal. Second, I disagree with his argument that other-oriented sympathy is ultimately the 'proper' form of sympathy. However, here I should say that I think he's right that this form of sympathy constitutes a genuine normative and psychological achievement, and his argument for *that* claim is both important and persuasive. As we will see, in each case, I also happen to disagree not only with the substantive theoretical claim Ben-Moshe is making but also with his arguments that these are claims that Smith would have (or could have) endorsed. I'll discuss the claims in order.

Ben-Moshe develops an account of moral reasons/normative standards according to which the source of these standards is the judgements of a universal impartial spectator. According to Ben-Moshe, universality is necessary so that our standards of correctness for moral judgements:

1) are not objectionably relativistic, that is 'not dependent on what each one of us, or even a collection of us, approves and disapproves of,' and
2) can make intelligible the idea that 'we might all be wrong' in our judgements (and perhaps always have been). (Ben-Moshe, p. 108.)

I agree that a universal impartial spectator of the sort Ben-Moshe describes would have these virtues, and I also agree with his argument that the standards derived from the judgements of such a spectator can be recognisable and motivationally efficacious for agents. I part ways with Ben-Moshe, however, insofar as it's not clear to me that the perspective of the impartial spectator needs to be universal to have these virtues. Put differently, I worry that Ben-Moshe runs together the concepts of impartiality and universality. While the former might be necessary to gain normative leverage on our practices that is sufficiently independent of our actual judgements and any biases that may infect them, it is not clear that universality is needed for this. Indeed, I worry that the aspiration for universal standards threatens to sever the connection to actual judgements and psychology that makes the sentimentalist picture so attractive. And even if it doesn't do this, I worry that the aspiration for universality creates intractable questions about the times, places, and agents that we do (and don't) want to be able to hold our moral judgements fixed over.

Of course, this isn't meant to be a knock-down objection. After all, Ben-Moshe is far from the first moral philosopher to suggest that universality is a necessary or desirable trait for moral judgements to have. I just want to know more about why we need to aspire to universality.

Perhaps more importantly for our purposes, though, I want to push back on Ben-Moshe's suggestion that Smith thought of the impartial spectator as providing universal judgements because I read him quite differently. Of course, this isn't to say that there's no support for the reading of Smith that Ben-Moshe presents. As he ably shows, there are several places where Smith seems to suggest that the impartial spectator we really aspire to create will have 'no connection at all' to either the agents being evaluated or to those affected by their actions.[3] But here I would note that there's a difference between aspiring for a judge that has no connection at all to the events being judged, and the presumption that the judgements we seek should always and everywhere be the same. While it may be true that we often aspire to a kind of universality, it's not clear that this is always true, nor are we discomfited by the fact that our moral judgements are sometimes parochial. Indeed, I think the most persuasive reading of Smith places the tension between the aspiration for impartiality and the need for normative judgements to be parochial at the centre of his thinking. Smith clearly thought this tension was inescapable, and my conjecture here is that he was concerned that taking this seriously makes the further demand for universality impractical and perhaps even undesirable. Consider for instance TMS III.2.31–35. These are the two paragraphs in the sixth and final edition of TMS that replace the passage Ben-Moshe cites, along with the following three paragraphs which were not revised. Here Smith explicitly contrasts the perspective of the impartial spectator (or man within the breast) with both the immediate and less reflective judgements of the 'man without' as well as with those of the 'all-seeing Judge of the world.' And although Smith makes it clear that the judgements of the latter play an important role in comforting us in the face of the unavoidable fact that we won't always get what we deserve, it's not obvious that he takes this perspective to be the operative standard for everyday social morality. Indeed, Smith explicitly calls attention to the 'demigod' like nature of the man within the breast, and in doing so, he makes a point of observing that aspects of the impartial spectator that distinguish it from the gods are precisely what make it an appropriate arbiter of human affairs.

More specifically, in the paragraphs just mentioned Smith notes that man – through his reverence for the sentiments and judgements of his brethren – has been rendered the immediate judge of mankind (TMS III.2.31). However, Smith reminds us that the immediate judgements of man tend to be founded on 'the desire of actual praise, and in the aversion to actual blame.' He goes on to suggest that these judgements provide only provisional normative standards as they are always subject to the scrutiny of the 'much higher tribunal' provided by the impartial spectator whose judgements are founded instead 'on the desire of praise-worthiness, and in the aversion to blame-worthiness.'[4] The verdicts rendered by the higher tribunal of conscience are not necessarily dispositive, though. While the man within is usually able to correct the false judgements of men in cases where we are praised or blamed for actions we did not perform (or motives that did not influence us), Smith notes that there are cases where this is not always so, and his discussion of these cases is nuanced enough to be worth quoting at length.

> The man within seems sometimes, as it were, astonished and confounded by the vehemence and clamour of the man without. The violence and loudness with which blame is sometimes poured out upon us, seems to stupify and benumb our natural sense of praiseworthiness and blameworthiness; and the judgments of the man within, though not, perhaps, absolutely altered or perverted, are, however, so much shaken in the steadiness and firmness of their decision, that their natural effect, in securing the tranquillity of the mind, is frequently, in a great measure, destroyed. We scarce dare to absolve ourselves, when all our brethren appear loudly to condemn us. The supposed impartial spectator of our conduct seems to give his opinion in our favour with fear and hesitation; when that of all the real spectators, when that of all those with whose eyes and from whose station he endeavours to consider it, is unanimously and violently against us. In such cases, this demigod within the breast appears, like the demigods of the poets, though partly of immortal, yet partly too of mortal extraction. When his judgments are steadily and firmly directed by the sense of praiseworthiness and blameworthiness, he seems to act suitably to his divine extraction: but when he suffers himself to be astonished and confounded by the judgments of ignorant and weak man, *he discovers his connection with mortality, and appears to act suitably rather to the human than to the divine part of his origin.*
>
> (TMS III.2.32, emphasis added)

Smith's analogy of the impartial spectator to a demigod requires some interpretation. One might think that Smith is here simply pointing out an imperfection in our actual psychologies, but that doesn't exactly square with Smith's suggestion that we should 'act suitably' by sometimes discounting the voice of our conscience.[5] More importantly, I think Smith's discussion in the subsequent paragraphs argues against a reading that privileges the perspective of either the spectator or something more idealised. Smith notes that when the impartial spectator is overwhelmed by the ordinary less reflective judgements of man, we are apt to appeal to the 'still higher tribunal . . . of the all-seeing Judge of the world, whose eye can never be deceived, and whose judgments can never be perverted' (TMS III.2.33). And, though such appeals are 'deeply rooted in human nature' and may well provide 'effective consolation' for us, as Smith also notes, they do so at the cost of making 'our happiness in this life' dependent on the 'hope and expectation . . . that there is a world to come, where exact justice will be done to every man.'[6] Moreover, Smith suggests that, as attractive as the notion that there may be a world in which cosmic justice is realised may seem, it is rightfully subject to derision insofar as its demands have been 'too frequently in direct opposition to all our moral sentiments.'[7]

To return to the conjecture with which this discussion began, what I think Smith is sketching in the passages discussed earlier is a picture of social morality and the reasons it offers us in which multiple perspectives have normative authority. Crucially, we should be hesitant to privilege the authority of the most idealised perspectives. Having spent quite a bit of time on these passages, I don't want to give the impression that the exegetical argument I'm engaged in here with Ben-Moshe hinges solely on the few paragraphs I've discussed earlier. Rather, I think one finds support for this view in the numerous places where Smith reminds us that the judgements of the impartial spectator are arrived at by weighing considerations and perspectives that may well vary from one place to another, and indeed in a handful of other places where he suggests that the judgements of the impartial spectator itself are weighed against other judgements. Consider, for instance, Smith's suggestion that not only utility but also the appearance of utility has an effect on the sentiment of approbation, as does our sensitivity to custom and fashion.[8] Of course, Smith does not go as far as Hume in founding our sense of virtue entirely upon such considerations, but by allowing that they might appropriately have some influence, Smith seems to make our normative assessments sensitive to considerations that will tend to vary significantly from one time and place to another. Or consider Smith's reflections in the final two sections of TMS where he clearly commits himself to the view that only some parts of morality – namely, the rules of justice – are amenable to being enumerated in a precise and accurate way, while all other virtues are 'loose, vague, and indeterminate.'[9] As I've discussed at length elsewhere, though, perhaps the most convincing evidence that Smith would have been sceptical of the degree of idealisation demanded by the aspiration for universality comes from his discussion of the role the impartial spectator plays in mediating our 'irregular sentiments' in TMS II.iii.[10] Perhaps even more directly (if less clearly) in his tendency throughout TMS to refer to the 'supposed impartial spectator' where it's not obvious that the 'supposed' qualification is being invoked as a way of discounting the impartial spectator's normative authority.

Of course, to be fair to Ben-Moshe, he doesn't claim to be offering an account of Smith's view. Instead, he's defending a view that is recognisably Smithian. And while I have my reservations about the way in which Nir depicts the impartial spectator, I wholeheartedly agree with him that Smith's impartial spectator and his account of sympathy allow Smith's account to overcome several challenges that plague Hume's account of normative judgements. For my part, though, I think the worry with Hume's account is less that our judgements will be parochial than that Hume offers a less persuasive account of how societies will come to converge on normative judgements, and a less persuasive account of how the general point of view gains motivational traction on us.[11]

It's perhaps also worth noting that Ben-Moshe doesn't consider himself to be presenting the kind of view that I (and perhaps more importantly Smith) are sceptical of. As Ben-Moshe notes in the introduction to his book, his motivation for developing a Smithian account of reasons is precisely that he believes Smith develops arguably the most promising version of a modest ideal observer theory within an anti-realist and naturalistic framework. So perhaps the complaints I've laid out here are an example of countenancing one man's modesty over another's licentiousness. That said, I want to reiterate my worry that the view Ben-Moshe presents is idealised enough that it risks losing the motivational grip on us that the commitment to modest idealisation is supposed to retain. Before moving on to other matters I also want to suggest that, insofar as Ben-Moshe's goal of developing an account of a universal impartial spectator is motivated by a desire to have the resources for grappling with the fact that the received consensus about the truth or falsity of our moral judgements might be wrong, it bears noticing that the demand that our normative judgements be universalisable is no guarantor that they are, in fact, correct.

Having registered my concern about universality, I now want to conclude by briefly turning to a second worry about the respective roles that Ben-Moshe ascribes to self- vs. other-oriented sympathy.[12] As Ben-Moshe describes them, self-oriented sympathy is derived from imagining oneself in another's position, while other-oriented sympathy derives from imagining *being the other person in their situation.* I want to spend some time on this distinction and the work it does for Ben-Moshe because I think he has produced an important and persuasive account of how other-oriented sympathy represents a psychological and normative achievement. However, there are several places where he seems to suggest that it is other-oriented sympathy alone that we ultimately want to use to construct the judgements of the impartial spectator, and that provides our normative standards, while self-oriented sympathy is merely important in helping us develop the capacity for other-oriented sympathy.[13] And while I agree with Ben-Moshe that other-oriented sympathy is important, I think he is too quick to discount self-oriented sympathy. Given my previous worry this probably isn't surprising, but the worry itself is distinct from my previous concerns and also has some different implications so I think it's worth sketching in more detail.

As I read Smith, the impartial spectator is meant to be a mechanism that mediates our judgements/sentiments and those of others. To do so, we utilise both self-oriented and other-oriented sympathy (as well as whatever other inferences we can make about what others think/feel based on what they say/do/outwardly express). So, while other-oriented sympathy is a normative achievement that is absolutely crucial to generating an impartial spectator that can deliver authoritative normative guidance, we shouldn't necessarily privilege 'what I think you would feel in your shoes' over 'what I would feel in your shoes.' Indeed, I don't think we should even entirely privilege what an idealised neutral party would feel in your shoes over those other perspectives. Instead, what we want (and, more importantly, what I think Smith thought we needed) was a way of mediating between all of these perspectives. But that requires holding on to a certain degree of partiality in all of our judgements. Or, at the very least, it requires holding onto the thought that all of our individual perspectives have a valuable normative contribution to make that deserves independent normative weight.

Of course, at this point, it bears repeating that Ben-Moshe's goal is not to present an account of Smith's view, let alone a defence of it. Rather, his goal is to defend a view that is recognisably Smithian. And the view he presents *is recognisably Smithian*. Furthermore, I agree with Ben-Moshe that Smith may not have fully appreciated the difference between self- and other-oriented sympathy, and, as a result, his account of sympathy is less clear and persuasive than it could have been.[14] My worry here is simply that, to the extent that Ben-Moshe has departed from Smith's own view in prioritising other-oriented sympathy, he's given up on something important. In fact, I think there are two real costs to embracing a view that downplays the *normative* significance of self-oriented sympathy. The first is that an account of the impartial spectator rooted entirely in other-oriented sympathy strikes me as less motivationally efficacious. As Ben-Moshe convincingly argues, the development of other-oriented sympathy is a normative achievement. And a fully developed impartial spectator requires that perspective. But while some individuals might be capable of reasoning from *and being motivated by* a perspective that doesn't privilege their own standpoint at all, most won't be. Second, and more importantly, I think giving up on the normative (as opposed to developmental) significance of self-oriented sympathy threatens to take away something of genuine normative value. It's not just that the average person is unlikely to fully take up an other-oriented perspective. Rather, the problem is that bringing our self-oriented sympathy to bear on the deliberations of the impartial spectator is perhaps the crucial mechanism through which we draw attention to the unique perspectives we bring to bear on the world. After all, individuals almost always have privileged access to their own feelings and motivations. And while their perception of these things might not be accurate, they are clearly of normative significance. Furthermore, individuals are often aware of aspects of events they are involved in that others are not aware of, and, more importantly, that others would still not have been aware of even if they had been in our position. My worry, then, is that privileging other-oriented perspectives over self-oriented perspectives encourages us to lose sight of the value of this information.

Notes

1 Stephen Darwall's (2006) *The Second-Person Standpoint.* is a notable exception here.

2 I say 'almost to a fault' here not because the precision isn't warranted (indeed it is necessary at times). Rather, I simply mean that I sometimes found the formulation of his view so precise as to be distracting, in the sense that it occasionally made it difficult to grasp the view of the forest through the trees.

3 See, for example, the passages from TMS III.2 that appeared in editions 2–5 that Ben-Moshe discusses at length on p. 125 (as well as earlier in chapter 4.3 at note 122). As is customary, all references to the *Theory of Moral Sentiments* are to the part, section, chapter, and paragraphs of the 6th edition of the Glasgow edition of the works and correspondence of Smith.

4 TMS III.2.32
5 Notably Ben-Moshe points to Smith's analogy of the impartial spectator to a demigod, and to the fact that this entails limits on the extent to which its judgements are idealized, in responding to Sayre-McCord's 'standards-for-standards' challenge to ideal observer theories. See Ben-Moshe, Idealization and the Moral Point of View: An Adam Smithian Account of Moral Reasons, chapter 4.5, especially p. 110., where he is referencing Sayre-McCord (2010), 'Sentiments and Spectators'; Sayre-McCord (2013), 'Hume and Smith on Sympathy, Approbation and Moral Judgment.' As my argument suggests, though, Ben-Moshe makes less of these constraints on the impartial spectator than I do.
6 TMS III.2.33
7 TMS III.2.33. Smith further reinforces this assessment in the final paragraph of the chapter (TMS III.2.35) where he contrasts the safe confines of a monastery within which a monk might pursue a life of virtue with the 'ennobling' hardships and hazards of war. 'To suppose that one day, or one hour, employed in the former should, in the eye of the great Judge of the world, have more merit than a whole life spent honourably in the latter, is surely contrary to all our moral sentiments,' he says. And, yet, it is this spirit which, 'has condemned to the infernal all the heroes, all the statesmen and lawgivers, all the poets and philosophers of former ages; all those who have invented, improved, or excelled in the arts which contribute to the subsistence, to the conveniency, or to the ornament of human life; all the great protectors, instructors, and benefactors of mankind; all those to whom our natural sense of praiseworthiness forces us to ascribe the highest merit and most exalted virtue.'
8 See TMS parts IV and V.
9 TMS VII.iii and VII.iv, especially VII.iv.1–2. Note that in section 4.3 Ben-Moshe points to Smith's claim that we can enumerate general rules of justice as evidence that the impartial spectator is capable of generating universal moral principles. But in doing so, he ignores Smith's subsequent qualification that this is not true of other aspects of morality.
10 See Hankins (2016). Here, it's worth noting that Ben-Moshe also acknowledges the relevance of these passages in the same section referenced above. Once again, though, he seems to think that these passages do less to reign in Smith's view than I do.
11 For these arguments, see Hankins and Thrasher (2022).
12 Ben-Moshe develops this argument at length in chapter 3.
13 See, for example, Ben-Moshe chapter 3.5, especially fn. 104, and his later discussion at pp. 153–154.
14 Ben-Moshe makes this conjecture at pp. 62–63 and then develops his argument for the claim in chapter 3.2.

References

Ben-Moshe, N. *Idealization and the Moral Point of View: An Adam Smithian Account of Moral Reasons*. Oxford University Press, manuscript.

Darwall, S. (2006) *The Second-Person Standpoint: Morality, Respect, and Accountability*. Cambridge, MA: Harvard University Press.

Hankins, K. (2016) 'Adam Smith's Intriguing Solution to the Problem of Moral Luck', *Ethics*, 126: 711–746.

Hankins, K. and Thrasher, J. (2022) 'Smithian Sympathy and the Emergence of Norms', *Philosophy and Phenomenological Research*, 105(3): 638–656.

Sayre-McCord, G. (2010) 'Sentiments and Spectators: Adam Smith's Theory of Moral Judgment', in V. Brown and S. Fleischacker (eds.) *The Adam Smith Review*, Vol. 5. New York: Routledge, pp. 124–144.

Sayre-McCord, G. (2013) 'Hume and Smith on Sympathy, Approbation and Moral Judgment', *Social Philosophy and Policy*, 30: 208–236.

Smith, A. (1982) 'The Theory of Moral Sentiments', in D. D. Raphael and L. Montes (eds.) *The Glasgow Edition of the Works and Correspondence of Adam Smith*, 6th edition. Indianapolis: Liberty Fund Inc.

22 Idealization and the moral point of view: an Adam Smithian account of moral reasons

Replies to my critics

Nir Ben-Moshe

Let me commence by thanking the three commentators: John Skorupski, Remy Debes, and Keith Hankins, who did a fantastic job of raising very insightful questions and objections. A version of these comments, along with my replies, was first presented at the 'Smith, Ferguson, and Witherspoon at 300 Conference' at the University of St Andrews in July 2023. I was fortunate enough to have this author-meets-critics panel on my book, *Idealization and the Moral Point of View: An Adam Smithian Account of Moral Reasons* (OUP), at an IASS conference prior to its publication. (I am grateful to Keith for organising the panel.) I did not make substantial changes to the book in response to these comments, and so, for those reading the published book, all the comments still hold. (In a few cases, I added a footnote that addresses a certain comment. Whenever I did so, I reproduced my response from this essay and thanked the commentator.)[1]

Reply to John Skorupski

I want to divide my response to John into three parts: the first clarifies the aim of my project; the second takes issue with John's own account of practical reason in Smith and its relation to Humeanism; and the third takes issue with the scope of the propriety of sentiments in Smith's account (i.e. with the question of whether Smith aims to provide a theory of the propriety of all sentiments or only of the sentiments involved in moral judgement). But first, let me make an important clarification. John talks repeatedly about 'Humeanism' in his comments. I will take this claim to encompass both the Humean theory of motivation and the Humean theory of reasons. According to the former, A's ability to be motivated to ϕ requires that A have a desire that would be furthered by ϕ-ing (e.g. Smith 1994).[2] According to the latter, p is a reason for A to ϕ only if A has a desire that would be furthered by ϕ-ing (e.g. Schroeder 2007). (Whether this condition is also sufficient for a reason-statement attribution is a point of contention.)

In terms of the aim of my project, John claims that I 'interpret Smith's theory of moral sentiments within the framework of a Humean, or "desire-belief," account of practical reasons.' He then argues that 'the Humean framework is unhelpful for understanding Smith,' since Smith has 'no reason to accept Humeanism,' nor 'does Smith anywhere discuss or endorse Humeanism.' John does note that he is 'not sure'

DOI: 10.4324/9781003767824-26

whether I think that Smith endorses Humeanism (454), and adds that I might say that 'Smithian insights' can be used to 'rebut or at least weaken the force of the standard objections' to Humeanism and that 'the Humean framework illuminates Smith's positions.' (455) I agree with the former claim, but not with the latter one. In particular, one of the aims of the book is to use key ideas from *The Theory of Moral Sentiments* (hereafter TMS) in order to offer an adequate account of moral reasons that is congruent with the aspirations of the informed-desire version of the Humean theory of reasons. Nowhere do I claim that Smith himself discusses or endorses Humeanism, nor that he has any reason to do so. Put differently, one of the aims of the book is to show that Smith illuminates Humeanism, without claiming that Humeanism illuminates Smith. John, for his part, remarks that the book 'does not show that either illuminates the other,' (455) but since he does not engage at all with the way I use Smith to defend the Humean theory of reasons, I find this remark quite uncharitable. I should add that while it may not matter for my purposes whether Smith endorsed Humeanism, there is a difference between Smith not endorsing Humeanism and Humeanism being inconsistent with Smith's philosophy: since I do want to develop a Smithian worldview, the latter would be troubling. However, I do not think that TMS contains any inconsistency with the Humean theory of motivation or the Humean theory of reasons for the simple reason that Smith does not present a well-articulated theory of either motivation or practical reason.

In the book, I build on the account of reasons in Bernard Williams' 'Internal and External Reasons' (1981). John claims that Williams is not a Humean. I agree that Williams deviates from the Humean theory of motivation in, among other things, maintaining that not only desires can motivate us: his notion of a 'subjective motivational set' includes 'dispositions of evaluation, patterns of emotional reaction, personal loyalties, and various projects . . . embodying commitments of the agent' (105). While Williams seems to have also allowed for more expansive forms of reasoning than the historical Hume,[3] his theory of reasons is Humean in that it combines (a) the thought that if p is a reason for A to ϕ, then p must be able to motivate A to ϕ (under the appropriate conditions),[4] with (b) the thought that the existence of a contingent psychological component in A's subjective motivational set is required to do the relevant motivational work. Of course, Williams thought that this explanatory dimension is inseparable from a justificatory one; hence, the addition of 'under appropriate conditions' in the formulation of point (a). These conditions include the fact that the agent has both no false beliefs and all the relevant true beliefs pertaining to the action, as well as the fact that she deliberates correctly. More specifically, the fact that p must be able to motivate A means that p can explain A's action, and the fact that the motivation needs to occur under the specified appropriate conditions means that p can justify A's action. So, if we bracket his deviation from the Humean theory of motivation, Williams belongs to the camp of those who endorse an informed-desire version of the Humean theory of reasons: the mere presence of a desire is insufficient for a reason-statement to apply to an agent – rather, the desire needs to occur under appropriate conditions in order to give rise to a reason, which for Williams means being sufficiently informed by the facts and by deliberation.

This brings me to the second part of my reply to John's comments. John identifies an account of practical reason in Smith, according to which there is a link between the propriety of sentiments and the propriety of actions. John thinks that there is a substantial deviation from Humeanism here, since the link is not only psychological but also normative; for example, justified fear is a reason for flight. I do not quite understand why the historical Hume (let alone some contemporary Humeans) could not hold this position in the following way: Hume could argue, for example, that sentiments experienced from the general point of view not only are justified but also give us a reason to perform certain actions. And he could do so in exactly the same way that, according to John, is available to Smith: 'Whatever facts give a person reason to feel a sentiment give that person reason to do the action "most immediately and directly" prompted by the sentiment.' (457) The fact that Smith does, while Hume does not, use the phrase 'most immediately and directly' does not mean that Hume (and some contemporary Humeans) could not use this strategy, since Humeanism does not necessarily rule it out.[5] John might insist that I am pointing to a mere psychological link when noting the possibility that is open for Hume's general point of view account. (The 'reason' in question might be a motivating rather than a normative reason.) But if that is the case, then I fail to see why Smith fares any better.

Now, at times it seems that John believes that Smith fares better because he is not committed to the Humean theory of motivation. For example:

> Suppose you go to a piano recital given by an acquaintance whom you thoroughly dislike. . . . You feel no admiration yet you see that there is strong reason to admire, because the disinterested man within your breast tells you so. . . . So you clap and praise even though you have no desire to do so. In other words, it's the sincere, fairminded belief that the performance is indeed worthy of admiration . . . that causes your praise. You clap because you believe that the sentiment of admiration is the proper response to this performance, and hence . . . that praise is proper action. This action, therefore, is caused by a normative belief, not a desire. (458)

John's thought is that it is the belief, without any aid from an independent desire, that is doing the motivational work in this example. Note, however, that this is a point of contention between proponents and opponents of the Humean theory of motivation. After all, a supporter of the Humean theory of motivation could easily argue that this is a misrepresentation of the phenomenon: despite appearances, there is an independent desire at work in this case. Humeans about motivation certainly have good arguments for this claim (e.g. Smith 1994; Sinhababu 2017). Furthermore, Adam Smith himself would argue that there is an independent desire at work here. As I argue in the book, Smith believes that it is the desire to be worthy of approval (TMS III.2.1)[6] that motivates us to moral action by making us adopt the standpoint of the impartial spectator. This standpoint provides a set of hypothetical and modestly idealised conditions that guarantee the authoritativeness of an agent's responses in constituting the standard of moral judgement. Thus, even if Smith does not endorse the Humean theory of motivation, he certainly thought that moral action is dependent on a certain background desire.

In any case, the normative connection that John identifies is rather weak, for surely a warranted sentiment can lead to all kinds of warranted actions. For example, warranted fear might rightly lead to flight, but it might also rightly lead to standing your ground and attempting to conquer the fear. What is required here, and is missing from John's account, is deliberation: given the specifics of the situation, we need to deliberate from warranted sentiments to warranted courses of action. Without deliberation, there is no practical reason. Williams (1981) understood this all too well; hence, for him, an account in which desires (or other psychological components) automatically give rise to reasons, without normative constraints such as deliberation, is 'sub-Humean' (102). Therefore, I do not see how the link in question constitutes a 'comprehensive sentimentalism about practical reason,' (457) as John calls it, for there is no account of practical reason here. At most, there is an account that tells us that we ought to do that which is typically associated with a warranted sentiment. This may be an improvement on what I call in the book 'the non-informed desire version of the Humean theory,' according to which a desire gives rise to a reason for action without any normative constraints. And perhaps this is the type of 'Humeanism' that John envisions as his (and Smith's) opponent. However, John's 'comprehensive sentimentalism' (457) gives us less than a Williams-inspired informed-desire version of the Humean theory, which includes deliberation, and which is the type of account that I defend. When joining this type of theory to Smith's sentimentalism, as I do in the book, one gets a stronger connection between the propriety of sentiments and the propriety of actions than the one provided by John on Smith's behalf: the propriety of sentiments is determined from the standpoint of the impartial spectator, but it is deliberation from that standpoint that yields certain reasons for action with the correct normative weights.

Finally, John takes issue with the scope of the propriety of sentiments in Smith's account. He argues that Smith's account is 'a general theory of the propriety of all sentiments' (456) and 'does not apply just to the sentiments specifically involved in moral judgement,' (456) adding that in Smith's theory 'desire becomes just one of the sentiments.' However, regardless of Smith's views on the role of desire in motivation – as I noted, he thinks that desire is crucial for moral motivation – Smith's focus is primarily on *moral* sentiments. This claim is the result of combining the following two observations. First, Smith believes that the objects of our sentiments of approval and disapproval merit that approval and disapproval from the standpoint of the impartial spectator (TMS II.i.2.2 & VII.ii.1.49; see also Sayre-McCord 2010, 2013). Second, and importantly, the standpoint of the impartial spectator, a standpoint which serves as our 'conscience' (TMS III.3.4, III.3.29, III.4.4), is supposed to serve as the standard of moral judgement in Smith's moral philosophy. In particular, the impartial spectator plays a key role in humbling our excessive self-love and makes us realise that our perspective is 'but one of the multitude, in no respect better than any other in it' (TMS II.ii.2.1 & III.3.4). This standpoint also allows us to 'see what relates to ourselves in its proper shape and dimensions' and to make a 'proper comparison between our own interests and those of other people' (TMS III.3.1), since we come to view all interests 'from the place and with the eyes of a third person, who has no particular connexion with either [us or others], and who judges with impartiality between us' (TMS III.3.3). Hence, the standpoint of the impartial spectator helps us appreciate that our own perspective and interests are no more privileged than other people's perspectives and interests, enabling us to consider the perspectives and interests of all concerned. In this sense, the standard of the impartial spectator is the type of standard that we tend to associate with moral judgement, and its purview is moral sentiments.[7]

Having said that, in two of the aforementioned passages, Smith does seem to suggest that the impartial spectator makes our sentiments proper quite generally. In TMS II.i.2.2, Smith speaks of the 'passions of human nature' quite generally seeming 'proper' when 'the heart of every impartial spectator entirely sympathises with them.' And in TMS VII.ii.1.49, Smith talks about the fact that 'the precise or distinct measure by which this fitness or propriety of affection can be ascertained or judged of' can only be found in 'the sympathetic feelings of the impartial and well-informed spectator.' However, I believe that to develop the thought that the impartial spectator can cover the whole gamut of the sentiments, we need to lean more heavily on virtue ethics. In particular, we need to build on Smith's claim that Aristotle's doctrine of the mean 'corresponds too pretty exactly' to his own account of 'the propriety and impropriety of conduct' (TMS VII.ii.1.12). Alexander Broadie (2010) has argued that, in the context of attempting to attain mutual sympathy (TMS I.i.2.1–6),

> the process of seeking a mean between undesirable extremes starts to take shape, with Smith showing how a compromise or accommodation is reached between the spectator and the person principally concerned by which each modifies the intensity of his own sentiment or passion where the change produced is in the direction of the intensity of the sentiment that the other has (81).[8]

The impartial spectator can constitute the standard of virtue by building on this process of mutual sympathy, which initially occurs between spectators and actors: 'The point of propriety, the degree of any passion which the impartial spectator approves of, is differently situated in different passions' so that 'the passions which the spectator is most disposed to sympathise with, and in which, upon that account, the point of propriety may be said to stand high, are those of which the immediate feeling or sensation is more or less agreeable to the person principally concerned' (and vice versa for the passions with which the impartial spectator is least disposed to sympathise) (TMS VI.iii.14). Smith is suggesting that the propriety of a given sentiment depends on the approval of the impartial spectator, but in a way that fosters mutual sympathy. And, assuming that this use of the doctrine of the mean can be extended to all the sentiments, we would in fact have 'a general theory of the propriety of all sentiments,' as John puts it.

Reply to Remy Debes

I want to thank Remy for his very kind words at the beginning of his commentary. Remy first notes that I do 'not spend much time discussing Smith's own use of the term "humanity" or its cognates,' nor do I discuss how my 'conclusions in this respect align with other interpretations of Smith on the subject of human worth and moral respect.' (459). In Chapter 5, I develop an account of *shared* reasons based on a *third-personal* perspective, namely, the perspective of the impartial spectator. I then ask, in Chapter 6: what am I to make of *my* perspective and *my* idiosyncratic reasons? And does the value I place on my perspective and my idiosyncratic reasons entail respect for *your* perspective and *your* idiosyncratic reasons? It is in this context that I develop a Smithian account of humanity. I see my discussion in that chapter as directly tied to the subject of human worth and moral respect. Indeed, I situate my Smithian account of humanity in the context of those sentimentalists inspired by Smith's moral philosophy, who have tried to show that one cannot have a perspective unless one can enter empathetically into other perspectives (Fleischacker 2019: ch. 2), or that one is committed to acknowledging the authority of others' 'affective perspectives' or 'emotional agency' (Debes 2012, 2017), or that one's reasons have normative authority over others (Stueber 2017). I clarify that these accounts are trying to establish a strong normative connection between one's perspective and/or reasons and others' perspectives and/or reasons, as a way of showing that we are reciprocally bound to, and ought to be engaged with, our fellow human beings. I understand the connection in question via Christine Korsgaard's (1996: 132) claim that 'valuing humanity in your own person . . . implies, entails, or involves valuing it in that of others,' which I shall call 'The Universality of Humanity Claim' (UHC). I believe this claim is about human worth and moral respect.

I offer a sentimentalist defence, based on Smith's moral philosophy, of a qualified, albeit adequate, version of UHC. In particular, valuing my humanity, understood as (my awareness of) my perspective and the reasons determined from within it, entails valuing your humanity, understood as (your awareness of) your perspective and the reasons determined from within it. The account is 'qualified' because it is conditioned on the premise that agents have certain psychological capacities, primarily the capacity, and the desire, for (mutual) sympathy. Nevertheless, the account is 'adequate' because it applies to the right set of agents, namely, those agents who are capable of being aware, qua spectator, of their own perspective, qua actor, and who are, therefore, distinctively human. The key premise in the argument for the proposed version of UHC is that an objective, third-personal point of view (the point of view of the impartial spectator) gives authority to a second-personal point of view in the form of a certain type of sympathy, namely, other-oriented sympathy [imagining being the *actor* in the actor's situation (TMS VII.iii.1.4)]. While it is true that I develop a *Smithian* account of humanity, and not Smith's *own* account of humanity, I do argue towards the end of the chapter that there is an interesting connection between the two accounts. Smith understands 'humanity' as the virtue of the spectator who attempts to augment his sympathy to match the experiences of the actor (TMS I.i.5.1). On my Smithian account, a key element in my ability to value your humanity – (your awareness of) your perspective and the reasons determined from within it – is, again, the ability to experience other-oriented sympathy. This type of sympathy helps us see the situation from the actor's perspective and is thus akin to the aspiration of humanity as Smith conceives of it, namely, the aspiration to augment sympathy to match the experiences of others.

Remy raises two sets of 'big-picture questions.' (460) The first set pertains to the authority, and recognition of the authority, of our ideal self. Remy asks: 'Must the judgments of the ideal self be made under suitable conditions *and* recognised as such? Or could either suffice? And what exactly *makes for* the "authority" of these judgements?' (460). He continues by noting that 'the relevant conditions are supposed to be normative for the *correctness* of the judgements,' but that 'without argument, it is not clear why these conditions render the judgement *authoritative.*' (460) A major theme of the book is that a standard of correctness – such as the standard of what is morally right – can be constituted by the responses of agents *who are under certain conditions.*[9] Of course, the conditions in question cannot be defined in terms of these agents getting the right results, on pain of circularity. But these conditions are required to guarantee that the agents' responses are in fact *authoritative*, and one strategy is to *idealise* these responses, for example, via an idealised observer. But how ideal should the observer be in order to be authoritative? Roderick Firth (1952) argued that the ideal observer should be, among other things, omnipercipient and omniscient with respect to the non-ethical facts so that 'any plausible description of an ideal observer will be a partial description of God' (333). The problem with Firth's suggestion is that it *over*-idealises the observer and detaches him from our human sensibilities. It therefore becomes unclear what epistemic access we have to the reactions of such an observer, or why his decisions should bind us or motivate us. In the book, I build on Smith and argue that his 'impartial spectator' makes use of the idea of spectators' responses under certain conditions to articulate a standard of correctness for moral judgements which, while transcending individual points of view, does not transcend the point of view of human beings. Importantly, I combine this 'modest ideal observer theory' with the thought that the impartial spectator is our (i.e. the relevant set of agents) ideal ethical self. In other words, the authority of the judgements of the impartial spectator is not only a function of the suitability of the conditions that constitute the standpoint of this spectator – although they are the *best* (i.e. idealised to the right degree) conditions – but this authority is also a function of the fact that these conditions constitute *our* (i.e. the relevant set of agents) ideal ethical *self.*

Now, this might still not answer Remy's worry, as Remy might be questioning the very authority of one's ideal (ethical) self. In the book, I note that the fact that some more idealised version of yourself would desire something different than what you presently desire may not strike you as relevant. For example, in medical contexts, one may well resent being subjected to physical assault (unwanted treatment, for instance) on the basis that this is what one's ideal self would desire; why should an agent be any less opposed to being subjected to the values of their ideal selves than to being subjected to the values of someone else altogether?[10] It is in the context of this question that I raise the issue of *recognition* with which Remy takes issue. In particular, I note that there is a crucial difference between a scenario in which the agent *could* recognise the authority of her alleged ideal self and one in which she could *not* recognise this authority: in the former, but not in the latter, she has a certain type of epistemic authority over the desires that constitute her ideal self. If the agent could *herself* recognise the authority of the standard in question, then not only are the verdicts of the ideal self authoritative because of the aforementioned reasons, but they are also authoritative because the actual self could endorse the deferral to the ideal self as the authoritative standard. Of course, there are various ways in which a person might be brought to recognise the authority of her ideal self: she might, for example, be hit on the head with a hammer or undergo some form of non-rational conversion. Presumably, the agent's epistemic authority is most respected if she could recognise the authority of her ideal self in a way that respects her *rational capacities*, that is, via *deliberation* from her actual self. The thought is that, in such cases, the agent could deliberate from the desires of her actual self to those of her ideal self, and endorse them. (This is how I interpret Williams' theory of reasons.) So, to answer Remy's question, judgements of the ideal self must be made under suitable conditions *and* recognised as such.

Remy's second set of 'big-picture questions' pertains to 'proportionalism,' (461) according to which the strength of a desire corresponds to the weight of a reason.[11] In the book, I explain why, given her commitments, a correspondence between desire strength and weight of reason is something that is natural for the Humean theorist of reasons to assume. First, given her scepticism about reason's ability, in and of itself, to determine the content of our fully rational selves and the content of our reasons, it is natural for the Humean theorist to assume that reason also cannot determine the weights of our reasons; rather, features of our contingent psychology would need to perform the task. Second, given her scepticism about the motivational efficacy of reason, it is natural for the Humean theorist, especially if she is committed to the Humean theory of motivation, to assume that the relative strengths of an agent's desires are the most plausible candidates for serving as the psychological components that determine the weights of our reasons. Indeed, note how proportionalism is natural when we focus on the agent's strongest desire: given the scepticism about the motivational efficacy of reason, the agent's strongest desire will motivate her, since reason cannot produce an opposing motivational force; and, given the fact that reason cannot determine the contents, or (therefore) the weights, of our reasons, what the agent is motivated to do is presumably what she has most reason to do.[12]

Remy asks whether proportionalism is true of the historical Hume, pointing to the work that the phenomenological peculiarity of moral feeling does for Hume in moral reasoning. However, I do not see how the mere peculiarity of moral feeling is helpful in addressing the issues that proportionalism is meant to address. First, by tying the weights of reasons to the strengths of desires, proportionalism can provide the Humean with a way of determining the normative weights of reasons. But how could the phenomenological peculiarity of moral feeling be helpful? Is this peculiarity supposed to show that moral reasons should have the greatest normative weight? If so, how? After all, we could have peculiar feelings in many domains: how would we then determine which type of reason, given the peculiar feeling associated with it, is weightier? Second, by tying the weights of reasons to the strengths of desires, proportionalism can provide the Humean with a way of explaining why weightier reasons are more likely to motivate us. But even if the weight of a reason could be determined by the peculiarity of a feeling, how would

Remy's proposal account for the motivational point: how would peculiarities of feeling explain why weightier reasons are more likely to motivate us? Indeed, Hume's point in T 3.1.2.4, which Remy cites, is primarily an epistemic one: we garner satisfaction from various kinds of objects, but, as Hume notes in this passage, the fact that the satisfaction from each kind is different 'keeps our sentiments concerning them from being confounded, and makes us ascribe virtue to the one, and not to the other. Nor is every sentiment of pleasure or pain, which arises from characters and actions, of that *peculiar* kind, which makes us praise or condemn.'

Now, in the book I actually argue for a *qualified* version of proportionalism – which I think is true of the *informed-desire* version of the Humean theory of reasons – according to which proportionalism does not necessarily hold for the desires of the actual self, but rather for the desires of the *ideal* self. The key idea, which Remy quotes, is analogous to entering a practice: we are familiar with practices in which, while it may be up to us whether or not to enter the practice, once we are in the practice, someone else gets to dictate what we ought to do. So, while one might choose whether or not to take Professor X's class, once one is enrolled in Professor X's class, one must adhere to the requirements that Professor X has specified in the syllabus. What I am suggesting is that committing to the authority of the ideal self ought to be conceived of along similar lines: given a certain desire that we initially have, and regardless of the strength of this desire, we enter into the practice of allowing our reasons (and their weights) to be determined by the desires (and their strengths) of our ideal self.[13] And if we focus on the ideal *ethical* self, the key thought is that we have, among our initial motivations, a desire that explains, regardless of its strength, why we are willing to enter the practice of *morality*; that is, it explains why we enter into the practice of allowing our *moral* reasons (and their weights) to be determined by the desires (and their strengths) of our ideal *ethical* self. The desire in question is, as previously noted, a desire to be worthy of approval (TMS III.2.1).[14]

Remy is worried that my talk of a 'certain desire that agents initially have' (462) sounds very similar to what would follow from the Humean theory of mind after one posits an original moral faculty, which could go against the naturalist and anti-realist bent of my project. I do think that if it were not for the desire to be worthy of approval, we would not, according to Smith, be distinctively human. As I note in the book, Smith argues that human beings have developed the desire to be worthy of approval, and not only the desire for mere approval, as the latter 'would not alone have rendered [them] fit for the society for which [they were] made'; rather, it is the desire to be worthy of approval that is 'necessary' to make human beings 'really fit' for society (TMS III.2.7). Therefore, the desire to be worthy of approval is needed in order to make us the type of social being that we are, and our social systems, or perhaps even our species, are so structured as to instil such a desire in each of us. I develop Smith's thought here and argue that the desire to be worthy of approval is constitutive of our social rationality – and, insofar as moral agency is a form of social agency, of our moral agency as well. Another way of putting the thought is that (a) intelligibility, understood as making sense of oneself, is constitutive of agency; and (b) insofar as our agency is social in nature, acting on a desire to be worthy of approval – by an appropriate, ultimately internal, other – is constitutive of the type of intelligibility in question. Nevertheless, I do not intend for the desire to be worthy of approval to act as an original moral faculty. It is a mere desire, which, as I argue in detail in the book, can develop from quite humble origins that initially merely track approval from actual people rather than from an internal spectator. (Alas, my account of the development of the desire to be worthy of approval is too involved and detailed to fully reproduce here.)[15]

A few thoughts about Remy's interpretive quibbles. In Chapter 2, I develop a novel *two-stage* reconstruction of Hume's general point-of-view account, modelled in part on his qualified judges account in 'Of the Standard of Taste.' In particular, I argue that the general point of view needs to be jointly constructed by spectators who have sympathised with (at least some of) the agents in (at least some of) the actor's circles of influence. In other words, sympathy with agents in the actor's various circles, which is the first stage in the process, provides a necessary, but not a sufficient, condition for attaining the standard of virtue. The full specification of the conditions under which judgements of virtue ought to be made includes an *idealisation* – in the form of full and unbiased knowledge of the effects of the actor's character traits on the interests and pleasures of the agents in all of her circles of influence – which spectators try to approximate, in the second stage of the process, through conversation and shared reasoning. Remy argues, regarding my proposed two-stage approach, that we need three, rather than two, stages. The first stage of a moral judgement, according to Remy's understanding of Hume, pertains to generalisations of causal judgements in the following sense: 'to attribute any action to a person, we must make a judgment from the relevant effects (in this case, some action) to the likely cause (some quality of character).' (463) I am sympathetic to Remy's observation, although my two-stage approach focuses on the *normative* account of correcting first-order value judgements. [As Remy himself notes when discussing the well-known 'virtue-in-rags' objection, 'by this point in Hume's argument, this "probability" use of the general point of view is normative: it *corrects* first order value judgements.' (463)] Hence, I do not think that the phenomenon that Remy notes is an additional stage *within* the normative account, but rather *preliminary non-normative* stage-setting for the normative account. Of course, stated this way, the disagreement between Remy and me may amount to an insignificant semantic dispute.

Remy then takes issue with my claim that sympathy, for Hume, is the *source* of approbation. What I meant is that Hume subscribes to the idea that we approve or disapprove of an actor's character traits, *given* certain sentiments we experience when sympathising with the actor and/or those affected by her actions. Therefore, I agree with Remy that (a) sympathy is 'the process or mechanism by which we come to feel the pleasures or pains of others,' and that (b) approbation is 'a sentiment entirely distinct from the one felt *by* sympathy.' (464). (The confusion may be the result of my commencing the discussion by relying on Hume's claim that sympathy is 'the chief source of moral distinctions' (T 3.3.6.1; SBN 618).)[16] Remy also notes that sympathy is not required for all sentiments of approval and disapproval, since Hume thinks that some actions and qualities of character elicit a sentiment of approval immediately. Wit seems to be an example of such a quality (see, for example, T 3.3.1.27, SBN 589–590 and EPM 8.3, SBN 262). Therefore, it might be more accurate to say that Hume subscribes to the idea that we *tend* to approve or disapprove of an actor's character traits, given certain sentiments we experience when sympathising with the actor and/or those affected by their actions.

Finally, Remy takes issue with my criticism of Hume's general point of view account in the *Treatise*. Hume suggests that the general point of view is a method for correcting our sentiments, via which we attain a conception of the character of the person in question in abstraction from both the proximity of that person to us and our own interests (T 3.3.1.15–18, SBN 581–584; T 3.3.1.30, SBN 591; T 3.3.3.2, SBN 602–603). In the book, I note, following others, that the general point of view may be susceptible to the following sources of bias: the actor might reveal different character traits to different members of a narrow circle; the actor's character traits can have different effects on different members of a circle; the members of a circle can be biased individuals; and spectators' sympathetic reactions can vary as a function of their distance from the members of a narrow circle.[17] Remy points to 3.1.2.4 in the *Treatise*, where Hume notes our ability to make use of the phenomenological peculiarity of moral approbation to distinguish moral approbation from the complications of self-love, and suggests that the inclusion of this 'critical claim' might 'greatly mitigate the supposed weaknesses of Hume's use of the general point of view.' (465) However, even if the peculiarity of moral approbation can help us distinguish moral approbation from self-love, why does this show, in and of itself, that self-interest is (or can be) overcome? Furthermore, even if the peculiarity of moral approbation can show that self-interest is (or can be) overcome, how would this help with most of the biases noted earlier, which do not necessarily pertain to the spectator's self-interest?

Reply to Keith Hankins

I want to thank Keith for his very kind words at the beginning of his comments. Keith has two main comments, and I'll reply to them in turn. But first, he notes that I should have been more ambitious in framing my project. I view the project as quite ambitious: I aim to do for Smith what Korsgaard has done for Kant, namely, to develop a novel and unique Smithian position within the contemporary meta-ethics and practical reason landscape. In the introduction to the book, I note, among other things, that Smith's moral philosophy and moral psychology, primarily as presented in TMS, provide a promising – arguably, the most promising – version of 'modest ideal observer theory,' particularly within a sentimentalist, anti-realist, and naturalistic framework. I also note that the book is geared primarily to those who are already sympathetic to a sentimentalist, anti-realist, and naturalistic framework and who hope to find a standard of moral judgement that can transcend subjectivism and relativism. The book does not offer a knockdown argument in support of this framework. I concede that, for all I say in the book, another meta-ethical position might, on balance, fare better. Nevertheless, I do discuss key aspects of this framework, especially in Chapter 4, where I develop Smith's impartial spectator account into a modest ideal observer theory. And, more importantly, I view the book as a whole as an argument for (a certain form of) sentimentalism – and for 'moral sentimentalism,' according to which the sentiments are the source of our moral judgements, in particular – even though the related anti-realism and naturalism are not my primary focus.

It is also worth noting that my point of entry into the book is not the meta-ethical debate in general or ideal observer theory in particular; rather, my point of entry is from the practical reasons angle, and more specifically, the Humean theory of reasons. The key idea in connection with the last point is the one I noted in my response to John's comments: Smith's thought can aid a Williams-inspired Humean theory of reasons by offering a novel and alternative account of moral reasons. I argue that the Humean theory of reasons is a natural counterpart to a sentimentalist account of normative and moral judgements, as it is congruent, like the sentimentalist account, with our contemporary naturalistic understanding of the world. Moreover, both the Humean theory of reasons (at least of the type championed by Williams) and sentimentalist accounts (at least of the type associated with Hume and Smith) make use of idealisation to account for the source of *normativity*: only when the relevant desires or sentiments are experienced under suitable conditions do they give rise to correct and authoritative normative reasons or normative judgements. While Williams makes use of idealisation to account for the normative dimension in his theory, a key claim in the book is that Williams' use of idealisation is insufficient for providing an adequate account of shared reasons, including moral reasons. Smith's 'impartial spectator,' and the idealisation inherent to it, can, on the other hand, provide us with such an account, and it can do so in a way that is congruent with the aspirations of the Humean theory of reasons. Thus, the meta-ethical component of the worldview is not only philosophically interesting in its own right but is also in service of a novel account of normative reasons for action. Hence, I am more than happy to endorse Keith's suggestion, according to which 'a fruitful way of approaching the book is as an attempt to show why the Smithian account of reasons it develops makes an anti-realist, naturalistic metaethical framework more attractive and plausible than the realists tend to think.'

Keith's first point of contention is with my claim that the moral point of view is universal. In the book, I discuss the question of whether each culture or society has its own 'societal impartial spectator' – where members of that group, if they continued to become more impartial and informed, would zero in on *that* spectator – or whether there is instead a single 'universal impartial spectator' that would emerge in any culture or society. While the former is a spectator *in* a given society – a spectator who applies that society's standards fairly and with knowledge of the facts – the latter is a spectator *of* that society and its standards, who can judge the social standards themselves. I suggest that, for Smith, a societal impartial spectator might only take into account the interests and perspectives of all concerned in a *qualified* way (e.g. only 'all men' or 'all white people'), but that a universal impartial spectator would take into account the interests and perspectives of all concerned in an *unqualified* way.

The emergence of the universal impartial spectator is important because, as I argue in the book, it can accommodate two key requirements to which our justificatory practices commit us. First, we want the standard of correctness of moral judgement to be more robust than a subjectivist or relativist standard; that is, we want to be able to say that this standard is not dependent on what each one of us, or even any collection of us, approves and disapproves. Second, and relatedly, we want to make intelligible the idea that we might all be wrong, and perhaps have always been wrong, when making moral judgements. When the standpoint of the universal impartial spectator has been achieved, the standard of correctness in question does not exclusively rely on the patterns of approval of actual individuals or, indeed, on the patterns of approval of collections of actual individuals. Accordingly, the proposed framework provides a standard of correctness that can transcend the patterns of approval, and hence the biases and prejudices, of both individuals and entire communities. This can lead to moral principles that hold everywhere and for everyone. Thus, an impartial spectator that universalises the scope of the *interests and perspectives* that are to be taken into account, and hence can transcend local biases and prejudices, can universalise the scope of the *principles* that it constitutes.[18]

Keith raises three other worries related to a universal moral point of view. First, Keith argues that impartiality, but not universality, is 'necessary to get normative leverage on our practices that's sufficiently independent of our actual judgements and whatever biases infect them.' (469) I agree that impartiality is necessary, but it is not sufficient. Consider a Nazi society. Such a society could have a societal *Nazi* impartial spectator, who, as the title suggests, is *impartial* in the sense that this spectator applies *that society's* standards fairly and with knowledge of the facts. But presumably we would not want to say that this impartial spectator constitutes the moral point of view. Why? Well, this particular impartial spectator might endorse discrimination and even genocide. This is the result of this spectator not necessarily taking into account the interests and perspectives of all concerned. On the other hand, a *universal* impartial spectator, whose impartiality amounts to taking into account the interests and perspectives of *all* concerned, would presumably not permit discrimination and genocide. And since these practices are allowed by the Nazi society, the universal impartial spectator is, as noted, an impartial spectator *of* that society and its standards and judges the social standards themselves.

Second, towards the end of his comments, Keith worries that 'the demand that our normative judgments be universalisable is no guarantor that they are in fact correct.' (474) Given all that I have said earlier, I am not sure what type of 'guarantee' Keith has in mind. Perhaps Keith means that realists and rationalists, for example, will argue that their account can provide a better standard of correctness. But within the proposed anti-realist and naturalistic framework of the book, the key thought here is that there is no higher standard for the correctness of moral judgement that would fare better: any higher standard, above and beyond the one set by the universal impartial spectator, would be unintelligible to us, since it would transcend the imaginative lives of beings such as us; alternatively, even if such a standard were intelligible, it would not have any resonance for us, since it would be detached from our human sensibilities.

Third, Keith worries that 'the aspiration for universal standards threatens to sever the connection to actual judgments and psychology that makes the sentimentalist picture so attractive.' As I have emphasised, I understand the idealisation that leads to the attainment of these universal standards in a minimal way: there is no assumption of any omnipercipience, omniscience, and so on, on the part of the universal impartial spectator. Indeed, in the book I note, much like Keith, that Smith emphasises the *human* nature of the impartial spectator, who is 'of mortal extraction' (TMS III.2.32) and who also experiences the 'irregularity of sentiment' inherent in the influence of fortune on our judgements of others (TMS II.iii.2.2; see also TMS VI.iii.30). I also offer several ways in which the universal impartial spectator does not lose the connection to our actual judgements and psychology with the aim of showing that the idealisation inherent in this spectator does not risk losing the motivational grip on us. Since these arguments are elaborate and encompass substantial chunks of the book, I cannot reproduce them here. But here are some of the key psychological and normative ideas: (a) as noted, I argue that the universal impartial spectator merely constrains one's societal impartial spectator, and the latter can determine many of one's values (as long as they do not conflict with the verdicts of the universal spectator)[19]; (b) I present an account of how the universal impartial spectator is itself constructed from within a given society and out of actual people's concerns; (c) I go to great lengths to tie the universal impartial spectator to our motivations, especially to the desire to be worthy of approval; (d) I present an account of why we should adopt the standpoint of the universal impartial spectator, given Smith's views on how we hold each other accountable.[20] I am sorry that Keith did not fully engage with these ideas, and I leave it up to the readers of the book to decide whether they are convinced by my arguments.[21]

But does Smith himself endorse the emergence of a universal impartial spectator? Keith engages in a lengthy discussion against the claim that Smith thought of the impartial spectator as providing universal judgements. I make my case to the contrary based primarily on Smith's claim that the impartial spectator is a judge whom we set 'between ourselves and those we live with,' a person 'quite candid and equitable . . . who has no particular relation either to ourselves, or to those whose interests are affected by our conduct,' but is 'merely a man in general,' an 'abstract man,' and 'the representative of mankind.'[22] Such phrases suggest a universal impartial spectator who is a *notional* or *hypothetical* other person – that is, any person – rather than a representative of a given society. This is an impartial spectator of *any* society, who can therefore serve as an impartial judge of the social standards of *any* society. I then discuss at length how a universal impartial spectator might come about in Smith's system.

Now, there is another idea in TMS that might seem to go against this suggestion, and I take quite seriously in the book. The idea is that some virtues may be culture-relative (e.g. TMS V.2.7). Indeed, Smith understands the point about the culture-relativity of virtues not as a mere *description* of the facts, but as a *normative* judgement, noting that 'in general the style of manners which takes place in any nation may commonly, upon the whole, be said to be that which is most *suitable* to its situation' (TMS V.2.13; emphasis added). I take this to mean that Smith believed that each culture or society does, in fact, have its own societal impartial spectator and that the many (potentially all) of the verdicts of this spectator should be respected. Which verdicts should not, and would not, be respected? Precisely those that contradict the verdicts of the universal impartial spectator. In other words, the universal impartial spectator merely acts as a type of normative constraint on local virtue (by taking account of the perspectives and interests of *all* concerned). Accordingly, the societal impartial spectator of 1930s Germany, for example, might retain many of the virtues considered worthy of approval in that society; however, these virtues would be constrained by norms that do not permit, as suggested, discrimination and genocide, when taking into account the perspectives and interests of all concerned. Thus, I am sympathetic to much of Keith's analysis, including his claim that 'while it may be true that we often aspire to a kind of universality, it's not clear that this is always true, nor are we discomfited by the fact that our moral judgements are sometimes parochial.'[23]

Nevertheless, as the preceding discussion suggests, I disagree with Keith that 'the further demand for universality' is, according to Smith, 'impractical and perhaps even undesirable' (470) across the board. Keith presents passages that show that 'Smith explicitly contrasts the perspective of the impartial spectator (or man within the breast) with both the immediate and less reflective judgements of the "man without" as well as with those of the "all-seeing Judge of the world"' (e.g. TMS III.2.31–35). (470) He emphasises passages that, according to him, show that 'the verdicts rendered by the higher tribunal of conscience are not necessarily dispositive,' (470) such as TMS III.2.32. Like other commentators (e.g. Sayre-McCord 2010, 2013), I take the standpoint of the impartial spectator to be authoritative. And there is good reason to do so: recall that Smith himself claims that the impartial spectator makes our sentiments proper quite generally (e.g. TMS II.i.2.2, VII.ii.1.49). And much of TMS III.2.32 further supports this claim by arguing for the normative authority of the judgements of the impartial spectator (as a 'much higher tribunal') over the judgements of actual spectators. Of course, given our all-too-human capabilities, even if we adopt the standpoint of the impartial spectator, we might not always adhere to its judgements. In particular, the impartial spectator, as utilised by us, might succumb to the voices of actual people (TMS III.2.32), or even to the violence of our own passions, especially self-love (TMS III.4.1–3). However, I take this to be a descriptive claim about what is the case, and not a normative claim about what ought to be the case. This just goes to show that acting morally can be a difficult endeavour. As for the 'all-seeing Judge of the world,' I do downplay any religious connotations in my interpretation of Smith, and I assume that Smith's moral philosophy and moral psychology can be interpreted in a naturalistic manner. Perhaps Keith will find this response unsatisfactory, but presumably one of the strengths of a sentimentalist framework is that it is generally congruent with a *secular* naturalistic understanding of the world (Fleischacker 2021: 64–65). And note that it is actually desirable for my purposes that Smith distinguishes between the impartial spectator and the 'all-seeing Judge of the world,' since it provides additional support for the aforementioned claim that, contrary to Firth's ideal observer, Smith's impartial spectator is neither omnipercipient nor omniscient.

In order to better understand Keith's second point of contention, let me provide a bit of background. In Chapter 3, I discuss Smith's rich accounts of sympathy and approbation. My aim is not merely to present Smith's views, but rather to solve two problems that seem to plague his accounts of sympathy and approbation. First, Smith's account of sympathy at the beginning of TMS appears to be inconsistent with the account of sympathy at the end of TMS. In particular, it seems that Smith did not appreciate the distinction between 'self-oriented sympathy' and 'other-oriented sympathy,' that is, between imagining being oneself in the actor's situation and imagining being the actor in the actor's situation (which I call 'the inconsistency problem'). Second, Smith's account of approbation, according to which a sentiment of approval arises when there is recognition of concordance between the spectator's sympathetic passion and the actor's original passion, does not work if we focus exclusively on either self-oriented or other-oriented sympathy. Since, according to Smith, the spectator attains both his own sympathetic passion and the actor's original passion by sympathising with the actor, the sympathetic passion of the spectator and the original passion of the actor will necessarily be identical. Therefore, there is no room to compare the spectator's feeling with what the actor does or does not feel (which I call 'the new sympathy-approbation problem').

In response to these problems, I offer a novel *developmental* account of sympathy in TMS: fully developed other-oriented sympathy – that is, other-oriented sympathy that is not distorted by the spectator's self-love or his idiosyncratic point of view – is a psychological and normative achievement, and the standpoint of the impartial spectator is needed in order to explain its development. Hence, while Smith emphasises self-oriented sympathy at the beginning of TMS (I.i.1.10–13), he had good reason to emphasise other-oriented sympathy only towards the end of the book (TMS VII.iii.1.4), after he has presented his account of the impartial spectator. This reconstruction of Smith's argument renders his account of sympathy consistent, thus solving the inconsistency problem. It also suggests what I will call 'the double-sympathy model of approbation': if the spectator imagines both what he himself would feel in the actor's situation and what the actor would feel in the actor's situation, he can compare these two passions and come to recognise whether or not there is concordance between them. In other words, Smith's account of approbation requires that the spectator employ *both* self-oriented *and* other-oriented sympathy, thus avoiding the new sympathy-approbation problem.

At the outset of his discussion, Keith writes that 'there are several places' where I seem to suggest that it is 'other-oriented sympathy alone that we ultimately want to use to construct the judgements of the impartial spectator, and that provides our normative standards, while self-oriented sympathy is merely important in helping us develop the capacity for other-oriented sympathy.' He adds that I am 'too quick to discount self-oriented sympathy.' (469) However, this is not my position at all! First, as noted, I argue that Smith's model of approbation does *not* work if we focus exclusively on either self-oriented or other-oriented sympathy:

the way to solve the new sympathy-approbation problem is by making use of a model of approbation that makes use of both types of sympathy. And insofar as the impartial spectator is constructed out of our patterns of approval, self-oriented sympathy, like other-oriented sympathy, will play a crucial role in its construction. Second, I demonstrate how the formation of the standpoint of the impartial spectator, through its various stages of development, *enables the emergence of fully developed other-oriented sympathy* that is not distorted by the spectator's self-love or idiosyncratic point of view.[24] In particular, I argue that the fact that the impartial spectator allows us to control our excessive self-love (TMS II.ii.2.1, III.3.4) explains how we come to be emotionally ready to experience fully developed other-oriented sympathy. Furthermore, I argue that the standpoint of the impartial spectator allows us to make a comparison between our interests and other people's interests by affording us an understanding of the aspects of the situation that pertain to us, but perhaps not to others. We are then ready to appreciate the difference between the situation as it confronts us and the situation as it confronts others (TMS III.3.1–3). Therefore, in addition to making us emotionally ready to experience fully developed other-oriented sympathy, the impartial spectator can make us cognitively ready to do so.

Other-oriented sympathy is not only a psychological achievement but also a *normative* one. This is because, when discussing other-oriented sympathy, Smith aims to show that while the account that 'deduces all sentiments and affections from self-love' arose 'from some confused misapprehension of the system of sympathy' – namely, self-oriented sympathy, which is 'founded in self-love, because it arises . . . from putting myself in your situation' – other-oriented sympathy is not rooted in self-love, because it is 'entirely occupied about what relates to you' (TMS VII.iii.1.4). Smith's insistence that other-oriented sympathy, rather than self-oriented sympathy, is not rooted in self-love suggests that it is the *proper* form of sympathy, especially given the association of self-oriented sympathy with the 'confused misapprehension of the system of sympathy.' More generally, given (a) Smith's account of the impartial spectator as a standpoint that humbles self-love and (b) the fact that the attainment of the standpoint of the impartial spectator leads, in turn, to the attainment of 'proper' sentiments (TMS II.i.2.2), Smith thought that a sentiment that is not founded in self-love is a more proper sentiment. But while I argue that other-oriented sympathy is ultimately the proper form of sympathy, I do not claim that this form of sympathy 'provides our normative standards,' (475) as Keith suggests. Rather, it is the impartial spectator that provides our normative standard. Hence, I am sympathetic to, and basically agree with, the remainder of Keith's analysis of these topics. Indeed, I agree with his claim that 'all of our individual perspectives have a valuable normative contribution to make that deserve independent normative weight.' (475) Recall that in Chapter 6, I argue that valuing my humanity, understood as (my awareness of) my perspective and the reasons determined from within it, entails valuing your humanity, understood as (your awareness of) your perspective and the reasons determined from within it. In other words, I believe that our individual perspectives are valuable and deserve independent normative weight.

Notes

1 The book is based in part on Ben-Moshe (2020a, 2020b, 2020c, 2021, and 2023).

2 Motivation also requires the agent having a *belief* that, were the agent to ϕ, she would further the relevant desire. The key point, which has its origins in Hume's arguments against the motivational efficacy of reason, is that a belief, in and of itself, cannot motivate; rather, a conative state, such as a desire, is required.

3 For example, Williams (1981: 104) famously argued that in addition to straightforward means-end reasoning, the following components should be included in the notion of correct or sound deliberation: 'Thinking how the satisfaction of elements in S can be combined, e.g. by time-ordering; where there is some irresoluble conflict among the elements of S, considering which one attaches most weight to . . .; or, again, finding constitutive solutions, such as deciding what would make for an entertaining evening, granted that one wants entertainment.'

4 This is called 'reasons/motives internalism' by Darwall (1997: 307), who defines it as 'a necessary condition of *p*'s being a reason for *S* to do *A* is that *S* can have, and under suitable conditions would have, some motivation to do *A* by virtue of a suitable awareness of *p*.' In the book, I discuss the motivational aspect in more detail. Among other things, I make much of Williams's (1995: 35, 2001: 91) later view, according to which p is a reason for A to ϕ only if A *could* reach the conclusion that he should ϕ by a sound deliberative route from his motivations.

5 John tends to use Smith's locutions elsewhere. For example, he writes: 'The general idea is that many sentiments prompt a characteristic action, the action that is both "natural and proper" to the sentiment. Thus, for example, the sentiment of gratitude prompts thanks, that of fear prompts flight, that of anger, aggression. That being so, reasonable fear (justified fear) is a reason for flight, reasonable anger (justified anger) is a reason for a hard retort, and so on.' Terms like 'natural and proper' are ones that Smith uses, but that does not change the key point that the philosophical strategy John attributes to Smith could be used by Hume and contemporary Humeans.

6 *The Theory of Moral Sentiments* is referenced as 'TMS,' with the part, section (if applicable), chapter, and paragraph in the Glasgow Edition (Smith 1976).

7 John makes his point about Smith's account being a general theory of the propriety of all sentiments by focusing on what he calls a 'disinterested spectator,' which determines the propriety in question, rather than on the 'impartial spectator,' which, according to John, tends to be viewed as 'specifically concerned with theories of ethical impartiality.' John claims that Smith uses the phrase 'disinterested spectator' although I could not find it in TMS; indeed, Smith uses 'disinterested' only a handful of times, mostly in connection with benevolence.

8 This process is plausible, for, as Smith notes, 'the propriety of every passion excited by objects peculiarly related to ourselves, the pitch which the spectator can go along with, must lie, it is evident, in a certain mediocrity. If the passion is too high, or if it is too low, he cannot enter into it'; and thus the 'mediocrity . . . in which the point of propriety consists, is different in different passions. It is high in some, and low in others' (TMS I.ii.intro.1–2).

9 As I argue in the book, there is a familiar worry for those who embrace a naturalistic picture of the world and are sceptical about the prospects of meta-ethical realism: an answer to the question what accounts for the correctness of moral judgement has proven to be elusive. Assuming one wishes to both (a) ground moral judgement in the *responses* of agents without paying the normative prices of subjectivism and relativism, and (b) attain a robust form of *objectivity* without paying the metaphysical, epistemological, and motivational prices of (especially non-naturalist) realism, one could opt for the position that it is the responses of agents *who are under certain conditions* that constitute what is morally right. Since actual agents may not meet these conditions, their responses, individually and collectively, might be in error. These observations are based in part on Vallentyne (1996: 101).

10 I discuss this example, and related issues, in Ben-Moshe (2022).

11 The term is borrowed from Mark Schroeder's *Slaves of the Passions*. Schroeder (2007: 97–102) takes the term to embody the thesis that the weight of a reason is proportional to the strength of the agent's desire *and* the degree to which a certain action promotes that desire. The first half of the thesis poses, I believe, the greater challenge to the Humean theory of reasons, and so is the one on which I focus. Schroeder, for his part, argues in his book that the Humean theory of reasons does *not* entail that the weight of a reason is determined by the strength of a desire.

12 Proportionalism is also natural if we consider the case of 'no desire.' As David Enoch (2011: 438–439) has argued (in response to Schroeder), the Humean theorist is committed to a close connection between desire-strength and reason-strength at one extreme of the desire/reason strength continuum: no desire entails no reason. There would thus be a discontinuity warranting an explanation if the Humean theorist were not committed to there being a similar connection between other points on the continuum, since the null-point is just a point on the continuum.

13 While not making all of these points, Williams (1995: 37) argues that the normative constraints on reasons are explained by components in the motivational set of our actual selves: his all-and-only-true-beliefs and sound-deliberation constraints are explained by the fact that 'any rational deliberative agent has in his S a general interest in being factually and rationally correctly informed' that is, by a desire to know things as they really are.

14 Remy writes that

> in partial answer to my foregoing confusion about what makes the dictates of the ideal self, authoritative, Ben-Moshe argues – consistent with the Humean theory – that the reasons of our ideal self are overriding when our *strongest desire* is to follow the dictates of that ideal self.

Note that this is a misrepresentation of my view, since I explicitly dissociate the weight of reasons as determined by our ideal self, ethical or otherwise, from the strength of the desires of our actual self.

15 Remy also writes 'If Ben-Moshe is willing to go in for one original faculty – namely, to explain why we recognise the authority of a certain practice of practical reasoning; then why not also accept a second faculty – namely, one that gives rise to the peculiar sentiment of approbation, and, in turn, all the benefits this peculiarity offers for moral reasoning?' I hope that the preceding discussion has shown that (a) the desire to be worthy of approval is not an original moral faculty, and that (b) an appeal to a 'peculiar sentiment of approbation' will not necessarily resolve the kind of issues that arise for the Humean vis-à-vis the weight of reasons and motivation.

16 *A Treatise of Human Nature* is referenced as 'T' with the relevant book, chapter, section, and paragraph in the Clarendon Edition (Hume 2007), followed by the corresponding page number in the Selby-Bigge/Nidditch (SBN) Edition (Hume 1978); *An Enquiry Concerning the Principles of Morals* is referenced as 'EPM' with the relevant section and paragraph in the Clarendon Edition (Hume 1998), followed by the corresponding page number in the Selby-Bigge/Nidditch (SBN) Edition (Hume 1975).

17 See Baier (1991: 212–213), Darwall (1994: fn. 37), Cohon (1997: 844), and Taylor (2002: 53).

18 As I also argue in the book, given the fact that the standpoint of the impartial spectator grows out of antecedent interactions with others, it is not likely that *all* of one's moral judgements will be wrong – indeed, as I discuss in these replies, the universal impartial spectator may endorse many of the local judgements that are made within a given society or culture – but this observation is probably true of any account of moral judgement that is sensitive to the texture of human life and human sensibilities. Nevertheless, the impartial-spectator account does offer a sound basis for the claim that any person or group of people in any era may be wrong about a given moral judgement.

19 In this regard, I also develop the following model: (1) we each have our own particular evaluative point of view with the reasons that are determined from within it (e.g., by our

contingent motivations and evaluative attitudes); (2) the relative weights of some of our reasons are determined from within a shared evaluative point of view (ultimately that of the universal impartial spectator); (3) these shared reasons have authority over and constrain our private reasons, those that are determined from within her own particular point of view.

20 While I cannot reproduce my argument here, it builds on Smith's claim that 'a moral being is an accountable being. An accountable being, as the word expresses, is a being that must give an account of its actions to some other, and that consequently must regulate them according to the good-liking of this other. Man is accountable to God and his fellow creatures.' These remarks can be found on p. 111 of the Glasgow Edition (1976).

21 Keith adds that he worries that 'the aspiration for universality creates intractable questions about the times, places, and agents that we do (and don't) want to be able to hold our moral judgments fixed over.' I do not quite see the force of this worry: we want the demands of morality to apply to everyone, apart, perhaps, from children of a certain age and some severely morally depraved grownups. In the book, I argue for *Modest Morality/Reasons Internalism:* Moral demands *necessarily* issue reasons to act on these demands for all *moral* agents – a subset of all reason-responsive agents that is large enough to include nearly every human being above a certain age.

22 These phrases are taken from a passage which first appeared in the second edition of TMS, remained with minor variations in editions 3–5, and was replaced by a slightly different passage in the 6th edition (III.2.31–32). The quoted passage can be found in a footnote on pp. 129–130 of the Glasgow Edition (Smith 1976).

23 Keith acknowledges Smith's claim that the impartial spectator aspires to, as he puts it, 'no connection at all' to either the agents being evaluated or to those affected by their actions. However, he adds that 'there's a difference between aspiring for a judge that has no connection at all to the events being judged, and the presumption that the judgments we seek should always and everywhere be the same.' To repeat, I do not claim that all normative judgements should always and everywhere be the same. Rather, some normative judgements should (and will) always and everywhere be the same. And it is the 'no connection at all,' which guarantees this: the Nazi impartial spectator yields the wrong results vis-à-vis the prohibition against discrimination and genocide – which presumably should always and everywhere be the same – precisely because this impartial spectator has a privileged connection to some groups.

24 When other-oriented sympathy contributes to the construction of the impartial spectator, it is not yet fully developed.

References

Baier, A. (1991) *A Progress of Sentiments*. Cambridge: Harvard University Press.

Ben-Moshe, N. (2020a) 'An Adam Smithian Account of Moral Reasons', *European Journal of Philosophy*, 28(4): 1073–1087.

Ben-Moshe, N. (2020b) 'Hume's General Point of View: A Two-Stage Approach', *Pacific Philosophical Quarterly*, 101(3): 431–453.

Ben-Moshe, N. (2020c) 'Making Sense of Smith on Sympathy and Approbation: Other-Oriented Sympathy as a Psychological and Normative Achievement', *British Journal for the History of Philosophy*, 28(4): 735–755.

Ben-Moshe, N. (2021) 'A Defense of Modest Ideal Observer Theory: The Case of Adam Smith's Impartial Spectator', *Ethical Theory and Moral Practice*, 24(2): 489–510.

Ben-Moshe, N. (2022) 'Internal and External Paternalism', *Canadian Journal of Philosophy*, 52(6): 673–687.

Ben-Moshe, N. (2023) 'An Adam Smithian Account of Humanity', *Ergo*, 10(32): 908–936.

Broadie, A. (2010) 'Aristotle, Adam Smith and the Virtue of Propriety', *Journal of Scottish Philosophy*, 8(1): 79–89.

Cohon, R. (1997) 'The Common Point of View in Hume's Ethics', *Philosophy and Phenomenological Research*, 57(4): 827–850.

Darwall, S. (1994) 'Hume and the Invention of Utilitarianism', in M. A. Stewart and J. P. Wright (eds.) *Hume and Hume's Connections*. University Park, PA: The Pennsylvania State University Press, pp. 58–82.

Darwall, S. (1997) 'Reasons, Motives, and the Demands of Morality: An Introduction', in S. Darwall, A. Gibbard and P. Railton (eds.) *Moral Discourse and Practice*. New York: Oxford University Press, pp. 305–312.

Debes, R. (2012) 'Adam Smith on Dignity and Equality', *British Journal for the History of Philosophy*, 20(1): 109–140.

Debes, R. (2017) 'The Authority of Empathy (Or, How to Ground Sentimentalism)', in R. Debes and K. R. Stueber (eds.) *Ethical Sentimentalism: New Perspectives*. Cambridge University Press, pp. 171–191.

Enoch, D. (2011) 'On Mark Schroeder's Hypotheticalism: A Critical Notice of *Slaves of the Passions*', *Philosophical Review*, 120(3): 423–446.

Firth, R. (1952) 'Ethical Absolutism and the Ideal Observer', *Philosophy and Phenomenological Research*, 12(3): 317–345.

Fleischacker, S. (2019) *Being Me Being You: Adam Smith and Empathy*. Chicago: The University of Chicago Press.

Fleischacker, S. (2021) *Adam Smith*, (Part of the *Routledge Philosophers* Series, ed. Brian Leiter). Oxon and New York: Routledge.

Hume, D. (1975) 'An Enquiry Concerning the Principles of Morals', in L. A Selby-Bigge and P. H. Nidditch (eds.) *Enquiries Concerning Human Understanding and Concerning the Principles of Morals*. 3rd edition. New York: Oxford University Press, pp. 167–323.

Hume, D. (1978) *A Treatise of Human Nature*, (eds.) L. A Selby-Bigge and P. H. Nidditch, 2nd edition. New York: Oxford University Press.

Hume, D. (1998) *An Enquiry Concerning the Principles of Morals*, (ed.) T. L. Beauchamp. New York: Clarendon Press.

Hume, D. (2007) *A Treatise of Human Nature*, Vol. 1, (eds.) D. F. Norton and M. J. Norton. New York: Clarendon Press.

Korsgaard, C. M. (1996) *The Sources of Normativity*, (ed.) O. O'Neill. Cambridge: Cambridge University Press.

Sayre-McCord, G. (2010) 'Sentiments and Spectators: Adam Smith's Theory of Moral Judgment', in V. Brown and S. Fleischacker (eds.) *The Adam Smith Review*, Vol. 5. London & New York: Routledge, pp. 124–144.

Sayre-McCord, G. (2013) 'Hume and Smith on Sympathy, Approbation and Moral Judgment', *Social Philosophy and Policy*, 30(1–2): 208–236.

Schroeder, M. (2007) *Slaves of the Passions*. New York: Oxford University Press.

Sinhababu, N. (2017) *Humean Nature: How Desire Explains Action, Thought, and Feeling*. Oxford & New York: Oxford University Press.

Smith, A. (1976) [1759] *The Theory of Moral Sentiments*, (ed.) D. D. Raphael and A. L. Macfie. Oxford: Oxford University Press.

Smith, M. (1994) *The Moral Problem*. Malden, MA: Blackwell Publishing.

Stueber, K. R. (2017) 'Smithian Constructivism: Elucidating the Reality of the Normative Domain', in R. Debes and K. R. Stueber (eds.) *Ethical Sentimentalism: New Perspectives*. Cambridge: Cambridge University Press, pp. 192–209.

Taylor, J. (2002) 'Hume on the Standard of Virtue', *The Journal of Ethics*, 6(1): 43–62.

Vallentyne, P. (1996) 'Response-Dependence, Rigidification and Objectivity', *Erkenntnis*, 44(1): 101–112.

Williams, B. (1981) 'Internal and External Reasons', in *Moral Luck: Philosophical Papers 1973–1980*. Cambridge, UK: Cambridge University Press, pp. 101–113.

Williams, B. (1995) 'Internal Reasons and the Obscurity of Blame', in *Making Sense of Humanity and Other Philosophical Papers 1982–1993*. Cambridge, UK: Cambridge University Press, pp. 35–45.

Williams, B. (2001) 'Postscript: Some Further Notes on Internal and External Reasons', in E. Millgram (ed.) *Varieties of Practical Reasoning*. Cambridge, MA: MIT Press, pp. 91–97.

Part IV

Book reviews

23 Adam Smith and the death of David Hume

Reviewed by Maria Pia Paganelli

The Letter to Strahan and Related Texts. Edited by Dennis Rasmussen. 2018. Lanham Maryland: Lexington Books/Fortress Academic. ix+97 ISBN-13: 978-1498586108

Adam Smith and the Death of David Hume is a much-needed addition to the existing scholarship on both Adam Smith and David Hume. As Dennis Rasmussen notes in the introduction of this small volume, *The Letter to Strahan* is not just a regular piece of correspondence between Smith and his publisher. It has been treated this way so far as it is incorporated among Smith's *Correspondence*. Yet, the *Letter to Strahan* is a carefully crafted piece meant for publication, explicitly under the name of Adam Smith. It was to be added to *My Own Life*, the short autobiography that David Hume requested to be added to all his publications.

The volume includes Rasmussen's detailed and pleasantly written introduction, Hume's *My Own Life*, Smith's *Letter to Strahan*, as well as three essays of comments on Smith's *Letter* published soon after the publication of Smith's *Letter*: an attack by George Horne, the Vice Chancellor of Oxford University, President of Oxford's Magdalen College, and a chaplain in ordinary to King George III; an attack by a certain 'E.M.'; and a defence of Smith and Hume by 'Idem.'

The introduction provides a useful context for the *Letter*. It explains that much attention was given to this *Letter* at the time of publication because all eyes were on Hume, to see how a great infidel would die. The bets were that someone without the comfort of religion would not be able to die peacefully. Hume's account of his own life and Smith's conclusion testified not only that an infidel can die in tranquillity and cheerfully but can also live and die 'as approaching as nearly to the idea of perfectly wise and virtuous man, as perhaps the nature of human frailty will permit' (p. 51). This was a scandal.

Rasmussen describes Smith's *Letter* as a moving eulogy, a paean to friendship, an attempt to vindicate Hume's reputation, and a defence of the morality of life without religion. This last explanation, topped by the last sentence of Smith's *Letter* cited above, is also one of the causes of the heat Smith subsequently had to take, as two of the other letters published in this volume indicate.

Despite all the criticisms and accusations Smith had to endure as a consequence of the publication of this *Letter*, Rasmussen notes that Smith 'never retracted the

DOI: 10.4324/9781003767824-28

claims he made in it, never expressed regret for having published it, and never responded to the critics' (p. 29). An additional indication, in Rasmussen's interpretation, that the friendship between Smith and Hume was not impacted in any way by Smith's refusal to publish Hume's *Dialogues Concerning Natural Religion.* After all, asking to be trusted to finish someone else's autobiography, and trusting someone else to describe one's own death by giving them complete freedom to do so, are two reciprocal acts of the most intimate and complete friendship possible.

The only aspect I wished Rasmussen had elaborated a bit more on in an otherwise carefully edited volume, is something he simply hinted at, but then quickly dropped. The description of Hume's life in his own pen does not include any reference to the *content* of his works. Maybe Hume did not think it necessary to summarise his work as people were familiar with it, speculates Rasmussen. What Hume does describe is his rise from 'not rich' (p. 35) to 'very opulent' (p. 42). This increase in personal wealth was the product of Hume's labour. He sold his services and his works and became wealthy. This same opulence is picked up by Smith in the *Letter to Strahan* as a comforting thought Hume may have as he would leave his friends and family in 'great prosperity' (p. 47). This very thought was eventually derided by Smith's critics. Nevertheless, this great prosperity and his 'love of (economic) independence' are part of the legacy both Hume and Smith want Hume to be remembered by. This was probably not an accident in an age of commerce and in works by two writers who sanguinely defended a newly developing commercial society.

24 Adam Smith and *The Wealth of Nations* in Spain

Reviewed by Julio Seoane-Pinilla

A History of Reception, Dissemination, Adaptation and Application, 1777–1840. Edited by Jesús Astigarraga and Juan Zabalza Abingdon (UK) & New York: Routledge, 2022, p. 278. ISBN-13: 0367716004-978

At first glance, a history of the introduction of *The Wealth of Nations* (*WN*) in Spain may seem to be a study of interest only to scholars or historians of eighteenth-century Spanish economic thought. And indeed, on a first reading that is what this book offers, but upon further reading some additional themes broaden the focus of interest in this work. The first of these is that, by following WN's passage through Spain, we are offered an authentic history of the Spanish Enlightenment, and it is the virtue of this book that it is possible to follow such history in a very pleasant way without detracting from detail and rigour.

The reading of Adam Smith in Spain was not based on very detailed theoretical discussions (and in this sense it is paradigmatic that discussion of WN was always outside the Spanish Universities), but on using him to bring Modernity to the governance of a country still anchored in a very *Ancien Régime* monarchy. During the reign of Charles III, the priority was to try to put some limits on the power of the Church, to establish a prosperous commerce that would overcome the chains of the guilds and to achieve the Enlightenment – education – of the country. To this end, were used all the Enlightenment works, and, as far as the field of political economy was concerned, one could not forget WN: a very important work for gaining strength so that Spain could place itself on the same level as the most advanced European nations. The great merit of the book discussed here is that in its reading, we can witness the struggles for economic, political and cultural modernisation through the way in which Smith was used or the tools obtained from WN were proposed. In short, through the recovery of WN we can reconstruct a time when Enlightenment was struggling to make its way in a country that had long forgotten its own enlightenment.

But it is not only for the value of presenting a history of Spain that this book deserves attention. We have been pointing out for many years that, although one of the main objectives of the Scottish Enlightenment was the construction of a *science of man*, it did not forget that it should also serve to educate and offer useful tools to the social world to make life less cruel and more pleasant (more just, in a sense).

DOI: 10.4324/9781003767824-29

The fact that after the 'Treatise' always comes the 'Essays,' that once the profession of anatomist has been exercised, space must be left for the work of the painter to show us the best way to live with the anatomy we have, is something that we have been reading for some time in the studies that underline the educating, sociability-building facet of the Scottish Enlightenment. In this sense, the book under review here allows us to pick up Smith not to argue meticulously (academically) with him, but to take his tools with us and see what we can do with them. This was the case of the reading of WN in Spain and it is the one that is reconstructed with rigour and detail in this book. Without forgetting, of course, the technical details that were discussed with WN in hand, nor the emergence of political economy in Spain generated by such discussions (both issues that are expressed in several chapters of the book), the general impression is that here we have an exercise in unravelling WN in the light of the applications that were made of Smith in Spain in the eighteenth and nineteenth centuries. And the 'applications' should be emphasised, for throughout this work we are shown not infrequently how WN's proposals were adapted and moulded to a country quite alien to the world that surrounded Smith. It is not that the modernity of an economically advanced commercial society was denied, but rather that an attempt was made to establish the novel proposals and visions of the commercial world through negotiation with a reality that still struggled to refuse to enter Modernity. Thus, while the first part of the book details the translations, introductions and compilations of WN, later and quickly we see how Smith was used to propose different economic policies that adapted WN to a situation very different from the one in which Smith had lived.

To say that Smith was introduced to answer questions of taxation is to imply that there was no deep theoretical discussion of WN. This is not to denigrate or ignore early economic thought in Spain, but it is the superlative merit of WN for providing several tools for a society that was already beginning to be very diverse and multiform. There are no detailed discussions of political economy in general, but there is a political and economic use of the tools provided by WN, as well as many nuanced economic and fiscal debates generated from WN. All this, of course, is not a task in the work of a pure anatomist, but the work of a thinker situated and eager to educate and help those around him to live better lives. This is, in my opinion, the educational facet that goes hand in hand with the science of man. In short, we cannot forget that political economy must be, in the end, both economy and politics.

As one of the detailed chapters in this book shows, WN was never the subject of strictly academic discussions that analysed each of its proposals. This makes it clear that the sphere of action and discussion that WN had in Spain was the fiscal discussions of the Ministers of Finance and their collaborators (indeed, they are the ones who commissioned the translation of WN, its summaries and its compilations), or the moments of constitution of the *Asociaciones de Amigos del País* (private associations that tried to industrialise the country, make it more productive and also educate in a new liberal and secular conception of economics, politics and morality). It would be overly simplistic to state that the consequence of this 'lack of academy' was that in Spain the discussion of philosophy and economics had a very low intellectual level. On the contrary, the situation described in relation to the position of WN in Spain is fully in line with what was really the aim of the Enlightenment: to use ideas in practice. It is true that such commitment is necessary to 'produce' thought, but overall in Europe, this production was done according to the needs that arose with the hopes expressed, indeed, through great works such as WN.

As I see it, in a way, it could give the impression that in this book we are witnessing the dismantling of WN in order to use some pieces and discard others, as if the precise fit of the pieces of WN was broken to seize only some elements appropriate to the context of Spain in the late eighteenth and early nineteenth centuries (sometimes even contradicting the internal coherence of WN) or taking the work as a storehouse of tools to be used according to the situation. This is undeniable insofar as the discussions focused on the application or not of tariffs in accordance with the industrial backwardness of the country or on the elimination of the guilds without breaking up the only centres generating wealth, however unproductive they might be. Smith really became a name – a myth – that gave strength to the pretensions of changing and modernising the economic and political structure of Spain, and for this reason it was not necessary to know WN thoroughly, but simply to know where in Smith's book to go to endorse some model of modernisation with the authority of WN. 'The famous Smith' was on the lips of those who thought of a new nation; it helped to compose part of the reflections on political economy aimed at turning Spanish policies around, and it inspired fiscal measures or economic organisation. Is it possible to think of a better sphere of influence? Is that not what the science of man should be for?

When one analyses classical Roman thought, it is usual to describe it as eclectic and to save only a few names (Cicero and Seneca mainly) from many centuries of political, economic, and cultural domination. There is no Roman thought, it is often assumed, because they took everything from Greece, and Rome only had practical (and not theoretical) interests; such is a statement that has always made me very uncomfortable, however useful it is for rendering unnecessary the study of many centuries of history in detail. The situation is repeated with respect to Spanish thought at least from the seventeenth century onwards, as there is a tendency to consider that what is most characteristic is still ultramontane and counter-reformationist. In the book reviewed here we learn that this is not the case. Although there were many voices anchored in the religious tradition, there was also a desire for change and the reading of new and different authors. The Spanish Enlightenment was precisely the adaptation, often eclectic, of these readings. And this adaptation has a value *per se* that should not be underestimated. Perhaps the thinkers studied in this book are not Smithians *tout court*, but with WN they are undeniably enlightened – and I am convinced that it is also an educational merit that the *literati* willingly pursued.

It would be unfair to conclude a review of this book without a detailed reference to each chapter, but that will be the case because this work is not a typical edited book. We are used to books that are published as collective works in which the chapters do not always relate to each other, even if they deal with not too dissimilar periods or themes. The editor has made a considerable effort to build a common body. Such is a commonplace in our cultural industry, and it is a pleasure that this is not the case with this book, which, in all its pages, shows signs of initial planning that has distributed the work among several contributors. One can really guess that what we have in our hands is the result of the same research project with very precise planning by J. Astigarraga and J. Zabalza, who have distributed the duties among the members of the project. For this reason, I have thought it appropriate not to refer to any of the collaborators in particular and I prefer to say something about the development of the book as a whole.

It consists of 14 new and unpublished chapters, written by eight historians of economic thought, which have been distributed in three parts. The first part focused on translations, compendiums, extracts, or extensive news of WN in Spanish. The second part refers to the tonalities and influences of WN around three historical periods: (a) the first serious attempt at modernisation in Spain (1770–1800), (b) the one following the French invasion, the proclamation of the first liberal constitution, and the subsequent international reintroduction of absolutism (1800–1820), ending with (c) the political struggles surrounding the triennium of the first liberal government in Spain (1820–1840). The third part of the book is an analysis of Spanish Smith at the institutional level, that is to say, the way in which Smith's work is applied to the Spanish economy and how it permeated the press, the Chairs, the constituent discussions of Cadiz (1808), or the liberal triennium, etc.

As the editors confess, 'the book aspires to restore the "Spanish Smith" to his time,' starting from his translations and summaries, but taking into account that the original was often read in English or through interpretations that came from France, which helps to explain why, in Spain, Smith did not manage to generate a strictly academic field of study. WN began to circulate in Spain through a work by Alcalá-Galiano (Fiscal del Consejo de Castilla and member of the Finance Minister's team) which incorporated a summary of Smith's work and whose main focus was the question of income taxation. Alcalá-Galiano was not a convinced Smithian (he was rather a man close to Necker in many respects, which underlines his eclectic approach to WN), but from him Smith began to be known as the 'famous Smith.' Following this summary, Martínez de Irujo translated Condorcet's *Compendium* of the work, and in 1794, 18 years after the original, the first translation by José Alonso Ortiz appeared (it was promoted by a ministerial commission and would be the only translation until 1956). This text, apart from making a work of great importance available to the interested public, was the trigger for stretching Spanish in terms of acquiring new vocabulary to account for the emerging economic world of the eighteenth century. Words such as 'commercial' or 'shares' were not in common use in Spanish, and Alonso's efforts began to put them into circulation. (It should not be forgotten that having words makes it easier to have a world.) It must be said that in this first translation, as was the case with WN's summaries or reviews, some parts were eliminated 'without adulterating the substance of the work' (89) so as not to disturb the sensibilities of the readers (generally questions referring to religion).

This first translation incorporates explanations and long notes by the translator in which he does not always follow Smith or, at times, simply opposes his proposals; these additions by the translator were to a large extent the basis on which the economic debate in Spain was subsequently generated, and it became clear that the introduction of WN had to be undertaken hand in hand with certain concessions and negotiations, the final result did not always fit with WN. This is the case of the guilds, which were admitted to be 'anachronistic institutions that functioned in a manner contrary to their original purpose,' and although it is acknowledged that 'in the face of Smith and the experience in Scotland, the alternative was not to abolish them or issue across-the-board regulations, but to implement Campomanes' gradual liberalising programme, which had in fact culminated in a system in which the guilds coexisted with freedom of labour' (p. 91); and it is also the case of the recognition that 'for an economy like Spain's, tariffs were the "only" or "main" means of compensating for the poor competitiveness of its manufacturing' (p. 93). These adaptations are the ones that the book goes through in order to make clear (in a meticulous, well-documented and well-discussed way) what the path that WN sowed was like, what was intended to germinate along the way, and what was harvested as the final fruit.

I have already mentioned that WN put into circulation a vocabulary and an authority (an enthusiastic Spanish liberal claimed that Smith was the 'patron saint of political economy' [p. 133]) that made it possible to fight for a new economic model for the country and to reinforce the changes that had begun with the Enlightenment in Spain. In this sense, Smith 'provided a model for the reorganisation of Spain's administrative and financial structure' (p. 109) and we can underline what was already mentioned at the beginning of this review: WN's reading was pragmatic and not dogmatic. It was pragmatic because its readers were policymakers who used WN to inspire new measures or to convince public opinion. It was non-dogmatic insofar as, for example, 'the supposed virtues of the 'invisible hand' as a channel for the 'maximisation of individual freedom within a framework of law and order' were obscured by the four Smithian principles of taxation, the idea in the WN that was most often repeated by the enlightened Spaniards' (p. 119). In this last sense, the final chapters recall that, in the Cortes de Cádiz and during the discussion of the first Spanish constitution, concepts that show clear Smithian traits are used, and the same happens during the Liberal Triennium, although 'the WN's theoretical issues are not present in the parliamentary debates' (p. 220).

To summarise each chapter would unnecessarily lengthen this review, as they are all as juicy as they are delightful to read. I prefer to conclude with the observation that WN accompanied the struggle for the Enlightenment and modernity in Spain, efforts that are 'a fascinating story of political struggle, enlightened efforts, ephemeral successes and big disappointments' (p. 181). Like all struggles, it had a lot of pragmatism, an eclectic bid to furnish a world very different from the one Smith lived in when he wrote WN. I am convinced that Smith himself would not reject such a reading at all – and such could be the envy of all *literati*. It is obvious that it was a partial reading, but it is also very clear that it was a reading interested in what I have no doubt was also the desire of the author of WN: to offer tools to manage in the world (which, at least, is a desire that every anatomist cannot help fondly appreciate).

In short, this book shows us with rigour and very careful discussions that in the three historical periods that are its object of research

> the reading of the WN remained fragmentary and eclectic – without any pejorative connotation. In Spain there were almost no pure Smithian economists, solely eclectic doctrinal positions that qualified the theories in the WN and intermingled them with those of the late Enlightenment Spanish economists. . . . Acceptance of the WN was patchy and uneven.
>
> (p. 135)

I see nothing but Enlightenment in this quality of 'patchy and uneven'; if this seems like a personal and controversial opinion, I think it can be valid with the evidence that this magnificent work presents a detailed knowledge of the history of economic thought in Spain during eighteenth and nineteenth centuries, of the beginnings of our political economy, which also offers us a rigorous and very enjoyable approach to the Spanish Enlightenment. It seems to me a success, and I can't help suspecting that a large part of this success is due to the conductors of the work, who have managed to combine excellent musicians in a very well-defined performance.

Notes for contributors

Submissions to *The Adam Smith Review* are invited from any theoretical, disciplinary or interdisciplinary approach (max. 10,000 words, in English). Contributors are asked to make their arguments accessible to a wide multidisciplinary readership without sacrificing high standards of argument and scholarship. Please include an abstract not exceeding 100 words.

Please send all submissions, suggestions, and offers to edit symposia to the incoming Editor, Craig Smith, School of Social and Political Sciences, The University of Glasgow, 42 Bute Gardens, Glasgow, G12 8RT. Email submissions are welcomed at adamsmithreview@glasgow.ac.uk. Alternatively, please send three hard copies in double-spaced type.

Please prepare your manuscript for anonymous refereeing and provide a separate title page with your name. Interdisciplinary submissions will be sent to referees will different disciplinary expertise. Submitted articles will be double-blind refereed and commissioned articles will be single-blind refereed. All contributions must be in English; it is the author's responsibility to ensure the quality of the English text. Where quotations in languages other than English are required, authors are asked to provide a translation into English.

Final versions of accepted papers will need to conform to the ASR Guidelines for Authors (Harvard reference system), but submitted papers are accepted in any format.

Submission to *The Adam Smith Review* will be taken to imply that the work is original and unpublished, and is not under consideration for publication elsewhere. By submitting a manuscript, authors agree that the exclusive rights to reproduce and distribute the article have been given to the Publishers, including reprints, photographic reproductions, microfilm, or any other reproductions of a similar nature, and translations.

Book reviews

Books related to Adam Smith or of more general relevance for Adam Smith scholarship will be reviewed in *The Adam Smith Review*. It is editorial policy to invite authors to respond to reviews of their work. Offers to review works published in languages other than English are welcomed. Please send books for review to the Book Review Editor: Craig Smith, School of Social and Political Sciences, The University of Glasgow, 42 Bute Gardens, Glasgow, G12 8RT

Craig.Smith@glasgow.ac.uk

The website of *The Adam Smith Review* is http://www.adamsmithreview.org/

For Product Safety Concerns and Information please contact our EU representative GPSR@taylorandfrancis.com
Taylor & Francis Verlag GmbH, Kaufingerstraße 24, 80331 München, Germany

www.ingramcontent.com/pod-product-compliance
Lightning Source LLC
LaVergne TN
LVHW010551300926
849162LV00002B/299
9781041290575